The Economic Development
of Modern Scotland
1950-1980

The Economic Development of Modern Scotland
1950-1980

Edited by
RICHARD SAVILLE
Lecturer in Economic History
University of St. Andrews

JOHN DONALD PUBLISHERS LTD
EDINBURGH

ISBN 0 85976 111 8

Exclusive distribution in the United States of
America and Canada by Humanities Press Inc.,
Atlantic Highlands, NJ 07716, USA.

Phototypeset by Burns & Harris Limited, Dundee
Printed in Great Britain by Bell & Bain Ltd., Glasgow

PREFACE

J. Steven Watson,
Principal of the University of St. Andrews

We have all been told that history never repeats itself and also that no two economists are likely to agree. It would seem that economic history, when it comes up to temporary problems, and even hints at the future, must prove a doubly difficult task. Economic historians in St. Andrews have nevertheless assembled a book which is enjoyable and instructive. I speak on the basis of having attended some of the original lectures by distinguished visitors and of having joined in talk about the rest.

It was practical experience rather than academic study which first quickened in me a sharp, even painful, interest in Scottish development. It was long before I had any idea I would ever be coming back north to preside over a university. As the end of the war came at last into sight, we in the Ministry of Fuel and Power commissioned a special survey of the future of energy supplies. Working on its findings, we then outlined a plan for moving miners and resources from Lanarkshire to Fife. As Secretary of the Minister I sat for many enervating hours in Glasgow hotels watching everything go down in arguments whose bitterness obscured the common need for self-preservation.

More than twenty years after this, when moving to St. Andrews, the picture seemed much brighter. Glenrothes, projected as a coal metropolis, had been built and had become one of the centres for electronics. Expansion and innovation were the keynote in wider circles as well as in the universities. Now, however, twenty years later again, we seem to have resumed the export of talent and to be incubating extremism. How far such impressions accord with the facts needs to be tested. Have the immigrants with new skills failed to outweigh those forced to leave the dead industrial yards?

Everyone knows Dr. Johnson's cruel quip that no prospect so allured a Scot as that of the road south into England: at the time he made it, a Scottish revival, both economic and cultural, was getting under way. And at that time, at all times, the Scots tramping off along the roads of the world have usually been looking back over their shoulders. Even when settled for generations overseas, they have still felt they must look back, for there was a secret left behind.

The present book, hard-headed as it is, was made possible by this romantic spirit. The St. Andrews Jubilee Trust was created by the late Gershom Stewart. To name him is to explain his motives. When Moses took refuge at Midian and lived with the priest's daughter, 'she bore a son, and he called his name Gershom, for he said "I have been a sojourner in a strange land"'. As Moses had been chased from his home, so these Stewarts were driven from Arran. From that time on, each first son in the family was called Gershom to remind him that to be out of Scotland is to be in exile.

v

The Gershom I knew was educated at Eton and at Christ Church, Oxford. He contrived, however, to spend much of his boyhood in Kintyre. At the end of each vacation he would journey south by rowingboat, by steamer and by train, grappling with a tin trunk which held all his treasures. From Oxford he went to the English Bar and then, with the war, to the Devon Yeomanry in which he became a major. At the war's end he was, for a while, the 'town major' for Padua. This caught at his affections. Italy, after Scotland, became his favourite country. But for his career in business he could not conveniently live in either. He bought a house on Arran so that his family could renew acquaintance with the cousins who had persisted there. His own highly successful career in the legal side of shipping and at Lloyds was conducted from a house in Buckinghamshire.

He sought out a chance to play some part in Scotland. He found this in politics. He had risen high in the National Liberal party. He stood as their candidate for Leith. He did not succeed in winning but he only lost after three recounts. At that election, he proudly recalled, his was the only constituency where there was any swing towards a Unionist. He came out of it all rejoicing in the friends he had made and with his delight in the tapestry of Scottish life renewed.

It was in continuation of this experience that he began to seek opportunities to talk with students at St. Andrews. He did not easily give up his hope of becoming a legislator. But gradually he accepted the idea of guiding those who could shape the future. Students, like the working men of Leith, gave him confidence in his country. He believed that he sensed a growing creativity. If this could be encouraged locally, it would burst forth at the right time and operate on a world stage. But to bring this about, the debates among ourselves badly needed enriching, needed more information. At an acute stage of decisions about devolution he was very happy to seize an opportunity to help publish a book, *The Crown and the Thistle*, which explored, from contrasted points of view, the cultural as well as the constitutional issues involved.

Above all, as a businessman, he wanted to bring about a more positive pursuit of social studies. He was tolerant of many opinions but they had to be based upon fact and had to survive close analysis.

There could be no fitter memorial to Gershom Stewart than this present record of the aspirations, achievements, and errors, of our recent past. It would have aroused him to pleasurable argument. I record the debt we owe to him and his Trustees for opening our eyes to what has been going on around us.

LIST OF CONTRIBUTORS

Sir Kenneth Alexander. Principal and Vice-Chancellor of Stirling University, former Chairman of the Highlands and Islands Development Board (1976-1980), and Govan Shipbuilders (1974-1976). He has written widely on business and economic development, and on industrial relations.

Dr. John Bryden. Formerly Head of the Land Development Division of the Highlands and Islands Development Board. He is a Director of the Arkleton Trust and now farms in Aviemore. His first book, *Tourism and Development: A Case-study of the Commonwealth Caribbean*, was published in 1973. He has written extensively on agrarian and development questions, and is co-author of *Agrarian Change in the Scottish Highlands*.

Dr. Neil Buxton. Depute Director of Glasgow College of Technology, formerly Professor of Economics, Heriot-Watt University, Edinburgh. He is well known for his work on British and Scottish economic development, and the history of the British coal industry.

Professor Maxwell Gaskin. Department of Political Economy, University of Aberdeen. Well known for his standard work on the history of the Scottish banks. Co-author and Editor of *North East Scotland*; joint author of *The Economic Impact of North Sea Oil on Scotland*; Editor of *The Political Economy of Tolerable Survival*.

Andrew Gibb. Department of Geography, University of Glasgow. He has worked for many years on housing and housing policy, and in 1983 published *Glasgow: The Making of a City*.

Professor Laurie Hunter. Department of Social and Economic Research, University of Glasgow. He is the Editor of the *Scottish Journal of Political Economy* (since 1966), and has written many books and articles on labour problems, and on regional and industrial economics.

Dr. Gavin McCrone. Chief Economic Adviser, Industry Department for Scotland, since 1972. In 1983 he was appointed Visiting Professor of Economics at the University of Strathclyde, Glasgow. Among his many publications are *Scotland's Economic Progress, 1951-1960* and *Regional Policy in Britain*.

Stuart McDowall. Department of Economics, University of St. Andrews. He has worked in recent years on the economic effects of the oil industry, the jute trade, the economic impact of the Open Golf Championship, and the role of regional incentives on the investment decisions of companies.

Duncan Maclennan. Department of Social and Economic Research, University of Glasgow, Director of the Housing Research Group, University of Glasgow. He has worked extensively on housing research and public policy questions in the U.K.

Professor Rosalind Mitchison. Department of Economic History, University of Edinburgh. Well known for her work on Scottish history, including *A History of Scotland*.

Professor Peter Payne. Department of Economic History, University of Aberdeen. Well known for his work on economic history, which has included *Colvilles*, the standard work on the Scottish steel industry, and publications on entrepreneurship, business development, and the labour market.

J. N. Randall. Economic Adviser, Industry Department for Scotland. His work has covered regional economic problems, the effects of the Scottish New Towns, and the impact of incoming manufacturing enterprises on the local economy.

Dr. Richard Saville. Lecturer in Economic History, University of St. Andrews.

CONTENTS

Preface by the Principal of the University of St. Andrews   v

List of Contributors   vii

Introduction   xi

1. The Industrial Background to the Post-War Scottish Economy   1
   Richard Saville

2. The Scottish Economy, 1945-79: Performance, Structure and Problems 47
   Neil Buxton

3. The Decline of the Scottish Heavy Industries, 1945-1983   79
   Peter L. Payne

4. The Scottish Financial Sector, 1950-1980   114
   Maxwell Gaskin

5. Scottish Agriculture, 1950-1980   141
   John Bryden

6. The Scottish Labour Market   163
   Laurie Hunter

7. The Hidden Labour Force: Women in the Scottish Economy since 1945 183
   Rosalind Mitchison

8. The Role of Government   195
   Gavin McCrone

9. The Highlands and Islands Development Board   214
   Sir Kenneth Alexander

10. The Scottish Development Agency   233
    Gavin McCrone and J. N. Randall

11. New Towns and New Industries   245
    J. N. Randall

12. Policy and Process in Scottish Housing, 1950-1980   270
    Andrew Gibb and Duncan Maclennan

13. Coal, Gas and Oil: The Changing Energy Scene in Scotland, 1950-1980 292
    Stuart McDowall

Index   312

INTRODUCTION

The general themes in the chapters of this volume cover the development of the Scottish economy since the end of the Second World War, and in particular in the three decades after 1950. While all the aspects of Scottish society discussed here have not been covered in the same detail, it is hoped that the interrelationships between different sectors will be understood and appreciated from the different approaches of the individual authors. Some reference has been necessary in several chapters to events before the War, though it is assumed that readers are familiar with the general outlines of Scottish development over the past century. Most chapters were first given as research papers to a series of seminars organised at the University of St. Andrews. They have been revised for the present symposium, in some cases substantially so.

It would not have been possible to organise the original series of discussions without the warm and enthusiastic support of Dr. J. Steven Watson, Principal of the University of St. Andrews, and it is more than a formal note of gratitude that is recorded here. We were fortunate to obtain financial support from the Jubilee Trust founded by Gershom Stewart, and the Carnegie Trust for the Universities of Scotland contributed generously towards various items of expenses. Regular comments were made on the seminar papers by colleagues at St. Andrews, notably Professor T. C. Smout, B. P. Lenman, Stuart McDowall, Dr. R. F. Fardon and Dr. L. Weatherill; and among others whose intellectual help has been encouraging and positive are Kirsten Ross of Cooper, Lybrand Associates, George Kerevan of Napier College and Professor John Foster of Paisley College. I also wish to thank Paul Auerbach of Kingston Polytechnic, Dr. David Bland of Sheffield University and G. R. Smith for their assistance at various points in the past two years. I am indebted to Robin Gibb of the St. Andrews University Cartographic Service for drawing the diagrams which accompany the text.

I have been asked to point out that the chapters for which Gavin McCrone and John Randall are responsible are of course their personal contributions to this book and should not be assumed to represent the views of their Department. John Tuckwell of John Donald Publishers has been generous with his advice and co-operation, and not least with his patient understanding of the problems of collecting together a symposium with many contributors; and finally, I would wish to register my own personal acknowledgement of the helpfulness and support which the contributors to this volume have shown to their editor. I can only offer my grateful thanks.

Richard Saville, St. Andrews

1

THE INDUSTRIAL BACKGROUND TO THE POST-WAR SCOTTISH ECONOMY

Richard Saville

In the early post-war years which preceded the period covered by this volume the Scottish economy maintained its long-established position as one of the leading industrial, commercial and financial centres of Europe. The industrial and trade reports of the 1940s and the first post-war Census of Production of 1948 confirmed that Scotland possessed a strong manufacturing base across most industrial classifications. In numerous products, especially in mechanical engineering, metal manufacture, shipbuilding and 'other' manufacturing industries, Scottish firms achieved internationally competitive standards of production and quality. Several trades made a significant impact on U.K. production figures and for shipbuilding and marine engineering on world output as well. Moreover, the commercial and financial sectors were competitive in merchanting and financial provision, and in the organisation and export of services, insurance and credit. It is important to acknowledge the strengths of Scottish industry at this time, which benefited from rearmament and war, and subsequently from the post-1945 export boom and the increase in demand from domestic sources. From the vantage point of the late 1940s it appeared that Scottish industry had a bright future, and that unemployment, the great scourge of the inter-war period, would remain at only a few per cent of the insured population. This important social fact, too easily forgotten in the 1980s, made a strong impression on contemporary thinking. Further, the determination of the Government and Scottish planners to deal effectively with the previous neglect of social provision, in particular with housing and the establishment of new towns, strengthened the widely held view that the post-war world was going to be qualitatively different, and better, from that of the inter-war period.

It has to be stressed that the industrial base for the post-war economy was, in general terms, inherited from the 1930s. It was the engineering, shipbuilding and metal working trades of Scotland which primarily benefited from munitions contracts, augmented in the 1940s by Government policies and expenditure, and after 1945 by more favourable export and demand conditions for the products of the engineering industries than had existed for the inter-war years.[1] This was widely acknowledged at that time.[2] By 1948 it was evident that, compared with the U.K. as a whole, manufacturing industry had consolidated its position in most of the sectors in which Scotland had been heavily represented in the 1930s, and indeed had strengthened this position in a number of respects.[3] One should stress that this was the case 'in general terms', as in a number of 'new' manufacturing fields Scotland had been able to

1

attract considerable investment from England and North America, a part of which had been directed north of the border in wartime.

By the late 1930s the general thrust of the industrial work of Government, and of a number of semi-official organisations, embodied an attitude to the Scottish engineering, shipbuilding and capital goods sectors which considered that these had little, if any, potential for growth, except in the short term for war production. This led to policies which encouraged 'newer' industries, and which tended to neglect the older and traditional strengths. This neglect of the latter, which was obviously untenable in the conditions of the late 1940s, derived from the demoralising experience of the inter-war years, and from the failure of the Scottish economy to grow as fast, and in the same way, as the British economy as a whole before the war. The general consensus of the 'thirties had been that industrial problems were essentially those which could be solved by restructuring and rationalisation, and by the development of new trades, and that therefore the problems of Scottish industry were not the result of a general failure of the economy and of aggregate demand, or of the lack of more substantial Government involvement in economic life.[4] We should just note that this view of the older and traditional industries as obsolescent was particularly appealing to the town and country planners and was used to support many of the planning proposals of this era. This was of importance for post-war Scottish planning, and is discussed below in sections 6 and 7.

We turn first in the present chapter to the reports on the Census of Production and Import Duties Inquiry Act of 1935 (published from 1938 to 1944). These reports (together with the Ministry of Labour employment data) dominated contemporary thinking and were the benchmarks used in discussions during the 1940s to measure industrial change and diversification.[5] They showed that during the inter-war years part of Scottish industry had been in a serious, and in some cases, deteriorating position relative to those industries in the U.K. as a whole. Adverse comparisons were made between Scotland and the U.K. for the 'newer' industries of vehicles, aircraft, and electrical engineering, as well as for longer-established trades in respect of insufficient utilisation of modern production technologies and market orientations. A mounting list of publications, among them the inter-war Censuses of Production of 1924, 1930 and 1935, were available in evidence. They provided a basis for post-war industrial planning, and in particular supported the case for increased Government intervention and the need for a shift in the proportion of investment in Scotland towards light engineering, consumer durables, and mass production technology, and away from the existing engineering base.

A great deal of effort was expended in the 1940s in dealing with industrial problems, particularly in respect of new industries, though the work done was much wider in its applications, and included industrial rationalisation, the development of energy supplies, infrastructural investment and large-scale planning of housing schemes and new towns. It will be noted that one of the main differences in Scottish public life after 1945 compared with the climate of opinion at the end of the First World War was the acceptance, and involvement, of Government at many levels of the economy. These matters are taken up in subsequent chapters for the decades after 1950. The final sections of this chapter cover the period from the end of the war to the close of the decade and focus on the industrial structure as shown in the 1948 Census of Production.

Several points should be briefly remarked upon. It is impossible to appreciate the ideological climate of the 1940s and the direction of post-war planning without reference to the awareness of the social problems and levels of unemployment of the inter-war years. After 1921 unemployment remained above 10% of the total insured workforce, and from 1930 to 1935 it was twice this level, reaching 27.7% in 1932, though many areas and trades experienced higher rates.[6] With unemployment went poverty: some twenty per cent of the adult population existed on an income of under ten shillings a week, as compared with ten per cent in Britain as a whole, and no less than 23% of Scottish families lived in overcrowded houses, as compared with 4% in England and Wales.[7] The fear of a return to depression gave a cutting edge to the efforts of planners and private organisations at the end of the war, and formed a crucial part of the appeal of the Labour Party in 1945. It is a measure of the success of the post-war economy and of the Government planning discussed in this book that it is difficult for a modern generation to envisage the poverty and hopelessness of parts of Scotland in the inter-war years. When one reads, for example, in the Clyde Valley Regional Plan of 1946, of the serious social condition of the Vale of Leven, then the focus on new towns, housing schemes, industrial diversification and full employment in that Plan and other reports of the time becomes more meaningful.[8]

The collection of data for Government publications normally contrasted Scotland with other parts of the U.K. These publications have provided benchmarks with policy implications, as did the reports of the Registrar General before the war, and the various housing statistics then and since. Some of these commentaries are well known to historians, as is the *Royal Commission on the Distribution of the Industrial Population* published in January 1940 (henceforth, the Barlow Commission) which gave a detailed series of regional comparisons in which to situate the adverse position of the West of Scotland and the other depressed areas compared with London, the Home Counties and the Midlands.[9] A number of these reports, indeed some of the most important at the time, came from business. The Earl of Elgin, for example, summed up a widespread feeling when he wrote in the preface to the volume by C. A. Oakley, *Scottish Industry Today* (1936), that 'in the world slump which followed the war Scotland suffered heavily, more heavily than many of her neighbours'. There are many similar views in the literature of these years, and most included suggestions for distinct Scottish remedies. The civil service in Scotland moved hesitatingly in these directions in the 1930s, and their experience of the opposition from Whitehall to serious ameliorative action proved useful in the wartime discussions on reconstruction. References to the situation in the U.S.A. and Canada were fewer in number, though several studies pointed to the benefits which could accrue to industry from the utilisation of American production methods and design techniques. By the 1970s the divergent rates of growth between the U.S.A. and Europe on the one hand, and Scotland and the U.K. on the other, had to some extent displaced the earlier England & Wales and Scotland comparisons.[10] These latter divergences still existed of course, as is made clear in the chapter which follows by Neil Buxton.

It is important to note the poor performance of most aspects of the Scottish economy before the war relative to the U.K. The figures for Scottish national income show that 'the growth of real income was relatively low, increasing by only one fifth over the period 1924 to 1937, a rate much lower than in the U.K. as a whole'.[11] In terms of the level of business activity, the Clydesdale and North of Scotland Bank index indicated that Scotland barely participated in the mild growth of the British economy of the later 1920s, and that total activity fell some 20% from 1929 to 1932, or twice the level for the whole of Great Britain, with only a modest recovery before 1936. The size of the insured workforce rose more slowly in Scotland for the years 1922 to 1939 than in Great Britain as a whole, and the number recorded as actually employed did likewise.[12] Unemployment in the country would have worsened more rapidly in the 'twenties had it not been for the high level of migration, which reached 111% of the natural increase for the period 1921 to 1931.[13] As is indicated by the figures in Tables 2 and 3 below, the rate of development of newer industries in Scotland had been slower than in England by 1935. They go a long way to explain the thrust of Government policies in the 1940s.

Furthermore, the problem of maintaining the Scottish industrial base had been exacerbated in the 1920s by the demise of a range of promising developments in cars and lorry manufacture, in aircraft and aircraft engines and in the large number of engineering suppliers which these products required. Taken together, and there are additional ways of looking at the adverse performance of Scotland, as Professor Buxton has phrased it, it would seem that 'there was a significant deterioration in Scotland's relative economic position compared with Great Britain as whole'.[14]

1. THE INTER-WAR PERSPECTIVE ON SCOTTISH INDUSTRY

The Census of Production for 1935 was conducted after the worst of the Depression, and before the main upturn of recovery in the late 1930s, associated primarily in Scotland with rearmament. Table 1 lists Scottish industries noted in the Census, with a number of exceptions where employment and output were below 1%. They are grouped under the general classifications used in 1935, which were changed in some respects in the 1948 Census, with some industries being amalgamated and others listed elsewhere.[15]

The figures indicate a wide range in the percentage of Scottish outputs and employment for the industries and product groups in each of the classifications.[16] Several key deductions were made at the time from these variations, in general around the idea that the figures emphasised the dangers of over-representation in heavy industries and under-representation in newer ones, and this led to policy implications designed to strengthen the latter. The figures also indicate under-representation at the consumer goods end of several long-established trades. Thus in the foundry and wrought steel category in Table 1 were several industries which had a long history in England, but which were weak north of the border; toolmaking, cutlery, domestic ware and needles come into this category. For the Iron and Steel trades as a whole, one of the most difficult questions concerned the rundown of domestic pig-iron production and the possible shift in location of steel-smelting to a site on the Lower Clyde. This is discussed in detail by Peter Payne in Chapter 3.[17]

The figures for Mechanical Engineering and Shipbuilding in 1935, when compared with those of the previous inter-war Censuses, show that the Scottish companies had maintained their position through the Depression, and remained important in U.K. production for many kinds of machinery outputs. The production for individual trades in the Mechanical Engineering sector ranged at the top end from 66.9% of U.K. output for sugar making and refining machinery, 65.3% for domestic and commercial sewing machines, 54.1% for non-ship boilers (mainly railway locomotives, coal central heating systems and steam turbines), and 41.8% for marine engines.[18] This last industry and shipbuilding increased their proportion of U.K. output by the end of the decade. A smaller part of U.K. output was provided by the other main sections of this classification, mining and hydraulic equipment (24.6%), laundry machinery (21.4%), power pumps (21.0%) and some textile machinery. As with the above trades, these are best described as quality products, which required considerable skill on the part of the workforce to adapt basic models to customer specifications. Even where volume output of the same product was undertaken, it was rarely possible to talk about mass production in the sense used in the 1930s. These trades, however, were part of an integrated, almost homogeneous engineering industry which linked hundreds of firms by purchasing and trading networks, and often by kinship ties as well. As the 1932 Board of Trade report on the South West of Scotland noted, the influence of the shipbuilding industry

> extends backwards to the steel, the iron and the coal trades, and forwards first and obviously to marine engineering and then to a very great number of other industries. In the modern passenger ship there is a vast amount of work to be done after the hull has been constructed; indeed, it is an instance of the growth of specialisation in industry that within a particular trade there is often a subdivision specially devoted to marine purposes. Thus firms are described as ships' cabinetmakers, ship electricians, ship flooring makers and manufacturers of sanitary and cooking appliances for ships. The manufacture of flags, of asbestos, of ropes, of paints, of engine cleaning waste, all depend very largely in this area on the amount of shipping and ship construction . . . cargo boats have likewise become specialised and some of these, as for instance refrigerating ships, bring into the picture new types of engineering or other industries. It follows that the state of shipbuilding, ship repairing and marine engineering cannot fail to have very important repercussions on a great number of other industries.[19]

Table 1 (a). *Census of Production 1935: Classifications 1-15 and Government Departments*

Industry	Gross Output Scotland % of U.K.	Net Output Scotland % of U.K.	Employment Scotland % of U.K.
1. Textiles	8.8	11.0	10.7
2. Leather	6.5	6.2	5.6
3. Clothing	3.6	3.7	4.6
4. Iron and steel trades	9.2	9.6	9.7
5. Engineering, shipbuilding, vehicles	8.4	7.9	8.9
6. Non-ferrous metals	2.5	3.7	3.0
7. Food, drink, tobacco	9.7	10.3	12.7
8. Chemicals and allied trades	7.8	7.9	7.9
9. Miscellaneous trades	8.4	8.7	8.3
10. Paper, print, stationery	10.2	9.7	10.5
11. Timber trades	8.6	7.8	8.7
12. Clay and building materials	5.6	5.6	5.9
13. Building and contracting	7.6	8.3	9.4
14. Mines and quarries	12.5	12.4	11.1
15. Public utility services	7.8	8.1	8.2
Government departments	6.8	6.0	5.7

Table 1 (b). *Census of Production 1935*

Classifications 1-3 Textile, Leather, Clothing	Gross Output Scotland as % of U.K.	Net Output Scotland as % of U.K.	U.K.	Employment Scotland	Scotland as % of U.K.
Jute	99.0	98.5	24190	23898	98.8
Carpets in (W.W.)	32.3				
Fancy Hosiery in (H.T.)	27.8				
Fell Mongery	27.6	27.7	2431	579	23.8
Canvas Goods and Sack	30.0	24.6	8844	2081	23.5
Lace	22.6	22.4	16342	3061	18.7
Rope, Twine and Net	21.4	22.2	15276	3564	23.3
Linen and Hemp	17.6	19.6	69152	11598	16.8
Hosiery Trade (H.T.)	9.6	11.8	115673	16706	14.5
Woollen and Worsted	7.7	10.6	242209	25176	10.4
Cotton Spinning and Doubling	4.6	9.3	182415	9679	5.3
Textile Finishing	9.4	9.3	100084	10488	10.5
Leather (Tanning and Dressing)	5.4	6.0	30286	1823	6.0
Mackintoshes, Oilskins, Proofed Garments	5.3				
Underwear (in H.T.)	5.2				
Fur	5.2	5.7	7647	547	7.2
Tailoring, Dressmaking, Millinery (T.D.M.)	4.1	4.4	362334	19874	5.5
Bespoke Tailoring (in T.D.M.)	5.0				
Undergarments (in T.D.M.)	3.9				
Wholesale Tailoring (in T.D.M.)	3.4				
Silk, Artificial Silk, Rayon etc.	2.8	3.6	81825	2313	2.8
Boot and Shoe	2.6	2.6	122734	3534	2.9
Cotton Weaving	1.7	2.3	166904	3891	2.3
Leather Goods	1.9	2.3	17816	443	2.5

Table 1 (b) (continued)

	Gross Output	Net Output	Employment		
Classification 4 Iron and Steel Trades	Scotland as % of U.K.	Scotland as % of U.K.	U.K.	Scotland	Scotland as % of U.K.
Iron and Steel (Foundries)	16.3	17.6	109643	20014	18.3
Wrought Iron and Steel Tubes (Small Arms Private)	E 18.2	E 15.2	28387 } 1399 }	E 5339	E 17.9
Iron and Steel (Smelting and Rolling)	11.0	12.4	135274	16216	12.0
Blast Furnaces	6.8	7.8	15815	1429	9.0
Wire	6.4	7.2	23427	20.75	8.9
Chain, Nail, Screw and Miscel- laneous Forgings	7.9	6.0	56783	3821	6.7
Metallic Furniture, Sheet Metal, Holloware	2.4	2.5	97778	2863	2.9
Tool Implements	1.2	1.4	25508	447	1.8
Classifications 5-6 *Engineering, Shipbuilding,* *Vehicles, Non-Ferrous Metals*					
Sugar Making, Refining Machines (M.E.)	66.9				
Sewing Machines, Boot and Shoe Machines (M.E.)	65.3				
Boilers (excluding for ships) (M.E.)	54.1				
Marine Engines (M.E.)	41.8				
Shipbuilding	29.3	25.9	82020	21353	26.0
Mining Machinery (M.E.)	24.6				
Laundering Machinery (M.E.)	21.4				
Pumps, Hand Power and Petrol (M.E.)	21.0				
Constructional Repair Work (M.E.)	12.0				
Textile Accessories (M.E.)	11.8				
Mechanical Engineering (M.E.)	14.6	13.3	432811	62855	14.5
Aluminium, Lead, Tin (Smelting and Rolling) (N.F.M.)	5.5	7.1	27238	1696	6.2
Machine Tools and Parts (M.E.)	5.9				
Prime Movers or Ship Engines (M.E.)	5.7				
Carriage, Cart and Wagon	4.5	5.7	6153	326	5.3
Textile Machinery (M.E.)	4.9				
Agricultural Machinery (M.E.)	4.9				
Finished Brass (N.F.M.)	3.9	3.8	34824	997	2.9
Railway Carriage and Wagon	4.6	3.3	20651	969	4.7
Motor and Cycle	2.3	2.6	279748	9172	3.3
Copper and Brass (Smelting and Rolling (N.F.M.)	1.7	2.0	28052	834	3.0
Electrical Engineering	1.2	1.1	347948	3299	1.3
Classification 7 *Food, Drink and Tobacco*					
Spirit Distilling	48.0	51.0	3220	1603	49.8
Fish Curing	40.6	39.8	5543	2355	42.5
Wholesale Bottling	28.3	30.2	23323	4505	19.3

Table 1 (b) (continued)

	Gross Output	Net Output	Employment		
Classification 7 (continued) *Food, Drink and Tobacco*	*Scotland as* *% of U.K.*	*Scotland as* *% of U.K.*	*U.K.*	*Scotland*	*Scotland as* *% of U.K.*
Biscuit	18.7	18.1	44001	8940	20.3
Bread, Cakes	17.8	17.7	110637	21593	19.5
Bacon Curing and Sausage	9.7	10.3	19695	2196	11.2
Preserved Foods	8.5	8.1	49970	4160	8.3
Sugar and Glucose	5.2	7.9	16507	1117	6.9
Aerated Water, Cider, Vinegar, British Wine	8.1	7.6	17861	1801	10.1
Grain-milling	7.3	6.4	30135	2275	7.5
Brewing and Malting	6.3	6.2	55809	4279	7.7
Cocoa and Sugar Confectionery	6.2	6.0	74169	7406	10.0
Butter, Cheese, Condensed Milk, Margarine	5.6	5.5	15085	1055	7.0
Cattle, Dog, Poultry Foods	5.5	3.5	9062	467	5.2
Tobacco	2.2	1.8	42859	1826	4.3
Classification 8 *Chemicals and Allied Trades*					
Explosives Petroleum	} 44.8	} 50.3	9870 4157	} E 5362	} 38.2
Fertiliser, Disinfectant and Glue	13.8	13.3	9619	1251	13.0
Starch and Polishes	8.6	7.2	8722	797	8.9
Chemicals, Dyestuffs, Drugs	5.4	5.2	77611	4445	5.7
Paint, Colour and Varnish	5.2	4.6	24893	1397	5.6
Oil and Tallow	4.4	3.4	9717	587	6.0
Seed Crushing	3.4	2.8	11542	465	4.0
Soap, Candle, Perfumery	2.9	2.2	29114	920	3.2
Ink, Gum, Typewriter Requisites	1.8	1.7	4999	147	2.9
Classifications 9-10 *Miscellaneous Trades and Paper,* *Printing and Stationery*					
Linoleum and Oilcloth	35.7	36.6	12455	4019	32.3
Paper	18.2	18.9	59748	13013	21.8
Rubber	9.8	9.3	55593	6995	12.6
Printing, Bookbinding, Stereo- typing, Engraving	9.4	9.2	169416	16989	10.0
Sports Requisites	9.7	8.6	8253	800	9.7
Printing, Publications, News- papers, Periodicals	8.2	8.4	79454	6629	8.3
Manufactured Stationery	6.3	6.0	44722	3570	8.0
Cardboard Box Trade	6.3	6.0	41899	2651	6.3
Scientific Instruments, Appliances, Apparatus	4.5	5.3	30059	1873	6.2
Coke and By-products	3.8	4.5	14061	621	4.4
Classifications 11-14 *Mines, Quarries, Timber Trades,* *Clay and Building Materials,* *Building and Contracting*					
Coopering	33.4	33.6	2775	879	31.7
Wooden Crates, Cases, Boxes and Trunks	17.8	15.6	11551	1709	14.8

Table 1 (b) (continued)

	Gross Output	Net Output	Employment		
Classifications 11-14 (continued) Mines, Quarries, Timber Trades, Clay and Building Materials, Building and Contracting	Scotland as % of U.K.	Scotland as % of U.K.	U.K.	Scotland	Scotland as % of U.K.
Non-Metaliferous Mines and Quarries (excluding coal, salt, slate)	14.3	14.8	56692	8870	15.6
Coal Mines	12.8	12.6	764175	84945	11.1
Timber (Sawmilling)	10.6	9.3	68074	7368	10.8
Building Materials	7.9	9.3	32406	3600	11.1
Building and Contracting	7.6	8.3	502278	47253	9.4
Brick and Fireclay	7.7	7.3	92074	7715	8.4
Glass	4.9	4.7	46201	1986	4.3
Furniture and Upholstery	5.1	5.5	109226	6970	6.4
Slate, Mines and Quarries	3.1	3.1	9598	327	3.4
China and Earthenware	2.5	2.6	68537	1338	2.0
Cement	1.7	1.0	10220	162	1.6
Classification 15 Public Utilities and Government Departments					
Trainway, Light Railway Undertakings	14.9	13.1	25359	3567	14.1
Canal, Dock and Harbour	13.2	13.0	14302	1890	13.2
Railway Companies	8.5	9.3	211219	20280	9.6
Local Authorities	8.3	8.0	191052	14986	7.8
Electricity	7.1	7.6	102945	7048	6.8
Gas	7.3	7.5	121249	7028	5.8
Water	6.5	6.8	31974	2108	6.6
Government Departments	6.8	6.0	102453	5808	5.7

The industrial linkage represented by shipbuilding and the supplying trades was the best known of the Scottish industrial patterns, though a detailed look at each machinery sector would feature a similar type of linkage.

Numerous machinery makers, faced with sharp cuts in purchases, survived the depression by basing their output on continued demand for only a limited range of goods. Beardmores, a case in point, mainly restricted outputs by the close of the 1920s to their foundry and steel plants.[20] But virtually the whole of the textile-making sector, machine tools, including those firms making automatic lathes, milling, planing and boring and drilling mills, pumping machinery and internal combustion engines were unable to extend their shares of the U.K. market, and with the closure of the passenger car firms, the aircraft engine industry and some chemical plants there was little incentive to invest in a broader output. An analysis of the lower end of the machine-producing sector, as in the case of the weaker side of the foundry and wrought-steel classification, indicates the degree to which the range of products remained geared to markets which were established earlier in the century, and especially to Scottish and colonial buyers. However, it must be stressed that Scottish engineering firms were able to remain among the most advanced in the world in the heavy machinery and individual products sectors, and the investment they made in the inter-war years ensured both an effective base for the industrial needs of the country in war, and for the successful export drive in the years following.

The most obvious examples of weakness in the metal-using industries (listed in Table 1) were in motor vehicles, with the virtual absence of cars and lorries (2.6%), of aircraft engines (nil), railway carriage work (3.3%), and the many branches of the chemical industry which normally supplied inputs for mass-produced consumer goods, particularly paints and plastics. These trades had been built up prior to and during the First World War in Scotland, and their rundown in the 1920s had serious implications in the metal and miscellaneous trades which supplied them. The small scale of the output of alloy and special steels, the wire trades, sheet steel, porcelain, non-ferrous metals (3.7%), the minor size of the textile and upholstery trade serving the vehicles sector followed from the closures of that decade. These trades had rapidly expanded south of the border, and the advantages of English sites gave the Ministry of Supply and the Board of Trade Control of Factory and Storage Premises organisation during the early years of the war a case for not shifting production to Scotland. We may take the matter further by looking at the size of the electrical engineering industry. In 1935 Scotland still produced virtually no electrically powered generators, and a small fraction only of U.K. output of electric motors, power transformers, and switch gear. No lighting accessories or fittings were produced, no wireless sets, telegraph or telephone apparatus, sound reproducers, radio gramophones, valves or batteries. The electrical engineering industry, such as it was, was tied up with shipbuilding, ship fitting and mining equipment, and nearly a quarter of the meagre total of net output was accounted for by repair work and maintenance.

Thus Scotland had not sustained many significant developments in a wide range of newer industries which had expanded in England. Virtually the whole U.K. production of motor vehicles, aircraft and their engines, electrical goods for industry, and the huge range of consumer electrical goods and building industry requirements was located south of the border. The engineering industry in Scotland in 1935 was oriented towards traditional linkages connected with shipbuilding, boilers, locomotives and assorted specialised engineering work, though, of course, we are talking about thousands of products here. Mass production and consumer goods were neglected, and even with particular developments in new industries in the 1930s, such as the initiatives of the Scottish Co-operative Wholesale Society, the view of Scottish entrepreneurship as cautious in the newer trades does not alter, advanced as they were in basic industries.[21] In aggregate terms Scotland's share of the newer industries in the U.K. in the inter-war years was under 5% by 1935, and the rate of development below half of that of the south. Summing up an analysis of the movement of industrial trends, Neil Buxton, in an earlier article, noted that the main features of the Scottish economy between the wars were the heavier commitment to industries that were stagnating or in decline . . . [and] at the same time, an inability to secure a share in the 'new' growth industries of the 1930s . . . in 1924 the 'new' industries in Scotland were conspicuous largely by their absence. Subsequently their development was so slow that over a decade later they were still less important in the Scottish economy than they had been in the U.K. in 1924. [Table 2] also emphasises the much greater weight of the staples in Scotland. As in the U.K. their contribution to total net output underwent some relative decline between 1924 and 1935, but even by the latter date they still accounted for well over one third of the region's production. Throughout the inter-war years the general course of the Scottish economy was still largely determined by these traditional industries.[22]

In summary, Table 2 shows the contribution of the 'new' and the 'staple' industries to the value of total net output in Scotland and in the U.K., at the three Census dates of 1924, 1930 and 1935.

Table 2

		1924	1930	1935
		(Figures expressed as percentage of net output of all Census of Production Figures)		
Scotland:	'New' industries	8.3	9.1	11.0
	Staple industries	43.2	40.9	36.8
U.K.:	'New' industries	14.1	15.9	21.0
	Staple industries	37.0	29.6	27.8

Source: Neil K. Buxton, 'Economic Growth in Scotland between the Wars: The Role of Production Structure and Rationalisation', *Economic History Review*, 2nd series, Vol. 33, no. 4 (1980). Table 6, p. 549

Table 3

	London & Home Counties	Lancs.	West Riding, Notts Derby	Staffs Warwick Worcs. Leics. Northants	North & Durham	Mid-Scot.	Glamorgan & Monmouth
Total industrial population in 23 industries, 1923	1342270	456750	329750	497910	139300	255220	83460
Number in the 23 industries as % of total insured population in area in 1923	55.5	26.9	23.5	41.1	22.5	32.2	18.3
Increase in the 23 industries 1923-1937 as % of total in G.B. in those industries	32.2	11.2	9.3	11.4	4.1	4.8	2.6

Source: Royal Commission on the Distribution of the Industrial Population, Cmd. 6153 (1940), adapted from Table on p. 39

The regional differences in the rates of growth of British industries were often pointed out in the inter-war years and, for example, comparative figures from different parts of Britain were given in the Final Report of the Barlow Commission. The figures given there came from Ministry of Labour employment data on twenty-three industries in which the rate of expansion between 1923 and 1937 was greater than the average rate of growth. The low rate of increase for Scotland, parts of Wales and the North of England need hardly be remarked upon.

2. THE DEVELOPMENT OF NEW APPROACHES TO SCOTTISH INDUSTRY

The evidence tended to suggest that, amongst other requirements, a radical diversification of the Scottish industrial base towards new industries was required. How this was to be achieved raises the question of the development of contemporary opinion and the change in public policy during wartime and why policy and expenditure took certain directions and not others. This is always a difficult problem of exposition, and we shall note only some aspects. The first is the work of local authorities and semi-official organisations, the main one being the Scottish Development Council founded in 1931, and its offshoot the Scottish Economic Committee of April 1936. This latter group worked with the general aim of the industrial development of Scotland, the promotion of its business image, and the attraction to the country of light engineering and consumer-oriented industrial products.[23] The second concerns the change in the attitudes of Government departments, including the Scottish Office, and organisations like the Special Areas Commission. There were some divergences of approach by the end of the 1930s between Government organisations in Scotland and those in London. Third, there is the question of how the war years culminated in a radical realignment of attitudes to the role of the public sector, and how this was focused on questions which were more concerned with town and country planning and demand management, and not primarily with industry. On a general note we have to remember that Scotland had a strong left-wing political presence which embraced many organisations, and these had a tradition of active support within the trade union movement. There is evidence to suggest that the political activities of the groups involved, and the spread of socialist ideas on nationalisation and state planning caused concern to the industrial circles involved in the Scottish Development Council and also to Government departments. This had a bearing on the interest shown by many industrialists in solutions to the economic crisis involving planning ideas which took an intermediate path between those of socialism on the one hand and legislation enacted by the post-1931 National Government on the other. Further, a discussion of ideas and policy relevant to Scotland in the 'thirties and in wartime has to acknowledge that most general economic policies which affected the whole of the U.K., such as tariffs and wartime control over production, were determined in London, and that Scottish influences were important only on occasion. The development of thinking about demand management and the ideas of J. M. Keynes and the inter-departmental discussions on the type of post-war policies to be carried out at the U.K. level were also centred on London, particularly in the Treasury and the Board of Trade.[24]

3. THE WORK OF THE SCOTTISH ECONOMIC COMMITTEE

The Scottish Economic Committee, by itself and in conjunction with state organisations, made several important contributions to the industrial discussion. Primarily it acted as a business-oriented forum which underpinned the arguments for industrial change, and coming as it did from a respectable establishment body, it was taken more seriously by the Conservative Party in Scotland and by business in general. Further, it emphasised that Scotland had to be treated as a separate entity with problems which only specific 'Scottish' remedies could solve. This was clearly stated in its reports, though it was careful not to antagonise existing firms, or raise the question of why so many firms had pulled out of 'newer' industries and halted diversification in existing trades in the 1920s. It provided evidence of entrepreneurial caution in light engineering and consumer industries which, it argued, would take a massive effort to resolve. On the technical and business level the Committee was crucial in bringing to the attention of planners the need to diversify effort for new plant investment, labour and management training, and expand their design work, advertising and marketing. Its report on 'Light Industries', published in 1938, is worth quoting from:

> The Economic Committee has elsewhere laid stress on the fact which is no doubt becoming generally appreciated, that an increasing development of light industry is desirable in Scotland in the interests of industrial stability. The manufacturer of consumer goods, in particular for the home market, is less liable to violent cyclical changes, involving acute variations in employment, than the heavy industries and shipbuilding, which depend mainly on the export market, and are therefore sensitive to the fluctuations of international trade. If a considerable development of light industry could be brought about in Scotland, it would form a most useful complement to the basic industries, and would tend to mitigate the unfortunate effects of depression in those industries by providing a reasonably constant source of employment and production. It is of course the case that Scotland already has a wide range of light industries in which many enterprises and successful firms are engaged. But there has been no development of light industry in Scotland since the war which is proportionate to the advances made by the principal light industries in England, especially in the Midlands, the South East area and Greater London.[25]

The point about the diversity of Scottish production in light industry is valid for the textile trades such as boots and shoes, hosiery, and underwear, but examples of modern developments were few, and comparisons with England only underlined Scottish weakness. The Committee's 1938 report on the furniture trade pointed to an inability to learn from changing market needs in existing consumer trades:

> With a few exceptions Scottish manufacturers have neglected the lower income groups. The requirements of the assured income classes, schoolmasters, ministers, public officials etc., are considered carefully, and the makers of bed settees etc., compete in all but the very cheapest lines, but for his living room, the working man is practically compelled to buy furniture made outside Scotland.[26]

With textiles and furniture the Committee was dealing with industries which were well established, with a labour process which emphasised the skilled nature of the trade and with the management difficulties involved in production of lower-quality goods for a mass market. Its reports on heating, ventilating and refrigerating equipment and the food-processing industry raised further problems faced by the management of these industries, though it was basically of the opinion that the existing trade and industrial base could be used to diversify to the lower end of the market. But with Electrical Appliances and Equipment, where 'interests further south have advanced . . . to an extent which makes expansion difficult in Scotland', it was deeply pessimistic.[27] One possibility the Committee could see for growth, given the reluctance of most indigenous capitalists to diversify, was to secure offshoots of existing English and North American companies, so that branches would avoid those start-up costs associated with non-factory management which new firms required. Background discussions to the establishment of the Scottish Development Council in 1931 pointed to advances in engineering and miscellaneous trades brought by foreign firms, and examples were given of the post-World War I reorganisation of the Inchinan aerodrome by the India Tyre and Rubber Co., the success of Babcox and Wilcox, of Singers at Clydebank, and the North British Rubber Co. This led to the need to consider the attractiveness of the Scottish environment to incoming business, to the establishment of Scottish Industrial Estates Ltd. in 1937, and to the Bellahouston Park Empire Exhibition of 1938 which emphasised the business amenities of the country in general and the focus Scotland provided for the Empire as a whole.

The Committee thus left several legacies: one was concern about a focus on new trades, based on the assumption that future growth would not be substantial in the older industries and in those where Scotland was already well represented. Second, it focused attention on the managerial difficulties of mass-production and consumer industries. Further, it is important to recognise the contribution its writings made towards a detailed 'feel' of the variety of problems facing industries of different types, and towards pinpointing the need to consider location policy, and advertising, research and investment.

An acceptance of the need for diversification into new industrial fields in the Scottish business world, or at least a part of it, by itself meant little, and the general lack of commitment of money and resources from private enterprise raises a number of fundamental questions about the workings of the private sector in respect of new enterprise, and how widely the positive view of this kind of diversification was shared. Moreover, there seems little doubt that considerable efforts were made within existing Scottish industries, especially in engineering in the later 1930s, to improve quality and expand the range of products, some of which activity was due to mergers and rationalisation. But this was a different matter to moving resources from older industry to new ones. This problem was approached in several ways by the Economic Committee. A sub-committee under the chairmanship of the General Manager of the Royal Bank of Scotland examined the question of finance for new industries, and in 1938 the Scottish Development Financial Trust was formed with the Earl of Elgin as Chairman, 'to assist in the provision of capital for new or existing enterprises in Scotland . . . so situated as to be unable to obtain financial accommodation through the normal channels'.[28] The provisions of the second and third Special Area Acts of 1936 and 1937 and the £2 million Nuffield bequest of 1936 for new industries in the Special Areas also covered this, but as indicating a recognition of the problems of securing capital for domestic Scottish industry by the financial institutions in Scotland it was of basic importance. Further, in *Scotland's Industrial Future: The Case for Planned Development* (1939) and in the evidence given to the Barlow Commission in March 1938 (and published later the same year) the Economic Committee advocated the establishment of a centralised planning authority for Scotland,

> with a view to securing a well balanced industrial structure throughout the country which would be better able to resist cyclical depression in international trade . . . Its primary duty would be to formulate national plans for the future layout and development of the country . . . a branch of the suggested Planning Authority should be created to deal so far as practicable with the question of the location of industry . . . should have powers enabling it to offer reasonable inducements to industry to establish itself in areas where there is an outstanding need for new developments . . . this branch of the Planning Authority might appropriately consist of a group of established personalities in industry, finance and labour.[29]

Moreover, in evidence to the Commission, Sir Steven Bilsland for the Committee made it clear that its proposed central authority would have to be independent of the Ministry of Health, the Board of Trade, and the Ministry of Labour, and would be responsible to the Secretary of State for Scotland. He agreed that

> the central planning authority would not essentially concern itself with what we know as town and country planning, but would plan in the widest sense. It would have full cognisance of everything that was necessary to overcome the difficulties of Scotland in true development . . . Secondly, as far as industry is concerned there would be constituted some body of trustees or person such as we have at the present time in the Special Areas Commission that would have regard to the development of industry only.[30]

The Economic Committee had arrived at this and other policy recommendations in part because of the weak effect of the Special Areas legislation in Scotland, as well as the failure of its own efforts and those of the Scottish Development Council to persuade existing industries to invest in new ones and to diversify to new lines. Such a clear 'Scottish' angle led a number of Whitehall officials to accuse the Committee of a nationalist bias.[31]

We must be quite clear about the landmark that these ideas represented for Scottish public life. Here was an influential business lobby pointing to the inadequacies of the existing framework of financial provision for industry and of the inability of the protectionist tariff system to help Scotland in an obvious way.[32] Moreover, it noted the failure of the Special Areas legislation of 1934 and after, and of the inadequacy of the private sector, left to itself, to move into new sectors of expansion. It spelt out, industry by industry, the problems of the country, and argued that State intervention in a wide range of matters was absolutely crucial for further progress. This was not a peripheral point but the core of the argument. There was no equivalent to this position among industrialists in England. One should add, of course, that the Committee recognised the influence on Scottish development of the First World War, of international trade and restrictions on the overseas markets for heavy industry products, of the distance of Scotland from markets in England, and that it was generally in favour of some protectionist legislation for newer trades. Its discussion of these matters, however, was limited to a desk-clearing operation which led to the scenario which it outlined in 1938 and 1939. It was not primarily concerned with the industries in which Scotland was most strongly represented in the inter-war Census, and the evidence it gave to the Barlow Commission strengthened the idea that future growth in Scotland would take place outside traditional sectors. As we shall note, this type of evidence was highlighted by the Commission.

It will be seen from the foregoing quotations that the Economic Committee suggested that the central authority was to be more than an industrial planning organisation. It understood the arguments about sites, location and amenities. The emphasis the Committee adopted was thus compatible in many respects with the town and country planning lobby which was on the verge of its wartime breakthrough in public policy and its writings show far more sophistication than, say, those of the Federation of British Industries.[33] The S.E.C. approach to planning would have made little headway in the general political conditions typical of the 1930s, yet within a few years these ideas were widely accepted as a basis for legislation. Before we turn to this, we need to mention the relevant administrative history, as there were parallel developments in ideas in Scottish Government departments in the years before the war. In general it is a record of the decline of ministerial and civil service opposition to a growing State presence in planning industrial change, and the emergence of a fairly responsive group of civil servants in Scotland who were convinced that industrial diversification could only really be brought about by positive Government action.

4. THE SHIFT IN GOVERNMENT ATTITUDES PRIOR TO THE WAR

The ideological shift in public sector attitudes has been the subject of much discussion, and only the outline need be noted. Until the mid-thirties the focus of the U.K. Government had been mainly on the employment situation and on the organisation of import duties and Imperial Preference, with some concern for location of industry and the role of Government in social provision. The Labour Transference scheme for state-assisted emigration was established in 1928, and five Special Areas were set up in late 1934 under the provisions of the Special Areas (Development and Improvement) Act.[34] Despite the statutory provision that the two Special Commissioners (one of whom dealt with Scotland) had powers to initiate, organise, prosecute and assist measures designed to facilitate the economic development and social improvement of the specified Areas, including the establishment of Trading Estate Companies, in practice the emphasis was on a strictly limited number of initiatives. The Scottish Economic Committee noted in its 1938 evidence to the Barlow Commission that

> a number of restrictions [were] applied in administrative practice to the work of the Commissioners, which together with the narrow delimitation of their functions in the Statutes, prevented them in general from carrying out any measures of direct assistance to industry, the work done relating mainly to the improvement of certain local authority services in the Special Areas, such as sewers and hospitals, and the amelioration of the conditions of unemployment by the encouragement of social service facilities and other palliatives. These limitations met with considerable public criticism . . .[35]

Matters were improved by two subsequent Acts. The first was the Special Areas Reconstruction (Agreement) Act, 1936, which set up the Special Areas Reconstruction Association Ltd. with limited powers to provide loans of under £10,000 for small businesses, a scheme supervised by the Bank of England. The Special Areas (Amendment) Act, 1937 expanded this, and the Treasury was authorised, on the recommendations of an Advisory Committee, to make loans to persons carrying on more extensive undertakings than under the original Act, and to offer concessions towards rents, rates and income tax. One positive result of the Scottish Commissioner's work was the North Hillington Trading Estate in Renfrewshire, close to the Glasgow conurbation. Work of a minor kind was carried out there in 1935 and 1936, and later in 1937, largely on the initiative of the Economic Committee and some Scottish civil servants, Scottish Industrial Estates Ltd. was founded with support from the Special Areas Fund run by the Commissioner. The capital expenditure and land purchase came to £932,500, and by May 1939, seventy-eight factories with 1,500 employees were in production. The 1936 and 1937 Acts included provisions for funding new industries, and Lord Nuffield added a third fund, of £2 million, in December 1936. Up to 30 September 1938 financial assistance for capital had been given from the three funds, 'for the establishment of new industries', to only 121 firms in all five Special Areas, at a total cost of £2,874,000 for an employment gain of 14,900. By that date some 290 firms had been assisted by capital and other inducements, such as factory buildings and sites, to start production in the Special Areas.[36] By 1938 the Economic Committee and the Scottish Development Council thought that something of a breakthrough had been achieved in bringing new industries to Scotland, though much of this, as they acknowledged, was a result of the munitions programme.[37] Their publicity, however, encouraged many firms to consider location in Scotland and, after the war, several of these transferred production north of the border.

From the middle of the decade there are signs, though these should not be exaggerated, that official thinking in the Scottish Office was coming round to the view that Scottish economic and social problems should be tackled by distinctive solutions, and that the powers required to implement these would have to be greatly augmented. Moreover, it was appreciated that the scale of unemployment required a more widespread approach than the works achieved under the first Special Areas Act and by the other legislation and aid which bore on this. In the discussions over widening the area covered by the Special Areas the Scottish Office argued that Scotland would have to be treated separately, and by the end of 1936, in regard to the Highlands and Islands, it pushed for increased powers for the Commissioner, 'to instigate, organise, prosecute and assist for the economic development of [all] areas of high unemployment in Scotland'. By June 1938 the Commissioner was prepared to suggest that

> For the Scottish Area the only real hope of some alleviation during the next depression lies in the diversification of its industries. That process is only beginning. Unemployment figures are apt to mislead. There has been a substantial improvement since 1934, but it is mostly in the heavy industries, and to an important extent is due to rearmament; and an area which depends almost wholly on the heavy industries ought properly to be treated as a special area even when its employment is comparatively good, because it will once again become a serious political and administrative problem as soon as trade recedes.[38]

The Scottish Office echoed this in September of that year, when it noted that the decrease in unemployment

> is mostly in the heavy industries, which show a fall of 55% compared with 19% in the remaining industries. The heavy industries will no doubt continue to benefit from the rearmament programme, but unless a considerable diversity of industries can be attracted to the areas they will be liable during the next depression to be as hard hit as before.[39]

Local authorities in Scotland were also pressing for action, and in evidence to the Barlow Commission in December 1937 the County Councils Association for Scotland went so far as to call for a coherent national policy on planning:

> It will be generally agreed that for the future every endeavour should be made to direct and plan the geographical distribution of the industrial population rather than that it should proceed on the haphazard methods of the past. There must therefore be some sort of national control, some sort of national survey, some sort of national town plan into which local schemes can be fitted, and some sort of scale beyond which the number of human beings, and consequently the number of industrial undertakings in any one district is not to be permitted. As against restriction, the creation of new towns and industrial centres should be properly planned.[40]

5. THE SUCCESS OF TOWN PLANNING

The Special Areas policy, and Government intervention to help depressed areas in the 'thirties, have, of course, been criticised as woefully inadequate for the size of the problem. The attempts of organisations such as the Scottish Economic Committee to encourage diversification into new industries had made only a minor impact on the situation; their problem was lack of powers, inadequate finance, and reliance on private sector initiatives within the protectionist system, and on persuasion. But this only raised the question of future industrial trends in a sharper form. It did not impede support for the idea of diversification as one of the central policies to be pursued. The 'something more' needed to achieve these aims was provided by the impending success of the town planning lobby which by the end of the 1930s was ensuring that many of the recommendations of the Scottish Economic Committee would be adopted as Government policy by the end of the war. The quotation above from the County Council Association was only one of many from officials in the 1930s who considered town planning as the solution to working-class illness, atmospheric pollution, and social problems in general.

The *Royal Commission on the Distribution of the Industrial Population* (the Barlow Commission) was established in March 1937 to help develop a broader appreciation of the problem of the Special Areas, and Neville Chamberlain thought it would temper criticism of the Special Areas policy. From the viewpoint of the planning lobby it could not have come at a better time. The evidence published from 1937 to 1939 and the report of January 1940 kept its arguments in the forefront of discussion of industrial questions, and was, with several other wartime reports, to dominate thinking on reconstruction. The Commissioners' recommendations are central to post-war Scotland, and it is useful to consider the main thrust of the report, bearing in mind what the Economic Committee had been striving to achieve.

The Commissioners defined their objectives as threefold: first to consider 'the geographic distribution of the industrial population, together with the probable direction of any change in that distribution in the future', with an emphasis on the main conurbations of the British Isles. This helped to define the problems as primarily urban, rather than, say, industrial. Town planners and health officials came forward with detailed evidence on the adverse consequences of inadequate urban and housing planning powers, and to argue for nationally uniform solutions. Second, the Commissioners were to consider the 'social, economic and strategical disadvantages of the concentration of industries and of the industrial population in large towns or particular areas of the country'.[41] The evidence taken on these matters strengthened the case for general planning powers. And lastly, they assumed they must offer remedial measures which, not surprisingly, were agreeable to the town planning and environmental health lobby.

The Commission in their opening remarks put forward the accepted opinions and attitudes of the planning lobby on British urban life, which considered the growth of population in great towns since the industrial revolution as 'marked by a disastrous harvest of slums, sickness, stunted population and human misery from which the nation suffered in mid-Victorian years and continues, though fortunately to a much lesser extent, to suffer today'.[42] There followed appreciative references to Ebenezer Howard's *Garden Cities of Tomorrow*,[43] the Town and Country Planning Act of 1932, the Council for the Preservation of Rural England, Letchworth and Welwyn Garden Cities, and the role of economists and town planners who had fought 'side by side for the last half century to make England if not the New Jerusalem of Blake's poem at any rate a fairer and sweeter country'. This is the dominant theme of the Barlow Commission, and the key to understanding the core of the report. It was after all the philosophy of the town planning lobby. It was careful to call for evidence from the Federation of British Industries, which remained opposed to strict planning powers and any direction of industry, and the Commission naturally agreed on the importance of industry for the national existence. But, it went on,

> when conditions affecting the health or well-being rather than the wealth of the State demand alteration, when slums, defective sanitation, noise, air pollution and traffic congestion are found to constitute disadvantages, if not dangers to the community, when the problem becomes social in texture rather than economic, then modern civilisation may well require a regulating authority of some kind to step in and take reasonable measures for the protection of the general national interests . . . An enlightened national conscience may well be heard to insist that while successful prosecution of industrial activities is vital to the life of the nation, due attention must be paid to social needs, and consideration given to the question how, with the co-operation of industry and those engaged in its management, grave social evils where shown to exist can be mitigated or removed.[44]

The Commission thus argued on social and health grounds against freedom of location for industry, and in favour of planning, a case it elaborated at length. The Barlow report accepted the arguments of commentators in the 1930s who considered that the heavy industries were no longer carriers of industrial regeneration, the newer lighter sectors being awarded this role. The Commission could thus specifically point to the S.E.C. evidence and report, as a consensus view, that

> It would not seem unreasonable to anticipate that the importance of the pre-war 'basic' industries in the national economy may decline, and that of other industries may increase and in that event the industrial areas containing the former will only be able to keep up with the national rate of general industrial progress, if they are able to stimulate within themselves a growth of the miscellaneous 'light' industries in excess of the rate of growth of such industries in the country as a whole. To what extent that growth can be stimulated, whether by Government action or otherwise, it is impossible to prophesy.[45]

The supposition was made that future industrial and commercial growth could follow the pattern of that in Letchworth and Welwyn Garden Cities, and there were no obvious reasons to suppose otherwise; indeed the report suggested a number of positive reasons why a suburban location would outweigh the disadvantages of not developing in existing conurbations. There is little in the Barlow Report up to this point which was not relevant to Scotland, and with which the S.E.C. and most Scottish civil servants would not have agreed.

In its conclusions the Commission unanimously accepted the need for action to establish a central authority to redevelop congested urban areas, and to decentralise and disperse industry and population. This programme would include an emphasis on garden cities and suburbs, satellite towns and trading estates, and would continue the development of existing small towns and regional centres. Development of industry in London would normally be halted.[46] The important outcomes of the majority report were the sweeping aside of the free market approach, and a stop to freedom of location and development. This was emphatically stated in the final remedies section, and was supported by the bulk of the evidence published from 1937 to 1939. There was some disagreement as to the nature of the central authority, both minority reports favouring some executive powers and speedier action, and the one signed by Patrick Abercrombie arguing for a new Government department or one evolved from an existing department. The detailed disagreements between the minority and majority reports are unimportant, however, for by the time post-war planning was on the agenda early in the war, most planners accepted the stronger line.

The Report represented a victory for the middle ground of the British establishment prepared to adopt interventionist policies, and reflected the strength of the town planning approach.[47] It also underlined the inability of the main industrial lobby, the Federation of British Industries, to see industrial requirements in other than a market framework. This is why the Scottish evidence and that from local authorities in the depressed areas was so interesting. Although the terms of the Commission's brief did not include industry first and foremost, its conclusions were especially important because there was no equivalent industrial blueprint. Barlow subsumed industrial development under the theoretical assumptions of general town planning, and the alternative arguments were either not put, or only feebly so. This must raise questions as to the adequacy of such an approach for a region like the Clyde Valley with a strong representation of heavy industries, in which employment and output were rising fast in the late 1930s.

6. WARTIME PLANNING IN SCOTLAND RELEVANT TO POST-WAR INDUSTRY

The Barlow report was published before the fall of France in the summer of 1940, generated much well-disposed comment, and was rapidly adopted as a part of the consensus of reconstruction thinking.[48] One must appreciate that the arguments involving reconstruction did not all go in favour of the town planners, and too much can be read into the influence of Barlow. There were many other pressures at work; in particular, as already noted, the proponents of deficit funding of Government expenditure had made considerable headway by 1945. This is all well known, and the fact of the matter is that many questions bearing on the State were thoroughly overhauled in wartime, though the type of physical planning of location and negative controls on industrial building was fully legislated for.

Developments at the U.K. level which affected physical planning in Scotland may be briefly noted. In April 1941 the Ministry of Works and Buildings set up a consultative panel on Physical Planning to which five members of the Barlow Commission, including Patrick Abercrombie, were appointed.[49] The subsequent Uthwatt and Scott reports of 1942 made recommendations on legal and other questions dealing with compensation to be paid for development and for rural land use.[50] In December 1942 a new Ministry of Town and Country Planning was announced. Led by the London County Council in April 1941, local authorities started a wave of investigations based on the assumption that in post-war years there would be comprehensive planning powers.[51] In 1943 legislation was passed which in effect instructed County Boroughs and Councils to each prepare a planning scheme, and the 1947 Town and Country Planning Act required all planning authorities to submit plans by 1951. The establishment of the new Ministry, and the subsequent New Towns (Reith) Committee of October 1945, and the New Towns Act (1946) and the Town and Country Planning Act (1947) ensured the success of the post-war planning proposals. Few adequate alternative perspectives were advanced on these matters, and the older approaches to industrial freedom made only a marginal impact. It was clear by 1945 that physical planning and questions of location within overall area plans would have considerable 'teeth', and would involve the main lines of policy advocated by town and country planners.

In Scotland there were several aspects of wartime planning which were relevant to post-war reconstruction. Production committees were established at the start for munitions industries and trades, and quickly embraced the rest of the economy. By the end of the war these committees had enabled the Government system in general to amass considerable information and expertise on the detailed functioning of Scottish industry. Further, as part of the specifically Scottish proposals for reconstruction, the Secretary of State in late 1941 established the Advisory Council of Ex-Secretaries of State on Post-war Problems in Scotland. It set to work on areas which in the inter-war period had been shown to be in need of attention, including hydro-electricity, gas and water, the fishing industry, housing, hospitals, hill sheep-farming, and some industrial questions. Specialist sub-committees were set up which worked with the production committees where relevant.[52] Their work was complemented by that of the Scottish Industrial Council of February 1942, later renamed the Scottish Council on Industry, which acted as a focus for industry, the trade unions and local authorities, and as meetings of the ex-Secretaries declined, the Council on Industry expanded its work.[53] There was also a group of national bodies, including the Scottish Distribution of Industry Panel, the Scottish Building Committee, and the Scottish Physical Planning Committee, which late in the war helped forge a coherent approach to the physical aspects of the transition to peacetime production, particularly in the allocation of building resources.[54]

Further, there were the Scottish equivalents of the town and country planning organisations covering long-term planning of localities and regions. The relevant agendas were arranged as early as 1942 for the more important industrial areas of Scotland, when the County Councils Association and local authorities agreed that post-war social provision, infrastructure and industrial location should be considered in a regional context with a detailed liaison with Government departments. The following year two important Regional Planning Committees, for the Clyde Valley and for Central and South-East Scotland, were established, in addition to planning arrangements authorised under the 1943 and 1947 legislation.[55] In the long term, taking the period after 1950 covered by this volume, these planning committees were arguably the most important of the wartime decisions for Scottish development, if we mean by this the development of structures for implementing the general objectives of the town and country planners.

7. THE CLYDE VALLEY REGIONAL PLAN

The task of the Regional Planning Committees was to mesh together coherent regional plans which fitted both local initiatives and the national needs worked out by the Ex-Secretaries Committee and Government departments and organisations on physical resources. Patrick Abercrombie was appointed consultant for the Clyde Report and Frank Mears for the Central and South-East, and this made it certain that the plans would be in line with those prepared elsewhere in the U.K.[56] By any standards the Clyde Valley Plan was an extraordinary achievement and involved recommendations which radically recast the whole idea of regional and national development in Scotland; we shall refer to this in some detail. Most of the ideas in the Plan were at the limit of the more advanced planning perspectives of the time, and provided a scenario for further extension of Government powers.

The Clyde Valley, as Abercrombie admitted in 1943, was his most difficult and ambitious consultancy.[57] After all, it had a quite different economic and social structure from any of the areas which comprehensive town planning had previously considered south of the border. Yet the size of the area and the differences did not hinder the writers of the Clyde Valley Plan from cutting through a mass of parochial vested interests or from planning for a region in a national Scottish context, and they showed what advanced town and country planning was capable of. The Plan still reads today with a freshness and vitality, and is a damning indictment of pre-war lack of planning in the life of the Clyde area. The underlying ideas embraced 'the complete expression of the needs of people in society', that is to say, health provision, housing, environment and infrastructure, as well as industry and employment.[58] A strong basis for these all-embracing views of town planning had been laid in the later 1920s and 'thirties, in which Abercrombie had played an important role. The report and the background papers attempted such integration, and many of the suggestions and comments on physical planning were subsequently enforced. Coal-mining, metal manufacture, shipbuilding, and marine engineering were given specific attention, though many other industries were referred to. All the known questions of industrial location, factory estates, infrastructure, energy supplies, housing schemes, agriculture, transport and new towns were discussed in a linked fashion. The Plan utilised the legal framework suggested by the wartime Uthwatt and Scott reports and the legislation for town and country planning which was on or near the statute book. Here was a sophisticated blueprint for the future which not only reiterated the known problems, but offered optimistic solutions.

This said, there were some serious implications for Scottish industrial development in the discussions on the engineering and shipbuilding sectors in which the country was well represented. The Plan argued the consistent line of the English town planning format with its 'model' of future industrial and factory growth, and applied this to the Clyde and its industries.[59] While it acknowledged the size of the engineering and shipbuilding trades, it adopted the view that these were declining, or at best had good prospects only in the short term.[60] This sort of thinking had put down deep roots in the inter-war years and, as mentioned earlier, assumed that the inter-war crises in the heavy industries were not caused by a general deficiency of demand but were primarily ones of technological obsolescence, and that it was the duty of Government to smooth the transition to a lighter industrial age. The most detailed and useful suggestions for change for the heavy industries covered coal and steel, which the Plan recognised would remain very important sectors of the Scottish economy. On engineering and shipbuilding, however, there were rather too many 'broad brush' assumptions about long-term development. To take an example, we may consider the section on general engineering. This was, as the Plan acknowledged, an enormously wide industrial group, which included

> a whole range of engineering products such as electrical coal cutting gear and colliery machinery, locomotives, railway wagons, hydraulic pumps, boilers, structural steel for cranes and bridge building, ventilating and refrigerating equipment, motor vehicles, sewing machines, machine tools and various types of specialised machinery for the sugar making and textile industries. The industry is, to a large extent, concentrated in and around Glasgow which is one of Britain's outstanding heavy engineering centres, but the surrounding towns of Motherwell and Wishaw, Coatbridge, Airdrie, Paisley, Renfrew and Johnstone are also important, and, in fact, the whole area extending from industrial Lanarkshire through Glasgow to North East Renfrewshire, Greenock and Dumbarton forms a highly complex and interrelated area of iron and steel production and the manufacture of specialised engineering equipment, much of it associated with shipbuilding.[61]

The conclusion to draw from this and the 1935 Census, and wartime production figures, is that the area's industries differed widely with respect to production techniques, market demands and investment needs, and thus each required the kind of planning and aid which was given to, say, the coal and steel industries, discussed at length in the report. In fact, the thrust of the argument lumped the general engineering sections together as 'primarily a capital goods industry', with pessimistic conclusions as to future demand. There is some careful drafting which covered the expected short-term post-war demand, but industrialists may well have felt that the conclusion that the pent-up demand for traditional products 'should not be allowed to interfere with the industry applying its experience . . . to the development of other lines of manufacture' showed a disregard for excellent prospects for many traditional sectors. About shipbuilding, to which much space was devoted, the Plan was quite blunt:

> This great industry has been a source of tremendous strength to the Region, but now to some extent it is a source of weakness. The need to concentrate so much upon quality rather than quantity and the high degree of specialisation required has tended to infuse a certain degree of conservatism into Clydeside industry generally, making it difficult to adapt itself to modern mass production methods. Shipbuilding has, perhaps, too much monopolised the inventive and engineering genius of the people and has tied down to it too many subsidiary concerns which share its vicissitudes, inducing over a wide area an atmosphere of uncertainty which tends to destroy industrial confidence. Not only has the industry too much monopolised the Region's resources, but the shipyards themselves monopolise practically the whole of the available water frontage west of the main docks. As a result the Clyde has never developed the great mixed industry waterfront area so typical of some of our big ports.[62]

Moreover, the Clyde Valley Plan fully supported what was described as the 'excellent summary of the disadvantages of an unbalanced industrial structure', presented in the 1944 *White Paper on Employment Policy* (Cmd. 6527). What-ever the merits of the White Paper — and the policy of full employment is not to be lightly passed over — some of the industrial comments were typical of the simplistic deductions made from inter-war trends which were current in Whitehall at the end of the war.[63] It briefly expounds a narrow doctrine of industrial imbalance which has 'in the past enabled certain areas to reach the highest peak of temporary prosperity', and put 'shipbuilding and heavy industries in the industrial belt of Scotland' into a category which also included coal and iron in Wales and cotton in Lancashire. With this definition there could be no other conclusion than an entirely pessimistic one for the Clyde Valley unless industrial diversification was undertaken. Thus we have two of the most prestigious documents on regional and employment policy ever written stating similar conclusions on the future prospects for the Clydeside region. The convergence of the main Treasury position, and what became Government post-war policy in general, with that of the town planners in Scotland was, of course, a very strong block to serious consideration of the particular characteristics of the Scottish engineering and shipbuilding in-dustries. In an entirely negative sense the Plan, and the others from this time, contributed to the lack of urgency about long-term investment in the largest industrial sectors of Scotland, employing somewhere around 250,000 workers by 1947, itself a sharp increase over pre-war days, in favour of the lighter engineering, rural and suburban options of Hillington and the other trading estates. At the risk of multiplying the questions to be asked about Scottish entrepreneurs (for which see Chapter 3), we may well ask whether industrialists felt that insufficient attention was paid at the end of the war to their needs. It may indeed be the case that some investment decisions in the private sector are to be explained by the rather distant and unsympathetic statements which abounded at the time on the future of the traditional Scottish trades.

One must point out that there were some detailed investigations of Scottish industries, including one into the foundry trades, and Scottish Office civil servants would have liked others. Moreover, the Clyde Plan called for more planning of the economy as a whole and for enquiries into the 'set up and location of each of the Region's industrial groups', and it was particularly emphatic about the need to reinforce the recommendations of the Barlow Commission on factory controls. The power of the Treasury and industrialists opposed to indicative planning is not specifically stated as a major problem to be overcome, though the well-argued section on 'Location of Industry and Full Employment' suggests that they were indeed a stumbling block. By 1947 and 1948 it was clear that the priorities of the Government, with investment cutbacks and the yielding to U.S. pressures, made diversification in Scotland, and indeed industrial development in general, very much a secondary economic objective.

Beyond the position on heavy industries and engineering and shipbuilding in general, it is unfair to criticise the Clyde Plan, or Scottish civil servants' appreciation of industrial development of the later 1940s. There are wider considerations to bear in mind. Planning and ideas, and the effective use of knowledge, have rarely resulted in successful initiatives in economic affairs unless the whole panoply of Government powers is involved and long-standing pressures are brought to bear. This fundamental lesson was understood by the town planning lobby by the 1920s, though it still took it years to break down parochial and business opposition. An indicative industrially oriented plan, on the lines of some of the post-war continental experiences, would have called for careful preparation. Many business groups were strongly opposed to additional State involvement, and the mainstream of British Liberal and economic ideas was ambivalent if not hostile.[64] To these groups Keynesianism and demand management, and the ideas of town and country planning, were a much more attractive proposition. The mainstream of the Parliamentary Labour Party lacked interest in stronger industrial planning, and in pushing the Treasury in a more progressive direction, and in any case the day-to-day problems of the post-war world soon swamped longer-term consideration of the economy.[65]

8. HYDRO-ELECTRICITY AND THE COMMITTEE OF THE EX-SECRETARIES OF STATE

Before we turn to the employment and output record of the immediate post-war years, it is necessary to say something about the activities of Government departments during wartime on other economic matters. The Regional Planning Advisory Committees were inaugurated after the start of post-war planning, and brought together the work of central and local Government. There were, however, several important initiatives which could only have come from central Government. The most spectacular of these was almost certainly the development of hydro-electricity. Before the war there were only three hydro-electric works in the Highlands used for industrial supply, those at Foyers, Kinlochleven and Fort William, and three for general purposes, at Rannoch, Tummel and Loch Wishart. Six privately initiated schemes for northern Scotland were turned down by Parliament, and others never reached Westminster, with opposition from landowners, the Association for the Preservation of Rural Scotland, and the coal owning interests uncertain about future demand for coal. As late as September 1941 Parliament rejected a hydro-electric scheme for Glen Affric.[66]

It was realised by the Scottish Office that Parliament would only move if an authoritative report was published, with suggestions for a statutory body to organise hydro-electric development. A Committee chaired by Lord Cooper was organised when it became clear that the Glen Affric scheme would fail, and it reported in 1942 with scathing criticism of the six main inter-war failures: 'all major issues of policy both national and local have tended to become completely submerged in the conflict of contending sectional in-interests'. In August 1943 the Hydro-Electric (Scotland) Act vested responsibility for all developments north of a line from Dumbarton to Montrose in a new Board. Within the first three years of work, building commenced on projects at Loch Sloy, Tummel-Gary, Fannich and Mullardoch-Fasnakyle and Glen Affric, with an estimated capacity of 374,000kW. By December 1950 some twenty-five building schemes under the auspices of the Hydro-Electric Board were either in operation or in process of construction. Eighteen of these were for water-powered generation, with an estimated capacity of 644,600kW. Other schemes under discussion at that date comprised 171,600kW. The Act was a victory for the general aims of economic development over parochial interests, it was specific to Scotland, and its results indicated what properly planned Government action could achieve.[67]

As the work of the Ex-Secretaries Advisory Committee continued into 1942, it got drawn into the immediate exigencies of wartime organisation, especially in support of the Secretary of State in arguments with Whitehall, and the initial focus of post-war reconstruction was rather diluted.[68] Moreover, it became clear that Whitehall could not be relied upon to put Scottish interests on an equal footing with those of other parts of Great Britain. This came up with especial force over factory building, the location of wartime dispersal plants, and the policy of industrial concentration. The argument of the Scottish Office was that Scotland, because of its relative backwardness, had a greater need to retain the management structures and labour nucleus in its infant trades than had England. In 1941 some 90.9% of non-essential factory space allocated under the Factory and Storage Premises Control in Scotland was used for storage, involving 4.5 million square feet so converted in 1941, as against 9.1% and half a million square feet for production, whereas in England the percentage was only 71.6% for storage, with 28.4% for production. English companies had been successful in persuading the Control that where production should be maintained in non-essential industries, this should be done in England. Moreover, English interests opposed a concerted move to Scotland during the factory dispersals early in the war which were intended to move industry away from vulnerable English conurbations. It was only pressure from the Secretary of State in early 1942, the Ex-Secretaries Committee, and the Scottish Council that persuaded the Factory Control and the Ministry of Supply to direct industry to sites in Scotland and also treat Scotland more equitably with respect to the few remaining industrial concentrations then to be dealt with. One effect of the sluggish movement of industry north of the border and the closure of existing factories was the movement of a net total of 15,000 women to factory work in England.[69] This may not seem important compared with the huge contracts which came north for the heavy industries, but the pervasive fear among Scottish civil servants was of a dying away of the new initiatives, which they argued would make it that much more difficult to escape the over-representation of heavy industries. By 1943 attention was focused on further measures which could keep the new trades in Scotland, and the complaints of early 1942 should be seen in this light.

9. THE EARLY YEARS OF POST-WAR POLICY

By 1944 the main aims of Scottish conversion policy had been laid out. They included obviously enough the continued development of new industries and the new trading estates with preferential allocation of building supplies. The others were (i) the development of the basic resources of the country, especially coal, steel and building materials; (ii) the efficient switching to peacetime work of the munitions industries and the shipyards; (iii) the reopening and re-equipping of the civilian industries which had been closed down and concentrated in the earlier part of the war (Table 4 lists the main trades which had cutbacks); (iv) the absorption of over 300,000 personnel from the forces and from munitions work; and (v) the planning of the battle for output and exports, in line with U.K. policy.[70] Further, an interdepartmental committee chaired by the Department of Health was established in 1945 to draw up priorities for the siting of new industrial developments and to recommend programmes for the improvement of housing, water supplies, drainage, gas and electricity, and road, rail and air communications in the redrawn Development Area. This planning had two objectives:

(a) 'To see that new industries are located so as not only to satisfy immediate needs of particular areas but also to fit in with the longer term development of Scotland as a whole, and to ensure that housing, communications, water supply and drainage, and other

developments necessary to properly balanced communities proceed hand in hand with industrial expansion.'
(b) 'To see that suitable sites for new industrial projects are available where they are needed.'[71]

Together with the plans of local authorities, for example the housing proposals of Glasgow Council, and the early drafts of the regional plans, these comprised the main aims of Scottish conversion policy. On the face of it the policy context of the U.K. Government would have been complementary. The main concerns of the *White Paper on Employment Policy* (1944), the *Distribution of Industry Act* (1945) and the papers of the Ministry of Town and Country Planning were full employment, industrial location, and the attempt by persuasion and by negative controls to move industry to the enlarged Development Areas. There were references in the White Paper to improving the efficiency of industries in which Scotland was strong, though the major aim was to influence the location of new and resited industries using a system of building licences with finance for factory building from the Board of Trade.[72] Overriding all of these considerations was the national battle for output. These were not the compulsory powers of industrial location which many Scottish civil servants would have liked, and fears for the future were underlined in 1945 and 1946 when a number of English companies closed their Scottish branches. However, within this admittedly limited context the civil service was able to make strenuous efforts to keep industries in Scotland, and to bring new ones to the country, as well as to meet the other aims of the conversion policy. The *White Paper on Industry and Employment in Scotland* (1946) summed up the more complex work that Scotland faced than, say, the south of England:

> Undoubtedly there is a considerable way to go before Scotland's economy is on an entirely sound basis. The evil effects of twenty years' lack of planning in Great Britain as a whole at a time when many new industries were developing was not quickly remediable. Sufficient progress has been made in securing projects for new industries in Scotland to give real grounds for hope in the future. But a sustained effort on the part of all sections of the community is needed in order to overcome as quickly as possible current shortages of materials and supplies which limit production and necessary expansion of industry. Scotland needs even more than the rest of the country to win the battle for output.[73]

As it stands, this looks tough enough, but in detail, apart from the coal and steel industries and some mention of shipyards, references to how the planning mechanism was expected to tackle the engineering and metal-using sectors were extremely vague, and by 1948 most Government reports fell back to the mere chronicling of events, and listing the export successes of these sectors.

It must be stressed that there were pressures from within Scottish industry and from the civil service for more detailed planning on heavy industry. By the end of the war these industrial sectors were well into a period of sustained growth which lasted, on a European scale, from the mid-1930s to the 1970s, and this was, in fact, the longest recorded capital goods and heavy engineering upswing since the industrial revolution. The figures given in Chapter 3 are an indication of this. The Clyde Valley Plan recognised that these sectors would remain the most important industrial component of the West of Scotland. The point which needs to be stressed is that properly organised efforts on the part of industry and the State in the decade after 1945 could have ensured steadily rising outputs and employment in these trades, though substantial investment and relocation would have been necessary. Neither the Treasury nor the main political parties were prepared to accept the detailed economic planning that this required. There were voices calling for a proper policy for the engineering and shipbuilding industries, the most important Scottish one outside the civil service being John Gollan, whose *Scottish Prospect* covered all the main industrial sectors. The book emphasised the responsibility of the Government in 1947 and 1948 for giving in to U.S. pressure to cut back on steel supplies to British shipbuilders, and for the subsequent abandonment of the policy to restore the British merchant fleet to its pre-war strength. There is now a great deal of evidence on many aspects of U.S. policy, and not only for convertibility and Marshall Aid, which has specified a number of the damaging consequences for British industry in the later 1940s. The effect on diversification within Scotland at this time is briefly noted in the next section.[74]

10. THE GROWTH OF 'NEW' INDUSTRY

The questions must be asked: what was achieved for newer industries? What were the emerging lines of Government policy both for industry and town and country planning? Were there in fact successes in industrial diversification, and moreover, how did the economy as a whole look by the 1948 Census of Production? Apart from the last question, these cannot be answered by reference to the 1940s alone, and are mainly dealt with in subsequent chapters. We may briefly note here the expansion of new factory building, and the estimates made about employment generated from new industries by 1950 which had not existed in Scotland prior to 1935.

As Abercrombie pointed out in 1946, 'compared with the South, Scotland has secured far less than her fair share of wartime factory building. She is thus greatly handicapped in competing for new industry with the areas which do possess these factories'.[75] To make matters worse, Scotland was weak in the building trades sectors, and especially in the production of cement, as was shown in the 1935 Census. As Table 4 indicates, the brick, cement and other building trades contracted sharply during the war. The resulting brick shortage was only remedied by the summer of 1947 and only after huge imports, and the shortage of cement continued for the rest of the decade.[76]

As far as possible the Scottish Office protected the new factory programme after 1945, but it had a very long way to go, because of the low level of new building in Scotland during wartime suitable for conversion to peacetime uses, compared with south of the border. All kinds of buildings were pressed into service, including church and scout halls, pre-fabricated huts, and office space, and the number of trading estates organised by the Scottish Industrial

Estates Company was increased to nineteen. This put pressure on supplies because the infrastructural work which had to be done on sewage, energy, water and roads was far greater than for building factories in existing urban areas.

Between 1945 and 1950, 9,617,000 square feet of factory space in units of above 5,000 square feet were completed in Scotland, compared with 57,374,000 square feet in Great Britain. This represented 16.8% of factory completions. However, pressure from English interests and the slacker enforcement of controls from the end of the decade resulted in a poorer showing thereafter, for in 1950 only 7.4% of G.B. factory completions were in Scotland. Table 5 lists the expansion of new industrial developments at the new factory sites from 1937 to the end of 1950, and the figures are divided into the Development Areas, and the rest of Scotland. By that date some 100,000 jobs existed in factories built after 1937, with an estimated future potential for 50,000 more.[77] This represented slightly over 10% of the total of industrial employees of all categories in 1950. The record was thus a strong one for the

Table 4 (a). *Employment in Scotland 1939-1945/6/7 (insured workers)*
Trades and services which were above July 1939 employment levels in July 1945

	1939 total	1945 total	% of total in 1939	1946 total	% of total in 1939	1947 total	% of total in 1939
National Government Service (exc nfs)	18,630	65,710	353	59,450	319	55,520	298
Motor Vehicles, Cycles and Aircraft	18,340	52,260	285	30,000	164	31,190	170
Explosives	9,690	24,080	249	9,930	103	10,030	104
Railway Service	14,690	30,050	205	34,730	237	35,290	240
Shipbuilding and Ship Repairing	37,880	65,070	172	56,180	148	51,700	136
General Engineering, Engineers; Iron and Steel Founding	70,170	114,750	164	90,760	129	95,220	136
Harbour, River and Canal Service	4,220	6,410	152	3,770	89	3,570	85
Shipping Service	16,790	24,710	147	16,240	97	14,850	88
Cast Stone and Cast Concrete Products, Patent Fuel, Stone Grinding etc.	1,060	1,480	140	2,200	208	2,910	275
Sawmilling and Machined Woodwork	9,600	12,670	132	11,290	118	10,690	111
Marine Engineering etc.	19,480	25,440	131	23,360	120	21,900	112
Chemicals	7,890	9,830	125	10,640	135	11,510	146
Metal Industries nss	11,170	13,240	119	13,550	121	15,630	140
Port Transport (Docks, Wharves etc.)	9,260	10,350	112	8,840	96	8,440	91
Glass Manufacture (ex Bottles, Lenses etc.)	1,160	1,290	111	1,380	119	1,440	124
Local Government Service	47,740	52,570	110	55,380	116	58,640	123
Cotton	13,240	14,300	108	15,690	119	16,510	125
Tramway and Omnibus Service	27,740	28,580	103	30,440	110	32,620	118
Goods Transport by road	16,430	16,550	101	18,320	112	20,440	124
Farming, Market Gardening etc.	78,400	79,500	101	77,900	99	78,610	100

Source: Industry and Employment in Scotland 1946-1948

Table 4 (b). *Trades and services which were below July 1939 employment levels in July 1945*

	1939 total	1945 total	% of total in 1939	1946 total	% of total in 1939	1947 total	% of total in 1939
Other Food Industries	17,010	16,810	99	19,220	113	21,220	125
Laundry Services	14,270	13,750	96	14,020	98	13,830	97
Steel Melting and Puddling etc.	22,240	21,320	96	18,870	85	20,140	91
Drink Industries	16,450	15,220	93	16,210	99	17,960	109
Professional Services	29,890	27,600	92	30,540	102	34,010	114
Coal Mining	92,300	83,760	91	82,440	89	84,900	92
All Other Insured Industries and Services	173,630	156,280	90	171,060	99	190,230	110
Hotel and Catering etc.	41,760	36,300	87	41,450	99	47,920	115
Tailoring	14,470	12,110	84	13,650	95	15,160	105
Entertainments, Sports etc.	11,470	9,210	80	11,120	97	12,360	100
Gas, Water and Electricity Supply	16,890	13,350	79	16,190	96	18,380	109
Paper and Paper Board	13,610	10,320	76	12,340	91	13,950	102
Distributive Trades	249,240	183,360	74	200,910	81	213,950	86
Shirts, Collars, Underclothing etc.	5,920	4,340	73	4,870	82	5,400	91
Commerce, Banking and Finance	13,140	9,460	72	10,850	83	10,700	81
Bread, Biscuits, Cakes etc.	33,510	23,790	71	24,920	74	26,360	79
Woollen and Worsted	15,080	10,430	69	12,740	85	15,420	102
Furniture Making etc.	9,540	6,430	67	8,620	90	10,600	111
Textiles, Bleaching, Printing, Dyeing etc.	9,740	6,440	66	6,010	62	7,420	76
Stoves, Grates, Pipes etc.	18,030	11,220	62	13,770	76	15,440	86
Printing, Publishing and Bookbinding	28,440	16,980	60	21,790	77	25,320	89
Linen	11,300	6,390	57	6,410	57	6,090	54
Brick, Tile, Pipe etc.	9,510	5,020	53	7,140	75	7,720	81
Jute	25,970	13,250	51	15,250	59	17,050	66
Hosiery	18,110	8,620	48	11,010	61	12,900	71
Cement, Limekilns, and Whiting	1,060	460	43	560	53	570	54
Building	99,220	41,760	42	77,470	78	97,680	98
Fishing	10,010	4,250	42	6,450	64	8,270	83
Civil Engineering Construction	38,350	15,370	40	26,160	68	27,290	71
Carpets	10,720	1,680	16	3,880	36	6,320	59

late 1930s and 1940s, though the Scottish Office and Abercrombie were of the opinion that more firms would have come north if extra space had been built during wartime. The growth can be stated in various ways, the Scottish Council (Development and Industry) estimated that from 1946 to 1950, some 554 new enterprises had started production, 460 of these in the existing main industrial areas. It confirmed that the rate of formation of new enterprises was down by 1950, and again in 1951 and 1952. It blamed this in part on Treasury policy which had cut building of advance factories in Development Areas in 1948, and had partly freed the granting of Industrial Development Certificates, and then halved regional policy expenditure from 1947/48 to 1950/51. By June 1951 the Scottish Council estimated that 92,453 persons were employed in the post-1945 factory space area, or 4.5% of the total insured

Table 5. *Number of Employees in New Industrial Developments (as defined below)*
Mid 1937 to 31 December 1950

Period	Type of Development	Development Area	Rest of Scotland	Scotland
Mid-1937 to Mid-1945	Industrial Estate factories built before Mid-1945	6,870	—	6,870
	Firms moved into existing premises, and other developments	3,700	2,150	5,850
Total (Mid-1937 to Mid-1945)		10,570	2,150	12,720
Mid 1945 to 31 Dec. 1950	New factories and extensions (5,000 sq. ft. plus), minor new factories, extensions and adaptations, Govt. factories now in industrial estates, Royal Ordnance factories and other retained Govt. factories, and all other developments	69,900	17,770	87,670
Total (Mid-1937 to 31 Dec. 1950)		80,470	19,920	100,390

Source: Industry and Employment in Scotland 1950, Cmd. 8223 (1951), p. 83

population. They confirmed that the impact of the activity had varied, with over 10.0% of the insured workforce in Dundee working in such new enterprises, 6.2% in Glasgow, and just over 5% in Falkirk, Stirling, Ayrshire and the South-West.[78] Given the emphasis on new industries and new factory space, the plans for increasing trading estates were ambitious and provided many important accretions to the economy. All this work, of course, appealed to the Ministry of Town and Country Planning, and its work north of the border.

The detailed industrial record was mixed, though by 1948 definite successes had been achieved by the combined efforts of the State sector, the Scottish Council, and local authorities, though in several industries the new trading estates were not the primary reason for location in Scotland. In the aircraft sector, for example, the Ministry had planned well before the war to disperse production. Over twenty-five main schemes came north, including the Rolls-Royce aero-engine plant at Hillington, which in 1943 employed nearly 25,000, and still retained 5,500 by 1947. By 1950 over thirty firms had direct contracts for aircraft components. This was an important gain, though it has to be said that much of it was organised as branch production for U.K. and U.S. firms, and was mostly the individual batch outputs typical of the Scottish engineering trade.[79]

The other main gains may be briefly noted. Before the war there was only one typewriter factory in Scotland, assembling imported components. A considerable effort was made to attract foreign and English companies, and by 1950 nearly 6,000 persons were employed in making these and other business machines and components. At that date some 25% of U.K. typewriter output was in Scotland, though all six firms were controlled from abroad. Pre-war only a handful of artisan-type workshops produced clocks and watches, but after the war two volume producers came from America, and three from England. Initially they were assembly plants, but by 1950 they had branched out into manufacture with a spin off to other firms, with something like 35% of U.K. output, and a higher net output per employee than south of the border. As noted before, electrical engineering products, and radio and allied electronic equipment were only manufactured in minute amounts in the 1930s. Dispersal and post-war controls brought many firms north, and by 1950 around 10,000 were employed in these sectors. There was a considerable increase in trades using steel and aluminium and light alloys; the new trades which came during the war were estimated to employ another 4,000 by 1950, and in one branch, office furniture, some 25% of U.K. output was made in Scotland.

While all these trades involved some linkage with domestic industry, the Scottish Office made particular efforts towards the end of the war to attract vehicle construction to Scotland, especially cars.[80] The high quality of a volume parts trade which is normally required in car component plants would have been a useful diversification of the engineering base, with a potential spin off for a large number of firms. Although there were attempts to achieve this, which in 1945 looked hopeful, without large-scale Government finance and the direction of industry the projects did not materialise. As it was, by 1950 Scotland was a modest producer of tractors and combine harvesters, hydraulic equipment, earth movers, and caravans. With parts production and some internal combustion engines and commercial vehicles, the total of the vehicles-related employment came to about 3,000 in 1950. This was a long way from the 1945 aim of the Scottish Office.

The relatively slow development of these new industries by existing Scottish companies led inevitably to a move away from local ownership. This had political repercussions in Scotland in subsequent decades, though less so than in some European countries. Foreign and English ownership was not new, and several of the most important and longstanding Scottish factories had been initially or still were controlled from abroad, including Singers of Clydebank with 12,000 employees by 1950, Babcock and Wilcox (by then British) which employed 8,000, and the North British Rubber Co. with 4,500. After the war the huge capital base of American companies and the shortage of dollars in Europe encouraged many to establish plants in the U.K. They thereby gained access to the sterling area on an equal basis with British producers, with the bonus of the right to convert after-tax profits to dollars. The reorganised Scottish Council made an energetic drive to attract North American companies, and this remained a key part of Scottish Office policy in later years. From 1937 to 1950 some 218 incoming firms were established in Scotland, and of these 120 came from the Greater London area, 115 from the rest of the U.K., mainly the Midlands, 36 from the U.S.A. and Canada, and 27 from the rest of the world. It was estimated by the latter date that 8,500 workers were employed in plants of overseas companies which had settled in Scotland since the war, and the total employment from all foreign-owned firms was around

40,000. The importance of new trades for the business structure of the country was undoubted, but the main bases of the Scottish industrial economy remained as they were before the war, and the evidence suggests that these had been strengthened, both in terms of employment and the range of products made.[81]

11. THE PATTERN OF EMPLOYMENT AND INDUSTRIAL STRUCTURE, 1947-1948

Table 4 (A & B) lists the employment of insured workers in all sectors of the economy, including industry, agriculture, the professions and services, and the percentage contribution of each to total employment in 1939 and from 1945 to 1947. The first column confirms the scale of the increase, noted in reports on the late inter-war economy, of the service and distribution trades since the First World War, and the rise of banking and finance, hotel and catering and miscellaneous services. Part A shows the employment of most of those sectors of the economy which expanded their production during the war because of the munitions effort, and related trades, and certain managerial sectors essential to production (columns 3 & 4). These figures confirm that re-armament and the Second World War coincided with the start of one of the longest booms in capital and engineering goods in Scottish history. The manufacturing sectors of motor vehicles, cycles and aircraft, shipbuilding, general engineering, marine engineering and metal goods increased their employment from 157,040 to 215,640, or by 27%. The table further shows that a modern war economy required a sharp increase in Government services and certain categories of distribution, national Government service rising from 18,630 to 65,710 and local Government to 52,570. Railways, shipping, ports, and road transport saw considerable employment increases, especially in railways, where the total doubled. Part B on the other hand lists the trades least required for war, and shows the possibility of sustaining the munitions programme by cutting existing trades. It was not possible to shift much in the way of physical resources from these trades, though labour and management and storage space were released for the armed services and war-related work. A number of sectors were kept at a relatively high level of work by substituting women, the unemployed and the elderly, and these included the food trades generally; agriculture, laundry work and many textile trades also came into this category. Many uninsured workers kept up distribution and services, though what numbers were involved is unknown.

The conversion to peacetime took place in economic conditions which were fundamentally different from those facing the country in the 1930s.[82] The level of peacetime and export demand for products from the main munitions industries, with the single exception of explosives, ensured that employment levels remained higher, usually substantially higher, than those in the summer of 1939. The only equivalent rates of expansion in industry over 1939 levels were in small employment groups within other categories, such as chemicals and concrete products. What is particularly interesting is the relative slowness of the wartime non-essential industries to reach and overtake their 1939 employment levels. Even with the building and cement trades, now seen as crucial, it proved difficult to increase numbers to the required levels, and these trades remained below pre-war employment levels two years after the war.

The main effort of the Scottish end of the battle for output went into import substitution, the export trades, engineering, shipbuilding, building trades and coal and steel, and some idea of the importance attached to these can be gained from the figures of physical output listed in Scottish Office publications for each year at the end of the decade. With a few exceptions these were trades in which Scotland was well represented in the 1935 Census. However, many engineering industries which produced both for domestic and overseas markets found themselves involved in the dollar drive required to support the June 1947 convertibility programme. Thus many requests from industry for steel, coal and building materials were turned down from 1946 to 1950 unless a case could be made that this would aid exports, and numerous requests from British purchasers of heavy engineering products were shelved. The policy was particularly felt in the heavier end of engineering such as hydraulic turbines for electricity generation, locomotives, and specialist castings, where foreign industry was given a preference. The adverse consequences of the U.S. pressure for convertibility and the Treasury investment restrictions of the late 1940s have been noted before. There were complaints after 1947 from Scottish civil servants that Treasury policies on convertibility were hindering Scottish industrial development and the improvement of infrastructure. There was little they or local industrialists could do about it, however, and these adverse consequences were seen in Whitehall as only temporary.

Before turning to the post-1950 period it is as well to say a few words about the overall Scottish economy at the time of the 1948 Census of Production. This may be seen in Tables 6 and 7. The former lists a comparison of the seventeen (new) industrial classifications of the 1948 Census compared with those in 1935. Although some qualifications must be made in the interpretation of these figures, they do suggest that 'Scotland may have caught up arrears during the war and that over the whole period of thirteen years between 1935 and 1948, Scottish industrial production may have shown the higher rate of increase'.[83] While a comparison of the figures for Scotland and Great Britain 'can only be made with great caution', they show that 'the highest rates of expansion whether due to increases in price or in output have been in the metal groups with a range of 254-345% for Great Britain and 218-467% for Scotland'. Some deterioration was evident in the overall figures of net output at the end of the 1940s, on the evidence of the Censuses of 1949, 1950, and 1951, and as Neil Buxton shows in the following chapter, this pattern continued into the 1950s.

Table 7 lists the gross, net and employment outputs of all the main industrial categories of the 1948 Census in Part A, and a detailed industrial

Table 6. *Percentage Increase in the value of net industrial output.*
Scotland and Great Britain, 1935 compared with 1948

Census of Production classification (1948)	Scotland	Great Britain
2. Mining and Quarrying	181	194
3. Treatment of Non-Metalliferous Mining Products	257	171
4. Chemicals and Allied Trades	160	181
5. Metal Manufacture	218	258
6. Engineering, Shipbuilding and Electrical Goods	422	345
7. Vehicles	319	264
8. Metal Goods (Miscellaneous)	459	323
9. Precision Instruments, Jewellery etc.	409	254
10. Textiles	158	185
11. Leather, and Leather Goods and Fur	287	234
12. Clothing	168	148
13. Food, Drink and Tobacco	160	121
14. Manufactures of Wood and Cork	278	203
15. Paper and Printing	134	133
16. Other Manufacturing Industry	174	247
17. Building and Contracting	302	231
18. Gas, Electricity and Water	133	128
Total Industrial Production	225	207

Source: C. E. V. Leser, 'Production' in A. K. Cairncross (ed.), *op. cit.*, Table 33, p. 73

Table 7 (a). *Value of Net Output in each Standard Industrial Classification order in Scotland in 1948,*
nos. 2-18

	Percentage of Scottish industrial production	Percentage of total for Great Britain
2. Mining and Quarrying	10.3	11.9
3. Treatment of Non-Metalliferous Mining Products other than coal	2.3	7.2
4. Chemicals and Allied Trades	4.0	7.2
5. Metal Manufacture	7.1	10.4
6. Engineering, Shipbuilding and Electrical Goods	20.3	11.4
7. Vehicles	4.0	5.2
8. Metal Goods not included elsewhere	2.2	4.8
9. Precision Instruments, Jewellery	0.5	3.7
10. Textiles	9.6	10.5
11. Leather, Leather Goods and Fur	0.7	7.1
12. Clothing	1.7	4.1
13. Food, Drink and Tobacco	11.6	12.3
14. Manufactures of Wood and Cork	2.4	9.9
15. Paper and Printing	5.5	9.9
16. Other Manufacturing Industries	1.9	8.5
17. Building and Contracting	11.8	10.7
18. Gas, Electricity and Water	4.1	7.6
Total Industrial Production	100.0	9.4

D

Table 7 (b). Breakdown of 1948 Census of Production Categories 4-8, 10-13, and 17

	Gross output Scotland as % of G.B.	Net output Scotland as % of G.B.	Employment Scotland as % of G.B.	Net output per person in Scotland	Net output per person Scotland as % of G.B.	Number of Establishments S./G.B.	Average number of employees in Scottish Establishments	Scotland as % of G.B.
No. 4 Chemicals and Allied Trades								
Explosives and Fireworks	49.2	44.9	37.0	539	121	9/49	1,023	201
Fertiliser, Disinfectant	18.6	17.7	20.3	615	87	31/172	100	113
Coal Tar Products	7.5	8.2	6.4	1,009	128	9/78	44	56
Seed Crushing and Oil Refining	5.2	6.2	7.5	507	83	8/44	92	41
Paint and Varnish	5.7	4.9	5.4	836	89	27/363	66	73
Coke Ovens and By-Products	6.0	4.8	4.7	761	100	7/88	125	60
Chemicals (General)	4.3	4.4	5.7	572	77	50/510	114	58
Glues, Gum, Paste	3.4	4.4	6.1	530	72	4/62	77	95
Soap, Candles and Glycerine	3.6	3.9	4.9	554	79	17/160	60	46
Drugs	3.9	3.6	3.3	817	108	21/299	75	48
Oils and Greases	3.0	2.9	3.0	879	98	11/171	26	47
Polishes	1.1	1.3	1.7	659	75	3/79	33	46
Nos. 5, 6, 7, 8 Engineering and Metals								
Marine Engineering	42.1	38.7	40.0	442	97	37/97	583	105
Shipbuilding and Repairing	30.2	23.1	24.2	476	96	149/678	375	110
Constructional Engineering	25.0	21.7	20.3	625	106	47/366	257	159
Iron Foundries	14.7	15.6	16.1	546	97	102/870	188	137
Mechanical Engineering	13.0	13.2	14.2	520	93	231/2,765	282	170
Iron and Steel (Melting and Rolling)	12.3	13.1	12.5	623	105	50/398	502	100
Railway Carriages, Trams	11.8	12.7	12.4	465[BR]	114[BR]	81/404[BR]	79[BR]	59
Mechanical Handling Equipment	12.5	12.2	13.5	505	90	20/162	197	109
Mechanical Engineering (Repairs)	12.7	11.5	11.9	450	97	103/826	35	97
Wire and Wire Manufacture	7.1	9.4	10.8	540	88	23/277	164	130
Motor Vehicles and Cycles (Repair)	9.4	9.4	10.0	396	94	119/1,304	60	110
Blast Furnaces	8.0	7.9	7.0	781	113	4/51	477	89
Brass Manufacturers	8.0	7.5	8.2	508	92	54/616	78	93
Textile Machinery and Accessories	6.5	6.6	7.3	462	90	32/423	155	97
Chain, Nail, Screw	7.8	6.3	7.1	492	90	44/640	126	103
non-Ferrous Metals (Smelting, Rolling)	5.2	5.3	5.7	621	93	34/475	174	79

Table 7 (b) (continued)

Nos. 5, 6, 7, 8 Engineering and Metals (continued)	Gross output Scotland as % of G.B.	Net output Scotland as % of G.B.	Employment Scotland as % of G.B.	Net output per person in Scotland	Net output per person Scotland as % of G.B.	Number of Establishments S./G.B.	Average number of employees in Scottish Establishments	Scotland as % of G.B.
Aircraft Manufacture	3.8	4.7	5.5	431	85	6/195	1,238	180
Electrical Wires and Cables	4.7	4.5	2.4	1,159	187	4/84	382	50
Radio and Telecommunications	4.0	4.2	4.0	482	108	13/421	624	131
Printing and Book Binding Machinery	3.6	3.7	4.2	501	87	3/104	211	147
Machine Tools	3.7	3.7	3.8	547	98	21/616	138	111
hardware, Holloware, Metal Furniture	3.6	3.6	4.1	440	88	87/1,951	83	92
Electrical Engineering (General)	2.9	2.6	2.8	459	93	49/892	147	51
Carts, Perambulators	2.0	1.9	1.7	495	111	5/100	25	35
Motor Vehicles and Cycles	1.1	1.2	1.5	450	80	31/1,024	157	51
Tool and Implement	1.1	1.1	1.3	418	84	7/333	55	64
Nos. 10, 11, 12 textiles, Clothing, Leather Goods and Fur								
Jute	98.0	97.8	98.8	366	99	67/72	254	106
Linen and Soft Hemp	87.6	86.9	89.1	373	97	51/75	195	131
Fell Mongery	54.7	47.7	41.5	754	119	13/44	50	140
Carpets	28.9	29.9	32.1	521	93	25/124	294	160
Canvas Goods	33.7	26.7	24.7	498	108	39/241	75	150
Lace	25.1	24.4	16.7	906	146	36/264	57	122
Rope, Twine, Net	21.7	21.4	23.2	422	92	37/163	84	101
Textile Finishing	13.3	14.8	17.6	402	84	62/596	210	169
Hosiery and Knitted Goods	9.8	11.1	14.2	368	78	172/952	79	79
Hair, Fibre etc.	10.1	8.7	10.8	577	81	4/87	135	235
Woollen and Worsted	6.8	8.2	9.4	548	88	141/1,457	122	97
Leather, Tanning and Dressing	6.8	6.6	7.6	822	87	32/459	80	109
Made-Up Textiles	5.2	6.5	6.4	550	103	8/102	33	81
Fur	5.0	6.3	8.3	386	75	26/212	25	68
Umbrellas	7.0	6.0	6.2	388	97	6/52	27	54
Cotton, Spinning and Doubling	5.2	5.5	4.9	490	114	19/730	389	184
Tailoring, Dressmaking	5.3	5.3	7.0	283	73	383/5,116	61	93
Flock and Rag	3.5	4.1	5.0	494	83	7/176	48	126

Table 7 (b) (continued)

Nos. 10, 11, 12 Textiles, Clothing, Leather Goods and Fur (continued)	Gross output Scotland as % of G.B.	Net output Scotland as % of G.B.	Employment Scotland as % of G.B.	Net output per person in Scotland	Net output per person Scotland as % of G.B.	Number of Establishments S./G.B.	Average number of employees in Scottish Establishments	Scotland as % of G.B.
Leather Goods	3.5	3.5	3.6	391	97	15/330	42	92
Narrow Fabrics	3.6	3.4	3.0	527	115	5/209	108	124
Rayon, Nylon, Silk	2.7	2.8	3.7	435	76	34/939	146	70
Boot and Shoe	1.7	1.9	2.5	356	74	39/894	83	66
Cotton Weaving	1.4	1.8	2.4	338	73	24/778	106	79
Hats, Caps, Millinery	1.7	1.2	2.5	196	48	6/268	68	109
No. 13 **Food, Drink, Tobacco**								
Spirit Distilling	66.5	70.2	64.2	1,225	109	84/94	35	73
Starch	41.8	48.3	42.6	634	113	3/19	361	270
Wholesale Bottling	28.9	40.2	26.5	1,470	152	84/502	83	158
Fish Curing	35.6	35.4	41.9	345	84	122/255	27	87
Ice	22.1	21.7	22.8	819	95	4/15	36	85
Biscuit	18.7	19.0	19.1	511	99	27/114	213	59
Bread and Flour	16.8	17.2	19.6	509	88	311/1,881	69	119
Wholesale Slaughtering	18.1	13.7	9.5	1,150	144	101/615	—	91
Bacon Curing, Sausage	15.1	12.1	12.1	616	100	46/346	48	144
Miscellaneous Preserved Foods	11.6	11.2	11.5	746	98	22/277	137	66
Grain Milling	12.7	10.5	10.3	857	102	53/338	57	63
Sugar and Glucose	9.8	7.8	8.6	689	91	7/51	222	120
Brewing and Malt	7.9	7.6	9.3	1,043	82	54/695	122	97
Soft Drinks, British Wine	6.9	7.5	11.1	487	68	60/527	38	62
Milk Products	7.5	6.9	7.6	514	91	71/581	48	94
Preserved Fruit/Vegetables	7.6	6.9	8.6	450	81	29/320	130	54
Ice Cream	5.0	6.1	5.9	1,091	105	4/37	32	61
Cocoa, Chocolate	5.7	6.1	7.4	460	82	38/313	105	31
Margarine	4.7	5.4	6.1	751	88	6/30	57	50
Cattle, Dogs, Poultry	5.9	5.4	6.8	531	80	24/178	34	

Table 7 (b) (continued)

No. 17 Building and Contracting	Gross output Scotland as % of G.B.	Net output Scotland as % of G.B.	Employment Scotland as % of G.B.	Net output per person in Scotland	Net output per person Scotland as % of G.B.	Number of Establishments S./G.B.	Average number of employees in Scottish Establishments	Scotland as % of G.B.
Tram, Trolley Bus etc.	38.5	36.5	42.0	283	87	6/20	473	140
Railways (Civil Engineering)	12.6	12.8	12.2	398	105	28/125	470	54
Building and Contracting	10.7	10.6	11.1	—	—	—	—	—
Local Authorities	10.5	9.4	9.9	304	95	94/970	205	102
Canal, Dock, Harbour (Civil Engineering)	8.8	7.4	8.5	314	87	11/100	183	78

breakdown of several of the main sectors in Part B. The industrial pattern of 1935 and the emphasis on particular trades is generally confirmed, with Scotland more heavily represented in a few trades. If we take Category 8 briefly, it is evident that once again the major industries dominating this category were shipbuilding and repairing, marine engineering, mechanical and constructional engineering, and certain specialised outputs in other sectors. Moreover, much of the output of machine tools and electrical equipment was not only a small proportion of the sector as a whole in Britain, but continued to be closely linked to coal machinery, shipbuilding, and machine-building firms.

Conclusion

The main bases of the economy of the late 1940s were the same as those of the 1930s. This was recognised at the time by the main regional planners, by the Scottish Office and by some local commentators. The policies of the Scottish Council and the civil service which had encouraged new industries had achieved some important successes by 1950, though post-war U.K. policy did cause serious problems, particularly after 1947. The development of planning in general at the end of the war ensured that the Government would play a much more important role in the economy after 1945 than in pre-war days, and this was generally accepted by political parties, both in Scotland and in the U.K. as a whole. There is some evidence of retardation in the economy by 1950 compared with the U.K., though if we wish to end on a more positive note, it would be to point to the disappearance of unemployment as a serious problem after 1945, which did not re-emerge as a major political and social question in Scotland for over two decades.

NOTES

1. A. Slaven, *The Development of the West of Scotland: 1750-1960* (London, 1975), Ch. 9, pp. 210-211; B. P. Lenman, *An Economic History of Modern Scotland* (London, 1977), pp. 232-3; C. Harvie, *No Gods and Precious Few Heroes* (London, 1981), pp. 54-55; *Economic Survey for 1947* (Cmd. 7046).
2. Scottish Office, *Industry and Employment in Scotland (I. & E. in Scotland) 1946*, Cmd. 7125 (Edinburgh, 1947); *ibid.*, for 1947, Cmd. 7459 (Edinburgh, 1948); Scottish Home Department, *ibid.*, for 1948 (Cmd. 7676 (Edinburgh, 1949); *ibid.*, for 1949, Cmd. 7937 (Edinburgh, 1950); *ibid.*, for 1950, Cmd. 8223 (Edinburgh, 1951), and sequence. While these Scottish Office and Scottish Home Department White Papers were optimistic in tone for the heavy industries, a number of Board of Trade reports and statements from Ministers show how deeply the experience of the 1920s and 1930s had affected them. See, in general, John Gollan, *Scottish Prospect: An Economic, Administrative and Social Survey* (Glasgow, 1948), Ch. 2.
3. See below, and C. E. V. Leser, 'Manufacturing Industry', in A. K. Cairncross (ed.), *The Scottish Economy* (Cambridge, 1954) and *I. & E. in Scotland, op. cit.*, Tables on Physical Outputs.
4. For the arguments provided by economists, see, in particular, E. A. G. Robinson, *The Structure of Competitive Industry* (rev. ed. Cambridge, 1935), Ch. 1.

5. *Census of Production and Import Duties Act Inquiry*, 1935 (London, 1938-1944). The fourth part of the 1935 Census was only produced in a photographic form after demand from Government planners. *Final Report on the Census of Production for 1948* (London, 1951). Ministry of Labour and National Service, *Tables Relating to Employment and Unemployment in Great Britain in 1939, 1945 and 1946, Regional and industrial analysis of persons insured against unemployment* (London, 1947). Central Statistical Office, *Monthly Digest of Statistics*. For discussions of Scottish post-war unemployment, *I. & E. in Scotland, op. cit.*

6. T. Dickson, *Scottish Capitalism, Class, State and Nation from before the Union to the Present* (London, 1980), pp. 280-282; A. Slaven, *op. cit.*, p. 199; C. Harvie, *op. cit.*, pp. 47-48; B. Lenman, *op. cit.*, pp. 219-220.

7. *A People's Plan for Scotland* (Glasgow, 1945), and see Registrar General's reports for Scotland, and Department of Health for Scotland publications.

8. *The Clyde Valley Regional Plan 1946*, A Report prepared for the Clyde Valley Regional Planning Committee, Sir Patrick Abercrombie and R. H. Mathew, H.M.S.O. (Edinburgh, 1949), Ch. 8 and Appendix 22; the Vale is described (p. 382) as 'a grim and depressing place'. The text of the interim report published in 1946, and the final version of 1949, are similar. The latter has maps, conclusions and appendices. See also G. D. H. Cole, *The Condition of Britain* (London, 1937); Ellen Wilkinson, *The Town That was Murdered* (London, 1939); W. H. Marwick, *A Short History of Labour in Scotland* (London, 1967).

9. Cmd. 6153 (London, 1940). For regional comparisons see Table 3.

10. D. I. Mackay (ed.), *Scotland 1980: The Economics of Self Government* (Edinburgh, 1977); S. Pollard, *The Wasting of the British Economy* (London, 1982); P. Armstrong, Andrew Glyn, J. Harrison *Capitalism Since World War II* (London, 1984).

11. Neil Buxton, 'Economic Growth in Scotland between the Wars: The Role of Production Structure and Rationalisation', *Econ. Hist. Review*, 2nd series, Vol. 33, no. 4 (1980), p. 539, discussing A. D. Campbell, 'Changes in Scottish Income, 1924-49', *Economic Journal* LXV (1955), pp. 225-40.

12. *Ibid.*, pp. 540-2.

13. D. J. Robertson, 'Population Growth and Movement', in A. K. Cairncross, *op. cit.*, Table 3, p. 13.

14. Neil Buxton, *loc. cit.*, p. 541.

15. Industries in Scotland were not always disaggregated in the country tables of the Census. Compilers thought that disclosure would lead to recognition of the firms involved.

16. C. E. V. Leser, *op. cit.*, Table 61, p. 126 for categorisation of strongly, normally and weakly represented industries in Scotland. The normal category went from below 14% to above 7%. *The Clyde Valley Regional Plan 1946* (1949), Table 18, p. 88, listed over-representation as above 22% and under-representation as below 4.2%.

17. See Chapter 3 below, and note *Clyde Valley Regional Plan 1946* (1949), pp. 80-1.

18. There are figures for industries included in the general category of Mechanical Engineering which relate only to gross output; the employment and net output figures were included in Mechanical Engineering. The categories adopted by the Census compilers may have reflected a culturally dismissive attitude to heavy industries which had been developing in Britain since the later 19th century. M. Wiener, *English Culture and the Decline of the Industrial Spirit, 1850-1980* (Cambridge, 1981).

19. Board of Trade, *An Industrial Survey of the South West of Scotland* (1932), written by W. R. Scott and colleagues from Glasgow University, pp. 145-146.

20. J. R. Hume & M. S. Moss, *Beardmore* (London, 1979); R. H. Campbell, *The Rise and Fall of Scottish Industry, 1707-1939* (Edinburgh, 1980), Part III; A. Slaven, *op. cit.*, pp. 200-1; and see also P. L. Payne, *Colvilles and the Scottish Steel Industry* (Oxford, 1979).

21. For entrepreneurship in general see P. L. Payne, *British Entrepreneurship in the Nineteenth Century* (London, 1974); R. H. Campbell, *op. cit*; A. Slaven, *op. cit.*, Ch. 9; B. P. Lenman, *op. cit.*, Ch. 7.

22. Neil Buxton, *loc. cit.*, pp. 549-50.

23. A. Slaven, *op. cit.*, p. 202 notes the work of the Development Board for Glasgow and District formed in 1930, the aim of which was to develop existing industries and help incomers. The Board is referred to in the Board of Trade, *An Industrial Survey of the West of Scotland, op. cit.*

24. For literature on the advance of demand management, P.E.P. (Political and Economic Planning) thinking and the changes inside the Treasury and the Board of Trade, see Paul Addison, *The Road to 1945; British Politics and the Second World War* (London, 1975); Alan Booth, 'The Second World War and the Origin of Modern Regional Policy', *Economy and Society* Vol. 11, no. 1

(Feb. 1982); G. C. Peden, 'Sir Richard Hopkins and the "Keynesian Revolution" in Employment Policy, 1929-45', *Econ. Hist. Review*, 2nd series, Vol. XXXVI, no. 2 (1983).

25. For example, Scottish Economic Committee, Light Industries in Scotland, a Case for Development (1938), p. 7; this report included papers on Hosiery, Heating, Ventilating, and Refrigerating Apparatus, the Canning Trade, Linen, Boots and Shoes, Electrical Appliances and Equipment and Furniture.

26. S. G. E. Lythe, 'Report on the Furniture Industry in Scotland', *ibid.*, p. 29.

27. *Ibid.*, p. 18.

28. Scottish Economic Committee (S.E.C.), *Scotland's Industrial Future: The Case for Planned Development* (1939), p. 9; *The Times*, 26 Oct. 1938.

29. Scottish Economic Committee, *op. cit.*, pp. 9, 35, 36-7 and Minutes of Evidence to the Barlow Commission, 1938.

30. Minutes of Evidence to the Barlow Commission, 3 March 1938, p. 457, paras. 3967-8.

31. See R. H. Campbell, 'The Scottish Office and the Special Areas in the 1930s', *Historical Journal*, Vol. 22, no. 1 (1979) for one such criticism.

32. Forest Capie, 'The British Tariff and Industrial Protection in the 1930s', in Charles Feinstein (ed.), *The Managed Economy* (Oxford, 1984); Forest Capie, *Depression and Protectionism: Britain Between the Wars* (London, 1983).

33. Minutes of Evidence to the Barlow Commission, Federation of British Industries, 30 March 1938, particularly good on subjective factors which influenced location of industry; *The Times*, 11 Nov. 1942, report of meeting of 120 industrialists on post-war industry opposing Government controls in peacetime; Paul Addison, *op. cit*; Sidney Pollard, *The Gold Standard and Employment Policies* (London, 1970); Nuffield College, 21st private conference 1946, 'Industrial Development and Regional Policy' recorded opposition to industrial direction.

34. Gavin McCrone, *Regional Policy in Britain* (London, 1969), pp. 92-101.

35. S.E.C., Evidence to the Barlow Commission, 3 March 1938, p. 454. A recent case has been made that the first Commissioner for Scotland was aware of the general industrial situation and more advanced in his views than the works carried out would suggest: R. H. Campbell, 'The Scottish Office . . .', *loc. cit.*

36. Barlow Commission, Final Report; G. McCrone, *op. cit.*, pp. 93-101; for private industrial estates, A. Slaven, *op. cit.*, pp. 204-5.

37. For economic recovery in Britain, B. W. E. Alford, *Depression and Recovery, British Economic Growth, 1918-1939* (London, 1972); H. W. Richardson, *Economic Recovery in Britain, 1932-9* (London, 1967); A. Slaven, *op. cit.*, Ch. 8; N. K. Buxton, 'The Role of the "New" Industries in Britain during the 1930s: A Reinterpretation', *Business History Review* XLIV (1975).

38. R. H. Campbell, 'The Scottish Office . . .', *loc. cit.*

39. *Ibid.*

40. Barlow Commission, Minutes of Evidence, County Councils Association for Scotland, 15 Dec. 1937, p. 210. The development of the Scottish interest in town and country planning is discussed in Ian H. Adams, *The Making of Urban Scotland* (London, 1978), Ch. 10. There were a number of Department of Health for Scotland reports in the 1930s relevant to this, including *Working Class Housing on the Continent* (1935); *Town and Country Planning* (1936); Scottish Architectural Advisory Committee, *Report on the incorporation of architectural quality and amenity in the layout, planning, and external treatment of houses for the working classes and erection of high tenements.* Andrew Gibb, *Glasgow. The Making of a City* (London, 1983).

41. Barlow Commission, Final Report.

42. *Ibid.*, pp. 7 and 8.

43. First edition, *Tomorrow* (London, 1898). See in general, W. Ashworth, *The Genesis of Modern British Town Planning* (London, 1954). Discusses Howard and the reception of his views.

44. Barlow Commission, Final Report, pp. 194-195.

45. *Ibid.*, p. 50.

46. *Ibid.*, Part IV, Remedies. With two minority reports and a further dissenting note from Patrick Abercrombie.

47. A. Marwick, 'Middle Opinion in the Thirties', *English Historical Review*, Vol. LXXIX, no. 311 (1964): Paul Addison, *op. cit.* and W. Ashworth, *op. cit.* both discuss this question.

48. *The Times*, 1 Feb. 1940, Leader. Also 19 Feb. 1940. Parliamentary debate reported 18 April 1940. *The Times* criticised lukewarm response of the Government. Abercrombie made it clear that planning schemes should not be under the immediate control of politicians. *The Times*, 19 Feb. 1940.

49. *The Times*, 9 April, 1941.

50. *Report of the Committee on Compensation and Betterment* Cmd. 6386 (1942) (Uthwatt Report); Ministry of Agriculture, *Report of the Committee on Land Utilisation in Rural Areas* BPP 1941/2 IV (1942) (Scott Report). There were divergences in the views of these committees. Sir Frank Mears, in the *Regional Survey and Plan for Central and South East Scotland* (1948), pp. 5-6, noted that the Scott Report aimed to try and stabilise rural life and population, whereas the Barlow report 'envisaged a drastic re-distribution of the industrial population, practicable only by the invasion of rural areas'.

51. *The Times*, 5 April, 1941; and see W. Ashworth, *op. cit.*, for details of the planning committees under the 1919 Town Planning Amendment Act, strengthened under the 1932 Act. There was still little these pre-war powers could achieve.

52. R. H. Campbell, 'The Committee of Ex-Secretaries of State for Scotland and Industrial Policy, 1941-45', *Scottish Industrial History*, Vol. ii, nos. 2-3.

53. The Scottish Council on Industry was merged in June 1946 with the old Scottish Development Council to form the Scottish Council (Development and Industry), and the relationship between this and the Scottish Office was described by Sir D. Milne, in *The Scottish Office* (London, 1957).

54. *I. & E. in Scotland 1946*, Cmd. 7125 (1947), Ch. 6.

55. Cecilia Miller, 'The Scottish Economy and the Post-War British Governments, 1945-51', St. Andrews M. Phil. (1982) for résumé of local planning at this time.

56. Frank Mears was the son-in-law of Patrick Geddes, the well-known planning utopian. See also Ian H. Adams, *op. cit.*, Ch. 10 and the 'map' of influences, 'The Search for Utopia', p. 204.

57. *The Times*, 8 Jan. 1944.

58. *Clyde Valley Regional Plan 1946* (1949 ed.), referring to the work of Patrick Geddes. As W. Ashworth, *op. cit.*, has pointed out, this view was relatively marginal to town and country planning thinking until after the First World War. 'It was,' writes Ashworth, 'in the 1920s that the concept of controlled large scale decentralisation of industry and population was first clarified. By 1930 it received sufficient attention for a group of British planners to produce a symposium about it' (p. 201); Ashworth notes, H. Warren and W. R. Davidge (eds.), *Decentralisation of Population and Industry* (London, 1930).

59. See Ian H. Adam, *op. cit.*, Ch. 10 shows how closely the Scottish plans fitted the English model. Also W. Ashworth, *op. cit*; D. Niven, *The Development of Housing in Scotland* (London, 1979); G. E. Cherry, *The Evolution of British Town Planning* (London, 1974); Andrew Gibb, *op. cit.*, esp. Ch. 7, 'Brave New World', and Table 7(iv).

60. This is stated at several points, especially Ch. 2, 'Industry' and Ch. 13, 'Summary of Conclusions and Recommendations'. See also William E. Whyte, *Report by the Advisory Committee to the Constituent Local Authorities* (1947), appended to the final report. This accepted the industrial arguments without query.

61. *Clyde Valley Regional Plan 1946* (1949), p. 66.

62. *Ibid.*, p. 84.

63. Reference to the White Paper on p. 86 of 1949 edition of the Clyde Valley Regional Plan, and note also Alan Booth, *loc. cit.*, on disagreements between the Board of Trade and the Treasury. Of course, there was little the Treasury could do to stop the post-war physical planning, though it could impede the development of more comprehensive regional policy measures.

64. It is appropriate to add that though the main lobby of industrialists and business was through the forward-looking Scottish Council (Development and Industry), there were groups of businessmen around the Scottish Society of Individualists and the press who opposed any form of planning.

65. W. Ashworth, *op. cit.*, for the support given by the Labour Party for the town planning approach.

66. B. P. Lenman, *op. cit.*, pp. 234-5; *The Times*, 10 Sept. 1941.

67. *I. & E. in Scotland 1954*, Cmd. 9410 (1955), Ch. 4. Each I. & E. report contained progress notes on hydro-electric development. *A People's Plan for Scotland, op. cit.*, pp. 8-9.

68. R. H. Campbell, 'The Committee of Ex-Secretaries . . .', *loc. cit.*, pp. 4-5.

69. *Ibid*. Official war histories are rather vague on dispersal and concentration in relation to Scotland, but see E. L. Hargreaves & M. Gowing, *Civil Industry and Trade* (London, 1952), Chs. 10, 11, and Table 12, p. 225; C. M. Kohan, *Works and Buildings* (London, 1952), Ch. 9, 'Trouble in Scotland in 1942', pp. 207-209; W. Hornby, *Factories and Plant* (London, 1958).

70. *I. & E. in Scotland 1946*, Cmd. 7125 (1947), Ch. 2. Three important Government publications in 1947 on the Battle for Output were: *Economic Survey for 1947*, Cmd. 7046 (1947), advertised as the 'important White Paper on the economic state of the nation. A Plain statement of

the difficulties confronting the country and of the efforts required to meet them during the year'; *The Battle for Output*, 'A special edition of [the above] with simple picture charts added'; *We Live by Exports*, 'A clear account of the national housekeeping with 11 picture charts. Provides the answers to "Why can't we have the goods first?"'

71. *I. & E. in Scotland 1946*, Cmd. 7125 (1947), Ch. 4, 'Town and Country Planning'.

72. Gavin McCrone, *op. cit.*, Ch. 4, pp. 106-113.

73. *I. & E. in Scotland 1946*, Cmd. 7125 (1947), p. 84.

74. For a recent overview of the arguments about U.S. pressure see T. Brett, S. Gilliatt and A. Pople, 'Planned Trade, Labour Party Policy and U.S. Intervention: The Successes and Failures of Post-War Reconstruction', *History Workshop*, Issue 13 (1982).

75. *Clyde Valley Regional Plan 1946* (1949), p. 91.

76. *I. & E. in Scotland 1947*, Cmd. 7459 (1948), Ch. 18; *ibid.* 1946, Cmd. 7125 (1947), Ch. 16.

77. *Ibid.* and sequence. Each report lists progress in factory building. Figures adapted in Table 5 from *I. & E. in Scotland 1950*, Cmd. 8223 (1951), Table 2, p. 84.

78. Scottish Council (Development and Industry), *Report of the Committee on Local Development in Scotland* (Edinburgh, 1952) for figures of new enterprises in main industrial areas, and the rest of Scotland.

79. *I. & E. in Scotland 1953*, Cmd. 9102 (1954), Ch. 4, 'Recent Development of New Manufactures in Scotland'.

80. David Sims & Michael Wood, *Car Manufacturing at Linwood: The Regional Policy Issues*, Department of Politics and Sociology, Paisley College (Paisley, 1984).

81. *I. & E. in Scotland 1950*, Cmd. 8223 (1951), Ch. 4, 'American and Canadian Participation in Scottish Industry'.

82. This was recognised by the Scottish Office at the time.

83. C. E. V. Leser, 'Production', in A. K. Cairncross (ed.), *op. cit*; *Censuses of Production* for 1949, 1950 and 1951.

2

THE SCOTTISH ECONOMY, 1945-79: PERFORMANCE, STRUCTURE AND PROBLEMS

Neil Buxton

1. INTRODUCTION

In this section the opportunity is taken to signpost the way to the main features of the Scottish economy and to the problems encountered since 1945. The issues raised will be discussed in greater detail in the remaining sections of this chapter and also find reflection in several of the chapters which follow. With the benefit of hindsight it is possible to draw up a crude balance sheet to illustrate the gains and losses made by the Scottish economy over the last thirty years. In assessing the profit and loss account, few other than the incurable optimists could argue that the former has outweighed the latter. Nor could many view the short or medium-term future with any degree of complacency. True, on the credit side, the Scottish economy experienced until the 1979 recession some growth of domestic product and industrial production. But such growth was generally sluggish relative to that of the rest of the U.K., and the U.K. herself was, in turn, performing badly in relation to her industrial competitors abroad. It might, however, be argued with justification that Scotland has since the Second World War undergone a process of necessary structural change in industry, reducing her previous over-dependence on heavy staple industries and embracing, albeit with varying degrees of permanence, several new specialisms. The result has been that the production structure of the Scottish economy no longer suffers from that degree of imbalance that so retarded development between the Wars.[1] Indeed, a strong innovative role has characterised Scottish industry over the past two decades; due to this type of development, industrial structure now resembles fairly closely that of the U.K. as a whole.

In large part this innovative function has since the War been supported by foreign capital and enterprise. One of Scotland's success stories has been the extent to which she has been able to attract incoming firms, particularly from America. These, concentrating on 'new' areas of industrial activity, have been primarily responsible for the diversification and advances into lighter, science-based industries that were so conspicuously lacking before 1945. Of course, as was underlined by the international recession from 1979, such an invasion of foreign capital and enterprise carried with it attendant dangers. Employment, and indeed whole localities, became in certain instances virtually dependent upon decisions reached literally thousands of miles away from the scene of the action. Foreign investment is notoriously fickle, particularly where it assumes the form of branch-factory creation with headquarters remaining firmly in the country of origin. Moreover, it is essentially footloose and can be quickly withdrawn when economic conditions are unpropitious or because of factors quite unrelated to the actual performance of the branch firm. Frequently, too, closures are effected with little regard for the region which originally welcomes such incoming capital with inducements and concessions.

Although the dangers of a 'branch-factory' economy have been fully brought home to Scotland over recent years, considerably less attention has been paid to certain of the side-effects. These include measuring the opportunity costs and the fact that, in part, foreign capital and initiatives have 'crowded out' domestic enterprise and ingenuity. One of the chief deficiencies since the war has, therefore, been the lack of indigenous developments and the accompanying lack of readily visible Scottish entrepreneurial talent. Parochial considerations aside, the very few specifically Scottish success stories in manufacturing industry since the War have inevitably meant a level of dependence on outside capital and managerial skills undreamt of in 1945. This is not to condemn the scale and importance of these imports: indeed the relevant question which might be asked is where would the Scottish economy have been without them? Rather, it is to point out that Scotland's success in attracting incoming firms must be tempered by knowledge of the new dangers and weaknesses which they have exposed.

Nor by any means are these the only factors which appear on the debit side of the account. Regional economic policy upon which so many hopes were once pinned presently stands in some disarray, discredited in some quarters and apparently unable to deliver the levelling-up between regions of either employment opportunities or *per capita* incomes. There has, moreover, been a growing conviction in the peripheral regions such as Scotland that economic policy-making not only remains firmly entrenched at the centre, but is still designed very largely with London and the South-East in mind. However one might view the debate over the desirability of devolving political and economic powers to the separate regions of the U.K., this much at least is certain: Scottish influence has been less than crucial in framing policies and decisions which nonetheless have had a vital impact north of the border. The post of Secretary of State carries with it far too many and varied responsibilities for any one person efficiently to carry out. As a result, in the crucial decision-taking areas, most notably the Cabinet itself, he finds himself representing too many interests and conducting a lone battle against Departmental Ministers concerned only with their specific areas of responsibility. Scotland, as is often alleged, may be over-governed at grass-roots level, but in the inner sanctums where it really counts, she is still markedly under-represented. To echo Bruce Millan's words, 'A Minister's power is immeasurably increased when he has actual responsibility for a function rather than just an interest in it'.[2] For too long, from the economy's point of view, Scottish Ministers of State have been concerned merely with implementing policy decisions taken elsewhere rather than with the more vital tasks of actually framing policy itself. Power does indeed depend on responsibility: it has been Scotland's misfortune that, in the new industrial age emerging over the last two decades, her Ministers have not carried that level of responsibility which would have enhanced their powers to 'get things done'.

Over a wide range of activity Scotland has since 1945 experienced in more acute form problems that have been common to other parts of the U.K. Rates of unemployment and net migration out of the region have been persistently higher than the national average. Again, the quality of the housing stock and extent of social deprivation compare unfavourably with the rest of the country but perhaps above all, in terms of significance for the future, Scotland has suffered her full share of the chronic 'deindustrialisation' experienced by the U.K. as a whole over the last twenty years. Defining deindustrialisation as the absolute number of jobs lost in industrial activity, especially manufacturing,[3] both Scotland and the U.K. have lost approximately one-third of their industrial employment between 1966 and 1981. For Scotland, this amounts to over three hundred thousands jobs. Over the same period, manufacturing industry's share in total Scottish G.D.P. has fallen progressively while the contributions of professional, scientific and miscellaneous services, along with public administration and defence, have steadily expanded.[4] In view of these trends, there has been an assumption that the welfare of the Scottish economy is dependent to a unique extent on the public sector. Although the share of public sector employment is certainly higher than that in the U.K. as a whole, Scotland does not have an excessive reliance on public sector jobs. Of the U.K. regions, the largest share is to be found in Northern Ireland, followed closely by Wales, with Scotland ranked fourth behind the North of England.[5]

Nonetheless, weak private sector initiative has made deindustrialisation an issue of some importance in Scotland, affecting the competitive strength of the economy in international markets. This long-term trend has been reinforced by short-term cyclical influences, notably the failure of relatively new specialisms in Scotland to withstand the rigours of competition during the downswing. Diversification slowed during the later 1970s due to an avalanche of closures. This swept away not only branches of some of the best-known multinationals, but also several Government-inspired enterprises including the pulp mill at Fort William, motor vehicle assembly plant at Bathgate and the aluminium smelter at Invergordon. These resounding collapses have, however, been only the tip of the iceberg: more pervasively, the toll of small businesses has been heavy, particularly in Glasgow and the West Central region and has included firms such as the Carron Company which go back to the early industrial revolution. By the end of the 1970s, the concern was to prevent the contraction of industrial employment reaching that level which in the short run would threaten potential recovery and in the longer run might prove irreversible.

It is difficult to assess the general impact which regional policy inducements have had on Scotland.[6] It may be noted that many new ventures launched under the auspices of regional policy in the 1960s subsequently proved abortive; and that Scottish firms have not fully capitalised on the opportunities available from the exploitation and development of North Sea Oil.[7] Certainly there is little merit in adopting a whingeing approach that conveniently and naively attributes the deficiencies of Scottish enterprise to the neglect of Westminster and the machinations of Whitehall. Indeed, it can be argued that Scotland has consistently received relatively favourable treatment within the U.K. framework in the form of greater political representation and higher public expenditure per head than most other regions of the U.K.[8] A proper assessment of the strengths and weaknesses of the Scottish economy can, therefore, only be obtained by examining in some greater depth the indicators of performance over time. The following section is devoted to this task.

2. THE INDICATORS OF ECONOMIC PERFORMANCE

An analysis of the movements of the level of activity in Scotland over time depends upon having some yardstick of comparison against which performance may usefully be measured. The most convenient yardstick is, of course, the U.K. economy for which comparable data are readily available. However, it must always be borne in mind that the U.K. economy itself has lacked impetus and has generally trailed behind the rest of the industrial world. This is illustrated in Tables 1 and 2.

Table 1. *Growth of Industrial Production, Selected Countries, 1960-80 (% per annum)*

	1960-73	1973-75	1975-79	1979-80	1960-80
Japan	12.6	−7.1	9.2	6.8	9.1
France	5.9	−2.4	4.2	Nil	4.3
W. Germany	5.5	−3.8	4.0	Nil	3.9
U.S.A.	4.9	−4.7	5.7	−3.1	3.8
U.K.	2.9	−3.8	3.6	−6.1	1.9

Source: A. R. Prest and D. J. Coppock, *The UK Economy: A Manual of Applied Economics* (1982), p. 193

Table 2. *Growth of G.D.P. and G.D.P. per Capita, Selected Countries, 1970-79 (% per annum)*

	G.D.P.	G.D.P. per Capita
Japan	5.4	4.1
France	3.9	3.3
W. Germany	2.9	2.8
U.S.A.	2.4	3.2
U.K.	2.2	2.1

Source: A. R. Prest and D. J. Coppock, *op. cit.*, p. 54

During the comparatively stable years up to 1973, industrial output in the U.K. expanded much more slowly than in the leading industrial nations abroad. With the return in the 1970s of the business cycle on the scale experienced pre-1945, output in the U.K. fell less dramatically than in several countries, but equally failed to revive as strongly during the strong upswing of the later 1970s. As a result, over the whole period 1960-80, industrial production in the U.K. grew at the meagre rate of rather less than 2% per annum. Equally disappointing, as Table 2 makes clear, was the growth of G.D.P. in relation to the achievement abroad.[9] It is against this background that judgements must be made when matching Scottish economic performance against the rather dismal U.K. record. As will be shown below, Scotland generally compares unfavourably with U.K. growth rates which were, in turn, poor when judged by international comparison.

Gross Domestic Product

This is the most commonly used index of general economic performance. The most acceptable index for Scotland has been compiled by the Scottish Economic Planning Department, measuring components of the income stream — income from employment (mainly wages and salaries), income from self-employment, gross trading profits and surpluses (less stock appreciation) and rent. Of these, income from employment is by far the most important so that, as we shall see below, the relationship between Scottish G.D.P. and U.K. estimates depends largely on comparative movements in employment levels and average earnings.[10] Since the Scottish Office Index only becomes available from 1960, estimates for earlier years have been provided by McCrone, who has aggregated the values added in all branches of manufacturing, agriculture, mining and the service trades. This method depends heavily on *Census of Production* statistics and is, therefore, subject to the limitations of that data source.[11] The figures must, therefore, be used with caution for this earlier period, although their comparability with post-1960 data, both in aggregate and in component parts, would suggest that they are not seriously in error. Table 3 provides details of G.D.P. per head in Scotland between 1951 and 1960 and relates these figures to comparable U.K. data.

For most of the 1950s, at a time when heavy traditional industries were rapidly expanding, Table 3 shows that Scotland managed roughly to maintain her share of G.D.P. in the U.K. as a whole. After 1957, however, a rapid deterioration set in, both in absolute and *per capita* terms, reflecting the abrupt ending of the more-or-less continuous expansion which the staple trades had enjoyed since the Second World War. Problems of unemployment and surplus capacity, so familiar during the inter-war period, began to re-emerge on a serious scale. Renewed impetus was therefore given to regional economic policy, with the result that Scotland became one of the principal areas after 1960 to receive preferential treatment. Partly due to the stimulus accorded by such regional measures, necessary diversification of the industrial base at last

Table 3. *Gross Domestic Product Per Head in Scotland and Gross Domestic Product, Scotland as a Proportion of U.K., 1951-60*

(£, Current Prices)

Year	Gross Domestic Product per Head in Scotland (£)	Gross Domestic Product per Head in Scotland as % of U.K. (%)	Scottish Gross Domestic Product as % of that in U.K. (%)
1951	243	91.8	9.3
1952	249	91.8	9.3
1953	262	91.3	9.2
1954	279	90.6	9.1
1955	300	90.1	9.1
1956	320	90.1	9.1
1957	340	91.6	9.2
1958	342	89.8	9.0
1959	353	87.8	8.8
1960	377	87.5	8.7

Source: G. McCrone, *Scotland's Economic Progress* (1965), pp. 31-2

took place with the emphasis on the heavy industries being reduced in favour of certain new specialisms. As noted below, the changes during the 1960s and 1970s in the type of industrial activities carried out in Scotland were sufficient to bring the structure of production more closely into line with that of the U.K. as a whole. These two decades brought to an end an era in which Scotland's wealth and prosperity had to a very large extent depended on the fortunes of a relatively narrow range of basic industries.

It is important, therefore, to emphasise that the almost continuous improvement in Scotland's relative position from 1965, as shown in Fig. 1, cannot simply be attributed to the prosperity and additional employment associated with the discovery and exploitation of North Sea Oil. The latter simply sustained, and accelerated, the relative improvement in Scotland's *per capita* income that was already taking place. Nor was the rise in Scottish G.D.P. per head in relation to that in the U.K. solely due in the 1960s to the beneficial effects of the restructuring the economy. The fact is that throughout the decade *aggregate* G.D.P. in the U.K., measured in current prices, still rose at rather faster a rate than it did in Scotland: that the latter managed to make up ground in *per capita* terms was largely due to comparative movements in the levels of population. Simply, total population north of the border was falling as a proportion of that in the U.K.

The position changed, however, during the 1970s when, as Figure 1 illustrates, the relative improvement in Scotland's *per capita* output was particularly striking. Scottish population continued to decline in relation to that of the U.K. but, for the first time, *aggregate* G.D.P. north of the border began to increase at a significantly faster rate than in the rest of the country. Clearly new forces were at work stimulating the growth of Scottish G.D.P.

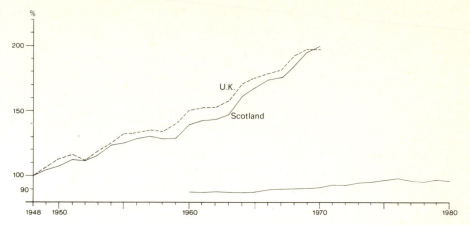

Fig. 1. Top: Index of industrial production, 1948-1970, Scotland and U.K. (1948=100). Bottom: Gross domestic product per head, Scotland, 1960-1980.

Principally, these consisted of the impetus provided by North Sea Oil and the influence of restructuring carried out after 1960. The effect of these was to lift *per capita* income in Scotland to a level close to the U.K. average. However, this improvement was not sustained during the later 1970s, the result once again of the particular vulnerability of the Scottish economy to the forces at work during the downswing of the cycle.

To appreciate why there was some 'catching up' on the part of Scotland over the period 1965-76, it is necessary to disaggregate G.D.P. into its principal component parts, income from employment, income from self-employment, gross trading profits and surpluses less stock appreciation and rent. Of these, the first is by far the most important, commonly accounting for some seventy per cent of G.D.P. in the 1970s. In turn, the largest contribution to income from employment comes, of course, from wages and salaries. It is this component that provides the main explanation of the relative improvement in Scotland's G.D.P. per head. Changes in industrial structure and oil-related developments had a stimulating effect on employment, and hence on income derived from employment. For instance, the number of employees in employment in Scotland rose much more rapidly than in the U.K. between 1972 and 1976. Along with this relatively faster growth of employment went a correspondingly greater increase in the value of wages and salaries, pushing up Scottish G.D.P. per head to a level virtually equivalent to that in the U.K. In the years following 1976, however, the rate of growth of Scottish employment was not sustained, with the result that the expansion of wages and salaries did not keep pace with that of the rest of the country. Therefore the level of *per capita* G.D.P. relative to that in the U.K. slipped back from its 1976 peak. Nonetheless over the decade as a whole Scotland had clearly gained ground within the U.K. framework. In 1971, Scottish G.D.P. per head of population was only the eighth highest amongst the U.K. economic planning regions. By 1980, it was third highest, behind only the South-East and East Midlands of England.[12] Whilst this was encouraging within the U.K. context, it must always be remembered that the U.K. as a whole performed poorly in relation to competitor countries abroad over the period.

Index of Industrial Production

Further evidence of some improvement during the 1970s in Scotland's relative standing within the U.K. is provided by movements in the index of industrial production. Such an index has existed since 1948 and provides a valuable guide over time to the level of activity in the Scottish economy. For the period 1948-1970 the series is formed by splicing together, on a standard basis, the indices for several sub-periods: 1948-54, 1954-58, 1958-63, 1963-68, 1968-70. Movements in the index are compared to those in the U.K. over the whole period 1948-70 in Fig. 1. Advantage is taken of the revisions made to the index in the 1970s (the year 1970 being used as a base) to analyse separately performance over the recent past. It should, of course, be borne in mind that the composite term 'industrial production' includes only manufacturing, construction, mining and quarrying, and the gas, electricity and water supply industries. Since major sectors such as trade, transport, finance and other service sectors are excluded, the index should not be regarded as a measure of *general* economic performance. Nonetheless, the Scottish series presently covers over forty per cent of the economic activity making up G.D.P. and, taken in conjunction with other indices of development, provides valuable insights into the wellbeing of the industrial sector of the economy. Moreover, it depicts the timing and broad magnitudes of change in industrial output and so allows useful comparisons to be drawn with the U.K. as a whole, as well as with countries abroad.

Fig. 1 makes clear that between 1955 and 1963 the performance of Scottish industry was relatively poor compared to that of the U.K. as a whole. Before 1955, Scotland had benefited from the prolonged post-war boom in demand for heavy industrial products, with the result that her industrial production grew at a rate roughly comparable to the rest of the nation. Between 1948 and 1954 output expanded by almost one quarter, at an average per annum rate of growth of about four per cent. Market conditions began to change in the mid-1950s, although only from 1957 did demand for the products of the traditional sectors rapidly decline. As a result, from 1954 to 1963 the rate of growth of industrial output fell to 2.2% in Scotland, this comparing unfavourably with the rate of almost 3% achieved in the U.K. Fig. 1 shows that a persistent, and widening, gap opened up between the Scottish and U.K. indices from the mid-1950s, the result of Scotland's heavy commitment to the staple trades and consequent lack of industrial diversification. These trends, along with growing concern over unemployment in Scotland and other relatively depressed regions, were largely responsible in the 1960s for the renewed impetus given to regional economic policy. The return of more vigorous regional policy, together with a steadily improving market environment, constituted something of a turning point in Scotland's industrial fortunes, not least because of its effects on Scottish business psychology. At last the Government was seen to be taking positive steps, so strengthening confidence in Scotland's industrial future. In the longer term this renewed optimism was to prove largely misplaced, with several of the major initiatives taken under the umbrella of regional policy coming to grief in the inhospitable economic climate of the later 1970s. However, in the short run Scotland was able to make up the ground that had previously been lost. The strong growth of industrial output after 1963 meant that by the end of the decade the Scottish index had overtaken that of the U.K. for the first time.

The relatively good performance of the Scottish economy during the 1960s can be attributed to widespread growth within manufacturing, particularly in food, drink and tobacco, vehicles, engineering and metal manufacture. In addition, the index for construction in Scotland began markedly to outstrip that for the U.K. from the latter part of the decade. Table 4 shows that Scottish industrial activity continued to rise at roughly the same rate as in the U.K. over the early 1970s. However, recovery from recession in the middle part of the decade was more pronounced in the U.K. than it was north of the border.

Table 4. *Indices of Industrial Production, Scotland and the U.K., Selected Years 1970-79 (1970=100)*

	Scotland	U.K.
1970	100	100
1973	109	110
1975	103	101
1977	104	103
1979	103	105

Source: Scottish Office, *Scottish Economic Bulletin*; *Annual Abstract of Statistics*

The indices in Table 4 exclude the influence of minimum list heading 104 of the Standard Industrial Classification. By omitting production relating to the exploration and extraction of petroleum and natural gas a more reliable comparison of domestic industrial activity is obtained.[13] As can be seen, in both Scotland and the U.K. industrial performance was weak over the 1970s, these trends representing a further erosion of the ability to compete effectively in the international economy. Moreover, recovery in Scotland from the recession starting in 1975 was less pronounced: gone were the faster growth and growing optimism of the previous decade. These trends in output are related to movements in employment and productivity to which we now turn.

Employment, Productivity and Wages

One of the most disquieting features of the post-Second World War Scottish economy has been the declining importance, in employment terms, of manufacturing industry and the extent to which employees in that sector have increasingly worked for foreign-based, or English, companies. 'Deindustrialisation' and the foreign ownership of the manufacturing base are recurring themes of this Chapter but emerged as central issues only in the latter half of the 1945-80 period. In the immediate post-war era, they had no place in the minds of Scottish industrialists who were concerned rather with short-run problems of scarcity of materials and skilled labour, and with coping with the system of 'controls' maintained by the Government after the war. Scotland benefited, along with the rest of the U.K., from the high replacement demand after the war for capital goods and manufactures, a demand reinforced by the exigencies of the Korean war in the early 1950s. By the middle of that decade, however, the familiar problems of structural deficiencies and the inability of industrial output to grow at a rate commensurate with that of the rest of the U.K. had resurfaced. Between 1954 and 1960 manufacturing output in Scotland grew by only 2.4% per annum compared to 3.4% in the U.K. as a whole. Modernisation of what was, essentially, a nineteenth-century industrial structure became imperative and was given impetus, as noted above, by the emphasis placed on regional economic measures in the 1960s. New developments were encouraged during the decade in an attempt to broaden the industrial base, including the Ravenscraig Strip Mill, two new motor vehicle plants, the Fort William Pulp Mill and the continued expansion of instrument and electrical engineering.

The process of structural change, coinciding with a period of buoyancy in industrial countries abroad, produced a stronger underlying growth in manufacturing output in Scotland, especially between 1964 and 1970. Inevitably, growth and structural change had major implications for trends in Scottish employment. First, the need to rationalise the old basic industries, mining and quarrying, shipbuilding, and textiles meant a rapid shake-out of workers. Due to differences in skill requirements and in location, these could not be readily reabsorbed elsewhere, despite the growth of employment opportunities in such new trades as motor vehicles, electronics, electrical engineering and scientific instruments. Moreover, many of the opportunities in new trades were for female employment: while the number of male employees in employment declined by 34,000 between 1954 and 1964, the number of females in employment increased by 52,000 over the same period.[14] The shortfall in the total number of jobs available for men contributed to the consistently higher level of unemployment in Scotland during the 1960s, although in absolute terms unemployment rates were not the cause for concern which they were later to become in the 1970s. Second, potential employment prospects were blighted by the apparent inability of indigenous economic enterprise to take advantage of the wide range of incentives available under regional policy and, in consequence, the persistent slippage of local control. Increasingly the level of Scottish economic activity came to depend on the policies and performance of incoming firms whose headquarters remained firmly based either in England or abroad. In the short run at least, this was less of a problem than the failure of locally inspired initiatives to take off from major foreign, or Government-directed, investments. In neither vehicles, electronics, nor later in oil, did local component suppliers develop on a significant scale in the 1970s. As a result, by the end of the decade, almost two-thirds of all employees were to work for companies controlled from outside Scotland.

Table 5 shows that in both Scotland and the U.K. the total employed labour force remained relatively stable between 1960 and 1979, and indeed in the '70s even showed some tendency to increase. However, this should not conceal the fact that, as noted earlier, important changes had taken place in the Scottish economy in structure (due in part to the dual influences of regional policy and oil-related activity); in the control of Scottish enterprise; and in the diminishing contribution made by native firms to the level of activity. Nor was that all. The main features of development in the 1970s carried with them additional implications for Scottish employment. Along with a weakening in the effectiveness of regional policies went the emergence of generally slower growth rates and a rapid reduction in the size of the labour inputs required by the manufacturing sector. The effect of such changes is largely reflected in Col. (2), Table 5, which shows for both Scotland and the U.K. the dramatic decline in employment in the production industries. Indeed, during the 1970s Scotland lost more than 100,000 jobs in manufacturing industry, with the result that by the end of the decade less than thirty per cent of the total workforce found employment in this sector.[15] To the extent that manufacturing is the engine of growth in an advanced economy, possessing growth-inducing characteristics that other sectors do not have, the dwindling size of the sector is a cause for concern. It has repercussions not only for the overall level of economic activity but also for unemployment. Unless the decline in industrial employment is compensated for by an expansion in other sectors, or by a decline in the size of the total workforce, serious unemployment must inevitably result. In Scotland and the U.K., some part of the job loss created by unfavourable market conditions and 'deindustrialisation' was indeed offset by a corresponding expansion in service employment. In both economies the service sector's share of total employment rose from just over one-half to around sixty per cent over the period 1970-79.[16] Equally, however, unemployment rates also began significantly to increase with the unemployment differential between Scotland and the U.K. as a whole widening once again during the latter part of the decade.

For Scotland, it is clear that the relative stability of the aggregate measurement, employees in employment, is achieved only by means of a series of compensating changes both within and between sectors. Within manufacturing, the more or less continuous loss of employment in the traditional heavy industries was partly offset for much of the 1960s and early 1970s by a corresponding growth in the workforce of the newer, technologically based industries. However, the persistent shedding of labour by both primary industry and manufacturing through the 1970s could only be partly compensated by a corresponding increase in service employment. This, along

Table 5. Employment, Productivity and Wages, Scotland and the U.K., Selected Years, 1960-1979

Year	Total Employees in Employment (1959/60 = 100)		Employees in Employment in Index of Production Industries (1959/60 = 100)		Labour Productivity in Index of Production Industries (1960 = 100, and 1970 = 100)		Total Registered Unemployment (%)		Average Weekly Earnings, Male Manual Workers At October[1] (£)		Average Weekly Earnings, Scotland as % of U.K. (%)
	(1)		(2)		(3)		(4)		(5)		(6)
	Scotland	U.K.	Scotland	U.K.	Scotland	U.K.	Scotland	U.K.	Scotland	U.K.	
1960	100.5	101.1	101.0	101.5	100	100	3.6	1.7	12.9	14.1	91
1963	100.7	103.6	98.2	101.2	109	105	4.8	2.6	15.5	16.8	92
1966	101.7	106.9	100.1	105.0	126	116	2.9	1.6	19.6	20.3	97
1969	99.5	103.8	96.8	99.8	147	134	3.7	2.4	24.1	24.8	97
1970	98.7	102.9	94.9	98.2	100	100	4.2	2.6	27.0	28.1	96
1973	98.3	101.9	89.2	87.8	116	116	4.6	2.7	40.4	40.9	99
1976	99.3	101.3	84.2	82.0	116	115	7.0	5.7	67.9	67.0	101
1979	99.8	102.6	83.7	80.9	117	121	8.0	5.8	95.4	96.9	98

Sources: Digest of Scottish Statistics; Scottish Economic Bulletin; Annual Abstract of Statistics

Note 1. Relates to all industries and services; the figures for 1960 refer to April.

with some expansion of the total civilian labour force (those available for work), resulted in an escalating unemployment rate during the 1970s.

These movements in employment help in part to explain the trends in productivity shown in Col. (3), Table 5. To obtain these figures, the index of industrial production was used in conjunction with an index of employees in employment. The latter was limited to those sectors covered by the production index, although problems of consistency associated with the latter index resulted in a break in trend between the two decades specified in Table 5. Movements in productivity in Scotland and the U.K. can, therefore, only be compared within, and not between, decades. It seems clear from Table 5, however, that throughout the 1960s the underlying growth of productivity in the Scottish production industries was consistently above that for the U.K.[17] This was the product of a faster rise in the Scottish index of industrial production during the decade (see Figure 1) while, at the same time, employment in the production industries fell more rapidly in Scotland than in the U.K. (Col. (2), Table 5). As a result output per person employed in Scotland rose by almost one-half between 1960 and 1969, at a time when an increase of only one-third was recorded in the U.K. Reflecting this better performance in Scotland, average weekly earnings rapidly made up ground on those of the U.K. during the decade.

The experience of the 1960s contrasts strongly with that of the subsequent decade. Over the 1970s the expansion of industrial output was lower in Scotland than in the U.K., the result in large measure of the failure of Scottish manufacturing output to recover from the recession in the middle of the decade. At the same time, employment in the production industries was, if anything, better maintained in Scotland. In consequence, the rate of growth of labour productivity north of the border fell back in relation to the U.K. average. The stimulus previously afforded the economy by the new capital-intensive industries had all but disappeared. With the latter experiencing much the same conditions of demand deficiency as the long-established basic industries, the dangers inherent in the extensive multi-national penetration of the Scottish economy were fully realised. Many of the brave new ventures launched in the 1960s foundered on the rocks of economic recession as companies with their headquarters in England or abroad sought to rationalise capacity by closing down their Scottish branches. Decisions to transfer investment elsewhere or delay development inevitably acted to the detriment of productivity growth in Scotland. Nor could the influence of these adverse economic circumstances be adequately offset by the continuing development of North Sea oil over the decade. Although some 60,000 new jobs were created in oil, and oil-related activities (some 3% of the total Scottish workforce), the bulk of direct expenditures on oil was in fact made outside Scotland altogether, and as such did not contribute to Scottish economic development. It was estimated in 1977 that the value of North Sea oil goods actually manufactured in Scotland, mostly by branches of multi-nationals, amounted to only 15% of the £1.9 billion spent in this sector.[18] As an ironical postscript, it may be added that by the same year, two or three times as many jobs had been created in the U.S.A. by North Sea oil activity as in Scotland itself.

In the final analysis, therefore, the achievements of the post-1945 economy have simply not been enough. It can be argued that by 1979 Scots were earning virtually the same average wages as in the U.K; that G.D.P. per head had risen to a level near to that of the U.K. before slipping back after 1976; that for a brief oil-boosted period the Scottish growth rate had actually outstripped that of the U.K; and that by the end of the 1970s the Scottish share of U.K. unemployment had fallen from one-fifth in 1960 to one-eighth. These are positive attributes but mean little when it is considered that on virtually every measurement of growth the U.K. itself has performed badly over the last two decades; that the acceleration of job losses in manufacturing has reached alarming proportions (a point we come back to in the next section); and that there has been a persistent failure in the 1970s to achieve a sufficiently high rate of new company formation *internally* or a sufficiently large importation of mobile new technology from *external* sources.

3. THE STRUCTURE OF PRODUCTION

Significant changes occurred in the structure of Scottish production during the post-Second World War era. This impetus to diversify in the 1960s and early 1970s stemmed from a number of factors, including a generally favourable market environment, the incentives available under regional economic policy and, subsequently, the opportunities provided by the exploitation and development of North Sea oil and natural gas. The consequent changes effected in established sectors and the introduction of virtually 'new' special-isms brought the structure of Scottish production much more closely into line with that of the U.K. as a whole. Gone was the excessive reliance on a narrow range of basic industries; instead a more balanced and diversified economy emerged, albeit one which owed too much, perhaps, to the skills, investment and enterprise provided by external sources. Despite such changes, Scotland by the end of the 1970s still remained more committed to traditional industries, agriculture and fishing, coalmining, textiles, shipbuilding and heavy engineering, than the rest of the U.K. As noted below, structural factors still account for part at least of the generally poorer Scottish economic performance during the last quarter of a century. Moreover, a new fear has emerged — that of deindustrialisation — stemming from the continuous decline of industrial employment and the apparent erosion of the manu-facturing base.

This section takes up such issues, starting with the changes which have been made during the last two decades to the structure of Scottish production. Thereafter, the problems posed by the process of deindustrialisation are examined and some explanation is provided for the persistence of this trend. Attention is subsequently drawn to the main features of existing production structure, emphasising those industries which, according to the 1973 input-output study of the Scottish economy, are likely to have maximum impact given an upturn in the level of activity. The section concludes by noting that while the distribution of industry in Scotland is now broadly similar to that in the U.K., structural weaknesses persist north of the border which inhibit growth.

To a large extent the severity of Scotland's economic difficulties in the inter-war period stemmed from an unfavourable industrial structure, with a relatively high proportion of resources concentrated in a narrow range of depressed staple industries. The result was a lower rate of growth of business activity than in the U.K., together with lower output per head and real income. Moreover, emphasis on the 'old' implied neglect of the 'new'. Since 'new' industries failed to develop on a significant scale in Scotland, there was no counterweight to set in the balance against the declining influence of old technology.[19] Of the total insured labour force in work in 1930, 47 per cent found employment in manufacturing, 36 per cent in the service industries, 9 per cent in mining and quarrying, and 8 per cent in building and contracting.[20]

These proportions changed significantly during the post-1945 era, but perhaps more striking was the extent to which Scotland's production structure, as distinguished by broad sectors, moved more closely into line with that of the U.K. The distribution of industrial population over the last quarter of a century for both Scotland and the U.K. is outlined in Table 6.

Table 6 makes clear that by the end of the 1970s sectoral shares of total employment were very similar in Scotland and the U.K. In both economies the service sector had steadily expanded its share of the workforce at the expense of employment in agriculture, forestry and fishing, extractive industry and manufacturing. The shake-out of labour in the primary sector has been more pronounced north of the border than elsewhere, although in absolute terms both agriculture and coalmining remained more important in Scotland. Increasingly attention has focused, in both Scotland and the U.K., on the persistent loss of jobs in manufacturing during the period specified in Table 6. By 1979 the share of the total Scottish labour force working in Services was double that of Manufacturing. Although the continuous nature of the decline in the latter sector caused some concern in the 1960s, this was heightened by the accelerating rate of job loss in the subsequent decade. Between 1954 and 1970 the number employed in manufacturing fell steadily, with 40,000 jobs being eliminated, a rate of decline which was, in fact, rather less than in the U.K. as a whole (see Table 6). However, during the 1970s alone a further 100,000 jobs were lost in Scottish manufacturing, at a rate faster than in the U.K.

These trends should, of course, be considered in proper perspective. The loss of Scottish industrial employment was faster than in the U.K. during the 1970s but, in turn, the decline in U.K. manufacturing employment was without parallel anywhere in the world economy.[21] On the one hand, it has

Table 6. Distribution of Employees in Employment between Main Sectors, Scotland and the U.K., 1954-1979

	Primary Industry[1]		Manufacturing		Construction		Services[2]		All Industries and Services	
	(000)	% of Total Employment	(000)	% of Total Employment	(000)	% of Total Employment	(000)	% of Total Employment	(000)	% of Total Employment
Scotland										
1954	213	10	748	36	156	7	991	47	2,108	100
1960	189	9	733	35	159	8	1,015	48	2,096	100
1970	98	5	708	34	173	8	1,080	53	2,059	100
1979	86	4	596	29	164	8	1,234	59	2,080	100
% Change 1954-79	− 60		− 20		+ 5		+ 25		− 1	
U.K.										
1954	1,573	7	8,974	42	1,358	6	9,499	45	21,404	100
1960	1,379	6	8,851	39	1,459	7	10,802	48	22,491	100
1970	876	4	8,342	37	1,339	6	11,921	53	22,478	100
1979	702	3	7,155	31	1,293	6	13,675	60	22,825	100
% Change 1954-79	− 55		− 20		− 5		+ 44		+ 7	

Sources: Scottish Office, The Scottish Economy 1965 to 1970: A Plan for Expansion, Cmnd. 2864, 1966; Scottish Economic Bulletin; Department of Employment, British Labour Statistics, Historical Abstract 1886-1968 (1971)

Notes   1. Comprises Agriculture, Forestry and Fishing, and Mining and Quarrying.
        2. Includes Gas, Electricity and Water.

been argued[22] that since manufacturing represents less than one-third of G.D.P. and of employment in Scotland, the sector is of particular relevance only if it can be shown to affect the economy in a significant way. If, for example, increased activity in manufacturing had a significant impact on services through multiplier effects, imparting a stimulus to manufacturing would be a strong policy option available to the Government. In a Scottish context, however, no convincing evidence exists to suggest a strong relationship between increased activity in manufacturing and employment change in the service sector. Indeed, it has been shown that in general the linkages between manufacturing and other sectors of the economy were not strong between 1962 and 1978.[23]

On the other hand, empirical investigation based on wider experience than simply that of Scotland suggests that there is a positive correlation between the size of manufacturing and the level of *per capita* income, and between the rate of growth of manufacturing output and the growth of G.D.P. Manufacturing has, therefore, been regarded as the 'propulsive' sector of the economy, providing the main impetus to growth. A decline in the importance of manufacturing, according to this view, is a matter for serious concern.[24] All the more so in the case of Scotland and the U.K. since it has resulted in a weakening of their respective trading and payments positions. Traditionally, both economies have been dependent on manufactured goods for export, these making a major contribution to the financing of necessary visible and invisible imports. Increasingly during the 1970s, however, services and oil revenues have been used to foot the import bill, a position which may be difficult to sustain unless further major discoveries are made. International competition in services like banking and insurance has developed rapidly and oil resources cannot, of course, last indefinitely. Such considerations make it necessary to monitor the 'deindustrialisation process' and the potential threat which it poses to the wellbeing of the Scottish economy.

Although the causes of this ongoing trend must await a full and detailed programme of further research, preliminary investigation would suggest that a number of forces have been at work. On the demand side, Scotland is heavily dependent on external trade. As a result, she is particularly vulnerable to a decline, or fall in the rate of growth, of U.K. or world demand. The comprehensive input-output analysis of the Scottish economy undertaken by the Fraser of Allander Institute for 1973 shows that, in that year, exports of goods and non-factor services, in value terms, amounted to 70 per cent of G.D.P, or 36 per cent of gross output.[25] Of total exports, some two-thirds went to the rest of the U.K., the remaining one-third to other world markets. Scotland possesses, therefore, a relatively open economy susceptible to fluctuations in world demand and more particularly to the deterioration in U.K. market conditions evident in the 1970s. Moreover, contrary to the dictates of traditional trade theory, natural resource endowment is no longer the main determinant of the nature and pattern of Scotland's external trade. Rather, the composition of trade is governed by the existence of multi-national companies, nationalised U.K.-wide industries and intra-U.K. links between private firms.[26] The needs and aspirations, particularly of the two former groups, do not coincide necessarily with those of the domestic economy. Since 1945, Scotland has therefore become increasingly susceptible to the vagaries of the decision-making processes of the multi-nationals and nationalised industries. In the former case, the essentially footloose nature of the enterprise has meant the dismantling of branch factories with few or no concessions being made to the domestic economy;[27] in the latter, closures have again been effected which reflect national economic needs rather than those of the local economy.[28] The great majority of Scots, between 65 and 88 per cent, employed in coal, petroleum, chemicals, aerospace, shipbuilding and marine engineering, were employed at the end of the 1970s by English-based companies, mainly nationalised.

The growing 'internationalisation' of capitalism with a few hundred global corporations emerging to dominate trade, investment, technology and industrial production makes it difficult for national economies effectively to control the level of activity or employment. In Scotland, however, the erosion of the manufacturing base has proceeded in the 1970s further than in any other advanced industrial nation, underlining the fact that particular problems have been encountered north of the border in addition to those shared by the rest of Western Europe. First, there has been a failure of indigenous firms to seize the opportunities offered by new technology, especially in the fields of oil exploration and development, electronics and instrument manufacture. Second, the degree of import penetration has served to deter venture capital from finding outlets, especially after 1973, in both established industries and in areas of more recent, 'high-technology', development. Finally, despite the efforts of the Scottish Development Agency, the thrust of regional economic policies in the 1970s has been to assist incoming firms rather than to assist, on a commensurate scale, local indigenous enterprise. Each of these has contributed, to a greater or lesser extent, to the progressive decline of manufacturing employment.

Thus far, examination of Scottish and U.K. production structures has been confined to employment statistics. Similar conclusions emerge from an analysis of the industrial origin of Gross Domestic Product. Between 1971 and 1979, the contribution made by manufacturing industry to Scottish G.D.P. fell from 30 to 26 per cent, while that of the service sector (including gas, electricity and water) increased from 53 to 58 per cent. The corresponding figures for the U.K. were a decline in the contribution of manufacturing from 32 to 28 per cent, and an increase in the share of services from 54 to 58 per cent. The dwindling importance of manufacturing activity was accompanied by a growing structural resemblance between the two economies, at least at broad sectoral level. This is confirmed by the findings of the Fraser of Allander input-output study of Scotland for 1973. It concluded that there existed 'only a modest degree of specialisation . . . in production and in trade with the rest of the United Kingdom'.[29] The economy by that year was highly diversified and, in contrast to the inter-war years, production was no longer so heavily concentrated on traditional industries such as iron and steel and heavy engineering.

At macro-level, it may therefore be concluded that since the 1950s Scotland's production structure has moved more closely into line with that of the U.K. as a whole. However, further disaggregation of the data to main order, and minimum list heading, level reveals that important differences still exist between the two economies. Within manufacturing there has been a steady expansion of employment in Scotland in Food, Drink and Tobacco between 1960 and 1979. By the latter date, the industry accounted for over 15 per cent of the country's manufacturing employment, while over the same two decades employment in the U.K. industry stagnated at around 9 per cent. Expansion has also been achieved within manufacturing in electrical engineering (including electronics) and in the broad industrial group coal, petroleum products and chemicals, although in both these latter categories Scotland is still under-represented in comparison to employment in the U.K. In the service sector, the outstanding feature has been the growth of employment in Professional and Scientific Services, its share of the total workforce rising from under 10 per cent in 1960 to over 17 per cent by 1979. At the other end of the scale it is still the case that Scotland is more heavily committed to traditional sectors that have for long experienced forces of contraction. Although there has been a rapid rundown in employment since 1960 in engineering and textiles, in each there is still a relatively high degree of concentration in Scotland.

These trends are summarised in Table 7, which shows the location quotients for Scottish industry in 1979. Within the manufacturing and service sectors, industrial groups are ranked according to their weight in the Scottish economy. Quotients are derived by dividing a region's share of employment in a given industry by the region's share of all industry. Where the value of the quotient is more than 1.0, the region has a more than proportionate share of a particular industry. The converse is true where the value of the quotient is less than 1.0. The findings to emerge from such an analysis are subject to certain qualifications. No account is taken of differences in regional income, and hence in expenditure patterns, nor of different production practices. Nonetheless at the level of main-order headings, the technique does provide a useful indication of relative concentrations.

Table 7 provides clear indication that the commitment in Scotland to traditional sectors, shipbuilding and marine engineering, agriculture and fishing, textiles and the extractive industries, was still relatively high in 1979. The slimming down of these industrial groups over the past two decades, while proceeding rapidly, has by no means eliminated the structural imbalance of the economy. This is confirmed, at the other end of the scale, by the fact that the country is still under-represented in industries of more recent origin, electrical engineering, chemicals and petroleum products, and vehicles. In part this reflects the failure of regional policy initiatives undertaken in the 1960s,

Table 7. *Location Quotients for Scottish Industry, 1979*

Industry Order (Based on 1968 Standard Industrial Classification)	*Location Quotient*
Agriculture, Forestry and Fishing	1.5
Mining and Quarrying	1.2
Manufacturing Industry	0.9
Shipbuilding and Marine Engineering	2.5
Food, Drink and Tobacco	1.4
Textiles	1.3
Instrument Engineering	1.2
Mechanical Engineering	1.0
Paper, Printing and Publishing	1.0
Metal Manufacture	0.9
Timber, Furniture etc.	0.9
Leather, Clothing and Footwear	0.9
Electrical Engineering	0.8
Coal and Petroleum Products/Chemicals	0.8
Bricks, Pottery, Glass, Cement	0.7
Other Metal Goods	0.6
Vehicles	0.5
Other Manufacturing Industries	0.5
Construction	1.4
Gas, Electricity and Water	0.9
Services	
Professional and Scientific Services	1.1
Miscellaneous Services	1.1
Transport and Communication	1.0
Public Administration and Defence	1.0
Distributive Trades	0.9
Insurance, Banking and Finance	0.7

Sources: Calculated from *Department of Employment Gazette*; *Scottish Economic Bulletin*; *Annual Abstract of Statistics*

particularly the lack of success in establishing a viable motor vehicle construction industry and the failure to induce related component-supplying firms to locate in Scotland. It also indicates the relative lack of movement of indigenous enterprise into electrical machinery and the high technology areas of radio and electronic components and computers, quite apart from the relatively low level of spin-off evident in Scottish manufacturing from the extraction of mineral oil and natural gas.

A detailed investigation of the importance of particular sectors and the inter-dependence of the industrial structure may be obtained from the input-output multipliers derived from the Fraser of Allander study. An increase in demand for the product of a given industry will require that industry to purchase additional goods and services from the rest of the economy. Such purchases stimulate further output which in turn require additional goods to be bought, and so on. In addition to the direct and indirect output requirements which a given industry imposes on other sectors, an increase in demand for the products of one industry also has income and employment effects. Calculating the magnitude of these effects (or multipliers), industry by industry, provides a detailed picture of the overall impact which a change in demand will have on output, income and employment throughout the economy. The analysis, conducted for 1973, showed that the output multiplier effects of agriculture, construction and forestry were high. Yet these industries exercised little influence through the income and employment multipliers. On the other hand the sector, meat and fish products, exercised a significant influence on the rest of the economy through all three multiplier effects. This is explained by the important domestic inter-industry linkages of the meat and fish products industries. Over two-thirds of the inputs into these industries were purchased from other industries in Scotland, whereas for all other sectors the proportion purchased from domestic sources was always below one-half, and averaged only 26 per cent. Hence, a change in final demand for meat and fish products results in relatively high demands being made on strictly Scottish industries which provide the necessary inputs. Moreover, the meat and fish products industries have a strong income multiplier effect, and the highest employment multiplier since they have a large indirect output requirement from other industries plus a low labour-output ratio.

As a further step, using techniques developed by Hirschman,[30] the backward and forward linkage indices of industries within the economy may be calculated in order to measure the structural inter-dependence of industries and to identify key sectors. Where the backward linkage index is greater than one, the demand of the sector generates an above-average response in the output of other industries. A higher than average forward linkage index means that the sector possesses an above-average dependence on demand from other industries. Table 8 lists the top 8 out of 75 industries in Scotland in terms of their backward and forward linkage effects on the rest of the domestic economy.

Table 8. *Domestic Linkages of the Scottish Economy, 1973*

| | Backward | | Forward | |
	Index	Rank	Index	Rank
Agriculture	1.300	4	2.110	2
Construction	1.230	7	1.989	3
Grain and Other Products	1.317	2	1.268	11
Meat and Fish Products	1.578	1	1.058	18
Electricity	1.104	13	1.546	9
Business Services	1.005	25	2.579	1
Timber Products	1.063	16	1.160	12
Iron, Steel and Aluminium	1.034	21	1.627	8

Source: Derived from Al-Ali and Burdekin, *op. cit.*, pp. 24-7, and based on the *Input-Output Tables for Scotland, 1973*

The key sectors of the Scottish economy in terms of domestic linkages are identified in Table 8. In all of these industries, backward and forward linkages are greater than one, signifying that their products are used as inputs by a wide range of other industries, as well as being used directly to satisfy final demand. In addition, they buy the products of a large number of other sectors in order to produce their own output. Multiplier/linkage analysis emphasises the crucial importance of the food and drink industry in Scotland. Increasing demand for the products of this sector in turn stimulates output, income and employment in the rest of the economy. Within the food and drink sector, meat and fish products, together with grain and other foods, stand out as activities which have the most significant 'knock-on' effects elsewhere. The evidence therefore suggests that in order to encourage economic growth in Scotland, policies should include measures which would stimulate demand for the products of some, or all, of these industries. Such measures would have a pervasive effect on the Scottish economy, given the high degree of structural inter-dependence of these industries.

In addition, the data contained within the 1973 input-output study can be used to consider the importance of leakages abroad which reduce the impetus to growth in the domestic economy. An expansion of output, given conditions of inelastic supply, may force industries to look outside the national economy for additional inputs. Moreover potential forward linkages may be frustrated by the export of intermediate output (such as bulk iron ore) rather than selling such output to domestic industries. In this context, the five electrical sectors[31] in Scotland were shown to be somewhat isolated from the rest of the economy. All were dependent to a greater or lesser extent on imports and appeared to have a significant potential for import substitution by domestically produced goods.

Finally, greater insight into the influence of industrial structure can be obtained by employing net shift analysis. Here, total net shift in employment over time is divided into two categories, differential and proportionality shifts. The former reflects regional growth differentials in the same industry, an upward shift representing a faster than national growth rate. The latter indicates the effects of a region's industrial structure. A relatively high concentration of depressed industries in the region results in a negative proportionality shift. A large share of expanding industries results in a positive proportionality shift. This analysis was applied to statistics for employees in employment for Scotland and the U.K. over the period 1960-1979 and for various sub-periods thereof. The results for the whole period are outlined below:

Scotland 1960-1979

	(000)
Total Net Shift:	
Real Change in Total Employment	− 16
Expected Change (1960 Employment × National Growth Rate)	+ 31
Difference	− 47
Differential Shift:	
Each Main order Heading × National Growth Rate for that industry to give net difference as above. The sum of shifts for all industries gives regional differential shift	+ 3
Proportionality Shift:	
Provided by Total Net Shift less Differential Shift	− 50

The analysis indicates that the Scottish experience did not differ substantially from that of the U.K. as a whole between 1960 and 1979. In terms of absolute employment, the total net shift in Scotland was relatively small between 1960 and 1979. Of the total shift which did occur in Scotland, all of it was 'explained' by structural factors rather than the failure of individual industries to match the growth rates of their U.K. counterparts. This was largely due to the fact that the effects of rapid structural change in the 1960s and early 1970s, bringing Scotland more closely into line with the national production structure, did not of course remove all structural deficiences. In addition, from 1973 the effects of structural change in certain sectors were eroded, even reversed. Closures in Vehicles, Paper and Printing and Publishing and in a wide range of small businesses helped to offset many of the positive effects of earlier structural adjustments.

With regard to the Differential component the most striking result is the faster contraction of employment in Scotland in certain of the service sectors, while in others there was a failure to match the growth of employment which was achieved in the U.K. In Transport and Communications and the Distributive Trades a more rapid decline in employment was experienced than might have been expected on the basis of national trends. On the other hand, the expansion of employment in Professional and Scientific Services, although large in absolute terms, did not match that in the U.K. as a whole. This confirms the findings presented in Table 6: the serious erosion of manufacturing employment has not made Scotland any more dependent on service employment than the rest of the nation.

4. REGIONAL POLICIES AND THEIR IMPACT

Regional policy in its modern form originated with the Local Employment Act of 1960 which repealed the Distribution of Industry Acts of 1945 and 1958.[32] An initial schedule of Development Districts was drawn up, representing those areas in need of preferential assistance. In this way, the 1960 Act increased the proportion of insured population in Scotland covered by regional policy measures from 55 to 62 per cent, and Scotland's share of the Great Britain total from 30 to 52 per cent. The Act also amended the system of control of industrial building through the issue of Industrial Development Certificates (I.D.C.s), the intention being to direct industrial development from the non-assisted to the assisted areas.[33] The revisions introduced by the Industrial Development Act of 1966, including the designation of Development Areas instead of Districts, brought virtually the whole of Scotland's insured population within the new assisted areas.[34] At the same time the Highlands and Islands Development Board was established to promote the economic and social development of the region through a system of grants and loans.

Two further categories were introduced in 1967 and 1970, Special Development Areas, which in view of exceptionally high unemployment received additional assistance,[35] and Intermediate or so-called 'grey areas' which lay outside Development Areas but suffer problems similar in kind, if not in severity.[36] Fundamental revisions in regional policy, as it affected Scotland, were made in 1972, 1975 and 1979. In 1972 the Finance Act greatly extended the amount of regional assistance on offer, while the Industry Act made provision for payment of selective assistance to industry. Industrial Development Boards were established for Scotland, Wales and the English regions with discretion to provide a loan of up to half a million pounds (subsequently raised in 1974 to one million pounds) in the form of selective assistance. In 1975, however, responsibility for regional selective assistance, together with powers for the provision and maintenance of Government factories and estates, was transferred to the Secretary of State for Scotland. In the same year the Scottish Development Agency was set up, introducing a new element into regional policy by being able to participate directly in industrial undertakings. As part of its remit, it was also to undertake derelict land clearance and environmental improvement schemes.

The haphazard progression of regional policy measures and the bewildering range of grants, loans and inducements available under such measures was to some extent 'rationalised' by the new Conservative Government in 1979. The intention was to reduce the overall level of Government involvement in industrial development and to concentrate regional aid more precisely in those areas where it was most needed. Specifically, the value of regional incentives and their availability were both reduced, the latter by raising the qualifying minimum expenditure levels and cutting down on the number of qualifying areas.[37] Of the three categories of assisted area — Special Development Areas, Development Areas, and Intermediate Areas — preference, in the form mainly of regional development grants and regional selective assistance, was given largely to the first two types of Area, while Intermediate Areas were eligible for very little assistance.[38] Rather than introduce new thinking on regional economic policy, these measures were confined simply to tinkering with its financial edges.[39] Over the long term, of greater concern have been the continuous changes which have been made to the definition of necessitous areas, the type of assistance on offer, and the scale of such assistance.[40] There have, too, been changes over time in the objectives of regional policy, ranging from eliminating disparities between regions in *per capita* incomes, industrial growth rates, net migration and, perhaps above all, unemployment. In addition, doubts exist about the efficacy of regional economic policy,[41] particularly in terms of job creation. According to Moore and Rhodes, net job creation in manufacturing in Scotland, Wales, Northern Ireland and the North of England amounted to 12,000 jobs per annum between 1972 and 1976. The inclusion of Merseyside and the South-West would raise this total to some 15,000 per annum: moreover, this figure excludes both the influence on service industries and the general multiplier effects. On the other hand, at the end of the 1970s Sir Keith Joseph, the Industry Secretary, estimated that only 10,000 net new jobs had been created annually by the operation of regional support measures in Great Britain as a whole.[42]

In terms of the Scottish economy, a huge absolute increase in the assistance provided under regional policy since 1960 has not been accompanied by significant changes in either the total size of the working population or the number of employees actually in employment. The relevant issue is, of course, how these indicators of the level of activity would have behaved had regional support measures not been available at all. The large increase in the annual Exchequer cost of special regional assistance to industry in Scotland is outlined in Table 9.[43]

If the objective of regional policy is taken to be a reduction in regional disparities,[44] it should ultimately have an effect on the main indicators of regional economic performance. Table 9 shows that total gross expenditure in the form of regional preferential assistance to Scotland rose from just over £3m. in 1960/61 to almost £200m. in 1980/81. This huge increase over the space of two decades was accompanied by a rise in industrial output; an increase in G.D.P. per head from 88 to 97 per cent of the U.K. average; and in an increase in average weekly earnings per head of male employees from 92 per cent to a level virtually equivalent to that in the U.K. However, at the same time, the total number of employees in employment stagnated while absolute numbers unemployed at June in 1980/81 showed a fourfold increase over those in 1960/61.[45] Moreover, precisely at a time when the greatest emphasis was being placed on regional policy measures, between 1966 and 1975, the closure rate of Scottish manufacturing plants was exceptionally high. It was higher than in the peripheral areas as a whole,[46] while in turn such areas experienced closure rates above those in the rest of the U.K. Indeed, over the period 1966-75, Scotland experienced a closure rate that was up to 35 per cent higher than in the U.K. as a whole amongst inter-regional moves[47] and up to 44 per cent higher amongst enterprises new to manufacturing (that is, the opening of a new unit by an enterprise not previously operating a manufacturing unit).[48] The closure rate was particularly high in Scotland in the Buildings Materials industry, Clothing, and Timber and Furniture, with Glasgow suffering an exceptionally high level of closures.[49]

Clearly, at a time when major emphasis was placed on regional policies, *per capita* income and average earnings were raised close to the levels obtaining in the U.K. as a whole, but the employment/unemployment statistics revealed a much less satisfactory situation. This does not necessarily mean, of course, that, in terms of job creation, regional policies 'failed'. As noted in sections 2 and 3, they were operating against a background of unfavourable market environment for much of the 1970s and rapid structural change over the whole period from 1960. In the absence of such measures, the labour market position in Scotland would have shown a significantly greater deterioration. For instance, over the last fifteen years there has been a cumulative shortfall of some 1,000,000 jobs in Northern Ireland, Scotland, the North-West, and the North of England relative to developments in the U.K. as a whole, despite the 350,000 manufacturing jobs shifted to these areas due to the operation of regional policies.[50]

Table 9. Expenditure on Regional Preferential Assistance to Industry in Scotland, Selected Years, 1960/61-1980/81 (£m)

Fiscal Year	Local Government Act			Industry Act 1972		Highland & Islands Development Board		Scottish Development Agency Act	Other Assistance			TOTAL GROSS EXPENDITURE
	Government Factory Building	Loans	Grants	Selective Financial Assistance	Regional Development Grants	Loans	Grants	Land & Factory Building	Regional Employment Premium	Investment Grants	Other	
1960/61	2.5	0.6	0.1	—	—	—	—	—	—	—	—	3.2
1962/63	2.8	10.1	1.5	—	—	—	—	—	—	—	—	14.4
1964/65	2.0	4.6	2.4	—	—	—	—	—	—	—	1.1[2]	10.1
1969/70	4.5	2.8	6.6	—	—	1.0	0.6	—	42.0	29.6	11.0[3]	98.1
1972/73	5.0		23.4[1]	0.1	3.0	1.2	1.5	—	37.1	17.3	—	88.6
1974/75	5.9		7.7[1]	5.1	61.6	2.3	1.6	—	56.4	2.7	2.4[4]	145.7
1979/80	—	—	—	14.7	70.2	6.9	4.6	37.8	—	—	9.0[4]	143.2
1980/81	—	—	—	22.6	113.3	5.0	6.4	47.3	—	—	3.9[4]	198.5

Sources: H. M. Begg, C. M. Lythe and R. Sorely, *Expenditure in Scotland 1961-1971* (1975), pp. 50-54; Scottish Office, *Scottish Economic Bulletins*

Notes
1. The arrangements for paying assistance under the Local Employment Acts were superseded by the Industry Act 1972. From 1972/73, estimates of gross expenditure on loans and grants were presented jointly.
2. Comprises Free Depreciation. No estimates for the differential value of the first-year tax allowances of 100% available from 1971 were made. The concession was extended to the whole country in 1972.
3. Comprises Selective Employment Tax Additional Payments.
4. Comprises in 1974/5 Department of Employment preferential assistance to industrial training and Tourism. In 1979/80 and 1980/81 the total comprises Small Firms Employment Subsidy and Tourism.

Empirical investigations of the effect of regional policy on the Scottish economy have been conducted by several observers, including Moore and Rhodes for the period 1951-71.[51] On the basis of shift-share analysis they conclude that there was a significant difference in the performance of the Scottish manufacturing sector between the 1950s, the period of dormant regional policy, and the subsequent decade when positive regional policies were pursued.[52] In the latter period, the strengthening of regional policy was responsible for some 70-80,000 new jobs in Scotland by 1971, about 12 per cent of the manufacturing workforce. This was far short of what *would* have been required to correct fully the unemployment disparity between Scotland and the more prosperous regions of the U.K. In order to equalise unemployment and activity rates between Scotland and the Midlands and South-East of England, and to eliminate net outward migration, some 230,000 further jobs would have been required over the period 1960-71. This represented some 21,000 new jobs per annum for eleven years in addition to the 7,000 jobs per annum which an active regional policy actually did create during the 1960s.

Hence the achievement of 70-80,000 jobs in the 1960s amounted to about one-third of what would have been required to produce a rough balance in the labour market. Of the new jobs secured, almost three-quarters came from the creation of new factories mainly by firms operating in other regions. The effect of regional policy on indigenous industry was therefore very limited, and employment in this sector continued to decline, relative to the same industries in the U.K., even in the positive regional policy period of the 1960s.

The question to be answered is, therefore, why policies which created 70-80,000 new jobs after 1960 nevertheless had only a small impact on the relatively high level of Scottish unemployment. The explanation is provided by changes in the behaviour of the non-active part of the working population (those in the working age groups but not registered as seeking employment) and of potential net outward migrants. After 1960, regional policy measures contributed to a decline, relative to the U.K., in the non-active part of the Scottish labour force. Increasing numbers were attracted into the active workforce, while at the same time there was a reduction in the hitherto very high rate of net outward migration. Simply, in view of the encouraging inflow of foreign capital, more people were persuaded to remain as part of the domestic working population rather than move outside Scotland. Hence, before an effective regional policy could have reduced unemployment in Scotland significantly, it would have had to generate sufficient employment opportunities to compensate for a probable reduction in net outward migration and in the relative numbers of non-active persons.

On the other hand, it may be appropriate to adopt an altogether wider view of 'regional policy' than simply direct expenditure on measures designed to influence the level of activity in particular regions such as Scotland. Direct regional expenditure in Scotland, for instance, represents only a small part of total Government spending undertaken north of the border.[53] In terms of output and employment, the effect of *direct* regional spending on Scottish manufacturing was relatively small between 1961 and 1978. However, other forms of expenditure by central Government in Scotland would, as noted above, include *some* regional policy component. When these wider aspects of spending were taken into account (capital expenditure by nationalised industries, grants to local authorities, wages and salaries in public administration and defence and expenditure on direct regional policy), they made a statistically significant contribution to employment change in manufacturing, although the extent of change was smaller for incoming firms than for indigenous firms.

If the analysis is broadened to include sectors of the economy other than manufacturing, the effect of Government spending in Scotland produced mixed results for the period 1961-78. In certain sectors the expenditure variables adopted were significant in explaining employment change: these included mining and the public utilities. However, in explaining output change, the expenditure variables were not statistically significant, nor can a satisfactory explanation be provided of either output or employment changes in the Services Sector.

In sum, the influence of direct regional policy expenditure was found to be limited, particularly with regard to manufacturing industry. A broader definition of Government spending in the regional context demonstrates that regional policy was significant in the longer-term restructuring of the Scottish economy: even here, the effect on employment was more important for indigenous than for incoming firms.

One further aspect of the effectiveness of regional policy is the extent to which the assistance provided by the Regional Fund of the E.E.C. helped mitigate the declining employment opportunities in Scotland during the 1970s. Under the Regional Development Fund set up in 1975 Britain had, by 1981, received 1.3 billion E.C.U. (European Currency Units), almost 24 per cent of the total 5.3 billion E.C.U. which had been distributed.[54] In addition, Britain of all countries had benefited most from loans provided for the rationalisation of coal and steel production under the European Coal and Steel Community Treaty (E.C.S.C.). Despite being a member of the E.E.C. only from 1973, Britain received almost 41 per cent of the 1.521 million E.C.U. in loans issued between 1961 and 1981. Other forms of assistance were made available through the Common Agricultural Policy, the European Social Fund and the European Investment Bank. At first sight this appears an imposing array of measures, but it has to be viewed, of course, in the context of the contributions made to the E.E.C. in the form of Agricultural Levies, Customs Duties, V.A.T. Contributions and M.C.A.s (Monetary Compensation Amounts, arising from the difference between market and 'green' rates for sterling). By the end of the 1970s Britain was, for example, contributing 20 per cent of the cost of the European Regional Fund and being allowed to withdraw 27 per cent. Again, since the vast bulk of total E.E.C. expenditure takes the form of agricultural spending, the funds available to assist industrial regions are severely restricted.

Table 10. *E.E.C.-Scotland Estimated Transfers, 1978*

Costs to Scotland (£m)		Benefits to Scotland (£m)	
Agricultural Levies	13.1	Agricultural Price Support and Other Agricultural	37.2
Customs Duties	60.1	Regional Fund	24.8
V.A.T. Contributions	56.6	Social Fund	10.7
Monetary Compensation Amounts	46.9	European Coal and Steel Community (Loan Differential)[1]	7.9
Total	176.7	European Investment Bank (Loan Differential)[1]	32.7
		Article 131[2]	27.2
		Research, Energy, Industry Intervention Payments	2.1
		Total	142.6

Source: D. Bell and N. Fraser, *The Scotsman*, 27-29 November 1979

Notes   1. The benefit from these loans is calculated by the differential between the interest rate actually paid and that which would have been paid on the U.K. capital market on all outstanding loans.

2. Payments under Article 131 reimburse 'new' members of the Community if their contributions rise above a specified limit.

For instance, during the lifespan of the first European Regional Development Fund, 1975-77, £650 million was available to help disadvantaged regions, of which 27 per cent was allocated to the U.K. The total benefit received by Scotland amounted to £38.4 million, hardly significant when measured against the £550 million (excluding loans) which Scotland received over the same period from the U.K. Government in the form of regional preferential assistance.[55] Nor have contributions made under the Fund constituted net *additions* to public expenditure in Scotland. These go to the U.K. Government rather than to the promoters of individual projects. Commonly, therefore, the E.E.C. comprises an *alternative* source of funding for grants that would otherwise have been provided by the U.K. Treasury.[56] The concept of 'additionality' is, indeed, crucial to the whole purpose of the E.E.C. Regional Fund, which is specifically designed to boost member states' own efforts to promote regional development. In fact funds made available to Scottish industry and local authorities are retained by the Treasury, so allowing the latter, in theory at least, to proceed with more regional investment than would otherwise have been possible. Whether this is the case in practice is debatable: at the very least the logistics of the exercise do not constitute the type of coherent European intervention on behalf of needy regions which the Community would wish. Rather than a regional strategy, the operation of the Regional

Fund up to 1980 resembled simply a resource-transfer mechanism.[57] Taking all direct benefits and costs into account, Bell and Fraser have concluded that on balance Scotland was probably making a net direct contribution to the E.E.C. by the end of the 1970s. The balance-sheet which they have compiled is presented in Table 10. Table 10 shows that in 1978 Scotland made a net direct transfer to the E.E.C. of some £34 million. This, though, takes account only of direct benefits-costs and makes no allowance for such indirect benefits as enlargement of the 'home' market brought about by the expansion of trade, the attraction of inward investment from countries outside the Community and looking for a base in Europe, and the stability of food prices. As Bell and Fraser conclude, however, while these may have improved Scotland's growth potential, there was no tangible evidence, given the poor performance of the economy over the second half of the 1970s, that such potential was being realised. That is, there were no conclusive signs that the indirect effects of Community membership had materially benefited the Scottish economy.

NOTES

1. Neil K. Buxton, 'Economic Growth in Scotland Between the Wars: the role of Production Structure and Rationalisation', *Econ. Hist. Rev.*, Second series, Vol. XXXIII (1980), pp. 538-555; A. Slaven, *The Development of the West of Scotland, 1750-1960* (London, 1975), Ch. 8; R. H. Campbell, *Scotland since 1707: the Rise of an Industrial Society* (London, 1965), pt. 3.

2. B. Millan, 'Scotland, the Scottish Office and the U.K. Economy', in C. Blake and C. Lythe (eds.), *A Maverick Institution; The Dundee School of Economics* (Dundee, 1981), p. 99.

3. A. P. Thirwall, 'Deindustrialisation in the U.K.', *Lloyds Bank Review*, No. 144 (1982), pp. 22-37.

4. See *Scottish Economic Bulletin*, No. 25 (1982); Table 6 below.

5. In 1977, Scotland had 750,000 public sector employees or 34% of the total workforce, compared to 7.8 million or 31.5% of the U.K. workforce employed in the public sector.

6. See Section 4 for an assessment of regional policy measures.

7. See Ch. 13.

8. In 1977-78, Northern Ireland's share of public spending per head of population was almost 54% above the English average, while in Wales it was 26% above and in Scotland 23% above.

9. See, for example, S. Pollard, *The Wasting of the British Economy* (London, 1983), p. 19.

10. A summary of sources and methods of estimation of Scottish G.D.P. is contained in the Scottish Economic Bulletin, No. 25 (1982).

11. See T. L. Johnston, N. K. Buxton and D. Mair, *Structure and Growth of the Scottish Economy* (London, 1971), pp. 42-3.

12. *Scottish Economic Bulletin*, No. 25 (1982).

13. For further details see the Scottish Office, *Scottish Abstract of Statistics* (1980), pp. 133-4.

14. Males in employment fell from 1,379,000 in 1954 to 1,345,000 in 1964. Over the same period, female employment rose from 728,000 to 780,000, Scottish Office, *The Scottish Economy 1965-70. A Plan for Expansion*, Cmd, 2864, H.M.S.O. (Edinburgh, 1966), p. 160.

15. Employees in employment fell from 708,000 in 1960 to 596,000 in 1979; the fall was almost as precipitate in the U.K. as a whole where employment fell from 8.3 million to 7.2 million over the same period.

16. In Scotland, Service employment increased from 1,080,000 to 1,234,000; in the U.K. from 11,921,000 to 13,675,000. For purposes of this calculation the category Gas, Electricity and Water is included in the Service sector. See also Table 6, and Ch. 6.

17. See also *Scottish Economic Bulletin*, No. 25 (1982), p. 5.

18. *The Scotsman*, 21 February 1980.

19. N. K. Buxton, 'Economic Growth in Scotland Between the Wars: the role of production structure and rationalisation', *Econ. Hist. Rev.*, second Vol. XXXIII (1980), pp. 538-555.

20. Calculated from Ministry of Labour data on the basis of the insured labour force in July minus the unemployed at June.

21. Comparisons with overseas experience are made in Thirwall, *loc. cit.*

22. M. Majmudar, 'Government and the Scottish Economic Performance: 1954-1978', *Scottish Journal of Political Economy*, Vol. 30 (1983), p. 154.

23. *Ibid.*, pp. 166-8.

24. Thirwall, *loc. cit.*

25. The value of exports of goods and non-factor services in 1973 amounted to £3,943 million, while total imports amounted to £4,196 million. Fraser of Allander Institute, *Input-Output Tables for Scotland, 1973* (Edinburgh, 1978).

26. D. R. F. Simpson and A. Jowett, 'The factor content of Scottish external trade', *Fraser of Allander Institute Discussion Paper*, No. 18 (June, 1980), pp. 8-9.

27. There are numerous examples, including such well-known names as Singer, Massey-Ferguson, Monsanto, Goodyear and Dunlop.

28. As, for instance, in coal, shipbuilding, iron and steel and motor vehicles.

29. *Input-Output Tables for Scotland, op. cit.*, p. 5.

30. A. I. Hirschman, *The Strategy of Economic Development* (New Haven, 1958).

31. These were electrical machinery, communications equipment, computers and electronics, domestic electrical appliances, and other electrical goods.

32. Details of regional policy measures, and of the grants, loans and other forms of assistance made available under these measures, may be obtained from G. McCrone, *Regional Policy in Britain*, (Oxford, 1969); G. McCrone, *Scotland's Future: the economics of nationalism*, (Oxford, 1969), Ch. 3; Johnston, Buxton and Mair, *op. cit.*, Chs. 12 & 13; Scottish Council (Development and Industry), *Committee of Inquiry into the Scottish Economy* (Toothill Committee) (1961); Scottish Office, 'Regional Assistance in Scotland since 1960', *Scottish Economic Bulletin*, No. 9, (1976); and see Ch. 8.

33. The strength with which I.D.C. policy was subsequently enforced varied considerably. Up to 1972, Industrial Development Certificates were required in *all* areas for projects above certain minimum size. From 1972 they were not required in Development Areas, and since 1976 I.D.C. control has not been strictly applied.

34. The only part of Scotland not included was the area in and around Edinburgh, defined by the Edinburgh, Leith and Portobello employment exchanges.

35. By 1971 the whole of West-Central Scotland and the new towns of Livingston and Glenrothes were indentified as Special Development Areas. In addition to capital subsidies, Regional Employment Premium was paid to firms in Development Areas from 1967 to 1976.

36. The Leith employment exchange was designated an intermediate area and therefore benefited from the assistance available under the Local Employment Act. It was joined in 1971 as an intermediate area by Edinburgh and Portobello.

37. Policies were designed to cut total regional expenditure in Britain by over one-third, from £609m in 1979 to £376m in 1983, and the proportion of the workforce in qualifying areas from over 40 per cent to 25 per cent.

38. Before the 1979 measures, regional development grants of 22 per cent were available in Special Development Areas for new machinery, plant and buildings; grants of 20 per cent were allowable in Development Areas; and a grant of 20 per cent on new buildings alone was available in Intermediate Development Areas. The effect of the new measures was to leave intact the regional development grants in the Special Development Areas; reduce grants in Development Areas to 15 per cent; and abolish altogether the building grant in Intermediate Areas. In future the only assistance available to such Areas was to come from a pool of money, withdrawals from which were severely circumscribed by stringent limits and conditions. Regional Selective Assistance usually takes the form of further, discretionary grants towards capital and training costs for projects conforming to job-creating criteria.

39. A new departure in policy was the subsequent introduction in 1980 of Enterprise Zones, very small districts, which were to receive special assistance. Such Zones were intended to help solve problems of economic and physical decay, primarily in older urban areas.

40. The most recent position, after implementation of the 1979 policy changes, is outlined in Department of Industry, *Incentives for Industry in the Areas for Expansion* (1981).

41. See, for instance, D. N. F. Bell and R. A. Hart, 'The Regional Demand for labour services', *Scottish Journal of Political Economy*, Vol. 27 (1980), pp. 140-151.

42. See *Financial Times*, July 20, 1979. It seems likely that this is an underestimate.

43. It should be emphasised that the figures in the Table relate only to Government expenditure

on direct regional policy. It has recently been argued that the concept of regional policy should be broadened to include grants to local authorities, capital expenditure by nationalised industries, and wages and salaries in public administration and defence. Each of these may be considered to include some regional policy component. See M. Majmudar, 'Government and the Scottish Economic Performance: 1954-1978', *Scottish Journal of Political Economy*, Vol. 30 (1983), pp. 153-169.

44. That is, regional incentives should increase investment and employment above the levels which would otherwise have been expected and have an influence on general growth rates, levels of income and the extent of unemployment.

45. Average unemployment in June amounted to 64.7 thousand in 1960/61; in 1980/81, June unemployed averaged 264.5 thousand.

46. Defined as Scotland, Wales, Northern Ireland, and North, North-West and South-West England.

47. That is, firms moving into Scotland from other regions of the U.K. and from abroad.

48. R. A. Henderson, 'An analysis of closures amongst Scottish manufacturing plants between 1966-1975', *Scottish Journal of Political Economy*, Vol. 27 (1980), p. 158. This analysis is based on the S.C.O.M.E.R. (Scottish Manufacturing Establishments Record) databank held by the Scottish Office. For a discussion of S.C.O.M.E.R. see Scottish Office, *Scottish Economic Bulletin*, No. 13 (1977).

49. Henderson, *loc. cit.*, pp. 169-70.

50. *Cambridge Economic Policy Review*, Vol. 6, no. 2 (1980), p. 36.

51. B. Moore and J. Rhodes, 'Regional Policy and the Scottish Economy', *Scottish Journal of Political Economy*, Vol. 21 (1974), pp. 215-235. This and the following paragraph rely heavily on this source. See also Moore and Rhodes, 'Regional Economic Policy and the Movement of Manufacturing Firms to Development Areas', *Economica*, Vol. 43 (1976), pp. 17-31.

52. Much the same conclusions are reached by R. R. MacKay and L. Thomson, 'Important Trends in Regional Policy and Regional Employment: A Modified Interpretation', *Scottish Journal of Political Economy*, Vol. 26 (1979), pp. 244-6. On the other hand, Majmudar, *loc. cit.*, pp. 161-3, has cast doubt on the positive effects of 'direct' regional policy for the period 1955-75.

53. Between 1961 and 1978, expenditure on 'direct' regional policy in Scotland amounted to just over 7% of total gross expenditure undertaken by central Government in Scotland. Majmudar, *loc. cit.*, pp. 156-7. This and the following paragraph rely largely on this source.

54. This share was second in size only to Italy which had received 40 per cent of the total. E.C.U. (European Currency Units) replaced European Units of Account with the introduction of the European Monetary System. By 1980 £1 = 1.67 E.C.U.

55. Between 1975 and 1979 the U.K. received £363.5 million, or 27 per cent of the total amount available under the European Regional Fund. Of this, Scotland was allocated £107.3 million, £75 million for infrastructure projects and £32.3 million for industrial projects.

56. The only net effect on the Scottish economy is therefore the marginal reduction of tax rates which might result from lower levels of British public expenditure.

57. See 'The Anatomy of a Euro-fraud', *The Scotsman*, April 10, 1980.

3
THE DECLINE OF THE SCOTTISH HEAVY INDUSTRIES, 1945-1983*

Peter L. Payne

There is a bitter irony in the fact that all those industries — coal, iron and steel, and shipbuilding — that once constituted the very sinews of the Scottish economy are now, after having been taken into public ownership, on the brink of extinction and can only survive as the direct result of political will. It is the object of this chapter to examine the course of, and the reasons for, this precipitous decline. That the relative diminution of the share of the heavy industries in the Scottish economy was inevitable has been apparent for many decades; the problem that confronts us is to attempt to determine whether the speed of the collapse need have been so rapid or so apparently complete.

1. DECLINE: ITS EXTENT AND CHRONOLOGY

The extent of the deterioration of Scotland's heavy industries is revealed by Tables 1-3. Both in absolute and relative terms, the severity of their problems is plain. It is equally clear that the onset of accelerating decline has afflicted the three industries at different times. Let us consider each of the interrelated industries in turn. Since it is accepted that the fundamental basis of the modern development of Scotland's manufacturing activities was the ready availability of indigenous resources, it is appropriate to begin with coal.

The peak of Scottish coal output, like that of Britain as a whole, was attained in 1913. From a total of 42.5 million tons in that year, output fell to an average of not much over 30 million tons between the wars, remained steady at between 23 and 24 million tons during the first quinquennium (1948-52) of state ownership, had slipped to about 18 million tons in the early 'sixties, and was barely half that figure by the mid-'seventies. In the year 1981-82 saleable output stood at 7.1 million tonnes. The fall in Scottish coal production since the Second World War has been steeper than that of the nation as a whole. From consistently providing 13-14 per cent of British output between the wars, Scotland's share had fallen to about 10 per cent by the late 'fifties, averaged about 8.75 per cent during the 'seventies, and was only 6.7 per cent in 1981-82. Employment in the industry has experienced a similar trend. The number of miners in Scottish coalfields, nearly 150,000 in 1920 or nearly one in eight of the industry's national labour force, had fallen to

* It will be obvious to the reader that this chapter relies heavily on the work of Professor Tony Slaven and Professor Neil Buxton, the former of whom kindly supplied me with additional unpublished data. I wish to record my sincere thanks to them both.

79

Table 1. *Coal: Output and Employment in Scotland, Selected Years, 1913-1982*

	Output (tons millions)		Employment (000's)	
	Scotland	Scotland/U.K. %	Scotland	Scotland/U.K. %
1913	42.5	14.8	147.5	13.1
1938	30.3	13.3	90.0	11.4
1948	23.8		82.4	
1951	23.6	11.2	82.2	11.8
1955	21.7	10.4	82.8	11.9
1961	17.2	9.6	67.8	12.1
1967/68	13.7	8.4	38.9	10.0
1971/72	10.4	9.5	27.4	10.2
1975/76	9.7	8.6	23.6	9.7
1981/82	7.1	6.6	18.3	8.4

Sources: 1913, 1938, Mitchell & Deane, *Abstract of British Historical Statistics*, p. 119; 1948-1981/ 82, National Coal Board, *Annual Reports*

81,600 in 1933. This total, after some recovery in the late 'thirties to about 90,000, receded during the Second World War to the 1933 level and has since fallen to about 70,000 in 1961, to around 30,000 in the early 'seventies, and to an average of about 21,000 in the late 'seventies. In the early 'eighties, the figure has fallen below 20,000, or less than 9 per cent of the national coalmining labour force, compared with about 10 per cent a decade earlier.

While the proportion of British coal raised in Scotland nearly halved between 1947 and 1982 (c.12 per cent to 6.6 per cent), the proportion of the nation's steel output made in Scotland had fallen by a similar factor from about 15 per cent after the Second World War to below 8 per cent in 1978. Since then there has been a slight recovery to almost 13 per cent of a much smaller national total in 1981. But whereas the absolute amount of coal raised in Scotland has shown a downward trend since 1913, the volume of steel produced in Scotland almost doubled between 1945 and 1970. There followed a decade of sharp contraction. Indeed, the national output of steel fell by about 50 per cent during the early 'seventies, and the numbers employed by the British Steel Corporation fell from over a quarter of a million shortly after the second nationalisation of the industry in 1967 to barely 100,000 in 1982. Scotland's share of the steel industry's labour force fluctuated about a mean of approximately 20,000 during most of the 'seventies, though current developments in the industry threaten to bring a reduction in even this dispiriting figure. In 1980 Scottish employees of the British Steel Corporation were barely 10,000, or 6.3 per cent of the Corporation's labour force.

If the picture revealed by the coal and steel statistics is acutely depressing, the position of the shipbuilding industry is even more painful. From launching nearly 60 per cent of the *world's* merchant tonnage in 1913 and over one-third of the world's total in 1938, the United Kingdom's share of the world's market was a pitiable 1.8 per cent in 1980. Meantime, Scotland's contribution to

Table 2. Iron and Steel: Output of Crude Steel, and Numbers Employed in Iron and Steel Industry in Scotland, Selected Years, 1913-1981

| | (1) Output of Crude Steel (tonnes millions) | | | | (2) Employment (000's) | |
	Scotland	Scotland / U.K. %	Scotland	Scotland / U.K. %	Employees of B.S.C.'s Scottish Division (in March of given year)	As %age of B.S.C.'s Employees
1913	1,493	19.2	—		—	—
1938	1,627	15.4	—		—	—
1948	2,290	15.2	—		—	—
1951	2,149	13.5	—		—	—
1955	2,382	11.8	—		—	—
1960	2,744	11.1	31.4	9.6	—	—
1965	3,102	11.3	31.4	9.9	—	—
1971	3,034	12.4	22.6		—	—
1975	1,965	9.7	22.8		—	—
1976	1,944	8.7	20.3		—	—
1977	1,945	9.5	21.0		15.0	—
1978	1,612	7.9	19.5		13.3	7.2
1979	1,741	8.1			11.6	6.8
1980	1,277	11.3			10.5	6.2
1981	1,976	12.7				6.3

Sources and Notes: (1) Iron and Steel, Annual Statistics and B.S.C. Statistical Services
(2) The figures for Scottish employment in the Iron and Steel Industry are necessarily crude and somewhat inconsistent between dates because of problems of definition, though every attempt has been made to compare like numbers in arriving at the Scottish proportion of U.K. employment. The data have been drawn from the Census; Iron and Steel; Annual Statistics; the Scottish Abstract of Statistics; and the Annual Reports of the British Steel Corporation.

Table 3. *Shipbuilding and Marine Engineering: (a) Gross Merchant Tonnage Launched (or under construction) and Numbers Employed in Scotland, Selected Years, 1913-1981; (b) Numbers employed in Scotland by British Shipbuilding, 1977-1983*

(a)

Year	(1) Gross Tonnage (000's)		(2) Employment (000's)	
	Scotland	Scotland U.K. %	Scotland	Scotland U.K. %
1909/13 (average)	535	35.2	50.9 (1911)	32.7
1929/33 (average)	298	29.0	77.8 (1931)	39.7
1938	487	47.3	n.d.	
1951	493	36.8	76.9	27.8
1955	569	36.9	n.d.	
1961	392	31.9	63.3	26.7
1966	325	30.0*	47.9	21.6ø
1971	455	27.8	40.6	22.5
1975	519	26.7	43	
1976	302	17.2	42	
1977	436	29.5	40	
1978	286	31.2	41	
1979	125			
1980	174			
1981	234			

* 1971/1981 Tonnage under construction in last quarter of each year.

ø Scottish employment for 1966 expressed as a percentage of U.K. figure for 1965 given by the *Geddes Report*, p. 172

Sources: (1) 1909-1938: N. K. Buxton, 'The Scottish Shipbuilding Industry between the Wars', *Business History*, X (1968-69), p. 119; 1955-1961: *Glasgow Herald* Trade Reviews; 1966-81: *Scottish Abstract of Statistics*; additional data kindly provided by Professor A. Slaven

(2) 1911-1961, 1971, C. H. Lee, *British Regional Employment Statistics, 1841-1971* (Cambridge, 1979); 1965, 1975-8, *Scottish Abstract of Statistics*

(b)

Period, or average for period ending	Employees of British Shipbuilders in Scotland	As %age of British Shipbuilders' total
July 1977-March 1978 (average)	24,000	27.7
March 1978	23,600	27.5
March 1982	27,632	26.5
March 1983	17,900	27.8

Source: British Shipbuilders, *Annual Report and Accounts*

British shipbuilding, 47 per cent in 1938, had fallen to something less than 30 per cent by the late 'seventies. The labour force in Scottish shipbuilding and marine engineering too has declined, from 77,070 in 1950 to 44,400 in 1970, and to 41,000 by 1978. The number of Scottish employees of British Shipbuilders was down to fewer than 18,000 by 1983.

The decline in the relative significance of the old heavy staples in the British economy is clearly a manifestation of the phenomenon of interrelatedness. Just as the growth of each of these industries in the nineteenth century served to boost the expansion of the others, so the decline of each of them has debilitated its industrial partners. In Scotland, at least, the sickness afflicting the related activities gives every indication of being terminal. To what degree has each industry succumbed to forces beyond its control, and how far has the deterioration of each contributed to the wasting away of the others? Could anything have been done to arrest the diminution of coal, iron and steel, and shipbuilding and marine engineering in Scotland? Need the erosion of Scotland's share of the United Kingdom's dependence on these old staples have been so pronounced? It is to such questions that we must turn. Once again, it is appropriate to begin with coal, although it will become increasingly apparent that the fortunes of the three activities that are our concern are at least partially intertwined.

2. COAL

The pernicious influence on the profitability of the Scottish coal industry of detrimental factors acting from both the demand and supply sides were already apparent between the wars. The belief, largely engendered by the experience of the immediate pre-First World War period, that Scottish coal was facing a prosperous future in the 'twenties, proved ill-founded. Far from increasing, demand began to fall off. Professor Slaven has provided several reasons for this that have a curiously modern ring.[1] Among them may be mentioned the check to aggregate demand by economies in the use of coal by the iron and steel producers; the growing substitution for coal of gas, electricity and oil in the home and in industry; the erosion of export markets by severe competition, and the failure of export and domestic demand for the products of the Scottish iron and steel, shipbuilding and engineering industries. In the light of severe contemporary and retrospective criticism of the entrepreneurial response by the coalmining industry, it is legitimate to examine, with Professor Neil Buxton, just how well the Scottish coalmasters coped with these dismal conditions.[2]

Believing that the downward movement in the demand for coal was merely a short-term characteristic of the trade cycle, the coalmasters vigorously pursued policies designed to reduce costs in the hope that lower selling prices would regenerate demand, leading, as in the past, to more prosperous times. Thus, there took place a continual increase in the proportion of coal mechanically cut and conveyed and a substantial expansion in the use of electricity. In these and in other ways, Buxton makes clear, the Scottish coalmasters were in the very forefront of the adoption of new mining technology. Nevertheless, it was not enough to increase productivity solely by the application of capital. Such was the depressed market for coal that wages, the largest single element in costs, had to be reduced. This immediately brought the coalmasters into conflict with the workforce, protected as they were by the minimum wage clause of the Agreement of 1921. The consequence was the General Strike of 1926. But even when the miners were forced to return to work on the owners' terms, losses continued to be made in spite of relatively high productivity. In no less than 'nine of the eighteen years between 1921 and 1938 the Scottish industry incurred deficits'.[3]

The relentless pressure on prices, profits and wages meant that there was no alternative but to reduce the entire scale of the industry from the levels attained in the immediate pre- and post-war years. Employment fell rapidly, as we have seen, a large number of high-cost pits were closed down, and production was concentrated in the more efficient pits. Ownership too became increasingly concentrated, and it was already apparent that the future of the Scottish coal industry lay with Fife and Clackmannan and the Lothians, and not with the older areas where the link with the heavy industries was closest and where the most economic seams had become progressively exhausted.[4]

But for all the promise of the Eastern coalfields, for all the low costs (with one exception, the lowest of any district in Britain) and high productivity (until the later 'thirties the highest in Britain), the inescapable fact was that in the long term the Scottish coal industry was in a precarious condition: its continued existence was dependent upon indigenous geological resources that were fast running out, certainly in the older Central Coalfield, or becoming increasingly costly to exploit. Ominously, output per man in Scotland, for decades higher than the figures for England and Wales, fell below the latter for the first time during the quinquennium ending 1950. At the same time the cost of coal-getting in Scotland had come to exceed the average cost in England and Wales and by an increasing margin.[5]

Part of the explanation of this relative loss of ground lay 'in the more rapid progress in mechanisation in Scotland before the war, and the loss of this lead after the war. In 1935, 72 per cent of the Scottish output was cut by machinery compared with 50 per cent for Britain: in 1951 these proportions had become 86 per cent and 81 per cent respectively. Scotland also had a slight lead in 1935 in coal conveyed by machinery (48 per cent against 42 per cent) but had lost it by 1951 (80 per cent against 88 per cent)'. But, as Leser once emphasised, 'differences in the pace of mechanisation do not provide the full explanation; in coal-mining the use of more machinery does not always bring higher output'. One important factor operating to keep down productivity in Scottish mines was their small average size. 'In 1945 only 58 per cent of Scottish miners (compared with 83 per cent in Britain) were working in collieries employing 500 or more wage-earners. The average output of Scottish collieries in 1950 was 120,000 tons per annum — the lowest for any division in Britain and far below the average for the English East Midlands (420,000 tons) or the North-Eastern division (371,000 tons)'.[6]

Thus when, on 1st January 1947, the National Coal Board assumed responsibility for the 275 mines previously owned and managed by no less than 120 separate colliery undertakings, the Scottish Divisional Board decided to leave 79 small mines under the direction of their previous owners, to whom they gave special operating licences, and to subject the remainder of its inheritance to searching examination with a view to comprehensive rationalisation. It was found that more than half the collieries in Scotland had exhausted their workable coal reserves and were in an advanced state of physical and economic decay. It was proposed to phase these out by 1965, the consequent annual loss of output being estimated at nearly 7 million tons of saleable coal. At the same time, the plan was to raise Scottish coal production from its post-war level of just over 20 million tons to the 30 million tons characteristic of the late 'thirties and the figure which constituted the basis for the calculations underlying the *Report of the Scottish Coalfields Committee* in 1944.[7]

To achieve this ambitious objective the National Coal Board proposed to sink no fewer than nine new deep mines in Scotland (compared with thirteen for England and Wales), to develop thirty-eight new surface drift mines, and to reconstruct and modernise nearly forty pits, mainly in the eastern coalfields, so that productivity would rise overall by about 40 per cent, to over 400 tons per head. In framing the *Plan for Coal*, published in 1950, the National Coal Board chose to ignore the adverse trends in costs and productivity apparent in Scotland for over a decade, but the urgency for radical reconstruction, the necessity for new sinkings and the belief in the buoyancy of future demand seemed more than justified by the fuel crisis of 1947 which appeared to confirm Britain's utter dependence on sufficient supplies of coal.

In the event, the hopes underlying the *Plan for Coal* were to be cruelly shattered, and the many assumptions, explicit and implicit, built into the plan were to be unfulfilled. Within a few years of the publication of the National Coal Board's proposals, Dr. Leser observed unhappily that 'output has fallen, . . . productivity is lower than ever, and the margin between Scottish and British costs continues to widen'.[8] Nor, contrary to all expectations, were these trends to be reversed. 'The modernisation programme was unexpectedly slow and expensive. Some old pits were closed faster than new capacity could be brought into operation, substantial manpower engaged in modernisation did not contribute to short-term production, and many highly uneconomic pits were kept in operation from fear of losing scarce manpower'.[9] There were some terrible mistakes too. 'The new show colliery, with associated mining housing, at Rothes in Fife, is the supreme example. Sunk [in the 'fifties] at punishing expense on the advice of outside experts, and in the teeth of local mining opinion, it proved utterly unworkable almost at once.'[10]

But the greatest error — one for which the National Coal Board can hardly be held wholly responsible — was in the assessment of the future demand for coal. In the late 'fifties the market for coal collapsed: the prop supporting the

Table 4. Coal Consumption in Scotland, by Sectors, 1947-1978

	Million tons				Thousand tonnes									
	1947	%	1955	%	1961	%	1966	%	1970	%	1975	%	1978	%	1981	%
Public Utility undertakings	6.93	33.5	7.51	35.0	6,404	33.7	6,071	37.8	6,695	47.7	8,580	67.3	8,180	67.7	8,103	70.7
Gas	2.29	11.1	2.43	11.3	1,655	8.7	959	6.0	536	3.8	10	0.1	6	—	—	—
Electricity	2.31	11.2	3.15	14.7	3,713	19.5	4,912	30.6	6,149	43.8	8,567	67.2	8,172	67.7	8,103	70.7
Railways	2.33	11.3	1.93	9.0	1,036	5.4	200	1.2	10	0.1	3	—	2	—	—	—
Coke Ovens	1.30	6.3	1.63	7.6	1,687	8.9	1,518	9.4	1,914	13.6	996	7.8	1,055	8.7	996	8.7
Industrial Consumers[1]	6.94	33.5	6.96	32.5	3,852	20.2	2,494	15.5	1,629	11.6	569	4.5	514	4.3	378	3.3
Iron and Steel	n.d.		n.d.		712	3.7	249	1.5	87	0.6	21	0.2	3	—	—	—
Engineering and other metal trades					292	1.5	183	1.1	142	1.0	51	0.4	67	0.6	53	0.5
Food, drink and tobacco					487	2.6	454	2.8	281	2.0	63	0.5	65	0.5	41	0.4
Textiles, leather, footwear and clothing					267	1.4	138	0.9	94	0.7	21	0.2	18	0.1	17	0.1
Paper, printing and stationery					744	3.9	648	4.0	463	3.3	126	1.0	85	0.7	80	0.7
Bricks, tiles and other building materials					236	1.2	71	0.4	17	0.1	10	—	7	0.1	4	—
Domestic	3.49	16.9	3.66	17.1	3,925	20.6	2,738	17.0	2,016	14.4	1,367	10.7	1,274	10.6	998	8.7
Miners coal[2]					495	2.6	349	2.2	275	2.0	222	1.7	196	1.6	179	1.6
Merchants disposals: House coal	n.d.		n.d.		3,364	17.7	2,347	14.6	1,707	12.2	1,075	8.4	1,015	8.4	776	6.8
Anthracite					66	0.3	42	0.3	34	0.2	70	0.5	63	0.5	43	0.4
Collieries[2]	2.05	9.9	1.68	7.8	488	2.6	294	1.8	177	1.3	60	0.5	50	0.4	40	0.3
Total	20.71	100.0	21.44	100.0	19,023	100.0	16,072	100.0	14,024	100.0	12,747	100.0	12,070	100.0	11,459	100.0

Sources: 1947-1955: National Coal Board, Scottish Division, *Short History*, p. 106
1961-1981: *Scottish Abstract of Statistics*, No. 9/1980, Table 12.19, p 153; No. 12/1983, Table 12.14, p. 109.

Notes: (1) A number of specific, 'other manufacturing' and 'non-manufacturing' users have been omitted. Thus the figures for the specific users given do not sum up to the total of 'Industrial Consumers'.
(2) For 1947 and 1955, the consumption given for collieries includes miners' coal.
(3) As 'miscellaneous consumers' have been omitted from the tabulated figures, they do not sum to the total given.

Table 5. *Scottish Primary Fuel Consumption, Selected Years, 1963-1978*
(in millions of therms)

	1963	%	1966	%	1970	%	1975	%	1978	%
Solid Fuels	4,304	64.6	3,639	51.5	3,337	42.5	2,909	36.5	2,765	33.5
Petroleum	1,725	25.9	2,516	35.6	3,619	46.1	3,561	44.7	3,748	45.5
Natural Gas	3	—	6	0.1	23	0.3	612	7.7	809	9.8
Nuclear Electricity	150	2.3	361	5.1	366	4.7	358	4.5	557	6.8
Hydro Electricity	385	5.8	487	6.9	514	6.5	420	5.3	445	5.4
Net Imports of Electricity	91	1.4	58	0.8	−7	−0.1	110	1.4	−81	−1.0
Total	6,658	100.0	7,067	100.0	7,852	100.0	7,970	100.0	8,243	100.0

Source: Scottish Abstract of Statistics, Vols. 1 (1963, 1966) and 9 (1970-1978)

Note: The highest share of Scotland's primary fuel consumption attained by petroleum was 50.6 in 1972 (4,019 million therms out of a total consumption of 7,936 million therms).

Table 6. *Number of Active Pits in Scotland, Selected Years, 1930-1981*

1930	400+
1947	275
1958	166
1967/8	47
1971/2	32
1975/6	21
1978/9	16
1981/2	14

Source: National Coal Board, *Annual Reports*

National Coal Board's vast investment programme for the Scottish coal industry — estimated at more than £200 million in 1958[11] — suddenly gave way. There occurred a remarkable shift towards the use of oil, gas and electricity,[12] the switch towards the first of which had been officially stimulated in the mid-'fifties.[13] This traumatic change in the relative importance of the various components of total energy consumption — which brought to an end 'the dominant role which coal had played in the economy since the Industrial Revolution'[14] — had a particularly devastating effect on the Scottish coal industry. For decades Scotland had used rather more coal and coal-based fuel per head of population than most of Great Britain, the excess being greatest in consumption by railways and collieries. Thus, the success of the policy of converting locomotives from coal-burning to diesel engines and the accelerating closure of inefficient high-cost Scottish collieries were particularly erosive of inland coal consumption, as was the conversion of iron and steel furnaces to oil-burning following the 1947 fuel crisis.[15] In the period 1955-66, consumption of coal in Scotland fell by 25 per cent to 16 million tons, or about half the production anticipated in the optimistic plans of the immediate post-war years (see Table 4). And as the demand position worsened,[16] as oil almost doubled its share of primary fuel consumption between 1963 and 1970, and as natural gas rose in importance in the national fuel budget (see Table 5), the National Coal Board, whose policy in 1959 became one of matching output to current demand, accelerated the closure of uneconomic pits (see Table 6), reduced open-cast mining and restricted employment.

Despite an extension of mechanically cut coal from 86 per cent of output to 90 per cent in the first decade of state ownership, productivity obstinately failed to increase until the 'sixties (see Table 7). Thereafter the desired increase in average output per manshift was achieved by a halving of the labour force, the decimation of the number of active pits, and a massive investment in power-loading equipment. Labour productivity, however, remained substantially below the British average, largely because of the persistence of a phenomenon which Professor Slaven identified as being operative in the nineteenth century:[17] the overall average output per manshift worked was being held down by the necessity of supporting each face worker, whose output rose threefold between 1951 and 1978, by an increasing number

Table 7. *Average Output per Manshift Worked, Scottish Mines, Selected Years, 1951-1982, with comparative figures for the U.K., 1970-82, in Tonnes*

	1951	1961	1966	1970	Scottish % U.K.	1975	Scottish % U.K.	1978	Scottish % U.K.	1981	Scottish % U.K.
Average output per Manshift Worked:											
Overall Scottish	1.13	1.17	1.62	1.89	84.4	1.99	86.9	1.95	87.1	2.00	83.4
Overall U.K.	n.a.	n.a.	n.a.	2.24		2.29		2.24		2.40	
Underground (Scottish)	1.47	1.44	1.99	2.33		2.38		2.33		n.a.	
At Face (Scottish)	2.64	3.24	4.87	6.22		6.97		7.83		n.a.	

Source: Scottish Abstract of Statistics, Vol. 9 (1980), p. 155, and National Coal Board, Annual Reports

of what were once called 'oncost men', those underground workers required to maintain the mine and convey the coal to the surface.

The lower productivity contributed to the higher production costs in Scottish pits, and to help the Scottish Division reduce its deficit on sales the National Coal Board instituted a differential price increase in favour of Scotland in 1962.[18] However well meant, this special regional surcharge accelerated the use of alternative fuels by both domestic consumers and the traditional coal-using industries. In the short run, each ton of coal raised in Scotland may have generated an income higher than elsewhere in the United Kingdom, but the effect on total demand was adverse. Had it not been for the fact that, as part of a comprehensive fuel policy, the electricity industry was forced to consume large and increasing amounts of coal, the Scottish coal industry might have succumbed. In 1955 power stations in Scotland had consumed 3.15 million tons of coal, or 15 per cent of the coal raised (see Table 4); by 1961 the proportion so used was nearly 20 per cent, a figure that had more than doubled by 1970 (43.8 per cent) and more than tripled by 1975 (67.2 per cent).

What is so depressing in the present situation, as Professor Johnston and his colleagues at Heriot-Watt observed over a decade ago, is that 'despite rationalisation, a pricing policy which discriminates in its favour, and the partial sacrifice of efficiency in electricity, the Scottish coal industry is still quite incapable of making a profit'.[19] During the 'sixties Scotland was responsible for almost half the total deficiencies recorded for the operating Divisions of the National Coal Board (Table 8a). Although Scotland's share of the deficits has subsequently fallen, the losses per ton of saleable coal remain quite horrifying; at £4.68 they were more than double the national average in the financial year 1981/82 (Table 8b). All the indications suggest that little improvement in Scotland's relative position can realistically be expected, rather the reverse. Already the 'smallest' area of the National Coal Board (in terms of 'turnover'), its operating costs per tonne are 8 per cent above the national average and its operating loss greater than any other area except South Wales. Nor can comfort be derived by ascribing the area losses to the operation of a few very uneconomic pits. *All* Scotland's collieries were uneconomic (Table 9). Only on seven occasions in the four years 1976/1977-1980/1981 did a deep mine in Scotland produce a small operating surplus, though it is perhaps significant that the Longannet complex — by far the largest of the Scottish pits — came nearest to breaking even. Conversely, Cardowan's losses per tonne in 1981-82 were exceeded only by Snowdon in Kent and six pits in South Wales.[20] While output per man shift over the Scottish area as a whole has remained almost unchanged since 1976-77, the upward trend in costs is steeper than any area save Doncaster and South Nottinghamshire.[21]

The recent inquiry by the Monopolies and Mergers Commission revealed that most of the National Coal Board's high loss-making collieries had an output per manshift of less than 2.0 tonnes, and almost all had saleable

Table 8. *Financial Results of the National Coal Board's Colliery Activities, Scotland and U.K. 1947-1982*

(a) *Surpluses (+) and Deficits (−) on Deep Mining Activities, Scottish Division and United Kingdom, 1947-1972*

| | £s million | |
	Scottish	United Kingdom
1947	+ 0.0	− 22.9
1948	+ 1.6	+ 2.5
1949	+ 1.0	+ 17.8
1950	− 1.0	+ 11.5
1951	− 2.5	+ 3.8
1952	− 5.9	+ 6.3
1953	− 6.2	+ 3.5
1954	− 7.9	− 5.0
1955	− 10.8	− 25.5
1956	− 10.2	+ 8.9
1957	− 15.5	− 14.6
1958	− 18.2	− 21.7
1959	− 17.9	− 27.7
1960	− 15.5	− 23.2
1961	− 19.1	− 20.5
1962	− 11.5	− 4.3
1963/64[1]	− 6.4	+ 20.1
1964/65	− 4.6	− 8.1
1965/66	− 5.9	− 30.8
1966/67	− 4.0	− 7.2
1967/68	− 6.0	− 6.8
1968/69	− 5.1	− 18.2
1969/70	− 8.0	− 41.1
1970/71	− 9.7	− 21.8
1971/72	− 18.9	− 165.2

Source: National Coal Board, *Report and Accounts, 1971-72*, Vol. II (Accounts and Statistical Tables), Summary C, pp. 6-7

Note: (1) Fifteen month period; when the financial year was altered from a calendar year to a fifty-two week period ending in March.

(b) *Profit (+) or Loss (−) on Colliery Activities, Scottish Divisions and United Kingdom, 1970-71 to 1981-82*

| | £s per ton[1] | | |
| | Scotland | | U.K. |
	North	South	
1970/71	−0.63	−0.34	+0.04
1971/72	−1.66	−1.34	−1.32
1972/73	−1.83	−0.65	−0.68
1973/74	−1.81		−1.23
1974/75	−0.96		−0.29
1975/76	−0.74		+0.17
1976/77	−0.42		+0.72
1977/78	−0.31		+0.63
1978/79	−1.47		−0.39
1979/80	−2.44		−1.27
1980/81	−3.25		−0.97
1981/82	−4.68		−2.09

Source: National Coal Board, *Annual Reports*

Note: (1) £s per tonne from and including 1978/79.

Note: Of the many series of National Coal Board Financial data, those above have been selected to *illustrate* the relatively poor performance of the Scottish division. Attempts to produce systematic comparative series covering the entire period have been frustrated by the impossibility of reconciling the available figures and reducing them to a common base. For example, the statistics presented for Scotland in Part (b) above are not identical with the data provided in the *Scottish Abstract of Statistics*, though the trend is similar. It has been assumed — without great confidence — that each of the two pairs of data are internally consistent and comparable. See also Note to Table 9.

Table 9. *Losses Incurred by N.C.B. Deep Mines in Scotland, 1976-77 to 1981-82, with additional Data for the Financial Year 1981-82*

| Colliery | Loss (Surplus), £'s per tonne | | | | | 1981-82 | | | | |
	1976-77	1977-78	1978-79	1979-80	1980-81	Saleable Output (000 tonnes)	Overall O M S (tonnes)	Net Proceeds (£/te)	Operating Costs (£/te)	Operating Loss (£/te)
Cardowan	9.7	13.1	21.6	21.8	27.0	267	1.30	31.6	69.9	38.3
Sorn	3.2	6.6	6.6	2.5	22.9	57	1.33	36.6	58.1	21.5
Barony	9.1	4.5	7.1	13.3	5.5	227	2.00	36.4	50.2	13.8
Killoch	4.3	5.1	6.6	10.8	10.2	698	1.38	32.3	49.0	16.7
Seafield	6.1	6.0	8.6	7.4	13.0	848	1.98	35.4	44.1	8.7
Bilston Glen	0.8	1.0	1.6	2.0	1.8	892	2.06	38.1	42.7	4.6
Frances	2.4	6.3	14.9	0.0	4.6	254	1.85	35.3	53.1	17.8
Highhouse	1.4	1.7	4.7	(0.3)	3.0	118	1.81	39.9	47.3	7.4
Longannet Complex	1.1	(0.5)	0.2	0.4	1.3	1,955	3.19	29.7	31.2	1.5
Polkemmet	(3.2)	8.2	(2.4)	5.0	6.5	390	1.39	45.5	54.5	9.0
Comrie	(2.1)	(1.1)	4.0	(3.5)	1.5	374	1.61	31.7	48.3	16.6
Monktonhall	(0.5)	0.3	(0.4)	(2.2)	7.6	895	2.31	30.1	38.3	8.2

Source: Monopolies and Mergers Commission, *Report on . . . the National Coal Board*, Cmnd. 8920 (1983), Vol. II. pp. 30, 42

Note: The entire basis of the NCB's accounting procedures relating to individual collieries has been strongly criticised. See David Cooper and Anthony Lowe *et al*, 'NCB Accounts: A Mine of Mis-information', in *Accountancy* (January 1985), and George Kerevan and Richard Saville, *The Economic Case for Deep-Mined Coal in Scotland* (Edinburgh, January 1985), especially pp. 26-31. See also Andrew Glyn, *The Economic Case Against Pit Closures* (N.U.M., Sheffield, December 1984).

outputs below 600,000 tonnes.[22] No less than six of Scotland's twelve collieries fell into both of these categories in 1981-82, and a further three had *either* a saleable output of less than 600,000 tonnes *or* an output per man shift lower than 2 tonnes. Three Scottish pits (Comrie, Barony and Sorn) were said to be 'in jeopardy' in August 1982, and the decision to close Cardowan was announced in August 1983.[23]

It is the relentless and relatively heavy and rising annual deficits made by the Scottish collieries that bring into question the future of Scotland's coal industry. Any further escalation of oil prices may give it an additional lease of life, but on purely economic grounds it would seem that coalmining in Scotland cannot long survive. The 1971 verdict of Professor Johnston and his colleagues on the future of the Scottish coal industry is still valid: 'If it does remain active, it can be due only to social or other such considerations'.[24]

3. IRON AND STEEL[25]

Perhaps the most important clue to an understanding of the evolution of the Scottish iron and steel industry during the immediate post-war years is to be found in developments in the 1930s. Following the acquisition of the Lanarkshire Steel Company in 1936, the firm of Colvilles Ltd. became almost synonymous with the Scottish steel industry.[26] There followed an intensive effort to secure the technical and economic benefits of concentrated ownership, initially hindered though they were by a scarcity of capital and an unpromising, if steadily improving, economic environment. But as the upswing of the mid-'thirties continued, Colvilles' response to mounting domestic demand was inhibited by a chronic shortage of coking coal, pig iron and scrap. Not until the acquisition of the collieries of James Nimmo & Co. had solved the immediate fuel problem — and its magnitude may be judged by the fact that in 1935 the constituent companies of the Colville Group consumed three-quarters of a million tons of coal, much of it coking quality — would Colvilles' Board go ahead with the integration of the blast furnaces at Clyde Iron with the melting furnaces at Clydebridge, thereby permitting the large-scale adoption of hot metal practice in Scotland for the very first time.

It should be emphasised that the plan for Colvilles' future development determined in the late 'thirties had been designed to eradicate many long-standing weaknesses of the Scottish iron and steel industry. The integration of iron-making and steel-making activities was the most important element in this programme, but increased efficiency stemming from the attainment of internal balance between the operations of the various constituent parts of the Colville Group represented an equally important objective. On the eve of the Second World War, it was clearly recognised that Colvilles still possessed an unacceptably high scrap/pig iron ratio in the charging of the melting furnaces and that ingenious *ad hoc* 'patching' of inadequate productive capacity could go only so far before more radical changes in both organisational structure and the provision of capital equipment were imperative.

The exigencies of war prevented further progress towards realising the full technical and economic potentialities inherent in the successful completion of Colvilles' merger policy in the mid-'thirties, and when the company was asked by the British Iron and Steel Federation in August 1944 to provide information on its post-war plans, it was decided to press for a number of schemes which represented the completion of the pre-war rationalisation programme. There was nothing radical about these proposals, and they were strongly criticised as being far too conservative. Certainly, they disappointed those who hoped for the revival of the plan — first formulated by H. A. Brassert & Co. in 1929 — for a huge integrated tidewater plant on the Upper Clyde. Urged to be more ambitious, Colvilles repeatedly drew attention to marked deficiences in the supply of pig iron and scrap, to grave uncertainties in the future supply of coking coal, and to the social dislocation which would follow the closure of existing works as their output was transferred to a 'hypothetical new works on the Clyde'. The firm's detailed rejection of the tidewater plant concluded that 'it can be assumed that existing locations have not survived without sound reason and that only the strongest evidence for immediate and ultimate economy can justify a change which would create irrevocably a social upheaval of the first magnitude'.[27]

There was no moving Colvilles' board on this point, and it is arguable that this decision made the long-term decline of the Scottish steel industry inevitable. But it was not simply pigheadedness and an undue tenderness for what Vaizey has called 'powerfully rooted local concerns'[28] that underlay this refusal to bow to the demand of those who saw the future in terms of a new tidewater plant. Colvilles entertained grave doubts as to the existence of an effective demand for steel on the scale assumed by the national planners. In the light of subsequent events, part of Colvilles' case is worthy of quotation:

> The largest steel-consuming industry in Scotland is shipbuilding which takes about one-third of the total steel. If marine, constructional, and mechanical engineering is included with shipbuilding, about 60 per cent of the total steel consumption would be covered by this group. This is about twice as high as the proportion for the rest of the United Kingdom, and is reflected in the production of heavy plates in Scotland, representing about 32 per cent of the U.K. aggregate. For light products, however, the percentage in Scotland is no more than 8 per cent and for sheets only 5½ per cent of the production in the country as a whole. As indicated previously, the main future expansion of demand is likely to lie with the lighter products and sheets.
>
> In a recent broad appraisal of the future demand for steel undertaken by the Planning Department of the Government, a decline was expected in shipbuilding steel, . . . Attempts are being made to develop other industries in Scotland. Some of these, particularly bolts and nuts, tubes, and light engineering, will increase the demand for steel but the main emphasis of the development plans seems to be rather on chemicals, tobacco, non-ferrous metal manufacture, the food industry, and consumption industries generally. So far, therefore, there would not appear to be an overall basis for a big expansion in the consumption of steel. These considerations suggest that, while it may be appropriate to expand Scottish production on the basis of the present proportion of a 16 million ton capacity for the country as a whole, it would probably be undesirable to incur additional expenditure at this stage to facilitate still further expansion at a later date.[29]

This argument proved decisive, especially when the Statistical Department of the Federation concurred: 'shipbuilding in particular [does] not offer prospects of expansion, so that unless the character of Scottish demand changes radically, and of this there was little evidence, consumption is not expected to expand so greatly as in the U.K. as a whole'.[30]

With this, Colvilles were permitted to persevere with what they claimed to be the socially responsible and practical schemes which culminated in the creation of the Ravenscraig complex in the late 1950s. But by this time it was becoming increasingly apparent that a major weakness in the Scottish steel industry was the lack of any modern facilities for the manufacture of light plates and sheet metal, essential materials for the manufacture of cars and consumer durables such as refrigerators and electric cookers. In the belief that mass-produced, high-quality steel strip would attract industrial development to the region within which a strip mill was located, vociferous local campaigns were mounted to have such a mill which, if approved, would be the fourth of its kind in Britain. Various sites in South Wales and at Immingham in Lincolnshire received support, but by far the greatest furore was raised in favour of a Scottish mill. The reaction of Colville's chairman, Sir Andrew McCance, to this campaign was brutally simple. The necessary coal for the new integrated plant at Ravenscraig *and* a continuous strip mill was just not available. Nevertheless, enormous pressure was put on Colvilles by members of the Government, including Mr John S. Maclay, Secretary of State for Scotland, who was supported, in the Cabinet, by Lord Mills, the Minister of Power, and Mr Ian Macleod, the Minister for Labour. In vain did Sir Andrew McCance point out that the limited demand for sheet in Scotland would force a new strip mill in Scotland to sell most of its products south of the border, and that the heavy freight charges on these products and the immense interest burden on a costly plant of this kind would prohibit the new mill from competing with existing mills without making substantial losses. These losses, Sir Andrew McCance estimated, might amount to £4.5 million a year for many years to come. Such technical and economic arguments were ineffective. Eventually, Colvilles were 'persuaded' to build a strip mill at Ravenscraig with the aid of a government loan of £50 million.

The politicians had won, but in simultaneously 'awarding' another strip mill to Llanwern in South Wales they created conditions which made the accuracy of Sir Andrew McCance's predictions inevitable. Commissioned in 1962, the mill at Ravenscraig, unanimously agreed to be a technical masterpiece, was a financial disaster. There was insufficient demand for its products, despite successful government inducements to Rootes and the British Motor Corporation to build branches at Linwood and Bathgate. Thus, when the Labour Government was returned and implemented its proposals to nationalise the industry in 1967, Colvilles, once one of the most profitable firms in the industry, was struggling under an insupportable burden of debt and was, technically speaking, bankrupt.

With nationalisation in 1967 the British Steel Corporation (B.S.C.) inherited in Scotland an industry which by national standards was technically in good shape, well managed and, its financial indebtedness notwithstanding, confident of its future direction. As an interim measure designed to enlist the loyalties of the thirteen major companies which had been taken into public ownership, the industry was organised on regional lines. To maintain efficiency the regions were encouraged to compete with each other. The Scottish and North-Western Group almost immediately announced its intention of building an ore terminal at Hunterston on the Firth of Clyde capable of taking vessels of up to 200,000 tons in conjunction with a £300 million scheme for a fully integrated iron and steel works with an ultimate capacity of five to six million tons on an adjacent site.[31] Only later, when British steel production failed to maintain the upward trend of the late 'sixties, was the economic unreality of the scheme fully exposed. At the time, it seemed to the infant B.S.C. to smack of a pre-emptive bid calculated to muster the vociferous support of all facets of Scottish opinion and harness the powerful political pressures which had contributed to the success of the campaign for a Scottish strip mill.

Table 10. *Indices of Crude Steel Production: Scotland and the United Kingdom, 1967-1981*

(1967 = 100)

	Scotland	United Kingdom
1967	100.0	100.0
1968	118.2	108.2
1969	126.8	110.6
1970	128.1	116.6
1971	113.1	99.6
1972	114.2	104.3
1973	123.1	109.6
1974	99.9	92.0
1975	74.4	82.9
1976	73.6	91.8
1977	73.6	84.1
1978	61.0	83.7
1979	65.9	88.5
1980	48.3	46.5
1981	74.8	64.2

Source: Iron and Steel: Annual Statistics

Sorely embarrassed, the British Steel Corporation sought to stifle this example of regional exuberance by implementing its intention of reorganising its activities on a product basis. The multi-product groups and their constituent companies were dissolved: what was once the Scottish steel industry was dismembered and the various works parcelled out amongst the new product divisions. Nevertheless, the steel industry in Scotland continued to be modernised and expanded (see Table 10). It was intended that Scotland would 'remain an attractive location for engineering and other steelmaking industries'.[32] Futhermore, the Government continued to be buffeted by political pressures, and the Hunterston project — put forward so startlingly in 1968 — was never really dropped. In 1973 work started on the development of an ore and coal terminal at Hunterston designed to accept vessels of up to 35,000 tons capacity. This was completed in 1978 and, shortly afterwards, Britain's first two Midrex direct reduction plants were completed on an adjacent site, thus enabling the Corporation 'to come to grips with the technology which is already the dominant iron-making method in the developing countries of the world'.[33] Hopes were expressed that the steel industry in Scotland would enjoy a 'glorious resurrection',[34] a hope that had undoubtedly been strengthened by yet another convulsive administrative reorganisation of the British Steel Corporation in March 1976 whereby the product divisions were superseded by a structure in which the Corporation's main iron- and steel-making activities were grouped into five manufacturing divisions, one of which was the Scottish Division. That which was torn asunder in 1970 was essentially re-formed.

Such hopes — like so many in the recent history of this troubled industry — proved illusory. The ore terminal, having been ceremoniously declared open by the Queen Mother, was instantly paralysed by an inter-union dispute lasting six months.[35] The two Midrex units were never operated because of rapid increases in natural gas prices and low levels of demand coupled with abandonment of the plan for the erection of the electric arc furnaces which the direct reduction plant was primarily designed to feed.[36] Thus Hunterston — far from being the nucleus of a reborn Scottish steel industry — has served only to 'enhance' Ravenscraig by making economies possible in the importation of iron ore. Furthermore, the re-establishment of Geographical Divisions in 1976 clearly revealed the magnitude of Scotland's comparative disadvantage in steelmaking. Expressed in terms of output, Scotland's net losses in the four years 1976/7-1979/80 rose from £29.8 to £67.5 per tonne of liquid steel production (see Table 11). These figures were far higher than those of any other Division and doubtless reflected the smaller scale of operations, the lower proportion of capacity utilised, and the higher fuel costs incurred in Scotland. Furthermore, it is *likely* that higher freight charges per unit of delivered output are a characteristic of the marketing of iron and steel products manufactured in Scotland: the marketing hauls are long and the bulk of the production units are inland.[37] Thus, the collapse in demand for steel since 1973, when British crude steel output attained a peak of 26.6 million tons, has been more damaging to the Scottish operations of the British Steel Corporation than to any other region. With policy decisions becoming increasingly influenced by financial criteria, the future of the iron and steel industry in Scotland is bleak.

Could its present condition have been avoided? Only a larger element of speculation than an economic historian can legitimately claim to employ can answer this question. Let it first be emphasised that the roots of the malaise afflicting the Scottish iron and steel industry go much further back than the nationalisation of 1967. It may well be that *the* critical decision was the failure of the various interests to agree to implement the Brassert proposals of 1929: a decision which, however rational in the short run, condemned the industry to an inland location and denied the industry access to the ever-increasing cost-reducing potential of a tidewater site. When, fifteen years later, Colvilles were given the rare opportunity of rectifying this error, if error it was, it too was spurned. Nevertheless, it is difficult not to agree with Colvilles' contemporary arguments. Only with the knowledge of recent development of the Japanese steel industry do serious doubts arise. It has to be remembered that Colvilles — perhaps unduly influenced by inter-war experiences — had no confidence in the national planners' demand projections on which the viability of the plan ultimately depended. In 1950, Sir Andrew McCance had produced detailed estimates of future national demand for steel. He calculated that 'provided there is no change in present trends', production of the United Kingdom would be 17.5 million tons in 1960, 20.7 million tons in 1970 and 24.6 million tons in 1980.[38] These national figures, considered in conjunction with the future supplies of coking coal and scrap available to Colvilles and the Group's heavy dependence on the demands of the shipbuilding industry, made him extremely suspicious of the output targets which underlay the optimistic plans of the British Iron and Steel Federation and the Iron and Steel Board, and these anxieties were strengthened by the contemporaneous O.E.E.C. report on *European Steel Trends* which concluded that 'if all the schemes at present underway in many countries are completed, there may not be a sufficient demand to keep all the plants employed'.[39]

Thus what has been described as a golden opportunity was let slip.[40] But was it such an opportunity? Was the social cost worth incurring? This we shall never know. What is known is that when forced — and this is not too strong a word to employ — to build the Ravenscraig strip mill, Sir Andrew McCance's gloomy forebodings concerning its financial viability and the future demand for its products came to pass, and the economic basis of the Scottish steel industry was irrevocably undermined. But a grave weakening of the Scottish iron and steel industry would have taken place even without the incubus of an uneconomic strip mill: the fact is that there is just not the demand for steel products in Scotland today to justify a Scottish iron and steel industry. The economies of scale in the industry make it cheaper to supply Scotland's requirements from south of the border.[41]

Looked at in this light, what kept the iron and steel industry in existence *was* the construction of the strip mill and all the ancillary investment associated with that ill-fated decision. Without this, there would not have been any overwhelming *economic* argument to do anything other than to permit the Scottish branch of the iron and steel industry to wither away. Throughout most of 1983, desperate attempts — instigated by Mr Ian MacGregor, Chairman of the British Steel Corporation — were made to induce the United States Steel Company to purchase the bulk of the steel slabs produced at Ravenscraig. Ravenscraig's finishing capacity would then be closed with a loss of 2,000 jobs. It was believed that only such a scheme could keep even part of Ravenscraig in operation. Without such an arrangement, MacGregor's original intention of shutting down the plant entirely[42] — thereby reducing B.S.C.'s expenditure by £100 million a year — seemed increasingly probable. But this 'lifesaving deal', as the press termed it, collapsed in the closing days of 1983. The steel unions in Britain and the United States had fought bitterly against it, and Government Ministers were reported to be unenthusiastic about that variant of the scheme which envisaged the British Steel Corporation taking a substantial interest in an American mill which would roll the bulk steel produced at Ravenscraig, thus circumventing the restrictions imposed by the United States Government on steel imports. Once again, the future of Ravenscraig is 'under review', and the closure of the plant appears to have been postponed only because its output can currently fill the gap produced by the temporary loss of capacity caused by the modernisation and repair of Port Talbot. Because of the bleak demand outlook, B.S.C. sees a future for only two of the three plants in the strip mill division. The two favoured plants are Port Talbot and Llanwern, with Ravenscraig regarded by Mr Robert Haslam, McGregor's successor, as 'the most likely casualty'. Although the government is still formally committed to keeping open the basic steel-making and slab-casting part of Ravenscraig, this commitment extends only to the end of 1985.[43]

The Scottish iron and steel industry has become the victim of forces largely beyond its control. It is suffering to a heightened degree from all the ills afflicting the British steel industry. In addition to the generally adverse conditions created by a surfeit of world steelmaking capacity (perhaps the most important of which has been an inability to produce at a level high enough to attain the volume of output necessary to break even), for many years the British Steel Corporation found it inexpedient — because of political pressures — either to reduce its labour force or adequately to raise its selling prices to cover escalating costs. The consequent losses retarded the adoption of the latest technology, and the fullest exploitation of the economies of scale have been inhibited. It is hardly surprising, therefore, that judged by output, productivity, price, profitability or share of foreign trade, the performance of the British steel industry has been comparatively poor. Since the advent of the Conservative Government in 1979, the British Steel Corporation's response to its various afflictions has been to curtail investment, accelerate the closure of works responsible for the heavier losses, and halve the labour force. To such policies the Scottish iron and steel industry was particularly vulnerable. During the period 1976-80 it was the smallest of the British Steel Corporation Divisions, and although vast sums were poured into Ravenscraig and into the provision of the deepwater ore terminal at Hunterston in the late 'seventies, to provide 'a modern and balanced plant configuration',[44] the low level of capacity-working caused by persistent weak demand has produced losses per ton of liquid steel much heavier than those incurred elsewhere (see Table 11).

In these circumstances, when successive chairmen of B.S.C. have been told

Table 11. *Annual Losses by Major Divisions of the British Steel Corporation, 1976-1980*

	(1) Net loss on manufacturing and selling Activities after interest (£ millions)					(2) Liquid Steel Production (tonnes, millions)				(3) Net loss per tonne £s				
	1976/77	1977/78	1978/79	1979/80	Loss attributable to 1980 strike	1976/7	1977/8	1978/9	1979/80	1976/7	1977/8	1978/9	1979/80	1979/80 excluding loss due strike
Scottish	50.6	83.2	83.0	96	15	1.7	1.6	1.3	1.2	29.8	52.0	63.8	80.0	67.5
Scunthorpe	1.9	50.9	27.8	43	20	4.1	3.8	3.7	3.0	.5	13.4	7.5	14.3	-7.6
Sheffield	(19.5)	30.1	25.7	54	35	3.5	3.0	3.1	2.3	(5.8)	10.0	8.3	23.5	8.3
Teeside	24.1	90.7	81.1	137	50	3.3	2.9	2.9	2.5	7.3	31.3	28.0	54.8	34.8
Welsh	56.4	137.1	96.6	144	75	5.9	5.0	5.2	4.3	9.6	27.4	18.6	33.5	16.0

Source: (1), (2): British Steel Corporation, *Annual Reports*
            (3): calculated from data in (1) and (2)

Notes: (i) The financial year runs from April-March;
           (ii) In the financial year 1976-77, the Sheffield Division made a profit;
           (iii) The Geographic Divisions of B.S.C. were created in April 1976 and replaced by a product-based management structure in September 1980.

to continue to reduce both the Corporation's capacity and its labour force, the Scottish Division has been an obvious target for cutbacks and redundancies. There is the faint possibility that, given massive investment and a major technological breakthrough that would permit the idle direct reduction plants at Hunterston to operate on coal (instead of natural gas), an entirely restructured Scottish steel industry based on Hunterston *could* emerge,[45] but the fate of earlier proposals for tidewater or coastal locations fail to inspire confidence. The future for steel in Scotland is as questionable as that for coal.

4. SHIPBUILDING

As with the steel industry, it is perhaps in the inter-war period that symptoms of acute industrial malaise — the germs of which are apparent even before 1914 — become painfully clear in shipbuilding.[46] Put simply, in these two decades 'the capacity of the world fleet was greater, and sometimes much greater, than was needed to carry the volume of goods moved by sea'.[47] The result was that British shipbuilders were almost suffocated by a massive unused capacity.[48] To this they responded by adjusting tenders for the scarce available business downwards, frequently at or below the cost of labour and materials[49] and, following the establishment of the Shipbuilders Conference in 1928 and National Shipbuilders Security Ltd in 1930, the reduction of capacity. Although a number of small yards were closed, the radical restructuring of the industry that conditions demanded did not take place.[50] In 1938 there remained 49 companies building ships in Scotland of which 39 had been in continuous existence throughout the inter-war period. Of these companies, only nine were public limited companies, six were owned by a single proprietor or by partnerships, and the remaining 24 were private limited companies, invariably owned and controlled by a dominant family.[51] It would appear that the parlous state of the Scottish — not to say British — shipbuilding industry is a direct consequence of this hallowed structure, the weaknesses of which became increasingly apparent after the Second World War.

Whereas the output of the coal industry in Scotland has displayed a pronounced downward trend since 1950 and that of steel has fluctuated, until the late 'seventies the tonnage of merchant shipping launched from British yards — of which Scottish yards consistently contributed between a quarter and a third — did not so much decline as fail to go up. Fig. 1 is a sufficient illustration of this point. In a period during which world launchings increased tenfold, the output of Scottish yards remained well below the figure attained once during the War (1942) and frequently in the 1920s. The most obvious explanation of this apparent inertia is the massive growth of shipbuilding capacity overseas, on the creation and support of which rival nations have lavished massive financial support. While this interpretation is undoubtedly

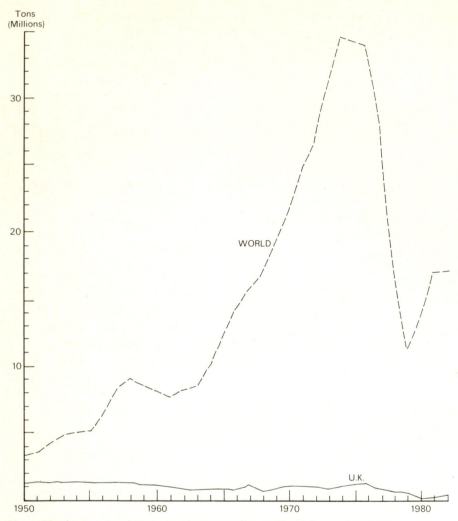

Fig. 1. Merchant tonnage launched, 1950-1982, U.K. and World (Source: Table 12).

valid, it is unconvincing for the immediate post-war decade when competition from Japan and Germany was temporarily extinguished. In the years after 1945, the demand conditions confronting the British shipbuilders can hardly have been more propitious: in retrospect an unpreceded opportunity seems to have been ignored.

It is arguable that an understanding of this apparent failure may constitute a key to later, even more depressing, developments. In the very short term there was, of course, no failure: for three years, 1946-48, Britain built and launched just over half the world tonnage of merchant vessels, over 50 per cent of it coming from the Clyde, but as world production doubled in the following quinquennium, British and Scottish output remained stationary, seemingly unable to move upwards, tethered to 1.3 million tons, despite years in which orders far exceeded this figure.

If demand was so buoyant, the constraints on output must have been rooted in supply factors. Of this the shipbuilders were in no doubt, and the greatest shortage was that of constructural materials, especially steel:

> The inadequate allocations of steel . . . are primarily responsible for the post-war plan of the industry falling behind.[52]

That this was so cannot be denied: Colvilles, the largest supplier of ship plates in the United Kingdom, were particularly conscious of the problem and of their own heavy dependence upon imported scrap and scarce coking coal to produce the required steel ingots.[53] But there were also exasperating shortages of skilled labour, not least experienced welders, all too slowly superseding in importance the traditional riveters and holders-on.[54]

Until the substitution of electric welding for riveting could be accelerated, the development of prefabrication was necessarily laggard, and the adoption of major change in technique was itself inhibited by the failure of Lloyds to grasp the significance of welding and to establish unambiguous rules about its use.[55] Meanwhile, outside Britain, progress was much more rapid, especially in American yards, whose share of world merchant tonnage tripled from 6.6 per cent to 20.2 per cent in the decade 1938-1949. But the slow development of welding and the associated expansion of prefabrication cannot be explained entirely in terms of a scarcity of skilled workers and conservative classification rules. The majority of the fiercely competitive Clyde yards hesitated either to raise the capital necessary for fundamental restructuring or to recruit specialists to senior positions,[56] predominantly because both courses of action might have eroded familial control. Perhaps this was the essence of the long-term problem.

The conscious decision not to expand — the difficulties of doing which are not underestimated — brought further problems. As orders for Clyde-built vessels piled up, there occurred an inevitable lengthening of delivery times and a desire on the part of the shipbuilders to negotiate contracts on a cost plus profits basis, rather than at a fixed price. These developments were to have adverse consequences as world shipbuilding capacity rapidly caught up with the demand for shipping. As Professor Slaven has pointed out:

> During the 1950's three factors came to play a critical role in obtaining new orders: credit arrangements, the quotation of fixed prices, and quick delivery dates. Clyde yards were at a disadvantage in all three. German yards benefited from special taxation relief and low interest rates: Holland and Sweden enjoyed long-term credit arrangements backed by either the government or local municipalities. In Japan the industry was officially controlled under a system of indirect subsidies on raw materials, low interest on loans, and reduced taxation. In Britain, the Ship Mortgage Finance Co. and the Export Credit Guarantee Department were weak supports compared with the range of subsidies and allowances available to builder and purchaser in foreign yards. The latter were frequently enabled to quote fixed prices and early delivery dates which Clyde and British yards could not meet, and orders were redirected to the recovering yards in Europe and Japan.[57]

If to the critical advantages enjoyed by foreign yards are added the benefits stemming from well-planned, heavily capitalised, modern yards erected on uncluttered sites fronting deep water, the supercession of the Clyde yards is readily explicable. Given such circumstances, it is unnecessary to exaggerate the retarding influence on change of the presence of no less than fifteen unions in the yards and the baneful inter-union demarcation disputes to which their activities so often gave rise.

One other major factor contributing to the eclipse of the British shipbuilding industry deserves consideration. In the post-war years there occurred a fundamental shift in the size and type of vessel ordered. In the mid-'fifties Cairncross was able to write:

> The small tramp has almost disappeared, the number of passenger liners has remained relatively low and the dry tonnage built has consisted increasingly of cargo liners of the larger sizes. The most striking change, however, has been the rise of the tanker. Half the output of the Clyde yards now consists of vessels of a type which, even in the 'thirties, represented only a small proportion of the total.[58]

The implications of this are twofold. Tankers were much simpler vessels than the traditional output of the Clyde, and their construction offered far fewer opportunities for the exercise of the established craft skills of the workforce; a major advantage enjoyed by Scottish shipbuilding industry was thereby significantly reduced. Furthermore, the essential simplicity of the tanker made its production amenable to flow-line methods utilising maximum prefabrication. In the adoption of such techniques the relatively small Scottish yards found themselves at an international disadvantage, and their comparative position deteriorated still further with the evolution of giant tankers and bulk carriers for which their crowded locations made it impossible for them even to tender.

Essentially, during the post-war years, the structure of the Scottish (and indeed British) shipbuilding industry had petrified at a level of development inappropriate for the new and rapidly changing conditions of the 'fifties and 'sixties. The reasons for this are patently complex, but not uncommon in the history of British industry. Prosperity — symbolised by bulging order books — has all too frequently preserved outmoded organisational structures, fostered complacency among managers and men, and encouraged a propensity to exploit short-term advantages. The historical observer, even with the benefit of hindsight, can all too easily fail to appreciate the corrosive influence of the helplessness experienced by the shipbuilding industry during the 'thirties: those who had owned and managed or had been members of the labour force of the industry during that acutely dispiriting decade were fearful of optimism, and were anxious to cash in while they could. Anything which might disrupt maximum immediate production — which the introduction of new building methods, more efficient yard layout, the restructuring of ownership and the refashioning of control and communication mechanisms threatened to do — was to be avoided.

There seems to have been an implicit belief that good times would not soon reappear, and they never did. When the market lost its buoyancy in the late 'fifties, the Clyde builders were ill-prepared to grapple with the severity of international competition. For a time, as Professor Slaven has emphasised, they were sustained by the loyalty of British shipowners, but when the significantly lower quotations and shorter and more reliable delivery times of Continental and Japanese builders forced British owners to look overseas in the early 'sixties and then to desert British yards, their last support was knocked away. Thenceforth the British shipbuilding industry survived only with the assistance of the State.

Within a few years many of the famous Clyde builders had gone. In 1963 William Denny of Dunbarton went into liquidation; Harland & Wolff abandoned their Govan yard; and Simons-Lobnitz closed.[59] In the following year the Blythswood Shipbuilding Co. and William Hamilton & Co. ceased trading. In the early 'sixties there were almost as many teams of experts inquiring into the state of shipbuilding as there were active companies within the industry. They could find little to please them, nor could they save the major yard of Fairfields from going bankrupt in October 1965. If Fairfields, with an order book of £32 million and a labour force of 3,000 men, could fall into the hands of the liquidator, what hope had the rest?

The new Labour Government, which had already appointed the Geddes Committee to examine the entire industry, rushed to the rescue. The Bank of England was asked to advance up to £1 million to meet Fairfields' immediate needs until the Geddes Committee could come up with a long-term solution. Simply to keep Fairfields going was felt by some to be too modest an objective: perhaps the Fairfields experiment could be used to instigate a new policy of co-operation between the State, private capitalists and the trade unions?[60] Mr Iain Stewart, invited by the Department of Economic Affairs to become Chairman of a reconstituted successor company to Fairfields, and Mr George Brown, the Minister concerned, envisaged a company in which half the shares would be purchased by private individuals and the trade unions, and the other half by the Government. Such a scheme would 'not merely . . . save a recently modernised Scottish shipyard from extinction, but would provide a proving ground for new relations in the shipbuilding industry which would change the whole image of our country'.[61] So began the 'Fairfields Experiment', the success of which is still hotly debated.

Meanwhile the Geddes report appeared.[62] Its major criticisms of the United Kingdom shipbuilding industry were that it operated with short-term attitudes to markets, men and money; exercised insufficient control over customers and suppliers; failed to negotiate constructively on labour relations and made poor use of its resources and skills in relation to marketing, purchasing, design and planning.[63] Detailed recommendations were made for action by the managements, the employers, the trade unions and the Government, and it was suggested that unless they were vigorously acted upon, the industry might be expected to decline. There would be 'no real gain in competitiveness, a decline to seven and a half per cent of the world market or less, and an output of little more than 1m gross tons per annum on average'.[64] Despite the implementation of the majority of the major proposals — the grouping of yards, the creation of the Shipbuilding Industry Board and the provision of massive financial assistance in the form of grants and loans — it was this prediction, the most unfavourable of those set out by the Geddes Committee, that came to pass.

In 1967 Scotts and Lithgows on the lower Clyde merged; in 1968, Upper Clyde Shipbuilders — an amalgamation of Fairfields, John Brown's, Charles Connell's, Yarrow's and Stephen's — came into being. On the East Coast, Robb Caledon was formed by the joining together of Henry Robb of Leith, the Caledon Shipbuilding Co. of Dundee and the Burntisland Shipbuilding Co. Government funds poured into the industry not, as was intended, to build up capital equipment and eliminate technical weaknesses but overwhelmingly to meet contract losses occasioned by uneconomic tendering exacerbated by inflationary pressures and excessive wage demands.[65] The industry stumbled from crisis to crisis.[66] Upper Clyde Shipbuilders (U.C.S.) went bankrupt in 1971, there followed the famous 'work in', and the emergence, phoenix-like, of Govan Shipbuilders in September 1972.[67] Governments and politicians, from both left and right, blew now hot now cold. Further reports were commissioned. More funds poured in to keep individual companies afloat; the trade unions appeared uncompromisingly unyielding in their response to appeals for flexibility and greater co-operation with management; productivity remained low. The proportion of the world's shipbuilding launched from British yards continued to fall, to reach a figure in 1973 less than half that of the Geddes Committee's most pessimistic estimate. Yet by 1976 Govan/U.C.S. ventures alone had absorbed no less than £80 million of public funds,[68] and if this was the most notorious of the 'lame ducks', it was only because of the sheer scale of its losses and the political furore that surrounded its short, chequered existence.

By 1976 there appeared to be no alternative to nationalisation even among the most rabid proponents of private enterprise: by any conventional accounting standards, the industry was bankrupt. Thus in 1977 British Shipbuilders was born. The last of the Scottish heavy industries had passed into the hands of the State. In case it be believed that public ownership in itself provided a guaranteed future for the industry, it is salutary to recall the words of Professor Slaven written at the very end of the 'seventies:

> In the 1970s, as in the 1930s, it is doubtful if even leadership in price, technology and efficiency can preserve the industry in a world context of huge excess building capacity and redundant shipping tonnage. Any price may be undercut by a determined competitor backed by government subsidy. The socialisation of the industry will, *for a time*, protect jobs, but neither the jobs nor the companies can pay their way in such conditions.[69]

What is so depressing is the speed with which the time has run out. In 1979-80, about half the £110m losses incurred by British Shipbuilders were attributed to Scottish yards, particularly Scott Lithgow,[70] and this accelerated the rundown of the industry's labour force in Scotland, the almost inevitable response to the intolerable pressures created by the contraction of the world's shipbuilding industry. In 1979 world launching of merchant ships was just a

Table 12. *Shipbuilding: Merchant Tonnage Launched, 1950-1982 ('000 tons)*
United Kingdom and World

	(1) U.K.	(2) of which Clyde %	(3) World	(4) of which U.K. %
1950	1,324	33.4	3,492	37.9
1951	1,341	31.8	3,638	36.8
1952	1,302	34.6	4,394	29.6
1953	1,317	30.2	5,094	25.8
1954	1,408	33.9	5,251	26.8
1955	1,473	32.9	5,314	27.7
1956	1,383	30.1	6,670	20.7
1957	1,414	26.8	8,501	16.6
1958	1,402	29.2	9,270	15.1
1959	1,373	28.2	8,746	15.7
1960	1,332	30.8	8,356	15.9
1961	1,192	27.8	7,940	15.0
1962	1,072	37.5	8,375	12.8
1963	927	27.9	8,538	11.4
1964	1,042	33.1	10,263	10.2
1965	1,073	30.6	12,215	8.8
1966	1,084	28.0	14,307	7.6
1967	1,298	29.6	15,780	8.2
1968	898	20.9	16,907	5.3
1969	1,039	29.2	19,315	5.4
1970	1,237	24.0	21,689	5.7
1971	1,239	22.9	24,860	4.9
1972	1,233	25.3	26,714	4.6
1973	1,017	30.6	31,520	3.2
1974	1,281	32.4	34,624	3.7
1975	1,294	25.2	34,203	3.8
1976	1,347	16.2	33,922	4.0
1977	1,124	28.7	27,532	4.1
1978	814	27.0	18,194	4.5
1979	608	14.1	11,458	5.3
1980	242	52.0	13,572	1.8
1981	342	50.0	17,033	2.0
1982	525	36.1	17,172	3.1

Sources:

Cols. 1, 3, 4, 1950-1974: A. Slaven, In Kuuse & Slaven (eds.), *Scottish and Scandinavian Shipbuilding Seminar: Development Problems in Historical Perspective*, p. 51

Cols. 1, 3, 4, 1975-82: A. Slaven, private communication to the author

Col. 2, 1950-71: A. Slaven, in Kuuse & Slaven (eds.), *op. cit.*, p. 51;

1972-78: *ibid.*, proportion based on merchant tonnage *under construction* in December each year;

1979-82: estimated by author (on basis of figures for merchant tonnage under construction on the Clyde, *Scottish Abstract of Statistics*, Vol. 12, 1983, p. 103)

third of the gross tonnage which went down the slipways only three years earlier. Although there was subsequently a modest revival in world output, completions in British yards in the 'eighties recorded their lowest levels since the early 'thirties.

In 1984 there are no signs of an end to the depression. In March 1983 British Shipbuilders were forced to announce — in what was ominously called their 'survival plan' — the loss of 9,000 jobs during the year.[71] They even suggested that the jobs of one-third of the industry's total workforce were at risk. In Scotland, Robb Caledon is threatened with closure; a thousand men could well be laid off at Govan; and at Scott Lithgows — where losses in 1982/83 amounted to £66m — the redundancies could be even higher. The demoralisation of the labour force at Scott Lithgows — where the workers were blamed for many of the problems afflicting the troubled yard — was such that in August 1983 trade union leaders were anticipating 'a massive rush for redundancy'.[72] The fate of Scott Lithgow seemed all but sealed when Britoil (January 1984) and British Petroleum (February 1984) cancelled orders for oil rigs because work was two years behind schedule. The yard was saved only by its sale to the Trafalgar House Group in March 1984, the reinstatement of the Britoil contract and the Government's assumption of Scott Lithgow's debts and losses, variously estimated at between £71m and £85m. Despite the men's agreement to new, more flexible working practices, further redundancies are anticipated, reducing the numbers employed from 2,900 in January 1984 to some 1,500 by the end of the year.[73]

5. DECLINE: AN EXPLANATION

At the beginning of this brief exploration of the decline of the Scottish heavy staple industries, the belief was expressed that a fundamental problem was to attempt to determine whether the rapidity of the collapse need have been so rapid or so apparently complete. Who, or what, was to blame? Except in the case of coal, it is still impossible to provide a fully satisfactory answer. The Scottish coal industry has declined because coal can no longer be mined at a cost lower than its selling price. Little that the old coalmasters did or could have done would have ameliorated the industry's present position, nor can the State, in the guise of the National Coal Board. The Government has, indeed, kept the industry alive in Scotland by the vast expenditure of public funds and by the artificial stimulation of demand for coal as an energy source for the generation of electricity. The past mistakes of private owners and managers and the occasionally ruthless exploitation by the miners of their power over the provision of labour, are mere contributory influences on the decline of Scottish coal. Perhaps the most that can currently be hoped for is that the coal industry in Scotland will be permitted to continue to contract in a manner and at a pace that causes the minimum social injury.

But what of iron and steel, and shipbuilding? Here hindsight permits a somewhat different verdict. In as much as the success of the Scottish iron and steel industry in the nineteenth century is to be explained in terms of a chronological sequence of favourable circumstances, including the use of cheap splint coal and blackband ironstone, rapid technical advances and the voracious appetite of the Clyde for heavy steel plate, then its subsequent relative decline was inevitable. As the supplies of coking coal ran out, as native iron ore deposits were exhausted, the long-term future of the industry became dependent on the creation of a deepwater terminal and a new location, and on a sufficiently buoyant demand to absorb the products of such a complex. The adoption of the radical Brassert proposals in the 1930s *might* have provided Scottish steel with a nucleus for future growth, especially when the demands of the shipyards remained highly important, albeit temporarily quiescent. But was the adoption of the Brassert proposals ever really plausible, given that the scheme had to meet commercial criteria? If the State had been prepared to help the embattled steelmasters in the 'thirties in the way that has more recently become acceptable and commonplace, the history of the industry might have been very different. As it was, those who subscribed the risk capital could not have been expected to assume responsibilities in the national, as opposed to their own selfish, interests. It was such considerations that influenced Sir Andrew McCance in his attitude towards both the renewed demand for an integrated steelworks on a tidewater site immediately after the war and the campaign for the strip mill in the 'fifties. Since he believed that the latter would never be commercially viable, he objected bitterly to Colvilles being forced to undertake its construction and operation: hence the long-drawn out arguments over the extent of Government financial assistance.

Thus, in apportioning responsibility for the decline of steel in Scotland, it is apparent that although there have undoubtedly been entrepreneurial failings, particularly in the determination of the relevant timespan within which to plan for the future, these must be accorded lesser blame than the erosion of the raw material base and the limited nature of Scottish demand for steel products, a factor that gains in significance with the decline of the shipbuilding industry. Given that the fortunes of the Scottish steel industry have been inextricably linked with the health of the shipbuilding industry, the decline of the latter has emasculated the former.[74] Here, 'blame' can be more clearly identified. Those who have owned, managed and worked in Scottish shipbuilding would appear to have contributed to its present parlous condition to an extent greater than those in coal or steel.[75] Few escape serious criticism in the Booz-Allen Report, or even in that of the Geddes Committee. The decline of Clyde shipbuilding is a sorry tale of shortsightedness, incompetence and selfishness, a counterpoint of weak management, greedy workers and meddling politicians.[76] In a world in which rival shipbuilding nations have undermined the British industry by 'unfair' methods, these deep-rooted weaknesses have brought shipbuilding in Scotland to the very brink of extinction and grievously damaged the prospects for steel.

The question remains: why did the steel industry not develop steel products for new and rising markets? Was it that to produce light steel or thin plates would have been beneath the dignity of those whose privilege it had been to clothe the warships of the Royal Navy?[77] Did Sir Andrew McCance — a brilliant technologist — ignore marketing and selling opportunities (albeit perhaps in anticipation of local demand) which he despised? Or was it that, conscious of input shortages on the one hand and social responsibilities on the other, he chose to concentrate on what Colvilles had always made — heavy steel plate and sections for shipbuilding and engineering construction — because to him these were the most important national requirements at a time when any diversification of output might have seemed frivolous? Alternatively, did the proud, dictatorial, obstinate and ageing men who controlled both steel and shipbuilding in the 'fifties and 'sixties fail to appreciate the fast-changing international environment within which the Scottish heavy industries would be required to operate?

The questions are almost limitless, and at the risk of once again straining the patience of those who have criticised my previous excursions into aspects of British entrepreneurship for the multiplication of questions rather than the provision of answers, is it conceivable that the present sickness of the Scottish steel industry is a direct consequence of its direction during a critical period by a highly qualified metallurgist? One is reminded of the suspicion, voiced by W. J. Reader, that the surest way to ruin a technological business is to put scientists in charge of it.[78] In answer — and I am conscious of its tangentiality — I would say that whatever their faults, technologists have had a less baneful influence on the Scottish heavy industries than the many politicians who have sought to exploit the condition of these related industries for their own narrow ends and then moved on to other things, leaving the problems they pretended to solve even more intractable. It is only right that the State should help to keep the coal, iron and steel, and shipbuilding industries alive in Scotland because the principal representatives of the State have contributed in no small measure to their sorry plight.

NOTES

1. A. Slaven, *The Development of the West of Scotland: 1750-1960* (London, 1975), pp. 195-6.

2. Neil K. Buxton, 'Entrepreneurial Efficiency in the British Coal Industry between the Wars', *Economic History Review*, Second Series, XXIII (1970), pp. 476-97.

3. *Ibid.*, p. 495.

4. R. H. Campbell, *The Rise and Fall of Scottish Industry, 1707-1939* (Edinburgh, 1980), pp. 111-18; see also Slaven, *op. cit.*, pp. 197-98.

5. C. E. V. Leser, 'Coal-Mining', in A. K. Cairncross (ed.), *The Scottish Economy* (Cambridge, 1954), pp. 115-6.

6. *Ibid.*, pp. 116-17.

7. National Coal Board (Scottish Division), *A Short History of the Scottish Coal-Mining Industry* (N.C.B., 1958), pp. 85-6; see also Slaven, *op. cit.*, p. 213; Scottish Home Department, *Scottish Coalfields. The Report of the Scottish Coalfields Committee*, Cmd. 6575 (1944).

8. Leser, *op. cit.*, p. 117.

9. Slaven, *op. cit.*, p. 213.

10. Bruce Lenman, *An Economic History of Modern Scotland* (London, 1977), p. 240.

11. National Coal Board, *Short History*, p. 88.

12. Neil K. Buxton, *The Economic Development of the British Coal Industry* (London, 1978), p. 237.

13. G. D. N. Worswick, 'The British Economy, 1950-1959', in G. D. N. Worswick and P. H. Ady (eds.), *The British Economy in the Nineteen-Fifties* (Oxford, 1962), p. 60.

14. Buxton, *Economic Development of the British Coal Industry*, p. 238.

15. Leser, *op. cit.*, pp. 110-12; P. L. Payne, *Colvilles and the Scottish Steel Industry* (Oxford, 1979), p. 312.

16. See 'Fuel Use and Fuel Costs', *Scottish Economic Bulletin*, No. 6 (July, 1974), pp. 8-9.

17. A. Slaven, 'Earnings and Productivity in the Scottish Coal-mining Industry during the Nineteenth Century: The Dixon Enterprises', in P. L. Payne (ed.), *Studies in Scottish Business History* (London, 1967), pp. 242-47.

18. T. L. Johnston, N. K. Buxton and D. Mair, *Structure and Growth of the Scottish Economy* (London, 1971), pp. 110-111.

19. *Ibid.*, p. 112.

20. Monopolies and Mergers Commission, *Report on the Efficiency and Costs in the Development, Production and Supply of Coal by the N.C.B.*, Cmnd. 8920 (1983), Vol. II, pp. 30-41.

21. *Ibid.*, Vol. II, pp. 27-8.

22. *Ibid.*, Vol. I, pp. 30-31.

23. A month after the decision to close Cardowan, Mr Ian McGregor, newly appointed Chairman of the National Coal Board, threatened to put Monktonhall on a care and maintenance basis if productivity was not improved. Despite an investment of £6 million, output per machine shift at Monktonhall during 1983 was 235 tonnes compared with 331 tonnes for the rest of Scotland and 356 tonnes for Britain as a whole. *The Times*, 23 August, 1982, 26 August 1983; *The Scotsman*, 21 September 1983; *Daily Telegraph*, 30 September, 1983.

24. Johnston, Buxton and Mair, *op. cit.*, p. 114.

25. Much of this section is based on the author's study, *Colvilles and the Scottish Steel Industry*, and, except for quotations, detailed references have been omitted. For a succinct and highly penetrating survey of developments in the Scottish steel industry in the two decades after the Second World War, see Kenneth Warren, 'Locational Problems of the Scottish Iron and Steel Industry since 1760', Part 2, *Scottish Geographical Magazine*, Vol. 81, no. 2 (September, 1965), pp. 87-103.

26. See the letter from Sir William McLintock to John Craig, 16 June 1936, quoted in Payne, *op. cit.*, p. 215.

27. Colvilles Ltd., 'Memorandum on Scottish Steel, 1947', section 39, quoted in Payne, *op. cit.*, p. 288.

28. John Vaizey, *The History of British Steel* (London, 1974), p. 141.

29. Colvilles' case, as presented to the Development Committee of the British Iron and Steel Federation by Robert Shone, February 1948, quoted by Payne, *op. cit.*, pp. 302-303.

30. British Iron and Steel Federation, 'Report of the Sub-Committee on Scottish Development', 10 March 1948, quoted by Payne, *op. cit.*, p. 304.

31. This episode has been examined by D. W. Heal, *The Steel Industry in Post-War Britain* (Newton Abbot, 1974), p. 154; K. Warren, 'Coastal Steelworks: A Case for Argument', *The Three Banks Review*, No. 82 (June 1969), pp. 36-7; and Chris Baur, 'The Future of Steel in Scotland', *British Steel*, Autumn 1974, pp. 16-17. See also J. Busby, *The British Steel Industry and its Expansion Plans in Scotland*, North Ayrshire Coastal Development Committee (October, 1971). For the background to Linwood and Bathgate, see David Sims and Michael Wood, *Car-Manufacturing at Linwood: the Regional Policy Issues* (Paisley College of Technology, 1984).

32. B.S.C., *Ten Year Development Strategy*, Cmnd, 5226 (1973), paras. 44-5.

33. Frank Fitzgerald, 'Direct Reduction at Hunterston', *British Steel*, Spring 1976, pp. 20-3.

34. David Murray, 'Scottish Steel. In the Melting Pot? Or the Graveyard?', *Scotland*, November 1972, p. 21.

35. *Steel News*, Scottish Division editions, Nos. 233-248, dated March 1979-November 1979.

36. Jim Love and Jim Stevens, 'The Scottish Lobby: Ravenscraig and Hunterston', in The Fraser of Allander *Quarterly Economic Commentary*, Vol. 8, no. 4 (May, 1983), p. 36.

37. It should be noted, furthermore, that the finishing mill at Gartcosh is about fourteen miles from the Ravenscraig complex. For some prescient comments on the disadvantages of Ravenscraig/Gartcosh as a location for strip steel production, see K. Warren, *The British Iron and Steel Sheet Industry since 1840* (London, 1970), p. 294.

38. Sir Andrew McCance, 'Production in the Steel Industry: Its Growth, Distribution and

Future Course', The Harold Wright Lecture at the Cleveland Scientific and Technical Institute, Middlesbrough, 28 November, 1950.

39. Colvilles Ltd., Annual Report for 1949, Chairman's statement, p. 15.

40. See, particularly, Kenneth Warren, 'Locational Problems', p. 102.

41. As early as 1954 Sir Archibald Forbes, chairman of the Iron and Steel Board, asked was it 'economic to carry steel production beyond a certain point as compared to manufacturing the excess in England?' Sir Archibald Forbes, 'Notes on the Modernisation and Development Proposals of Colvilles Ltd.', 22 May 1954, section 7, quoted Payne, *op. cit.*, p. 344.

42. Defeated it is said, by the so-called Scottish Lobby, a diverse coalition that included 'Conservative Scottish Office Ministers, Labour M.P.s, trade unionists and clergymen'. Love and Stephens, *op. cit.*, p. 33.

43. Extensive press reports on these developments were made throughout the summer and winter of 1983. The collapse of the negotiations with U.S. Steel was reported in most papers on 28 December, 1983. See also Love and Stevens, *op. cit.*, p. 33; and *The Economist*, 7-13 January, 1984, p. 25. It was reported in April 1984 that E.E.C. officials were pressing for the closure of one of Britain's three strip mills: Ravenscraig's operating loss of £44 million in 1983 coupled with the desperate efforts to keep the plant open during the miners' strike emphasised its vulnerability.

44. British Steel Corporation, *Annual Report and Accounts*, 1977-78, p. 17. Total capital expenditure on the Scottish Divisions in the two years 1977-79 was £133 million.

45. See Love and Stevens, *op. cit.*, pp. 33-37.

46. For a clear statement of the comparative position of the Scottish Shipbuilding industry in the inter-war period, see Neil K. Buxton, 'The Scottish Shipbuilding Industry between the Wars', *Business History*, Vol. X, no. 2 (July 1968), pp. 101-120.

47. J. R. Parkinson, 'Shipbuilding', in Neil K. Buxton and Derek H. Aldcroft (eds.), *British Industry between the Wars* (London, 1979), p. 79.

48. For the details, see A. Slaven, 'Growth and Stagnation in British/Scottish Shipbuilding, 1913-1977', in Jan Kuuse and A. Slaven (eds.), *Development Problems in Historical Perspective: A Report on the Scottish and Scandinavian Shipbuilding Seminar*, Glasgow, 21-23 September 1980. Professor Slaven's paper has been immensely valuable in the preparation of Section 4 of this paper.

49. See the interesting analysis by R. H. Campbell, 'Costs and Contracts: Lessons from Clyde Shipbuilding Between the Wars', in A. Slaven and D. H. Aldcroft (eds.), *Business, Banking and Urban History* (Edinburgh, 1982), pp. 54-79.

50. Although Buxton has identified a number of reasons for the Clyde's better performance than other shipbuilding areas in the period 1918-1939, he concludes that although the level of concentration rose relative to the remainder of the U.K., 'the organisation of yards on the Clyde hardly changed throughout the period and labour proved no more adaptable to new techniques'. Buxton, 'The Scottish Shipbuilding Industry', pp. 108, 110-111. See also A. Slaven, 'Self-Liquidation: The National Shipbuilders Security Ltd. and British Shipbuilding in the 1930s', in S. Palmer & G. Williams (eds.), *Charted and Uncharted Waters. Proceedings of a Conference on the Study of British Maritime History*, 8-11 September 1981 (London: Trustees of the National Maritime Museum in association with the Department of History, Queen Mary College, University of London).

51. Slaven, 'Growth and Stagnation', p. 19.

52. Quoted by David Clark, 'Steel Supplies Post 1945; Price, Supply and Demand: Some Observations with Reference to the British Shipbuilding Industry', in Kuuse and Slaven, *op. cit.*, p. 251.

53. See, for example, Payne, *op. cit.*, pp. 279-80.

54. A. M. Robb, 'Shipbuilding and Marine Engineering', in J. Cunnison and J. B. S. Gilfillan (eds.), *Glasgow* (Glasgow, 1958), p. 193.

55. Slaven, 'Growth and Stagnation', p. 29.

56. A. K. Cairncross, 'The Economy of Glasgow', in R. Miller and Joy Tivy (eds.), *The Glasgow Region* (Glasgow, 1958), p. 239.

57. Slaven, *Development of the West of Scotland*, pp. 218-19.

58. Cairncross, *op. cit.*, pp. 239-40.

59. See the accurate prediction made by the Shipbuilding Correspondent of the *Glasgow Herald Trade Review*, January, 1963, p. 173.

60. frank Broadway, *Upper Clyde Shipbuilders* (London: Centre for Policy Studies, 1976), p. 19.

61. Quoted by Broadway, *ibid.*, p. 20.

62. *Shipbuilding Inquiry Committee* (Geddes Committee), *1965-66*, Cmnd. 2937 (1966).

63. The criticisms as subsequently summarised by the Booz Allen Inquiry, Department of

Trade and Industry, *British Shipbuilding, 1972: A Report to the Department of Trade and Industry by Booz, Allen & Hamilton International BV*. H.M.S.O. (London, 1973), p. 84. In May 1983 Professor Slaven presented a highly illuminating paper to the Business History Seminar held at the Polytechnic of Central London on 'Marketing Practices in British Shipbuilding: 1945-1975' in which he argued that 'the failure to develop market research imprisoned British shipbuilders in a weak information environment, limiting their ability to identify trends and plan adaptations. The failure of British shipbuilders, generally, to select market segments: and make clear product choices suited to their own experience, resources and abilities, placed British yards at a severe disadvantage in competition with foreign builders who developed more positive market and product policies. From this stemmed the inability to perceive the advantages of a positive sales policy based on direct selling to clearly identified customers . . . The failure of marketing . . . is arguably the root source of the failure of British shipbuilding to sustain itself against the challenge of the Japanese and European builders' (pp. 20-21).

64. Geddes Report, p. 152.

65. There were, however, substantial differences between the various companies in this respect. Of the £160m provided by the Government to the industry between 1967 and mid-1972, only a third was devoted to capital expenditure. In Scotland, Robb Caledon employed three-quarters of their small grant of half a million pounds from the Shipbuilding Industry Board in this way; Scott Lithgow used a like proportion (72.4 per cent of £5.24 millions); but Govan/U.C.S. — the largest beneficiary of Government funds (£65m) — utilised only 19 per cent of its total assistance in capital expenditure. *Booz Allen Report*, p. 89.

66. A succinct account of the history of the Scottish shipbuilding industry between c.1965 and 1971 is provided by Johnston, Buxton and Mair, *op. cit.*, pp. 118-127.

67. Govan Shipbuilders Ltd — which formally acquired the Govan, Linthouse and Scotstoun yards from the liquidator of U.C.S. — was totally owned by the Government from the outset.

68. Broadway, *op. cit.*, p. 52.

69. A. Slaven, 'Shipbuilding', in David Daiches (ed.), *A Companion to Scottish Culture* (London, 1981), p. 355.

70. British Shipbuilders, *Report and Accounts, 1979-80*; see also Fraser of Allander, *Quarterly Economic Commentary*, Vol. 6, no. 2 (October 1981), p. 12.

71. Fraser of Allander, *Quarterly Economic Commentary*, Vol. 8, no. 4 (May, 1983), p. 23.

72. *Daily Telegraph*, 29 July, 1983; see also *Ibid.*, 23 August 1983.

73. The cancellation of the order for a semi-submersible rig being built for Britoil by Scott Lithgow's, the ensuing crises and the subsequent sale of the yard to Trafalgar House occasioned extensive press coverage. See particularly *Sunday Times*, 23 October, 1983, 18 December, 1983; *The Economist*, 7-13 January, 1984, p. 22; *Daily Telegraph*, 18 January, 1984, 29 March, 1984; *Glasgow Herald*, 25 January, 1984; *The Times*, 30 March, 1984; [Aberdeen] *Press and Journal*, 27 April, 1984.

74. Although the total consumption of steel by the U.K. shipbuilding industry represented only about 4 per cent of total U.K. steel consumption in the years 1967-71 (on an average of 650,000 tons per year), this demand mainly comprised steel plate, and the shipbuilding and marine engineering sector generated nearly 20 per cent of the U.K. demand for this product. (Booz Allen Report, p. 188. See also *Iron and Steel: Annual Statistics*). Since shipbuilding plates had traditionally been a speciality of the Scottish steel industry, demand for this item was of major importance in loading the Scottish rolling mills.

75. Professor Slaven has listed a number of propositions concerning the causes of the decline of British shipbuilding: each of them deserves detailed study. Slaven, 'Growth and Stagnation', pp. 45-8.

76. On the role of politicians in the shipbuilding industry, see Brian W. Hogwood, 'Government and shipbuilding in Britain, 1959-77', in Kuuse and Slaven, *op. cit.*, pp. 270-283, and the same author's *Government and Shipbuilding: The Politics of Industrial Change* (London, 1979).

77. This question was asked by W. J. Reader in a review of the author's *Colvilles, Economic History Review*, Second Series, Vol. XXXIII (1980), p. 429. I must acknowledge my indebtedness too to Professor R. H. Campbell, who suggested numerous avenues of inquiry in a review of the same work which appeared in the *Scottish Historical Review*.

78. W. J. Reader, *op. cit.*, p. 429.

4

THE SCOTTISH FINANCIAL SECTOR, 1950-1980*

Maxwell Gaskin

Scotland has long since enjoyed a measure of financial development and independent financial enterprise unusual among the regions of the U.K. where financial markets and the direction of financial institutions are heavily concentrated in London. The result, during these three decades, was that we had in Scotland a financial sector which presented an unusual mixture of native and expatriate financial institutions. It was a mixture that, almost uniquely, included its own set of retail banks — a system which, despite structural changes and the growth of strong external ownership interests, retained operational independence and which, in its central activities, was still largely geared to a Scottish market. But Scottish financial enterprise has been notably active in insurance and in the promotion and management of investment trusts, and in 1980 Scotland remained the principal centre for both these activities outside London. In both cases, however, Scotland was their home but not their sole or even their main market. And, of course, alongside and in many cases competing with the native institutions were all those institutions based elsewhere which operated in Scotland through branches and agencies forming parts of national, even international, networks of offices. Among the more important of these were the building societies. But also significant were the finance houses, the non-Scottish insurance companies and — not least — the numerous non-Scottish banks which had entered the country since the mid-60s.

All these institutions, indigenous or otherwise, saw immense changes in their market environments during these three decades, partly from exogenous events like government policy or inflation, but also from a growing competitive interaction between institutions. From the late 1950s onwards financial institutions were widening the scope of their activities so that by the end of our period almost all were multi-product firms, and the area of competitive overlap between what were formerly quite distinct organisations had extended greatly. So, the Scottish clearing banks saw their traditional market areas invaded by English and overseas banks, by a restructured Trustee Savings Bank movement, and above all by the building societies, whilst they, in their turn, extended their activities into areas such as instalment lending, house purchase finance and insurance broking.

This picture of a regional financial sector composed partly of locally based

*In preparing this chapter I have been greatly helped by the ready co-operation of financial institutions in Scotland and elsewhere, and by particular members of them who have provided information and answered my questions. In thanking them I must emphasise that any errors that remain are my sole responsibility.

financial enterprises partly of national or international institutions which were increasingly contesting this or that area of the domestic market, poses a number of questions. One concerns the consequences, beneficial or otherwise, to Scotland of this financial structure, and of the changes to which it was subjected. Such a question naturally tends to focus on the place and activities of the indigenous institutions, but in the light of all developments in the sector that is too narrow a focus. Another concerns employment effects. Employment, *per se,* hardly ever figures in discussions of financial structure, but it is important in Scotland where, as everywhere, financial employment grew rapidly in the last of these decades, and where all sources of new employment had a special importance.

Any historical survey of finance must proceed by first examining its individual sub-sectors, and we shall begin here with banking and banking-type institutions like the building societies. In discussing banking in Scotland, the later developments of the period demand an approach on functional rather than institutional lines, and the following two sections deal respectively with 'retail banking' and 'wholesale and merchant banking'. Following that we turn to the institutions more prominently concerned with long-term finance: the insurance industry, the investment trusts and the stock exchange. In the final section we assess the outcome of the changes of these three decades, and their implications for the general questions about the Scottish financial sector raised earlier, and also glance briefly at some future prospects, as they appeared in the early 1980s.

THE RETAIL BANKING SECTOR

In 1980, retail banking — that is, the gathering of deposits from and lending to the whole spectrum of transactors large and small, personal and commercial, and the operating of a money transmission system — was conducted in Scotland almost entirely by the three Scottish clearing banks and the Trustee Savings Banks (T.S.B.s), with a small but probably increasing contribution from a few of the recent incomer banks. Until the late 1960s it was the exclusive preserve of the clearing banks, then known as the 'Scottish joint-stock banks', and they continued collectively to have the lion's share of the business. By the end of the period retail banking far from comprehended the full range of the clearers' activities, but they remained in the first place retail banks, and we shall consider them mainly in the next section.

THE SCOTTISH CLEARING BANKS

The period 1950-80 saw striking changes in the structure as well as the activities of Scottish clearers. When 1950 opened there were eight joint stock banks, and that number had subsisted since 1910. The Scottish banking system had early consolidated itself into a small number of nationally operating banks — early, that is, compared with the Anglo-Welsh system which as late as 1900 comprised over a hundred banks. However, the consolidation of that system was then proceeding fast, and the expansive energies of the resulting banks were soon carrying them beyond their national bounds, so that between 1917 and 1924 four of the eight Scottish banks became wholly owned, though independently operating, 'affiliates' of three of the London clearing banks.[1] The first amalgamation of our period, in 1950, united two of these banks, the Clydesdale and the North of Scotland, both of them owned by the Midland Bank. These were the last Scottish banks with marked regional orientations: the mergers that followed in the 1950s and '60s, whilst frequently involving some differences of regional balance, were essentially amalgamations of (in Scottish terms) nationally operating banks.

The merger of the Bank of Scotland and the Glasgow-based Union Bank of Scotland, in 1954, was the first on this pattern, uniting two of the remaining 'independents' — banks that were unaffiliated to any of the London banks. It left the situation where the next two obvious candidates for amalgamation by their size, the British Linen Bank and the National Bank of Scotland, were affiliates of Barclays and Lloyds respectively. However, this supposedly complicating factor was shown to be surmountable when, in 1958, the National merged with the independent Commercial Bank of Scotland, to produce the National Commercial Bank. Lloyds emerged with a 37 per cent interest in this bank, but agreed not to increase it, and to allow the National Commercial to operate as a wholly independent Scottish bank — which, in the spirit of its Commercial Bank forbear, it very much did. And this union set a pattern which was repeated eleven years later in the two mergers that produced the present three-bank structure: that of the Royal Bank of Scotland with the National Commercial, and of the Bank of Scotland with the British Linen Bank. One effect of these mergers was to alter the pattern of English interests in Scottish banking, extending it by the introduction of Barclay's 35 per cent stake in the enlarged Bank of Scotland, diluting it by the relative contraction of Lloyd's interest to 16 per cent in the group formed by the Royal-National Commercial union — a group which included the Royal Bank's two English subsidiaries, Williams Deacons and Glyns, Mills & Co., later united as Williams and Glyns. The deposit and note liabilities of the three Scottish clearing banks (as in 1971 they first called themselves) in 1980 are shown in Table 1.

Table 1. *Deposits and Note Issues of the Scottish Clearing Banks, 1980*

	£ millions	
	Total Deposits	*Notes in Circulation*
Bank of Scotland	1810.4	164.0
Clydesdale Bank	1297.1	97.5
Royal Bank of Scotland	2867.2	251.6

Note: Totals are taken from annual balance sheets and relate, in order, to 28 February, 31 December and 30 September.

These later mergers produced two banks (the Royal Bank, and the Bank of Scotland) with much enlarged resource bases, and with prospects of economies through the rationalisation of branch networks. Other advantages, then largely in the future, were scale economies in the use of electronic data processing (E.D.P.) systems, and those in the banks' extending operations in wholesale and international banking and corporate financial services.

RESTRUCTURING BRANCH SYSTEMS

One advantage offered by almost all the mergers was some rationalisation of branch systems. Scotland had long been regarded as heavily if not over-banked. In 1951, with one branch office for every 3,000 of her population, her banking density was half as high again as that of England and Wales; in 1979, with a ratio of 1 branch to 3,350, it was still a third higher than south of the border. But absolute numbers of branch offices fell substantially in this period, from 1700 to 1500; and as this was a net reduction, concealing a substantial number of new openings, the actual number of closures was greater than the numbers suggest. Movements of population as well as developments in the market for banking services — including attempts to develop the potential market among manual workers — have required the opening of new offices in new housing areas and also in such places of work as hospitals, universities and colleges, offices and factories.

BORROWING AND LENDING

The pace of the change in the British financial system, especially since the early 1960s, has been reflected in the Scottish banks' balance sheets. The central mass of banks' resources, to finance their lending and acquisition of other assets, has traditionally been provided by the deposits which the public hold with them in current and time deposits. The intensive gathering of deposits has long been a distinctive feature of Scottish banking: the success of the joint stock banks in attracting a high level of funds, originally by way of deposit receipts,[2] in recent decades in deposit accounts, has been reflected in a traditionally low proportion of non-interest bearing — mainly current — account balances. In the 1920s these were as low as almost one-third of the total; in 1980, after much intervening fluctuation, they were almost back to that level, and appreciably lower than the 40 per cent of the London clearing banks. But this similarity of the present and past figures conceals important differences. For example, there is now considerably more use of deposit accounts effectively as current accounts — 'pass book banking' as it is termed — than formerly, which involves the banks in costs over and above the interest payable on these accounts. But even more significantly, by 1980 about one half of the clearing banks' total deposits were not retail deposits at all, but funds

taken up in the wholesale deposit and currency (i.e. 'Eurocurrency') markets
— or accepted at rates related to those prevailing in these markets.

An important feature of our period has been the upsurge of competition
from the building societies, so that for the Scottish banks they have replaced
the savings banks as their most potent competitors for retail deposits. In the 15
years 1965-80, shares and deposits in building societies increased almost
tenfold, and in Scotland by a much higher factor than that. This compared
with a threefold increase in the combined deposits of the English and Scottish
banks, though with a sixfold increase for the Scottish banks alone. And the
comparison would be even less favourable if one allowed for the banks'
increasing resort to the wholesale money markets during the 1970s. The comparative movements of banks' and building societies' deposits, between 1951
and 1982, are shown in Table 2.

Table 2. *Deposits, 1951-1982: Banks and Building Societies*

£ millions

	London Clearing Banks[1]	Scottish Clearing Banks[1]	Scottish Trustee Savings Banks[2]	Building Societies U.K.[3]	Building Societies Scotland[4]
1951 December	6,060	782	260	n.a.	n.a.
1955 December	6,251	694	274	1,959	n.a.
1960 December	7,156	738	326	2,925	n.a.
1965 December	8,477	823	445	5,159	77
1970 December	10,297	1,015	543	10,142	396
1975 December	22,518	2,305	794	22,696	1,226
1980 December	39,439	4,817	1,037	49,950	2,958
1982 December	59,191	6,882	1,133	67,421	4,012

Sources: Bank of England Quarterly Bulletin; B.S.A. Bulletin; T.S.B. Group.

Notes: 1. 1951 to 1970: current and deposit accounts. 1975 and later: total sterling deposits held in
U.K. (including current deposits).
2. Figures at 20 November. First figure is for 1950.
3. End-year figures: shares and deposits.
4. B.S.A. figures relate to a group of societies accounting for most Scottish business.
Variations in the group may affect the comparability of the series.

During the last decade of our period the banks were indeed competing more
vigorously for retail business, both among themselves and with other institutions. In this the banking policy regime introduced in 1971 under the title
'Competition and Credit Control' (C.C.C.) marked a turning point in that
whilst it did not remove previous inhibitions on the banks' competition with
the societies for deposits — and indeed new restraints were imposed on their
deposit-gathering activities in 1974, with the introduction of Supplementary
Special Deposits — it placed all banks on an equal competitive footing,
removed quantitative controls on their lending, and positively encouraged
them to compete actively with one another and with other financial institutions. As part of this (and along with corresponding action by the English
banks) the Scottish banks ended their one hundred and fifty year-old practice

of agreeing and publishing a common list of interest rates and other charges —
a move designed to increase competition in banking.

THE SCOTTISH BANKS' NOTE ISSUES

One of the superficially most distinctive features of the Scottish banks is their
right to issue banknotes. This is a relic of Sir Robert Peel's banking legislation
of 1844-45,[3] and as far as the Scottish banks are concerned, the effective
principle of regulation has remained unchanged: they are free to issue their
own notes provided they hold Bank of England notes (or certificates for such
notes, deposited with the Bank) one for one against all but a small fiduciary
element — £2.7m. in the aggregate — of their total notes in circulation.
Scottish bank notes have no monetary significance as such: the banks issue
them to the extent of the demand for them, and as the 'covering' Bank of
England notes form part of the Bank's own fiduciary issue, Scottish bank
notes may, except for the small fiduciary element, be regarded as simply
'standing in' for Bank of England notes.

However, that is not quite the whole story. Before the changes in the banks'
reserve requirements introduced under the 1971 measures, the Bank of
England notes, held by the Scottish banks as statutory cover for their own note
circulation, actually performed a dual function in that they also 'stood in' for
at least part of the reserve assets which the Scottish banks were expected to
hold under the pre-1971 regime. To the extent that this was so, a certain small
monetary effect was attributable to the note-issuing powers of the Scottish
banks — though it operated through the total of bank deposits generated by
the system rather than through the currency circulation[4] — and their ability to
lend and hold other earning assets was somewhat increased. With the 1971
changes and then again following the abolition of C.C.C. in 1981, the position
was outwardly altered but the monetary and other effects effectively remained.
However, these effects now flow from the fact that the banks do not need to
hold cover against unissued notes held in branch tills, and can thus supply a
large part of the float of cash required in branch tills (and equal to about 1½
per cent of deposits in the London clearing banks) at no other cost than that of
printing them. This undoubtedly releases bank resources for such purposes as
lending, and the Scottish bankers regard it as something which, by reducing
branch costs, makes many of their smaller branches viable.[5]

THE BANKS' ASSETS

Turning to the Scottish banks' use of the resources placed with them, the
prime question to ask is how the changing composition of their portfolios, as
well as the scale of their resources, has affected their lending to the private
sector and to public enterprises. Banks do not commit all their resources to

such lending: a proportion must be kept in highly liquid assets to meet outflows of deposits and to conform to Bank of England requirements designed for varying purposes,[6] and this liquidity reserve has traditionally been reinforced by holdings of gilt-edged securities. During these three decades the Bank of England's requirements have been an important determinant of the proportion of liquid assets held, though up to 1971 these lay very lightly on the Scottish banks. For example, they were never subject to the 8 per cent cash reserve ratio agreed between the Bank of England and the London clearing banks in 1946. Later, in the mid-1950s, when it was recognised that the significant asset ratio for control purposes was no longer that of cash but of total liquid assets — cash, bills, money lent 'at call' to the London discount market — to deposits, the so-called 'liquidity ratio', the Bank asked the English banks to observe a 30 per cent minimum ratio of these assets, a figure which they had broadly maintained in the 1930s. Subsequently the Scottish banks, along with other domestic banks, were asked to observe their 'usual' minima in the holding of liquid assets. Whatever their usual minima were reckoned to be (and this was never revealed), the Scottish banks were allowed to include two balance sheet items which very much moderated the effect of this requirement on them. These were cash held as cover for their own note issues, and items (cheques etc.) in the course of collection. In 1960 these two groups of assets amounted to over 20 per cent of deposits, and this meant that, whether or not they took advantage of it, the Scottish banks were in a position to lend and invest (i.e. place in gilt-edged and similar securities) a significantly higher proportion of their deposit based resources than the English clearing banks. And in other ways too, in the pre-1971 years, they were less restricted by policy than the English banks. Following the introduction of Special Deposits in 1958, as an additional means of controlling bank liquidity, the Scottish banks were consistently subjected to calls of only half the ratios required of the English banks. This moderation of the policy was prompted by the regional problems of Scotland, which also produced some exemptions of the Scottish banks from lending ceilings in force from time to time in the pre-1971 period.

Following the publication of C.C.C. in 1971, the system of controls applied to the banking system was almost completely reshaped. As part of the move towards equality of treatment of the various groups of banks operating in the U.K., which had multiplied during the 1960s, reserve requirements were reformulated: all banks operating in the U.K. were required to maintain a uniform ratio of 12½ per cent of reserve assets as newly defined.[7]

As far as the Scottish banks were concerned, the new requirement ended the relatively advantageous position in which they had been placed under the pre-1971 regime. Cash held as note cover and items in course of collection were excluded from reserve assets and indeed it appeared that, in contrast with the English banks, the Scottish banks would have to liquidate other assets in order to meet the requirement. In the event increased liquidity in the system as a result of government financing and policy made this unnecessary, and there was certainly no compression of their lending power. Indeed the 1970s saw a strong expansion of Scottish banks' advances, both absolutely and as a proportion of total assets, so that by the end of the decade the advances ratio stood at an all-time high.

In 1950 bank advances in Scotland, as elsewhere, had made only a partial recovery from their steep decline during the war years (caused by the methods of wartime finance of industry), and it was not until 1959 that the aggregate advances ratio recovered its 1938 level of 34 per cent of deposits. However, from that year it rose sharply to a peak of 53 per cent in 1965. With the release of the banks from lending restrictions — shortlived as it proved — in 1971, advances once again surged upwards, propelled largely by the massive growth in bank deposits in the so-called 'Barber boom', but also by another upward leap in the advances ratio. By the mid-1970s they stood at an unprecedentedly high 70 per cent of deposits, and by 1980 were somewhat higher again.

The obverse of this movement was an equally dramatic decline in the banks' holdings of gilt-edged securities. The Scottish banks had long held relatively high ratios of government stock, and in 1970 these holdings amounted to 20 per cent of deposits: by 1980 they were down to 3 per cent. It is interesting to note that recurrently between 1950 and 1970 doubts were expressed — by bankers as much as anybody — about the possibility or the wisdom of pushing the advances ratio up further, or letting the proportion of investments decline, from some contemporary position. Repeatedly such doubts have been falsified or ignored: all banks have proved able eventually to live with balance sheet positions that even their most recent predecessors would have shied at. Viewed from one angle, such action appeared to reflect an ever-growing confidence of bankers in the unassailable safety of the system — or in the

Table 3. *Scottish Clearing Banks: Main Assets, 1955-1980*[1]

	Liquid Assets[2]		Investments[3]		Advances	
	£m.	%	£m.	%	£m.	%
1955	272	31	378	43	200	23
1960	299	32	266	28	342	37
1965	366	34	191	18	503	46
1970	472	37	266	21	585	46
1975	718	27	149	6	1,446	55
1980	1,196	22	196	4	3,471	65

Source: Bank of England Quarterly Bulletin.

Notes: 1. All figures relate to December of the years given. Pre-1970 figures refer to the 'Scottish Joint Stock Banks'. Percentages are of the total of gross deposits plus notes in circulation; this produces smaller figures than the percentages of deposits only, given in the text. Throughout, the figures include liabilities and assets in sterling only.
   2. Up to 1970, figures include cash (including note cover) balances with other banks, money at call and bills. After 1970, totals include reserve assets as defined in C.C.C., plus market loans and bills other than reserve assets.
   3. British government stocks and other investments, including investments in subsidiaries. After 1970 British government stocks up to one year maturity are included in liquid assets. To include these in investments would increase the investments ratio by one percentage point in 1975 and 1980.

assurance of its safety by the central bank. From another angle, it pointed to the responsiveness of the banks to the financial needs of the private sector: during the 1970s, business turned to the banks on a massive scale for funds that a declining profit rate denied them, and that were obtainable on the capital market only at unacceptably high nominal rates of interest. Yet again the growth of advances was undoubtedly welcome to the banks in a period when rapid inflation, rising real costs and a fluid competitive environment were making life difficult for them.

The relative movements of the clearing banks' main assets during our period are shown in Table 3.

THE SCOTTISH BANKS AS LENDERS

Before turning to some qualitative aspects and the composition of Scottish bank lending, one other quantity should be noted — the proportion of total lending actually made within Scotland. In 1977 it was stated that 69 per cent of lending commitments, and rather more of actual lending — a total of £1,433m. — were then made within Scotland.[8] Most of the remainder went to Government, or to businesses and individuals dealing with their London offices, a high proportion of whom, it was said, had 'a historical connection' with Scotland. This reflects a trend which has marked Scottish economic life for more than half a century: the drift of control of Scottish industry and commerce to England or elsewhere. When head offices have removed to London, or Scottish firms have merged with English companies, the Scottish banks' London offices have afforded a means for retaining at least some of the business.

INNOVATIONS IN LENDING

The period of this survey saw some major departures in bank finance, and the first was launched almost at the beginning of this period by a Scottish bank. In 1954 the Commercial Bank of Scotland became the first U.K. bank to acquire a direct stake in hire-purchase finance by its acquisition of Scottish Midland Guarantee Trust Ltd., a finance company specialising in this business. Banks were by then advancing considerable sums to hire purchase companies, but the advantages of participating in the profits of the business, rather than simply earning interest on the lending which supported it, were becoming apparent. At the time the Commercial's coup incurred the displeasure of the Bank of England, which vetoed any immediate imitation. In 1958 the veto was withdrawn, and all British banks immediately followed the Commercial Bank's example. The resulting acquisitions brought the Scottish banks a stake in a rapidly expanding form of finance which, after an early rough passage marked by heavy losses in 1959-60, continued to be an important field of lending and became a significant source of finance for the producer as well as the consumer. The business financing side of the finance companies' activities was greatly extended in the 1970s with the strong growth of leasing and factoring,[9] both of them devices for injecting finance into enterprises without impairing their ability to borrow from other sources.

Two important innovations in bank lending also made their first appearance in the late 1950s. One was the institution of 'personal loans', that is the lending of fixed sums, repayable at specified intervals, to personal borrowers to finance the purchase of durable consumer goods, and later such developing activities as home improvements. This departure coincided with the banks' direct move into hire purchase, and indeed personal loans were designed to compete with the hire-purchase system.

The other leading innovation, important to business finance, was the 'term loan' first introduced in Scotland in the late 1950s, but only developed on any scale after 1971. In Scotland, as generally in Britain, the overdraft has been, and remains, the predominant form of banking lending to all classes of borrowers. From the banker's point of view it is essentially a short-term engagement, a vehicle for providing finance of the 'seed-time to harvest' variety rather than for fixed capital purposes. In practice most overdrafts are simply 'rolled over' at each review period, and can become quite long-term in character; but they remain in principle repayable on demand.

However, quite apart from the banks' traditional reluctance to make overdraft finance available for other than fairly short-term purposes, borrowers may be averse to financing medium or longer-term capital investment with funds that are subject, however remotely, to the possibility of recall. The term loan, an importation from the U.S., was devised to overcome this difficulty. It is made for fixed periods, usually for three to five, but in some cases up to ten years; it is usually repayable by instalments; and it is recognised as an appropriate instrument for financing plant and buildings. Individual Scottish bankers were advocating the term-loan concept in the 1950s, but only the Clydesdale produced a formal scheme at that time. The full exploitation of this and other lending innovations of that period — for example, the personal loan — was restrained by the controls on bank lending applied during the 1960s.[10] The removal of restraints in the policy change of 1971, coupled with developments on the borrowing side to be examined under 'wholesale and merchant banking', provided the release and the means which the banks required, with the expansionary consequences for total advances already described. In the expansion term loans, now made at variable interest rates, rose strongly, from under 3 per cent of Scottish banks' total advances in 1971 to over 13 per cent in 1976,[11] and higher still in the later 1970s when business turned on an even larger scale to the banks for finance which at the high nominal interest rates prevailing they were unwilling to raise on fixed interest terms in the capital market. But personal loans and other lending to the personal sector also expanded, encouraged by the spread of credit card and similar facilities and boosted in the late 1970s by the banks' entry into house-purchase finance. Despite the growth in term loans and other forms of corporate lending, lending to the manufacturing sector declined sharply as a proportion of total advances, reflecting the increasing difficulties of this sector as the 1970s progressed, with the result that by the early 1980s the Scottish banks' total lending to manufacturing industry was greatly exceeded by their lending both to the personal and service sectors. This major change in the composition of Scottish bank lending, from 1967 when regular statistics of this began, up to 1983, is shown in Table 4:

Table 4. *Scottish Clearing Banks: Analysis of Advances, 1967-1983*[1]
per cent of total

Sector	1967	1970	1980[2]	1983[2]
Manufacturing	34.0	37.1	23.6	16.4
Other Production	22.8	19.9	22.5	19.2
Services	22.5	23.7	28.8	27.2
Financial	10.3	9.4	8.9	9.4
Personal	10.3	9.8	16.8	27.8

Sources: Bank of England Quarterly Bulletin; Scottish Economic Bulletin.

Notes: 1. Figures relate to August in each year.
2. 1980 and 1983 figures include both acceptances and foreign currency lending to U.K. residents.

COMPETITION FOR THE CLEARERS

For the Scottish clearing banks a notable and novel feature of the second half of our period has been the extension of competition into some traditional preserves of retail banking. The banks have long had to meet competition in deposit gathering from the savings bank movement, which had its beginnings in Scotland and is a strong force almost everywhere. A new development was the appearance of competition in current account services — chequeing facilities, money transmission and cash provision — and in personal and other types of lending. An early challenger was the National Girobank established in 1968 to offer a chequeing and settlement[12] system, and later limited overdraft facilities. But the major competitor emerged from the Savings Bank movement, though in a progressively restructured form.

The movement of the Trustee Savings Banks into full retail banking proceeded from a series of extensions in their statutory powers, beginning with the institution of current accounts in 1966, and continuing in the 1970s with powers to provide overdraft, personal loan and credit card facilities, and, eventually, mortgage lending and small business loans. The movement itself has been structurally transformed. Originally composed of numbers of local banks of varying size, a process of amalgamation of smaller with larger T.S.B.s had begun before 1975; but that year saw the statutory consolidation of the whole U.K. system into seventeen regional banks, four of which were in

Scotland — the Aberdeen, South of Scotland, Tayside and Central, and West of Scotland T.S.B.s. The final step was taken in 1983 when the four Scottish banks were merged to form T.S.B. Scotland, which is a subsidiary of T.S.B. Group plc, a holding company for all the arms of the T.S.B. and itself to be sold off to the public. By 1980, with some 300 branches, and total deposits equal in 1980 to over one-fifth of the clearers' total (see Table 2) and only a little below that of the Clydesdale Bank, the T.S.B. structure was clearly a 'fourth force' in Scottish retail banking. Furthermore, the traditional strength of the movement in serving small savers gave it a decided advantage in the developing market among working-class people who had previously not looked to the clearing banks for any services.[13]

But interest in retail banking was not confined to the clearers and the T.S.B.s. Between 1964 and 1980 some thirty banks of several nationalities opened branches or offices — fifty in all — in Scotland, and whilst most came to conduct wholesale or merchant banking business, those that had retail banking interests inevitably collected some business of this kind, if only from previous client connections, whilst some came with the specific object of engaging in retail business. The principal competitors here were the big English clearing banks, all of which opened Scottish offices in this period, plus one or two American banks. For the English clearers the opening of branches in Scotland was part of a wider movement to fill gaps in the banks' branch networks, in the U.K. and worldwide. None were disposed to challenge the Scottish clearers countrywide, but by opening offices in Edinburgh and Glasgow they placed themselves within range of four-fifths of Scotland's population and business, whilst the addition of Aberdeen offices moved them into Scotland's most rapidly developing region. This pattern of operation would tend to be biased to larger accounts, and towards commercial rather than personal customers, but at least some of these banks saw themselves as full retail bankers in Scotland.

At the very end of our period, and into the early 1980s, newer sources of competition were arising in some areas of retail banking. The larger building societies were beginning to offer partial current account services, with chequeing and credit facilities, and cash dispensers, in some cases in co-operation with clearing banks. Whether ultimately they would be able to sustain a full retail banking service on interest-bearing accounts was a question to which it seemed technology in the form of electronic funds transfer might eventually provide an answer. The interest-bearing chequeing accounts beginning to be offered by various money dealing firms — 'money funds' as they are termed — but also by the Bank of Scotland, raised fewer doubts on this score because of limiting conditions on their use. But the payment of interest on 'sight' deposits of these kinds was a trend with large potential consequences for all banks. Finally, we should notice the founding, in 1983, of an entirely new retail banking institution in Scotland, by a group of Scottish institutions and individuals. Adam and Company (the name taken from Adam Smith), a 'licensed deposit taker', was designed to serve a relatively small, 'exclusive' clientele, on the lines of some of the smaller London banks, offering them the more personalised attention that a small bank can provide, together with a range of financial advisory services likely to attract customers with more than average amounts of assets to manage.

WHOLESALE AND MERCHANT BANKING

The development of term loans and other forms of corporate lending after 1971 was facilitated by the existence by then of active 'wholesale' money markets, in which the banks could bid for deposits made for fixed periods of time. The 1950s saw the beginnings of a set of interrelated markets in which funds were lent in large blocks, between banks themselves (in the 'interbank market'), between companies, and to local authorities and finance companies. The markets, which grew up in close association with the 'Eurodollar' — later Eurocurrency — market, in which bank deposits denominated in the major currencies are lent and borrowed, were joined in the 1960s by the market in certificates of deposit. They also broadened considerably in the 1960s with the local authorities becoming prominent borrowers, following official encouragement to use the market rather than the Public Works Loans Board. The interbank market grew up as the many 'outside' banks in London began to lend funds to one another in ways and on terms not available in the traditional London money market centred on the discount houses.

The original operators in these markets were the so-called 'secondary banks' which, loosely interpreted, embraced the merchant banks, the large and growing number of foreign banks established in London, and various finance companies which had developed a broader lending business. In the early 1960s they were joined by subsidiaries established for the purpose by the English and Scottish clearing banks. Before 1971, the latter were prevented by official controls from operating directly in these markets, but competition for funds — especially after their hire-purchase acquisitions in the 1950s — compelled them in the early 1960s to set up 'bidding subsidiaries' to bid for wholesale deposits, at market-determined rates. These funds were then onlent, at first to their own hire purchase subsidiaries, but later to the whole range of borrowers drawing on these markets.

Following C.C.C., in 1971, the clearing banks were able to deal in these markets directly, and this access to deposits fixable for longer periods than retail deposits, coupled with the removal of lending restraints, encouraged them to expand their term lending. This tie-up between wholesale deposit-taking activities and lending to industrial and commercial customers presents one aspect of a trend prominent in the second half of our period — the extension of wholesale and merchant banking activities within Scotland and a blurring of the distinction between them.

The institutions which entered Scotland after the mid-sixties were for the most part a mixture of commercial and merchant banks, and while they came from a variety of motives, most were attracted by the opportunities for wholesale deposit taking, together with one or more elements of merchant banking. With increased competition for deposits and for lending outlets for them, market operators (including some money brokers) saw advantages in establishing offices near the Scottish financial institutions and larger commercial companies, which were important sources of funds, and near also to the local authorities, by then important as borrowers. At the same time London-based merchant banks as well as some overseas banks identified a latent demand in the U.K. provinces for all the services comprising merchant banking: corporate finance and advisory services, portfolio management, development finance, acceptance credits and international trading and financial services. This development was not confined to Scotland, but with its exporting industries, its needs of industrial restructuring and its successes in attracting immigrant industry, the region clearly presented a potential market for these services, and more of these banks came to Scotland than to any other region. North Sea oil seems not to have been a significant draw, at least in the early stages, since the major financing of offshore operations is arranged in London, if not abroad.

The expansion of merchant banking and related wholesale banking activities has not been confined to the incomers. As we have seen, the clearing banks all had wholesale banking subsidiaries — or were associated with them through parent banks — which offered a resource base for extension into wider merchant banking business. In 1973 the Bank of Scotland decided that these services could best be marketed by setting up a new organisation, and this was given the revived name of the British Linen Bank. However, the first 'true' Scottish merchant bank to be established in our period was Noble Grossart, founded in 1969 by a mixture of individual and (non-bank) institutional enterprise. Then in 1974 the James Finlay Corporation began operations as a merchant banking offshoot of the historic textile and trading group of that name, whilst a fourth native institution, McNeill Pearson, also began operating in this field.

One element in merchant banking, though not present in all these banks, is development finance — the provision of finance to smaller, usually private, companies with potential for growth, and in some cases with a view to their eventually going public. Two early institutions operating in Scotland in this field were the Industrial and Commercial Finance Corporation (I.C.F.C.) and Glasgow Industrial Finance (Development) Ltd. (G.I.F.(D.)). The latter was set up in 1948 by a group of Scottish investment trusts along with an issuing house, Glasgow Industrial Finance (G.I.F.), to arrange new issues of shares or public flotations of private companies, for native Scottish enterprises. G.I.F.(D.) seems to have been before its time — at any rate it found smaller scope for its activities than had been expected, it was not able to operate on the scale that this difficult and risky area of finance demands, and in 1964 it was taken over by I.C.F.C.

I.C.F.C was established in 1946 by the English clearing banks, the Scottish joint-stock banks and the Bank of England, as a finance company providing development finance for small growing companies whose capital needs could not be met from existing sources such as the banks themselves, or the new issues market.[14] In the 1950s Scotland accounted for a relatively low proportion — under 7 per cent — of the I.C.F.C.'s total lending, but in the 1960s this increased, and by the early 1980s was 10 per cent. By then the I.C.F.C. had been combined with other companies with the same parentage to form the Investors for Industry Group, a group which offers the range of services of a typical merchant bank.

Finally in the area of merchant banking we should note here the important place in Scottish finance which the Scottish Development Agency assumed as a financier of new ventures as well as of not-so-new enterprises in need of restructuring: a full account of the Agency's various roles is reserved for Chapter 10.

THE BANKS, INTERNATIONAL BANKING AND NORTH SEA OIL

In the last two decades of our period there were a number of important financing developments in which the Scottish banks participated. The 1970s saw the joining of banks in large international syndicates to finance specific large-scale projects, of which the development of offshore oil and gas fields in the North Sea presented important examples. Some of these syndicates were based on international groupings or 'clubs' of banks which co-operated by pooling expertise and facilities in various aspects of international banking. In other cases international groups established 'consortium banks' to conduct large-scale international financing frequently of a specialised or regional nature on a continuing basis. A prominent example of the latter is the International Energy Bank which specialises in financing energy-related projects, and of which the Bank of Scotland was a promoter along with European partners.

Much consortium lending by British banks is made in currencies other than sterling, the member contributing either from foreign currency deposits made with them, or from funds borrowed in the Eurocurrency market. However, the borrowing and lending of currencies, which grew remarkably in the 1970s (for the Scottish banks from almost nothing), was by no means confined to consortium activities. So, the Scottish banks made currency loans for the financing of North Sea operations and to meet the needs of other borrowers, for example overseas companies established in Scotland, and indeed the Treasury itself in 1974 and 1975.[15]

All three clearing banks have been heavily involved in the finance of North Sea oil and gas-related developments, and through a variety of channels. Besides the syndicated loans referred to, they were involved through traditional lending channels, as well as through less traditional — in some cases quite novel — equity participations, and through their development finance and leasing subsidiaries. In the mid-1970s they were estimated to have some

£200-£300m. committed to oil-related activities; and there is no question that all the Scottish banking institutions showed great initiative and flexibility in meeting the opportunities created by the offshore developments, and that the offshore experience greatly extended their financial expertise and range.

THE BUILDING SOCIETIES

The clearing banks' most potent competitors in the market for retail deposits are the building societies and, as we have seen, by the end of our period they were beginning to offer partial current account services. The indigenous building society movement has always been weak in Scotland. There has been no lack of Scottish societies: in 1900 there were 140, but even this was only 6 per cent of the total number in Great Britain. By 1950, in line with a national trend towards concentration, the number had declined to 45, and in 1980 it was down to 14. But the striking fact is that no major institution had emerged from the movement in Scotland.[16] There was only one Scottish-based institution of any size, the Dunfermline; this society, which operated wholly within Scotland, through 19 branch offices, had £70m. of assets in mid-1979, which at that time placed it somewhere below fiftieth in order of size. Of the other 13 societies with head offices in Scotland, all but one operated from a single office.

Table 5. *Building Societies in Scotland, 1965-1980*

Year	No. of Scottish-based societies	No. of non-Scottish societies with offices in Scotland	Total No. of all society offices in Scotland
1965	30	16	98
1970	30	16	130
1980	14	29	399

Source: Building Societies Year Books.

The outcome of this situation was that by the end of the 1970s the undoubted importance of the building societies in Scotland, in the financial and housing markets, was sustained almost entirely by non-indigenous institutions operating through a rapidly growing number of branch offices, and an even larger number of agencies. As Table 5 shows, between 1965 and 1980 the number of non-indigenous societies with full branches in Scotland doubled, whilst branch offices quadrupled. Between 1970 and 1980 Scotland's proportion of the total number of branches rose from 5 to 7 per cent, indicating a particularly fast rate of expansion. One reason for this fast growth was the well-developed market for small savings which Scotland offered, a market in which large national societies were clearly able to compete.

However, equally attractive was the comparatively low, but rising, level of owner-occupation and the opportunities this offered the societies to extend their mortgage lending, and further the aims of the movement as a promoter of home ownership. An indication of the buoyancy of Scottish demand for housing finance appears in the figures of the sources and uses of building society funds in Scotland, as reported by the Building Societies Association (B.S.A.) and shown in summary form in Table 6.

Table 6. *Building Societies: Supply of and Demand for Funds in Scotland*

£ millions

1 Years	2 Total Funds Available[1]	3 Contribution to Liquidity	4 Net Funds Available = 2-3	5 Lending	6 Surplus (+) or Deficit (−) = 4-5
1965-69	384	43	341	281	60
1970-73	730	97	633	549	84
1974	213	76	137	186	−49
1975	389	86	303	310	−7
1976	360	—	360	396	−35
1977	587	164	423	450	−27
1978	530	−18	548	579	−31
1979	604	58	546	595	−49
1980	703	128	575	685	−110
1981	809	80	729	840	−111
1982	1,055	186	869	1,076	−207

Source: Building Societies Association Bulletin.

Notes: 1. Net receipts of deposits, plus interest credited and repayments of principal.
2. Estimates derived from the annual changes in aggregate liquid reserves of the movement, and an apportionment of these changes to the societies' Scottish operations.

It has tended to be assumed that the activities of the movement have led to a net outflow of funds from Scotland.[17] From the figures presented in Table 6, it appears that this was only unequivocally the case up to 1973. In 1974, the figures (see column 6) show the country as moving into net deficit on building society fund flows, though in most years this was only after reducing the gross funds available by estimated contributions to central liquid reserves (see column 3). What the figures certainly indicate is that since 1973 Scotland has attracted a large share of lending relative to the quantity of funds accruing from the societies' Scottish operations.

FINANCE HOUSES

Finance houses formed another important group of banking-type institutions, engaged principally in the extension of instalment credit to finance the purchase of producers' and consumer's goods. The hire-purchase finance of cars was a big part of their business, but the financing of ships, aircraft, vehicles and heavy plant, either through conventional extended credit, or through 'leasing', increased greatly in the 1970s. Before the secondary banking crisis of 1974-75,[18] finance houses obtained some funds by way of deposits from the public. Following that episode this source, never large, shrank further, and the houses relied on the banks and the wholesale money markets. In February 1980, 3 per cent of the Scottish banks' advances — £115 million — was lent to finance houses.

Most finance houses operated nationally through branch offices and field agents. The main Scottish involvement in this area of financial enterprise was through the ownership interests which all Scottish banks acquired in finance houses in the 1950s. These interests were mostly in companies based outside Scotland, and there was in fact only one major finance house, Lloyds and Scottish, with its head office in Scotland. This company, in 1980 about the third largest in the U.K., was owned jointly by Lloyds Bank and the Royal Bank of Scotland, the latter's interest, incidentally, deriving from the original pioneering acquisition of the Commercial Bank of Scotland.

INSTITUTIONS IN LONG-TERM FINANCE: INSURANCE

Insurance is an area of financial enterprise in which Scotland has traditionally been prominent, especially but by no means wholly in ordinary life assurance. In 1980 the Associated Scottish Life Offices (A.S.L.O.) had nine members, six of them based in Edinburgh, three in Glasgow; and this group was reckoned to account for about one-sixth of the life assurance and other business, notably pensions business, conducted by all British life offices. In the other main branch of life assurance, 'industrial' or 'home service' assurance, Scottish institutions have been much less active; in 1950 there were only three small collecting societies, based in Glasgow, and a subsequent merger reduced them to two.

In another main branch of insurance, 'general' insurance — a term covering such business as accident, fire and motor insurance — Scottish companies have been active, and indeed the Perth-based General Accident Fire and Life Corporation is the largest general office in the U.K. In the early 1950s there were four other significant Scottish companies in this field, all of them 'composite' offices, that is combining life assurance and general business, but in a countrywide wave of amalgamations in the 1950s, three of these merged with English offices. In 1957 the Caledonian amalgamated with the Guardian, and the resulting company united with the Royal Exchange, in 1959, to form Guardian Royal Exchange which, though London-based, retained a subsidiary head office in Edinburgh. Also in 1959 the Glasgow-based North British and Mercantile was absorbed by the Commercial Union and the Scottish Union and National by the Norwich Union. Finally, in 1966, the Northern and Employers Assurance, originally founded in Aberdeen, but for long having head offices in London and Aberdeen, was taken over by the Commercial Union.

In most areas of business, insurance institutions operate in a nationwide market, and the larger U.K. companies have extensive overseas businesses. For all Scottish offices, Scotland is only a fraction of their total market: the life offices, for example, commenting in the mid-1970s on a Scottish National Party paper on financial management in an independent Scotland, pointed out that 80 to 85 per cent of their business was in England and Wales. At the same time the greater part of insurance business within Scotland has long been in the hands of non-Scottish companies, operating through branch offices and agents like insurance brokers and banks.

The products of the insurance industry changed greatly during our period. Thus, a decline in industrial life assurance was more than counterbalanced by a long sustained expansion in ordinary life business which, coupled with a strong trend to endowment assurance with its major savings element, led to a vast growth in the assets controlled by the life offices. But other business also expanded, notably group pensions schemes and, in the 1970s, 'personal' pensions policies (these cover small group schemes as well as individual policies). Yet another feature of the 1970s, stimulated by inflation and the desire to build some hedge into endowment and pensions policies, was the growth of insurances linked to equity funds managed by the offices themselves, or simply to units of existing unit trusts — creating yet more examples of the trend towards the overlapping of institutions and their activities. In these developments the Scottish life offices have been more active than average, and by 1981 the funds controlled by them amounted to over £8½ billions, or nearly 18 per cent of the total of British non-industrial life funds.

MARINE UNDERWRITING

One interesting specialist branch of insurance, conducted throughout this period in Glasgow, is marine underwriting. Much of the underwriting (i.e. insuring) of marine risks in Scotland during these years was placed through the Glasgow underwriting market. This was an 'agency market' in which brokers, acting as underwriting agents, accepted risks which they placed with insurance companies whom they represented, although in the case of hull business some portions of large risks had to be placed with Lloyds syndicates. Formerly there were private underwriting syndicates in Glasgow, but the last of these ceased in 1958. In 1980 hull and cargo business was still important in the city, though hull business was declining with the shrinkage in the British merchant fleet. By then also the underwriting of shipbuilders' construction risks had gone, following the nationalisation of shipbuilding.

INVESTMENT TRUSTS

Another area of institutional long-term finance in which Scottish financial enterprise has been prominent is the promotion and management of investment trusts and, to a much lesser extent, unit trusts. The first Scottish investment trust was promoted over a hundred years ago in Dundee, by Robert Fleming, a pioneer of the movement, and today Scotland remains the principal centre of investment trust promotion and management outside London. In 1982 the Scottish trusts accounted for over £3 billions of the £8½ billions of assets held by all British trusts; and they were located in all four Scottish cities, though with their major concentrations in Edinburgh and Glasgow. During this period the number of Scottish trusts listed on the stock exchange declined from 82 in 1954 to 61 in 1964, and to 47 in 1982.[19] However, as the 1982 figure included 16 trusts formed after 1961 (including 12 in 1980-81), it is clear that more than one trend was in progress. Throughout our period numbers were being reduced by mergers among trusts formed mostly before 1939. Most of these amalgamations were of trusts with a common management[20] and were aimed at securing administrative economies of scale. But countering this there was a movement in the final years of this period to promote new trusts with portfolios concentrated on particular groups of securities — for example Japanese or offshore oil-related or 'high technology' shares. This trend followed important structural changes in the management of the industry.

Historically investment trusts were promoted either by groups of businessmen, who proceeded to run them with managers employed by the company, or by legal or accountancy partnerships, who promoted them often as an extension of managing clients' assets, and who ran them on a management fee basis. Since the mid-sixties, however, there has arisen a number of specialised fund management groups, most of them hived off from law or accountancy partnerships, with the eventual dropping of any formal connections with these professions. The present position is that some Scottish trusts continue as 'free standing' companies employing their own management; some continue to be managed by accountancy or law partnerships; but a significant number, including almost all the recent formations, are run by some twelve specialist management groups, some of which have become limited companies.

Scottish enterprise has been much less prominent in unit trust promotions, but by the early 1980s there were some forty trusts managed by a dozen groups, divided almost entirely between the specialist fund managers referred to and life assurance offices. For the fund managers unit trust promotion was a natural diversification of their activities — as also, incidentally, was the provision of pensions fund management services into which some moved. For the life offices it was an offshoot of their development of unit-linked assurances.

As with insurance, the obvious effects of the local investment trust industry for Scotland were in the employment and income it created. But also like insurance, it did have some local financial significance, as we shall argue later.

THE STOCK EXCHANGE

Finally, in the area of longer-term finance, these three decades saw far-reaching changes in the organisation of the stock market in Scotland. The organised market in stocks and shares is conducted by the Stock Exchange, a term usually attached to a place where traders meet to conclude bargains, but which actually denotes a self-governing association of stockbrokers and jobbers. Indeed, the stock market is primarily a set of trading relationships, conducted through various channels, and a physical trading 'floor' is not a necessary part of it — a fact well illustrated in Scotland where after 1971 only Glasgow had such a venue where brokers met to trade in person (and was one of only five trading floors outside London).

In the nineteenth century Scotland had acquired five stock exchanges with trading floors — in Glasgow, Edinburgh, Dundee, Aberdeen and Greenock.[21] In 1950, all but the Greenock exchange were still functioning, but the volume of business put through the local exchanges was already shrinking — a trend associated with the declining significance of the private investor and the rising importance of the large institutions, most of them based in London or increasingly inclined to channel their dealings through the London exchange. A concomitant of this trend was a fall in the number of stockbrokers and partnerships operating in Scotland — see Table 7 — and with this the smaller local floors ceased to be viable. The Aberdeen floor ceased trading in 1963, those in Dundee and Edinburgh in 1971.[22] However, major changes in the organisation of the stock market were carried through in this period.

Table 7. *Numbers of Stockbrokers and Firms in
all Scottish Exchanges, 1964-1980*

Year	Stockbrokers	Firms
1964	202	62
1970	195	34
1980	160	18

Source: The Stock Exchange

In 1964, with the object of improving efficiency by eliminating the duplication of facilities, all the Scottish local exchanges federated to form the Scottish Stock Exchange. Then in 1973 all the exchanges outside London amalgamated with the London Stock Exchange to form a single nationwide Stock Exchange, with a common membership, a common body of rules governing practice and trading and a single list of securities that may be traded in this national market. Of course, ever since the telephone was invented stock exchanges throughout Britain have been interlinked to form, in effect, a single national market. The local exchanges, however, besides remaining active in national securities, retained a particular role in providing a market for the securities of the smaller local companies that, because of their local nature and name, were not listed on the London Stock Exchange. These securities are now listed on the general list and may therefore be traded anywhere; but such dealings tend to be localised, and in Scotland they were facilitated after the restructuring by the existence of two specialist jobbing firms which combined dealing in the securities of the smaller Scottish companies with jobbing in major stocks.

REGIONALISATION AND INTEGRATION IN SCOTTISH FINANCE

With hindsight it can be seen that the later 1950s saw the opening of one of the most eventful phases in British and world financial history, and it remains now to assess the outcome for Scottish finance in the context of the advantages to Scotland of its financial structure. In doing so it would be a mistake to concentrate attention on the home-grown institutions. For a regional economy like that of Scotland the efficiency of all the channels of finance by which it is served is important. This requires that finance and financial services should flow freely both into and out of the Scottish economy, as well as within it; and implies that the efficiency of the non-indigenous elements is as important as that of the native institutions. In fact, almost all the changes recounted here seemed to strengthen these flows, an outcome that increased the integration of the Scottish financial sector with the national (and through that the international) system. Coupled with the survival, almost wholly intact, of its locally based institutions, this arguably brought the country the best of two worlds.

INCREASED INTEGRATION

The Radcliffe Committee, surveying the U.K. financial system in 1959, saw it as less than perfectly integrated.[23] Using a geological metaphor, the Committee noted 'faults' in the structure — institutional divides which transactors crossed with difficulty because of 'ignorance, custom or prejudice' or greater inconvenience or cost. Regionalism in finance could and did contribute to such 'faulting' in the British system, and the financial developments recounted here, some of them already beginning as the Committee sat, have undoubtedly diminished this kind of market segmentation.

The Scottish banks' adoption of term lending was important, given that the retail banks remain, even for many business borrowers, the most accessible sources of finance. But particularly important was the growth of merchant and wholesale banking activities. The developing provision of corporate finance and corporate financial services to large Scottish borrowers, by indigenous and incoming banks, opened up a supply of financial products previously undersupplied in regions remote from the City of London. But the growth of wholesale banking also increased the financial integration of Scotland with the rest of the U.K., for although there was some internal circuiting of these funds within Scotland, the bulk of these operations were channelled through

London. And the same integrating effect has proceeded from the increased activities of building societies in Scotland: these have decisively plugged the country into the national markets for household savings and deposits, and for housing finance.

THE REGIONAL SYSTEM: EMPLOYMENT AND FINANCIAL EFFECTS

Besides becoming more closely integrated with the national and international systems, Scottish finance emerged from this period with its core of indigenous institutions largely intact. It remains to consider employment and the financial significance of this.

In 1981 the Scottish financial sector employed 60,000 people, or 22 per cent more than in 1971, an increase which compared with a national (G.B.) figure of 28 per cent. As Table 8 shows, the increase was concentrated in banking and 'other financial institutions'; employment in insurance was unchanged between the two years, though it had dipped in the intervening period and was rising in 1981.

Table 8. *Employment in Scottish Finance, 1971-81*

| | | *thousands* | |
	1971	*1976*	*1981*
Insurance	22.2	20.9	22.1
Banking	22.0	27.9	30.3
Other financial institutions	5.0	5.3	7.5
Total	49.2	54.1	60.0

Source: Department of Employment.

Note: Figures are from the Annual Census of Employment, and relate to the Standard Industrial Classification Minimum List Headings 860, 861 and 862 respectively.

However, any distinctive employment effects of locally based financial institutions must derive from employment in head offices and other central servicing departments. These functions produce layers of activities and employment, both within the institutions and outside them (for example in the professions and in services like printing)[24] that are absent in regions served entirely by branches of institutions based elsewhere. Thus, rather more than half the employment of life assurance offices is typically in head offices and central units, which meant that the Scottish life offices contributed about 5,000 such jobs in 1980. In the clearing banks, with their large branch networks, head office employment is proportionately smaller — probably in the region of a fifth of their Scottish employment, or around 4,500 in 1980.

But of course there are also important qualitative effects in that the head offices, especially of financial institutions, house disproportionate numbers of highly qualified and highly paid staff. During the 1960s and '70s, with the development of new services and the increasing application of electronic data processing systems, the concentration of specialist and highly qualified staff in central departments increased, enhancing these qualitative effects. These trends have also caused head office staff to increase both relatively and absolutely; and should the further application of E.D.P. halt or even reverse the growth in financial sector employment, it is probable that head office employment will prove most resistant to reductions:[25]

FINANCIAL EFFECTS

Since during these decades the clearing banks were largely engaged in the direct finances of Scottish business and households, it might seem reasonable to look in their direction for any special advantages that Scotland's financial structure might have conferred — rather, that is, than to the insurance companies and investment trusts which could not for various reasons show special preferences for Scottish investments. But this, though broadly the case, was not the whole story.

One financial advantage that the presence of the non-bank institutions may have brought was a marginal easing of the raising of long-term capital by the smaller local companies. For such companies one of the easiest and cheapest means of doing this is by an issue of unquoted securities placed privately with institutional buyers, and a Scottish company raising capital by this means would almost certainly enjoy some advantage with the Scottish institutions, who would have ready means of acquiring information about it. And this advantage probably extended, however marginally, to public issues of securities in that the Scottish institutions, again from the basis of local knowledge, would be the more ready to underwrite such issues. More directly, the indigenous institutions assisted the provision of financial services in Scotland by their support of new local institutions. G.I.F. and G.I.F.(D.), active in development finance and new issue business in the 1950s, were established by investment trust managing groups in Glasgow. Later, Scottish institutions, both bank and non-bank, helped to establish some of the newer crop of indigenous merchant banks. Such initiatives were facilitated by the numerous links that existed at board level between all types of native institutions.

However, the financial advantages to Scotland of her separate clearing banking system were more apparent and probably more substantial than those of the non-bank institutions. One flowed simply from these banks' reportedly more relaxed view of the time period of their lending than used to be customary in the south. In the 1950s the Radcliffe Committee found that the Scottish banks 'have traditionally been more willing to acknowledge the long-term nature of some of their advances and have not been reluctant to act accordingly'.[26] Later, the Monopolies and Mergers Commission, considering the proposed merger of the Royal Bank with either the Standard Chartered Bank or the Hong Kong and Shanghai Banking Corporation, was told that 'the Scottish banks [have] a good record in backing smaller projects in manufacturing and commerce'.[27] But an undoubted advantage of their being *based* in Scotland is that in their lending the Scottish banks can operate very closely to the ground. There is certainly impressionistic and anecdotal evidence to suggest that, compared with their southern counterparts, they are more flexible and responsive in their lending conduct, and this must be attributable to shorter (and fewer) lines of communication between head office and branches. Furthermore, the structural changes of these three decades must have affected favourably the competitive climate in Scottish banking. Any adverse effects of the reduction in the number of indigenous banks from eight to three were more than counterbalanced by the influx of non-Scottish banks, some of them ready to engage in retail as well as corporate business, and by the transformation of the T.S.B.s. Indeed, the widening scope of competition between all financial institutions put new competitive pressures on all the clearing banks, English and Scottish, so helping to minimise the adverse consequences that the decline in the number of independent decision-making units could have led to.

CONCLUSION

The conclusion to which this survey points is that the structural and other changes in the Scottish financial sector during these three decades were favourable to its role in the economy of Scotland. The range of financial services broadened immensely, whilst increased integration with the U.K. system diminished any remaining sectoral barriers in the market. Some deficiencies in financial provision probably remained — for example, in the supply of high risk capital to small firms — but the position at the end of the period seemed to be uniquely favourable to Scotland: she retained the special employment and financial advantages afforded by her indigenous institutions, whilst enjoying the greater range of services which the changes of the last two decades of our period produced.

How long this favourable conjuncture would continue were questions for the 1980s. Immediately after the close of our period the competing proposals for mergers with the Royal Bank revealed the dissatisfaction of that institution with its situation and scope, and in 1983 the Royal Bank Group announced the impending merger of the Royal Bank and the Group's English bank, Williams and Glyn's, to form the first truly Anglo-Scottish bank. But before this both the Royal Bank and the Bank of Scotland had opened branches in English cities, opening up the prospect of a continuing attrition of the boundary between Scottish and English banking. But a heightening competition for retail deposits coupled with technological developments in the electronic transfer of funds — developments which, by permitting other institutions to develop money transmission services, could shake up the whole retail banking and deposit-taking system — portend even more momentous changes.[28] The implications for Scottish finance are as yet obscure; the only certainty is that the last two decades of the century will be at least as eventful as 1950-1980.

NOTES

1. Following the Report of the Treasury Committee on Bank Amalgamation, published in 1918 as Cmd. 9052, an informal mechanism was established whereby all bank mergers or acquisition proposals were voluntarily submitted for the approval of the Treasury. Today, as recent events involving the Royal Bank of Scotland show, they can be submitted to the Monopolies and Mergers Commission.

2. Deposit receipts are a documentary acknowledgement of a deposit which the depositor presents on encashment, or annually to obtain the interest which accrues at simple interest. Deposit receipts are now confined to specialised uses, for example the temporary holding of clients' funds by solicitors.

3. Bank Charter Act, 1844 (7 & 8 Vict. c. 32) and the Bank Notes (Scotland) Act, 1845 (8 & 9 Vict. c. 38). The Currency and Bank Notes Act, 1928 (18 & 19 Geo. 5, c. 13) introduced modifications necessitated by the withdrawal of gold coin from circulation.

4. For an argument to this effect, see M. Gaskin, *The Scottish Banks* (London, 1965), pp. 97-99.

5. As far as branch costs are concerned, the so-called 'till-money effect' actually operated to convert the costs of till money into a fixed central cost, unrelated to the scale or business of individual branches. See Gaskin, *ibid.*, pp. 95-97.

6. Up to 1981 such requirements were for purposes of monetary control. Since August 1981 the sole continuous obligation — as distinct from discontinuous Special Deposit calls — has been for banks to hold balances with the Bank equal to 0.5% of eligible liabilities. The purpose of this is simply to contribute to the Bank's running costs.

7. Under C.C.C. reserve assets were defined as Bank of England balances, Treasury Bills, money lent at call to the Discount Market, commercial bills up to a defined amount, and gilt-edged securities of less than one year's maturity.

8. Committee of Scottish Clearing Bankers, *Evidence to the Committee to Review the Functioning of Financial Institutions*, Memorandum 1, Part 2, Appendix 1.12 (April, 1977). The figures relate to February of that year.

9. Leasing is a form of finance in which the leasing company retains ownership of the items involved, though this is usually nominal, responsibility for maintenance etc. being with the lessee. Once the lessors' costs (including profit) have been recovered, payments typically revert to a nominal rent. The system has tax advantages for both parties. In factoring, the financing company takes over the book debts of a business plus costs of collection. In both cases the finance effectively involved does not appear as a debt on the balance sheet of the company to which it is extended.

10. See J. S. Fforde's paper, 'Competition, innovation and regulation in British Banking', in the *Bank of England Quarterly Bulletin*, Vol. 23, No. 3 (September 1983), pp. 364-5. The significance of these restraints and of the effect of their removal in 1971 in permitting 'a more positive attitude towards term lending' is confirmed in the Scottish bankers' evidence to the Wilson Committee: see *Evidence* of the Committee of Scottish Clearing Banks, *Memorandum* 1, Part 1, paras. 4.7 and 4.8, p. 20.

11. *Ibid.*, para. 4.10, p. 21.

12. In a giro system the payer issues a direct order to the giro bank to transfer funds to the payee, as distinct from handing the instruction in the form of a cheque to the payee. The London and Scottish Clearers set up a giro system of their own as an alternative to their cheque system, following the establishment of the National Girobank.

13. One savings institution which is not given attention here is the National Savings Bank (N.S.B.). Originally the Post Office Savings Bank, the N.S.B. conducts a savings bank operation through the post office system, and in 1966 its headquarters were moved to Glasgow as an act of regional policy. Its presence in Scotland is very important in job terms: in 1979 more than 4,000

people were employed in the Glasgow centre. It has no particular financial significance for Scotland.

14. It was in fact designed to reduce the 'gap' in financial provision identified by the Macmillan Committee in 1931: see *Report of the Committee on Finance and Industry*, Cmd. 3897 (H.M.S.O., 1931), para. 404.

15. On the currency lending of the Scottish clearers, see their *Evidence* to the Wilson Committee, *Memorandum* 1, Part 1, paras. 5.11-5.13.

16. Two reasons may be suggested for this gap. One is the early and sustained strength of the Scottish savings banks pre-empting one side of the building societies' role. The other is the high proportion of flats in the Scottish housing stock: only recently have these come to be regarded as suitable subjects for owner occupation by the societies or their occupiers.

17. See, for example, the Scottish clearing bankers' *Evidence* to the Wilson Committee, *Memorandum* 1, Part 1, para. 3.8.

18. The secondary banking crisis involved finance houses which, in the late 1960s and early 1970s, had become heavily involved in lending to property developers. Tightening monetary policy in 1973, followed by a collapse of property values in 1974, placed numbers of these houses in difficulties. By means of the 'Lifeboat', a joint lending operation, organised by the Bank of England and financed by the clearing banks, those institutions capable of eventual solvency or reconstruction were propped up. Apart from the Scottish banks' involvement in the Lifeboat, no Scottish institutions were involved in the collapse, though some Scottish money must have been lost in it. However, previously, there had been a 'one-off rescue operation' to deal with financial difficulties of the Banking Department of the Scottish Co-operative Society. These difficulties arose as a result of dealings in the money market, and the support was shared by the Bank of England and the Scottish and English Clearers: see Wilson Committee, *Evidence* of the Committee of Scottish Clearing Bankers, *Memorandum* 1, Part 1, para. 4.49.

19. 1954 and 1964 figures are taken from H. Burton and D. C. Corner, *Investment and Unit Trusts in Britain and America* (London, 1968), Tables 6.2 and 6.8, pp. 95, 112; 1982 figures are from *Investment Trust Companies*, published by Laing and Cruickshank, Stockbrokers (London, 1983).

20. See Burton and Corner, *op. cit.*, p. 113.

21. See R. C. Michie, *Money, Mania and Markets* (Edinburgh, 1981), Ch. 16.

22. It is not known when the Greenock floor ceased trading; the Greenock Stock Exchange did not join the Scottish Stock Exchange in 1964, and was wound up in 1965. After the Aberdeen floor ceased to operate there was for a time a daily 'call over' of local stocks, with member firms taking it in turns to provide the venue.

23. *Report of the Committee on the Working of the Monetary System*, Cmd. 827 (H.M.S.O., 1959), para. 319.

24. See *Memorandum to the Monopolies and Mergers Commission* (on the Royal Bank merger bids), para. 6.10, submitted by the Fraser of Allander Institute, and reprinted in the Institute's *Quarterly Economic Commentary* (July 1981). The *Memorandum, in toto*, presents a strong view of the advantages to Scotland of its indigenous financial institutions.

25. For a fuller account of employment and possible future employment trends in Scottish finance, see M. Gaskin and B. P. R. Gaskin, *Employment in Banking, Insurance and Finance in Scotland*, Economic and Statistics Unit Research Paper No. 2, Scottish Economic Planning Department (Edinburgh 1980).

26. *Report* . . . (Cmd. 827), *op. cit.*, para. 153.

27. The Monopolies and Mergers Commission, *The Hong Kong and Shanghai Banking Corporation, The Standard Chartered Bank Ltd., The Royal Bank of Scotland Group Ltd.: A Report on the Proposed Mergers*, Cmd. 8472 (H.M.S.O., 1982), para. 10.14 .

28. See J. S. Fforde, *op. cit.*, pp. 371-3.

5

SCOTTISH AGRICULTURE, 1950-1980*

John Bryden

INTRODUCTION

The post-war period has been one of the most intensive periods of change in the history of Scottish agriculture. Both technical and structural change has been extremely rapid, if uneven in its impact. Prices, particularly over the past decade, have risen rapidly for both inputs and outputs. The labour force has been decimated as a result of technical and structural changes, of shifts to less intensive production in some marginal areas, and of increases in real wage rates. Production has become more concentrated on fewer, larger, farms and also geographically. Agriculture has also had to contend with a series of shifts in policy partly, but not only, as a result of accession to the E.E.C. and largely consequential changes in public attitudes towards the industry.[1]

We can usefully delimit three broad sub-periods. The first, the immediate post-war period, from the late 1940s to 1960, was a vital and important period of policy formation, and in many ways a quietly successful period for the industry. Not only did gross output expand and self-sufficiency improve, but net output rose, labour productivity increased by about 30 per cent (at a time of low unemployment), and prices for many agricultural commodities fell in both money and real terms. This very success heralded some of the problems of the succeeding decade, the middle period from 1960 to the early 1970s when the agricultural support system devised after the war came under increasing pressure as a result of falling world market prices for many primary commodities and increasing physical production on farms. Thus while the then Secretary of State for Scotland, The Rt. Hon. James Stewart, M.P., was able in 1952 to tell farmers that 'We must extend our tillage acreage and, as far as we can, strive towards self-sufficiency in feeding stuffs. Maximum feed from every farm must be our slogan . . .',[2] by 1961 the Chancellor of the Exchequer was saying that 'We shall have to look critically at the level of agricultural support during the 1962 Review',[3] and in February 1963 the Prime Minister referred to 'the need to re-examine the present system of open-ended subsidy on a number of commodities with a view to bringing the Exchequer's commitment under greater control'.[4] Limitations on the guarantees introduced at the beginning of the first period were brought into effect by the device of quotas, or standard quantities, for the key commodities — cereals, meat, and milk.

*My thanks are due to John Norris for help with the collation of statistics, to George Houston who read the first draft, and to Scott Johnstone of the National Farmers' Union (Scotland). The financial assistance of the Carnegie Trust for the Universities of Scotland is gratefully acknowledged.

141

Thus the guarantee price only applied to a predetermined quantity of production and if production exceeded this level, actual prices to farmers were progressively reduced. But, despite this, production of most commodities continued to expand rapidly during the 1960s.

The third period, from the beginning of the 1970s to the early 1980s, started with a shift in the emphasis of policy to meet the new conditions arising from E.E.C. entry. The most notable feature of this shift was a renewed emphasis on output expansion in an attempt to ensure that U.K. agriculture was in a position to benefit from the Common Agricultural Policy. Thus, in the 1971 Annual Review, the value of agricultural guarantees was increased by £138 million, representing 'full recoupment of increased costs of all the main commodities except eggs'.[5] The general level of agricultural prices in the first part of this period increased rapidly and the production of most commodities, particularly cereals and milk, expanded apace. However, costs also increased very rapidly after the oil crisis of 1973, reinforced by increases in demand for machinery, fertilisers and other inputs from the now increasingly prosperous end of the farming spectrum. The change in the method of supporting agricultural prices from the deficiency payment system, based on recouping farmers for all or part of the difference between target or guarantee prices and market prices, to the E.E.C. system of import controls and levies plus intervention purchase to remove any surplus on the market above market clearance levels, had two major effects. The first was to bring consumers into much sharper and more direct conflict of interest with farmers. The second was to bring the U.K. and the E.E.C. into sharper conflict with the traditional agricultural exporters, particularly the U.S.A. and the Commonwealth. A third source of conflict arose out of the effects of continuing concentration and intensification of agriculture on the natural environment, and the growing political strength and credibility of parts of the environmental lobby. By the end of the period, these effects had reached significant proportions, producing a period of uncertainty within the agricultural industry, perhaps unparalleled since the assurances given by the post-war Labour government. The cause of agriculture has been further damaged by the technological and structural changes which have taken place within it. Although the whole period can be seen as one of unparalleled technological change, the effects of this have been uneven: between commodities, between regions, and between different farm sizes. Similarly, price support and, if to a lesser extent, structural support, have been uneven in their effects. The question is whether these two sources of unevenness have been additive or compensating in their effects.

There is a good deal of evidence to suggest that the effects of technology, price support, and structure support have been additive, tending to favour arable and dairy farms as against beef and sheep farms, tending to favour larger as against smaller farms, and tending to favour the geographically more favoured agricultural areas. Research and development spending over the period has been heavily biased in favour of arable crops. Technological advances in machinery have been most marked in relation to large-scale machinery suitable for large arable farms. Price support has tended to favour cereals, sugar beet (not relevant in Scotland after 1973), oilseed rape (a recent introduction) and milk as compared with beef cattle and (until the early 1980s) sheep, and the larger the farm the more support the system gives. What is known as structures support, with its emphasis on farm enlargement and aids to full-time farms, its lack of geographical differentiation, especially important in cattle and sheep subsidies, and the lack of effective limitation as to support given to very large farms, has also had similar overall effects.

The consequence has been that the most rapid rates of output growth and of technological change have been on large arable farms which became noticeably more prosperous during the 1970s. In the less favoured areas, technological change has favoured the larger upland and hill farm with relatively dense stocking rates, ability to achieve good control over stock and grazing management, and the capacity to adapt new techniques of grassland conservation for winter keep. Geographically, production has shifted towards the South-East, and away from the least favoured areas in the North-West. A growing structural and geographical dualism has been apparent.

Thus it appears that the policy and support system designed after the war to give farmers a certain income security in the longer term became increasingly a mechanism which favoured a minority of farmers in richer farming areas. Not only did this increase the public scepticism about the claims of the farming lobby and place politicians who supported the original aims of policy in increasing difficulty, it also led to increasing apathy and disillusionment on the part of smaller family farms in poorer areas which have been threatened most.

There can be little doubt that agriculture made a significant contribution to the post-war economic recovery. Not only did output, self-sufficiency and labour productivity increase rapidly, but substantial resources were released to other sectors of the economy which, up until the 1970s, needed them. But for this growth, agriculture and the economy in general would have been less well placed at the beginning of the 1970s to take advantage of E.E.C. entry, and it seems likely that the U.K.'s net contribution to the E.E.C. budget would have been higher than it has in fact been.

However, by the early 1980s the case for policies which encourage the replacement of labour by other inputs had been substantially weakened by the presence of large-scale unemployment, and the case for open-ended support for agriculture had been brought into question by the evident prosperity of some of its most visible sections and by the scant regard shown by an important minority of farmers for what was increasingly regarded, sometimes codified, as 'good practice' by the wider community. This showed itself in the removal of hedgerows, burning of stubble, industrial farming techniques, use of hormone growth promoters, and heavy antibiotic dosage. Moreover, the changes in support systems had brought the consumer into direct conflict with farmers. Finally, the farmer, again through the effects of the support system, had been largely separated from the market, producing what the signals of the support system told him to produce, quantity rather than quality, rather than responding to market signals. By the time that E.E.C. agricultural policies came up for review in 1983, the case for greater differentiation in policies, including those which recognised environmental, regional and structural effects which were undesirable from a broader point of view, and policies which recognised the consumer, seemed, from a practical point of view, very substantially strengthened. By the early 1980s there hardly appeared to be a significant political voice in the U.K. which was prepared to speak up in support of agriculture, and the media appeared almost at one in their condemnation of it.

It was surely ironic that all of these various pressures on agriculture, and on agricultural policy makers, arose at a time when, objectively, large sections of the farming industry fared relatively badly. After the peaks reached ·in the mid-1970s, the evidence is that Net Farm Income declined in real terms at a time when borrowings increased substantially, and other costs rose faster than prices received, the rate of technological advance slowed down, and natural conditions were more than normally adverse.

1. AGRICULTURAL PRODUCTION, OUTPUT AND INCOME

Scottish Agricultural Output in current prices increased from some £100 million in 1950 to some £1,000 million in 1981. Most of this massive increase resulted from increased prices for agricultural commodities, particularly marked during the 1970s. However, significant increases also took place in the physical output of most commodities produced by Scotland's farmers; the tonnage of cereals more than doubled, output of milk rose by some 68 per cent, that of all fatstock by about 74 per cent. For arable crops, yields per hectare increased substantially; cereal yields doubled, potato yields nearly so. However, as far as can be judged from the available data, increases in the physical productivity of livestock were less marked, although apparently significant in eggs, milk and (more difficult to measure) sheep. Table 1 summarises the changes for the main commodities. Livestock and livestock products dominated the structure of Scottish agricultural output in 1950 and, despite the growing importance of cereals over the period, this remained true in 1981, as Table 2 illustrates. The fortunes of the livestock sector are thus of great significance to Scottish agriculture as a whole, the more so because of the complex production chain in both cattle and sheep which links the specialist breeders of 'store' stock, often located in poorer farming areas, with the rearers, fatteners, and finishers of stock, often in better areas. It might be thought that the old adage 'up corn, down horn' thus gives a clue to the fortunes of Scottish farming in the post-war period, but this, if applied only to relative prices, gives a misleading interpretation.

Comparisons of Gross Output, Agricultural Inputs, and Net Output over time are fraught with difficulty due to changes in definitions which have taken place over the period. According to MacKenzie,[6] Gross Output at current

Table 1. *Scotland: Indices of Total Output, Physical Output, Prices Yield, Crop Area, Livestock Numbers (1950/51=100), 1980*

Commodity	A Index of Total Output (Current Prices)	B Index of Physical Production	C Index of Prices (A/B)	D Index of Yield	E Index of Crop Area/ Livestock Numbers
Cereals	1,346.8	224.8	599.0	204.8	109.5
Milk, Milk Products	554.5	167.6	330.9	145.2[a]	115.4
Fatstock	1,068.7	174.1	613.8	129.2[b]	134.8[c]
Clip Wool	194.0	104.2	186.1	102.1[d]	109.1[e]
Eggs	288.4	133.6	215.9	140.9[f]	82.1[g]
Potatoes	516.0	83.2	620.1	174.0	47.9

Source: Derived from data contained in various publications of the Department of Agriculture and Fisheries for Scotland (D.A.F.S.), most notably *Scottish Agricultural Economics (S.A.E.)*, published annually from 1950 to 1979; *Agricultural Statistics Scotland (Ag. Stats.)*, also an annual publication which ceased in 1978; and the less informative volume which replaced these from 1980, *Economic Report on Scottish Agriculture (E.R.S.A.)*.

Notes: a Milk Marketing Board (M.M.B.) data used for the basis of this index.
b Production of Beef and Veal ÷ Total Cattle (June census).
c Total Cattle.
d Production of Clip Wool ÷ Ewe Numbers (June census).
e Ewe Numbers.
f Egg Production ÷ Total Fowls *less* broilers and other table birds.
g Total Fowls *less* broilers and other table birds.

Table 2. *Contribution of Main Products to the Value of Total Output in Scotland, 1950/51 and 1980/81*

Commodity	Value of Output (£m) 1950/51	1980/81	% Contribution 1950/51	1980/81
Cereals	12.2	167.0	10.4 ⎫	17.0 ⎫
Potatoes	12.1	59.6	10.3 ⎬ 26.1	6.1 ⎬ 26.7
Other Crops and Horticulture	6.4	35.1	5.4 ⎭	3.6 ⎭
Fatstock	37.7	428.5	32.1	43.6
Store Stock	3.7	39.7	3.2	4.0
Milk and Milk Products	31.5	180.2	26.8	18.4
Eggs	12.7	38.6	10.8	3.9
Other Livestock Products	3.2	26.1	2.7	2.7
TOTAL OUTPUT	117.4	981.8		

Source: Derived from data supplied by D.A.F.S.

prices increased by about 40 per cent in the decade to 1961-62. It would appear that Net Output increased at a somewhat lower rate over this period, the volume of inputs apparently rising somewhat faster than the volume of output. The volume of physical output of most commodities expanded significantly during the decade; production of cereals increased by some 17 per cent, that of milk and milk products by 43 per cent, and that of fatstock by 43 per cent. Cereals prices declined, but those for fat cattle and sheep increased significantly. In the following decade, Gross Output increased by about 65 per cent and, since Inputs increased at a slightly lower rate, Net Output rose by nearly 70 per cent, all at current prices. Once again significant increases occurred in production, but this time cereals showed the greatest increase at 50 per cent, with fatstock increasing by 15 per cent and milk and milk products by only 3 per cent. Production of mutton and lamb, wool, and potatoes all fell during the decade. Most commodity prices increased, including those of cereals; the price of barley, rapidly becoming the dominant Scottish cereal in place of oats, increased by nearly 30 per cent, that of milk by just under 20 per cent, that of fat cattle by 50 per cent, that for fat sheep and pigs by about 40 per cent. Evidently, then, over the two decades the corn/horn price ratios had moved in favour of horn — yet it was the production of cereals which was expanding, rather than that of meat.

The final decade from 1971 saw an apparently massive increase in Gross Output of some 316 per cent — from £340 million in 1971-72 to £1,075 million in 1981. However, Inputs increased by 378 per cent over this period, reflecting massive price increases in the range of raw and manufactured materials used by Scottish farmers, and Net Output increased by only 218 per cent. Since general consumer prices increased by just under 350 per cent in the same period (using the All Items price deflator used in the National Accounts), it is evident that Net Output fell in real terms over this last period. The increase in Gross Output was largely due to price changes. Although production of most commodities increased, all, with the notable exception of milk, showed lower rates of expansion than were evident during the 1960s: cereals 28 per cent, milk 13 per cent, and meat 5 per cent. Due to the continued dominance of livestock and livestock products, and the decline in production of some important minor commodities like eggs and potatoes, the real output of Scottish agriculture appears to have increased by under 10 per cent. The substantial rise in commodity prices over the decade — 385 per cent for barley, 340 per cent for milk, 390 per cent for fat cattle — have produced an impression of rapid expansion over this last period, but when Inputs and the rise in general price levels are taken into account, this impression is misleading.

Net Output, in the definition now employed, is equivalent to value added in agriculture and comprises wages and salaries, net rents, interest on commercial debt and the net profits from farming. The distribution of this Net Output between these 'primary inputs' appears to have changed significantly over the period. The proportion of value added absorbed by rent and interest, in particular, has increased significantly, particularly during the 1970s, while the share of the residual Net Farm Income or net profits before depreciation has fallen. In retrospect, the period from 1972 to 1977 appears to have been one of relative prosperity; value added increased rapidly, and the share of value added going to Net Farm Income was as high as 66 per cent in 1973-74. The share of labour appears to have fallen up to 1973-74, and risen again thereafter.

The increased share of labour over the whole period occurred alongside substantial reductions in the input of labour in physical terms. By 1968-69, labour input was only 30 per cent of its average from 1954-55 to 1956-57, and

Table 3. *Composition of Agricultural Value Added, 1962/63 to 1981: Scotland*

	1962/63	1966/67	1971/72	1973/74	1977	1980	1981
Labour[a]	36.0	34.7	31.1	22.6	28.8	40.6	35.4
Rent[b]	8.3	11.7	8.8	5.9	8.4	10.6	10.2
Interest[c]	3.0	5.0	3.7	5.7	5.8	20.0	16.5
Net Farm Income	52.6	48.6	56.4	65.8	57.0	28.8	37.9

Source: Derived from *S.A.E.* 1969 to 1980 and *E.R.S.A.* 1981 and 1982.

Notes: a Including inputed labour income of farms and family workers.
        b Gross Rent, actual and inputed.
        c Interest of commercial debt — excludes interest on land purchases.

although the rate of labour loss slowed during the 1970s, it has been generally about 2 per cent per annum. Relative wages in the industry have increased significantly over the period. Scottish agriculture is overwhelmingly a family affair, and it has been pointed out that the full-time hired male labour force contributed only 37 per cent of total labour input in 1975, with occupiers providing 40 per cent.[7]

2. COMMODITY ASPECTS OF AGRICULTURE

(i) Crops

The most notable change in crop production has been the growth in cereal output. Production increased from just under 1.1 million tonnes in 1950/51 to about 2.3 million tonnes by 1980/81, and most of this increase took place after 1960/61. It was barley which made the major contribution, increasing from 180,000 tonnes to over 2 million tonnes over the period. Production of wheat also practically doubled, from some 90,000 tonnes to 165,000 tonnes, but that of oats declined significantly.

The reasons for these changes were mainly related to technical changes of two main kinds — first, mechanisation, particularly the increasing use of combine harvesters which almost totally replaced the binder during the 1950s and 1960s, and which preferred early ripening cereals; second, yield advances which were particularly related to barley and wheat, in both of which winter hardy varieties were developed. Average barley yields increased from 2.75 tonnes/ha in 1950/51 to 4.64 tonnes/ha in 1980/81, an increase of 161 per cent. Average wheat yields increased from 2.86 tonnes/ha to 5.99 tonnes/ha over the same period (209 per cent). Yields of oats on the other hand increased from 2.13 tonnes/ha to 3.84 tonnes/ha, still well below the averages for other cereals, and still suffered from added disadvantages of late ripening and, normally, lower market prices.

The increase in the area of land devoted to cereals, at just over 10 per cent, was modest. The area devoted to oats declined steadily throughout the period, whilst that devoted to wheat fluctuated, increasing in the 1960s and declining during the 1970s, ending the period slightly lower than in 1950/51. Barley, however, showed a steady growth throughout, especially from 1960. Most of the increase in the overall area devoted to cereals took place in the 1970s, and this on full-time units. Perhaps surprisingly, the greatest percentage increases in the area devoted to cereals took place on farms which were classified as Intensive, Upland, and Hill Sheep Farms in the Farm Type Classification of 1968. In absolute terms, however, it was full-time intensive farms, Upland Farms, Rearing and Arable Farms and Cropping Farms, in that order, which jointly accounted for 93 per cent of the increase on all full-time farms from 1970 to 1977. There has also been a growing concentration of cereal production on the larger farms.

Potatoes are the most important commercial crop after cereals on Scottish farms. Although output declined somewhat over the period, yields increased by about 93 per cent, while the area under production roughly halved. Varietal changes have not only contributed to these yield increases but have also improved resistance to some of the common diseases. Production of potatoes has also benefited from improvements in machinery in planting, harvesting and post-harvest handling and storage. As with milk, the Potato Marketing Board was empowered to control physical imports to maintain producer prices, to intervene in the market by removing surplus stocks for animal feed and manufacturing, and also, through the issue of licences, to act as the instrument of production control. This role was weakened at the end of the transition period of E.E.C. entry, but was used to good effect prior to that. Just before the end of the transition period, producers had two boom years for prices, and roughly an additional £100 million of purchasing power accrued to potato producers over these two years. There has been a strong trend towards increasing concentration and specialisation in the industry over this period. By 1968 'seed potato crops were already heavily concentrated onto cropping farms which accounted for 76 per cent of the acreage, and since then there has only been a very small increase in this percentage. In the ware sector, however, increasing farm type concentration is rather more noticeable: cropping farms accounted for 55% of the ware area in 1968, but 58% in 1975'.[8] Potato production also became more concentrated on fewer and larger farms. Whereas even in the late 1960s over half of all significant holdings grew potatoes, this proportion had fallen below 40 per cent by 1977. Moreover, as Dunn points out, the practices of seasonal letting of potato land to merchants or merchant-growers, and of forward and contract selling pre-harvest, imply a higher degree of concentration than the statistics, based on individual farms, suggest. Dunn concluded that the benefits of the boom of 1975 and 1976 in potato prices 'have not been evenly shared even among Scotland's 3,000 cropping farms'. In fact, most of the benefit probably accrued to fewer than 1,000 producers. This means that the additional resources made available in the mid-1970s, when other arable crops were also fairly profitable, were obviously highly significant to a few fairly large cropping farms, and contributed to a sizeable investment boom at the time which may well have significantly affected machinery, fertiliser and probably also land prices, all of which increased rapidly in the second half of the 1970s.

Cereals and potatoes account for 86 per cent of the value of all crop and horticultural sales in 1980/81, a higher proportion than in 1950. Crops grown mainly for stock feed — turnips, swedes, cabbages, kale and rape (some of which are also used for provisioning of farm households) — are an important user of arable land in Scotland, and accounted for some 53,000 ha in 1980. This was a considerable reduction on the 134,000 ha recorded in 1950, reflecting primarily the shift to silage production over the period, but also some yield increases. For example, average yields of turnips and swedes increased from 41 tonnes/ha in 1950 to 64.4 tonnes/ha in 1980. Other commercially significant crops were vegetables for human consumption and, until 1972, sugar beet. The British Sugar Corporation's factory at Cupar in Fife was closed in 1972, signifying the end of sugar beet production in Scotland. The '4,575 hectares of sugar beet grown in Scotland in 1971 were mainly replaced by more cereals, stockfeeding crops, temporary grass and peas'.[9] The area of vegetables for human consumption remained fairly static at 4,500 to 5,000 ha up to the mid-1960s, after which, with improved techniques of chemical weed control and mechanisation of planting and harvesting, it increased steadily to around 8,000 ha, most of which was located in South-East Scotland from Angus to the Lothians. Since the end of the 1970s, due to high E.E.C. prices, oilseed rape, with its characteristic yellow flower, has been a rapidly expanding crop in more favoured arable areas as far north as Morayshire, but it was not recorded in the agricultural statistics until 1982, when 1,606 ha were given, again mainly in the South-East.

Table 4. *Scotland: Area of Land in Principal Crops, 1950-1980*

	1950 (000 ha)	1960 (000 ha)	1970 (000 ha)	1980 (000 ha)
Crops and Grass, Total	1,781.0	1,753.1	1,683.8	1,688.0
Permanent Grass[a]	481.4	364.2	412.3	576.5
Temporary Grass[b]	583.7	762.1	676.4	490.2
Wheat	31.9	38.3	39.6	25.6
Barley	60.8	102.9	286.6	443.5
Oats and Mixed Grain	374.5	277.0	130.8	39.0
Potatoes	76.8	61.7	43.9	35.3
Sugar Beet	4.1	6.5	5.4	nil
Turnips and Swedes[c]	116.4	98.9	56.9	44.9
Cabbage and Kale[c]	5.7	7.5	3.2	15.2[e]
Rape[c]	11.8	12.4	9.4	
Vegetables[d]	4.6	5.3	5.9	8.7

Source: Ag. Stats. 1950, 1960, 1970, 1980.

Notes: a Grass over 7 years old for 1960 and 1970 and grass over 5 years old for 1980.

b Grass less than 5 years old for 1960 and 1970 and grass under 5 years old for 1980.

c For stock feeding.

d For human consumption.

e 'Other crops for stock feeding'. Rape is thought to have fallen to 7,700 ha by 1980.

It is a measure of the importance of grazing livestock to the Scottish agricultural economy that a total of 1,126,800 ha or 67 per cent of the total area of crops and grass was devoted to grazing, conservation and fodder crops by 1980. In 1980 about 351,000 ha of grass was cut for conservation of one kind or another. Average production in the five years to 1979 was 1,034,000 tonnes of hay and 3,390,000 tonnes of silage. This compares with an average production of about 600,000 tonnes of hay and 298,000 tonnes of silage in the 1950s. In 1959 about 246,000 ha was mown, so that the area of grass cut for conservation has increased significantly over the period. That, together with increased grass yields, largely due to the practice of double or even triple cropping for silage and much heavier fertiliser applications, accounts for the increased production. In this area also, mechanisation has been important. The development of balers and handling equipment for hay and silage has probably reduced the labour input of hay or silage making to about one-sixth of its levels as compared with the 1950s when the practice of curing hay in 'coles' and storing it loose in barns and stacks was prevalent. However, silage making is relatively energy-intensive and requires, for the common technique employed, relatively powerful and heavy machinery because of the weight of wet grass to be removed from field to store over short periods. Costs of making and handling silage have, therefore, increased rapidly with energy and machinery prices in the 1970s.

(ii) Livestock

Physical production of milk increased by about 170 per cent over the period, despite a sizeable decline of about 23 per cent in dairy cow numbers. There have, therefore, been significant increases in milk yields, although figures from different sources give conflicting quantitative estimates for this increase. Figures from the Milk Marketing Boards suggest increases of the order of 45 per cent, but given the decline in dairy cow numbers recorded in the Agricultural Statistics and the production figures for milk, this would appear to be an underestimate of the increases in yields per cow on an annual basis.

A marked concentration had taken place in the dairy industry by 1981, with 45 per cent of dairy cows in Scotland found on farms with over 100 cows, compared with under 9 per cent of cows in this size group in 1961. The herd size group 60 to 100 cows has been rather stable over the period, but herd size groups below 60 cows, which accounted for 65½ per cent of cows in 1961, accounted for only 20 per cent in 1981. Only 2,174 farm units had herds in excess of 60 dairy cows, and these accounted for 80 per cent of all dairy cows and 60 per cent of all farms with a commercial dairy herd, defined as 5 or more dairy cows. In 1961, by comparison, there were 8,707 commercial dairy units, and the size group over 60 cows accounted for only 34.5 per cent of cows and 18 per cent of commercial units. Milk production has also become more concentrated regionally over the period, and nearly three-quarters of all dairy cows were in South-West Scotland by the later date. Almost all of the increased production of milk since 1950 has gone to the manufacturing of milk products, the proportion of milk sold on the liquid market having fallen from 74 per cent in 1950/51 to about 50 per cent in 1980/81. With dairying, an almost total switch from Ayrshires to Friesians and Friesian-Holsteins took place over the period, the latter having higher milk yields and the capacity to produce more saleable surplus calves for both beef producers (for example, the Friesian x Hereford female) and rearers and fatteners. Much effort has been devoted to sire improvement, particularly of Friesians and Holsteins, mainly by the Milk Marketing Boards, through progeny testing and the use of artificial insemination. These changes, together with improved techniques of meeting the nutritional needs of the lactating cow through better silage and improved concentrate balancers, account for the yield increases which have taken place. Beef breeding cows have had mixed fortunes over the period. Physical output of beef and veal (the latter is of marginal importance) has increased fairly steadily over the period, reaching a peak in 1975/76, after which some decline took place, if not to pre-1970 levels. In 1980/81 production levels were about 75 per cent higher than in 1950/51. Beef cow numbers also increased steadily up to the mid-1970s, declining thereafter. In fact, the numbers of beef cows increased from 140,000 in 1951 to 480,000 in 1980. It is impossible to measure productivity changes in beef breeding and finishing in any precise way because of the flows of cattle and calves into and out of Scotland, and the difficulty of separating beef deriving from the dairy herd and that deriving from the beef herd. Certainly if we relate the number of animals under one year old to the total breeding herd, or the total beef and veal output to the total number of beef and dairy cattle, an increasing trend is evident, but again one must remain very uncertain about the significance of such trends. Suffice to say that the indications — and they are just that — are of some increases in physical productivity over the period.

Substantial changes have taken place in the nature of beef production. The post-war period saw the heyday and decline of pedigree beef breeding herds like the Aberdeen Angus, and the growth of cross-breeding with the use of Continental breeds of bull — Limousin, Charolais and Simmental becoming increasingly popular at the end of the period. In the 1950s and 1960s, herds of black cattle (mainly Angus or Angus cross, but sometimes Galloways or crosses like the 'blue-grey') were a common sight in beef-breeding areas like Orkney, Grampian and Speyside. It seems that, through no obviously deliberate act of policy or advice, a new era of commercial beef breeding crept in, more akin perhaps to the type of circular cross-breeding to be found, for example, in Canada than to the British tradition, manifest in Bakewell-Watson-McCombie inbreeding combined with highly selective cross-breeding.[10] The use of Continental bulls has meant calves with higher growth and finished weight potential, and the market has sought dams (again, usually crosses) with the capacity to bear and rear such calves. This has meant a decline in the demand for traditional breeds and crosses, perhaps also a tendency to rear more replacements at home. An examination of frequency

Table 5. *Bulls of British and Continental Breeds sold at the Perth Bull Sales of MacDonald Fraser &*
Co. Ltd., 1969-1983

Year	Continental Breeds[1]	British Breeds	Total, All Breeds	Continental Proportion %
1969	8	1,009	1,017	0.8
1970	53	889	942	5.6
1971	0	832	832	0.0
1972	21	1,004	1,025	2.3
1973	58	928	986	5.9
1974	72	891	963	7.5
1975	100	862	962	10.4
1976	204	923	1,127	18.1
1977	366	752	1,118	32.7
1978	397	624	1,021	38.9
1979	525	559	1,084	49.4
1980	530	466	996	53.2
1981	585	422	1,007	58.1
1982	736	404	1,140	64.6
1983	908	346	1,254	72.4

Source: MacDonald Fraser & Company Ltd. Livestock Salesmen, Perth. Auction records (R. L. Fraser: Personal Communication, March 1984).

Note: 1. Charolais, Simmental, Limousin and Others.

distribution data for the period since 1961 shows some tendency towards concentration on beef breeding herds, but this has been modest by comparison with dairying. Herds of over 60 cows accounted for 58.7 per cent of all beef cows in 1981 compared with only 20.8 per cent in 1961. However, beef breeding was a very widespread activity in Scottish farming, with 13,769 significant units rearing beef cows in 1980.

As with most other commodities, regional changes have been significant. Whereas the greatest rates of increase in beef cows between 1968 and 1971 were in the South-West (+36.9 per cent), the South-East (+14.9 per cent) and East-Central Regions (+10.7 per cent), the greatest rates of *decline* from 1975 to 1980 were in the North-East (−16.1 per cent) and the Highlands (−12.4 per cent), and the lowest were in the South-West (−5.5 per cent) and the South-East (−9.5 per cent). The South-West significantly increased its share of beef cow numbers between 1961 and 1980, and both the South-West and the South-East showed a marked resilience — by comparison with the northern half of Scotland — in face of hard times for beef producers in the period from the mid-1970s. One may reasonably suggest that the former areas were those best placed to take advantage of such technological advances as did occur in relation to beef breeding and grassland conservation.

Whereas the North-East had about 16½ per cent of beef cows in 1980, it had over 34 per cent of feeding cattle, an enterprise in which it has remained pre-eminent. However, numbers of feeding cattle in the South-West have increased significantly over the period. Although the practice of feeding cattle is widespread among Scottish farmers — even in 1980 14,639 farms had feeding cattle — there has been some tendency towards concentration, with 42 per cent of feeding cattle on farms with 100 or more such animals compared with 27 per cent in 1970. The losses have been on holdings with less than 50 animals.

Sheep are one of the most widespread enterprises on Scottish farms, and are of particular significance as the principal output of the hill and rough grazings which dominate the Scottish landscape. Sheep are therefore of particular importance to farms in marginal areas. Breeding ewe numbers increased significantly during the 1950s when considerable efforts were made to improve the position of 'marginal' producers through the operation of the 1946 Hill Farming Act, the introduction of the Marginal Agricultural Production (M.A.P.) scheme and various forms of 'differential' support aimed at this group. Part of the stimulus for this came from the Report on Marginal Land Problems prepared after the war by the Department of Agriculture for Scotland.[11] From the mid-1960s to the mid-1970s, however, ewe numbers fell steadily, and by 1976 they were only about 5 per cent higher than in 1951. After 1976 they began to increase slowly again as a result of higher market prices following access to the French market and restrictions on New Zealand imports and, more recently, as the result of the more secure returns offered under the E.E.C. sheepmeat regime introduced in 1979. Nevertheless, whilst production of sheepmeat tended to follow trends in ewe numbers up to the beginning of the 1970s, it did increase significantly during the 1970s and by 1980 was about 50 per cent above the 1951 level. This suggests that there has been some increase in the productivity of sheep over the period and particularly during the 1970s. An analysis of two indices of productivity strongly suggests that there has been a slow but significant trend in meat output per breeding ewe of about 1 per cent per annum, and of lambs produced per breeding ewe of about ½ per cent per annum over the period from 1950 to 1983. Regression coefficients on both trend lines are highly significant. Thus, over the 33-year period, the trend line suggests a growth in meat output from the ewe population of about 36 per cent, and we may hypothesise on the basis of the two series that about half of this has been due to improved lambing percentages and half due to improved carcase weights. Again, some uncertainty attaches to these results because of the uncertain effects of any changes in cross-border trading which may have occurred over this period. If true, one of the principal reasons for the improvement appears to be the relative shift of sheep production from the least favoured agricultural areas, where lambing percentages are low, to the more favoured hill and upland areas of Scotland which have been able to take advantage of improved techniques of management.

Output of wool, on the other hand, has shown little significant change over the period. Wool prices have increased by less than any other agricultural commodity, falling substantially in real terms, so that whereas wool accounted for about 16 per cent of all sheep and wool sales in 1950/51, this proportion had fallen to 7½ per cent in 1980/81. The position of wool was not helped by its classification as an industrial product within the terms of the E.E.C.

Common Agricultural Policy, which has left it exposed to world market competition.

Despite the widespread nature of sheep production, it has also shown a tendency towards concentration over the period. There has been a steady increase in the proportion of the breeding flock in flocks of over 1,000 ewes, at the expense of flocks below 300 ewes. The middle range of flock size has been the most stable.

The relative position of the more marginal sheep producing areas has been exacerbated by the changing balance of overall support to producers. Until the 1970s payments on sheep per head represented a substantial proportion of hill sheep farming income. After 1980, however, the balance of overall support for sheep has shifted to price support on lamb output through the variable premium mechanism. This has shifted the relative balance of support to sheep-meat output as opposed to ewe population, and has consequently favoured the more productive areas. The cessation of support for wool prices has had a similar although less significant effect.

In the recent past, and in the forseeable future, technical changes in sheep farming seem to favour those farmers who are able to improve control over the ewe flock management through fencing, pasture management, housing, flushing, and oestrus control. It is in these areas that new techniques are emerging which improve performance and lower costs — in-wintering, in-lambing, oestrus control, development of more productive ewes, identification of ewes with twins prior to lambing and better control of feed intake, con-trolled grazing during the crucial summer growing period, and so on. These, after all, are the areas which promise commercial rewards from research and development effort. This inevitably suggests that those in the best position to benefit will be farming in the better upland or 'green hill' areas in the southern parts of Scotland and parts of the North-East. Those for whom the benefits of these new techniques are and will remain elusive will be the 'true' hill farms in the harder areas of the North-West and Central Highlands, with more exten-sive grazing, low proportions of arable ground, poor grazing and flock control, and few existing buildings suitable for conversion as sheep housing. It remains to be seen whether new support arrangements, either under the Less Favoured Areas Directive, or under the sheepmeat regime, or in some combination, will help to redress this balance by greater effective 'differentiation' of support, or whether it will be further exacerbated.

Pigs and hens stand in direct contrast to sheep and beef cattle in so far as they are now highly concentrated activities both between farms and regionally. Whereas in the 1950s practically every farm in Scotland had pigs and hens, and production was moderately spread throughout the country, by 1980, 86.4 per cent of laying hens and pullets were on only 104 production units with flock sizes of over 5,000. In 1966, only one-fifth of hens were in this size group. Whereas, even as late as 1966, 31,377 units had more than one hen, by 1980 this number had fallen to 8,735. Regional concentration of hens — layers and broilers — has also proceeded apace; by 1980 about 80 per cent of all hens

Table 6. *Units Returning Crops and Livestock in Scotland (June Census)*

Crop/Livestock	Units Returning in 1970	1982	Percentage of Units 1970	1982
Wheat	2,822	1,851	7.4	6.0
Barley	13,427	14,664	35.0	47.4
Oats	20,002	5,925	52.3	19.2
Potatoes (Ware only)	15,859	7,609	49.2	24.6
Sugar Beet	588	nil	1.5	nil
Vegetables for human consumption	1,655	1,200	4.4	3.9
Soft Fruit	1,448	835	3.8	2.7
Dairy Cows	9,667	4,311	25.3	13.9
Beef Cows	19,172	12,802	50.1	41.4
Breeding Ewes	18,574	14,599	48.6	47.2
Breeding Pigs	3,647	827	9.5	2.7
Feeding Pigs	4,119	1,066	10.8	3.4
Laying Hens etc.	19,293	7,550	50.4	24.4
Broilers etc.	1,030	347	2.7	1.1
TOTAL UNITS	38,256	30,906		

Source: D.A.F.S. Agricultural Statistics, 1970; Economic Report on Scottish Agriculture, 1982.

Table 7. *Approximate Number of Units responsible for 75 per cent of the Acreage of Each Crop or Number of Each Livestock Group, and the Proportion of Units returning Each Crop or Livestock which these Units represent*

Crop/Livestock	Number of Units with 75% of Area or Number 1970	1982	Proportion of all Units Returning 1970	1982
Wheat	1,150	780	40.8	42.1
Barley	4,400	4,725	32.8	32.2
Oats	8,100	1,870	40.5	31.6
Ware Potatoes	1,872	1,050	11.8	13.8
Dairy Cows	3,215	1,840	33.3	42.7
Beef Cows	5,372	4,040	28.0	31.6
Breeding Ewes	4,655	4,120	25.1	28.2
Breeding Pigs	903	161	24.6	19.5
Fattening Pigs	670	150	16.3	14.1
Laying Hens	377	40	2.0	0.5
Broilers etc.	22	16	2.1	4.6

Source: Estimated from Frequency Distribution Tables in *Ag. Stats.* 1970 and *E.R.S.A.*, 1982.

were in the South-East and South-West of Scotland, and places like Orkney, which had a flourishing egg business until the 1970s, produce almost no eggs now. Pigs show a similar picture: by 1982, the South-East and North-East accounted for 82.3 per cent of all feeding pigs and 86 per cent of female breeding pigs. About two-thirds of all feeding and 86 per cent of female breeding pigs were accounted for by a mere 116 units in these two regions. By 1980, only 1,164 units in Scotland had any pigs. Although producers might reject the idea, both pigs and hens have become more like an industrial product than an agricultural one. Labour-saving innovation has been very important to both, and the creation of carefully controlled environmental conditions, regular disease control and immunisation, and mechanised feeding

systems have all contributed to the increasing scale and industrial characteristics of these sectors. Numbers of both pigs and poultry have increased
since 1950/51, although both pigmeat and egg production declined during the
1970s. Although on the face of it this might be due to high cereal prices, it is
notable that numbers of both pigs and hens on the largest size units increased
during the 1970s. In both cases, the decline in this period was due to smaller
units going out of production.

With the exception of barley, the growing of which has become more evenly
distributed, the number of units responsible for three-quarters of the area of
each crop, or three-quarters of the relevant numbers of livestock, fell more
rapidly in the 1970s than the total number of units, and this indicates the
process of concentration which took place in this period. Comparison with
earlier periods is hampered by lack of frequency distribution data, but we may
infer from the evidence which does exist that this continued trends which were
apparent for the earlier period.

3. REGIONAL ASPECTS OF AGRARIAN CHANGE

One cannot pass, in space and time, through Scottish farming without recognising the validity, even today, of Carter's argument that agricultural history,
more than any other branch of the art, conforms to Simpson's statement that
'Scottish History is at bottom a provincial history, yet it has suffered from the
failure of historians to grasp this fundamental truth'.[12] Unfortunately, the data
on regional aspects of agriculture (not to say other aspects of economy and
society) are fraught with lack of comparability over time due to changes in
regional boundaries and other definitions.[13] We even lack an adequate series of
regional gross and net output. Nevertheless, some broad judgements can be
made on the basis of an interpretation of the available data, and Table 8 summarises the main results of such a comparison in relation to regional shares of
production of the various commodities. The most striking point to emerge is
the consistently poor relative performance of the North-West, which contains
the largest number of holdings of any region, the smallest average farm size,
and, in general, the poorest land. The 'old' Highlands region and the new
North-West Region had a smaller proportion of every significant crop and
livestock enterprise in 1980 than it had in 1950, and this trend was consistent
throughout the period, each decade showing a similar pattern. No such consistent picture emerges for the other regions which tended, rather, to show a
strengthening of their positions in individual specialisms — potatoes, pigs,
sheep, dairying and fattening cattle in the North-West, arable crops and
poultry in the South-East, and all forms of cattle and sheep in the South-West.
The South-West has reduced its share of all arable crops, pigs and poultry,
and the South-East has reduced its interest in cattle, while the North-East has
done relatively badly in vegetables, beef breeding and poultry.

MacKenzie's analysis of agricultural output by regions concluded that

Table 8. *Regional Trends in Scottish Agriculture: Proportion of Crop Areas and Livestock Numbers in Different Regions, and Direction of Change, 1950 to 1980*

Commodity	North-West	North-East	South-East	South-West
Cereals	Down	Down Sl*	Up**	Down
Potatoes	Down*	Up*	Up***	Down
Vegetables	Down	Down	Up*	Down
All Cattle	Down	Up	Down	Up
Dairy Herd	Down**	Up**	Down**	Up***
Beef Herd	Down*	Down	Down	Up
Other Cattle	Down*	Up***	Down***	Up**
All Sheep	Down***	Up*	Same**	Up**
Breeding Ewes	Down***	Up	Up Sl	Up
All Pigs	Down	Up*	Down	Down
All Poultry	Down	Down**	Up	Down*

Notes: Sl= Slowly, i.e. a less than 1 per cent change in the regional share appears to have occurred.

Indicators of Regional Specialisiations:
*** Regional Output greater than 20% of Total Regional Output in 1961/62.
** Regional Output between 10 and 20% of Total Regional Output in 1961/62.
* Regional Output between 5 and 10% of Total Regional Output in 1961/62.

between 1951/52 and 1961/62 'the value at current prices of the gross output in Scotland has risen by some 40 per cent. Close comparison of the regional figures is not possible, but data available suggest that in the North East, South East and South West Regions the increase in value of gross output between 1952 and 1961/62 was much the same as in Scotland as a whole. In the East Region, however, it was more, and in the Highland region, less, than average'.[14]

Work on the 1971/72 figures for the Highlands and Islands concluded that 'it seems that over the period 1951/52 to 1971/72 a significant decline occurred in the share of Scottish Output coming from the Highland region', although the extent of the decline over the period 1961/62 to 1971/72 was moderated by relative improvements in production grants of special significance to the Highlands and in prices of sheep and cattle relative to other commodities.[15] In the period 1971/72 to 1980, on the other hand, not only did the share of the North-West decline in every significant indicator of physical output for individual products and, by inference, in gross output in physical terms, but relative prices moved against the region's main commodities, production grants of special significance to the region were eroded by comparison with those more generally available, and technological advances in the main commodities, sheep and cattle, seem to have been relatively favourable to other more fertile areas in addition to being more favourable generally to arable and intensive products produced, predominantly, elsewhere in Scotland. These factors suggest that the relative position of the North-West in terms of gross and net output deteriorated significantly in the final period from 1971/72 to 1980. No such firm conclusions can be reached for other regions, although it seems likely that the South-East has yet again improved its position whilst that of the North-East and the North-West has remained roughly as before.

It is obvious, then, that the changes within Scotland are not uniform across or even within regions or commodity groups, and this lends weight to Carter's argument that local studies are important for improving our understanding of agrarian change. The changes have not just been the effect of 'market forces' either; policy — at National and E.E.C. levels — has also had an important influence, as have such things as agrarian structure and the pattern of land ownership and control. Thus, the erosion of 'differential' support mechanisms for marginal land, much of which was in the North-West, has had an impact on the relative position of marginal farms as they were defined in the immediate post-war period, and the bias within research spending has favoured arable crops and the better upland and hill farms. Within regions, patterns of change also differ from area to area. In the North-West, for example, the largest declines in livestock numbers took place on the large estates rather than in the crofting areas, and the evidence for the Lochaber area of the North-West showed that in the period 1963 to 1974 most of the decline in livestock units carried in the area could be accounted for by only six units, each with over 5,000 ha, and that these units accounted for one-third of the loss of employment in the area over this period.[16]

4. FARM LABOUR

The regular farm labour force declined by some 53,000, or 60 per cent, from 1950 to 1980, and the casual and seasonal workforce by nearly 11,000, or 66 per cent. Occupiers accounted for about 40 per cent of the agricultural labour input in Scotland by 1977, and that proportion rose from about 30 per cent in 1960. Moreover, whereas only about 20 per cent of regular male workers were members of the occupier's family in the early 1960s, this approached 25 per cent by the later date. The converse, however, was true of female workers and, overall, the proportion of male and female regular workers taken together who are members of the occupier's family has declined gradually. Dunn pointed out that 'if the full time hired male labour force is taken to represent the main career groups of workers, it is particularly noteworthy that it now contributes only 37 per cent of the total labour input (and is represented on only 30 per cent of agricultural holdings.[17] Most farms in Scotland therefore depend on the occupier and his or her family for their labour input. Although average wages for agricultural labour in 1983 were still somewhat lower than those for industrial labour, the relative wages of agricultural labour improved significantly over the period, rising more rapidly than most other sectors of the labour force other than miners. Minimum wages are set annually (sometimes more often) by the Agricultural Wages Board in Scotland, a Board comprising representatives of farmers, agricultural labour, and the civil service. There are few significant regional variations in earnings of farm labour. According to survey data, general agricultural workers earned an average of £10.33 per week and had statutory hours of 46 per week in 1962/63, whereas in 1981/82 earnings were £80.19 per week and statutory hours were 40.[18]

The common explanation for loss of labour relates to the undoubtedly rapid process of mechanisation. The major impact of this process cannot be underestimated, but it has not been the only factor at work, and, as suggested earlier, the effects of this process have not been evenly spread across every commodity, every type and size of farm, and every locality. Nevertheless, labour-saving innovations of one kind or another have been important in every area of farming. In 1950 there were still 57,677 horses for agricultural purposes on Scottish farms. By 1960 this number had fallen to 8,383 and by 1970 to 1,402. Tractors, on the other hand, increased from about 37,000 in 1950 to 60,000 in 1961, after which they remained at about this level, although important changes took place in both the average size (horse power) of tractors and in their capacity to undertake additional tasks through the development of the three-point linkage and hydraulic drive systems, pioneered by Harry Ferguson.[19] Many of the labour-saving items of machinery followed the introduction and development of the tractor during the 1950s and early 1960s — hay and straw balers expanded rapidly during the 1960s, as did forage harvesters for silage, which were almost unknown in the 1950s. As noted before, the combine harvester for cereal harvesting began to replace the old binder during the 1950s, but the main period of expansion was during the 1960s. This development was paralleled by an expansion in the number of ventilated silos, bins and floors for grain storage which was a necessary accompaniment to the move from storage in the sheaf and stack to separation of grain and straw at harvest. The use of potato harvesters also expanded rapidly during the 1960s. The loss of labour implied directly through the replacement of horses with tractors was therefore quickly followed by further heavy losses related to the development of the tractor and crop-harvesting equipment. The new methods of harvesting and storage and handling bulk and concentrate feeding stuffs required and allowed the development of new methods of keeping livestock. However, during the 1970s, when the rate of labour loss began to slow down, it was evident that the process of labour replacement through mechanisation was slowing down.

The effect of these changes on the farm, and particularly on the arable farm, in Scotland was dramatic. I have a photograph taken as a boy in about 1953 on an arable farm in Perthshire at haymaking time. There are nine people, excluding myself, in the photograph, and the records show that we were harvesting about 25 acres. Today, the same area for hay or silage would probably be handled by one man.

But these were not the only changes which led to labour losses. That same farm still had a regular labour force of four in 1970, necessary because it had some ten separate enterprises on its 160 arable acres. However, during the 1970s these ten separate enterprises were reduced to two or three, the predominant one being cereals, and the labour force was reduced to about one. Moreover, even although that farm provided a perfectly adequate family income in 1970, it has since been amalgamated with another farm. The shift to specialisation on arable farms concentrated labour requirements at certain peak periods, and made the use of contractors for spraying and harvesting more prevalent. Even if many would still argue the technical merits of mixed cropping and rotations, the economic rationale, the spreading of risks from both weather and market conditions, was eroded by greater certainty of return, firstly by the system of guaranteed prices and, perhaps more significantly, by E.E.C. entry in the early 1970s. The shift in the relative importance of different farm enterprises, with different labour requirements, has also had some impact. Bryden and Houston, comparing the labour requirements in 1951 and 1973 with the use of standard man day coefficients, concluded that 'changes in the relative importance of different farming enterprises would have led to a lower requirement for labour on farms in 1973 than in 1951, irrespective of technological and other changes. In the Crofting Counties the drop in theoretical labour required was of the order of 2,550, whilst in Scotland it was of the order of 4,600'. By comparison, productivity changes over the period accounted for the loss of around 4,800 full-time jobs or their equivalent in the Crofting Counties, and 45,300 or thereby in Scotland.[20] Evidence for Morvern and Lochaber suggests that, at least in the context of the West Highlands, rates of labour loss were highest on holdings of over 2,500 ha in extent, and this is confirmed by an analysis of changes in 25 parishes of the Highlands and Islands which experienced a decline in livestock units over the period from 1968 to 1978.[21]

5. FARM STRUCTURE

Scotland had, in 1980, 31,413 significant agricultural units and a further 18,332 insignificant units which were excluded from the agricultural statistics after 1973 and which had less than 40 standard man days of work. Since 1950, between 20 and 25 thousand holdings appear to have either gone out of production or been amalgamated in Scotland. This loss of holdings has occurred in every size group except the largest; only the number of farms with over 200 hectares of arable land has actually increased over the period. Between 1970 and 1977 alone, large farm units with over 1,250 standard man days each (about 5 man years) increased their share of production by about 20 per cent, to 60 per cent of the total, and their share of arable land from 45 to 52 per cent of the total.

Ignoring the insignificant holdings, the greatest loss of holdings was in North-East and South-East Scotland, the lowest loss in the North-West. This latter fact is due largely to the protected nature of crofting tenure, which is unique to the North-West and Argyll (the old crofting counties). Of the 31,413 units and 5,579,446 hectares of agricultural land, 274 units and 2,308,283 hectares were tenanted or mainly so. In 1959 there were 61,911 units recorded in the June census of which 38,790 were tenanted or mainly so. Taking the modifications to the census coverage into account, we may estimate that some 12,531 tenanted units were lost in this period, and that this accounts for all of the loss of holdings in this period. Despite this very high rate of loss, the tenanted sector in Scotland, accounting as it does for 45 per cent of holdings and 41 per cent of land, is still very significant.

Why has a loss of this magnitude in let farms taken place? In October 1945, the three Farmers' Unions of England, Scotland and Wales met and agreed upon four main principles of policy, one of which was 'Efficiency in husbandry and estate management, with security of tenure for the good farmer'.[22] No doubt this statement was somewhat weaker than the Scottish farming leaders would have wished, and the 1947 Agriculture Act, whilst giving improved security to tenants by removing from the landlord the decision as to whether an efficient tenant could be evicted, left some sizeable loopholes which remained unsolved, and were a source of much acerbity with the Landowners' Federation until the 1967 Act, which gave security of tenure to heirs and successors and put the onus on the landlord to establish a need to deny these rights and resume land, other than for forestry, a problem which has remained. Farmers had fought hard for security of tenure, but it has undoubtedly been an important factor in the loss of tenanted farms in recent years, for the principal reason that tenanted land has its value on the market discounted by as much as 60 per cent compared with land in vacant possession. Estates have therefore taken tenanted farms falling vacant into their own hands, attempting to farm larger and larger units themselves. Measures which had benefited a generation of existing tenants were increasingly seen as being an important part of the cause of losses of farms and farm families in rural areas, which had social and economic effects both within and beyond farming. The problem — not least for the Farmers' Union — is how to reverse the loss of farms without losing the hard-won benefits of security of tenure.

6. SOME CONCLUDING REMARKS

In conclusion one might highlight six main themes which seem, from this near viewpoint, to be significant in any account of Scottish agriculture in the post-war period. First is the expansion of output, undoubtedly substantial, which has taken place. Second is the significant reduction in labour input over the period. Third is the phenomenon of differential technical progress, favouring some types of crop and livestock products over others, some types of farm over others, and some regions, or parts of regions, over others. Fourth is the growing structural dualism within agriculture, with the loss of small and medium family farms and the growth of large farms. Fifth is the growing spatial dualism between rich and poor agricultural regions. Sixth, and very significant, is the changing policy, and political, framework within which agriculture has had to function.

NOTES

1. See also M. Tracy, *Agriculture in Western Europe: Challenge and Response, 1880-1980* (2nd edition, London, 1982). This volume gives an excellent account of the development of E.E.C. agricultural policy formation.

2. The Rt. Hon. James Stewart, M.P., Secretary of State for Scotland. Foreword to the *Annual Review of the National Farmers' Union of Scotland* (Edinburgh, 1952).

3. The Rt. Hon. Selwyn Lloyd, M.P., Chancellor of the Exchequer, reported in the *Farming Leader*, Edinburgh, 1 September 1961.

4. Harold MacMillan, Prime Minister, reported in the *Farming Leader*, April 1963.

5. *Annual Review and Determination of Guarantees*, 1971. Cmd. 4623 (H.M.S.O., 1971).

6. A. M. MacKenzie, 'Agricultural Output in Scotland by Regions, 1961/1962', *Scottish Agricultural Economics (S.A.E.)*, Vol. XV, p. 336, Department of Agriculture and Fisheries for Scotland (D.A.F.S.) (Edinburgh, H.M.S.O., 1965).

7. J. M. Dunn, 'Some Aspects of the Structure of the Agricultural Labour Input', *S.A.E.*, Vol. XXVI, pp. 8-9, D.A.F.S. (Edinburgh, H.M.S.O., 1976).

8. J. M. Dunn, 'The Changing Pattern of Scottish Potato Production', *S.A.E.*, Vol. XXVII, p. 98 *et seq.*, D.A.F.S. (Edinburgh, H.M.S.O., 1977).

9. N. F. Toulouse, 'Some Aspects of Land Use Changes in Relation to Sugar Beet and Peas, 1971-75', *S.A.E.*, Vol. XXVII, pp. 96-97, D.A.F.S. (Edinburgh, H.M.S.O., 1977).

10. A. Fraser, *Beef Cattle Husbandry* (London, 1959 rev. ed.). Robert Bakewell (1726-1795) practised, some say initiated, selective inbreeding used by Hugh Watson (1789-1865) and William McCombie (1805-1880) in the development of the Aberdeen-Angus breed.

11. *Scotland's Marginal Farms* (H.M.S.O., 1947). The report quantified the problem of marginal farming in Scotland and made tentative recommendations for enlargement/amalgamation, encouragement to make better use of advisory services, improved financing, afforestation, and the encouragement of part-time occupations outside agriculture in marginal areas.

12. W. D. Simpson, *The Castle of Kildrummy* (Aberdeen, 1923), cited in Ian Carter, *Farm Life in North East Scotland, 1840-1914* (Edinburgh, 1979). The holding of such a position is surely not to deny the need for more global generalisations.

13. For statistical purposes, Scotland is now divided into four agricultural regions — the North-West (broadly the old Crofting Counties except Argyll, and including all of the Highland Region, the Western Isles, Orkney and Shetland), the North-East (Grampian Region), the South-East (Tayside, Fife, Lothian and Borders Regions) and the South-West (Central Region, Strathclyde, Dumfries and Galloway). Prior to the changes in Regional Government in 1975, there were five agricultural regions — Highlands, North-East, East-Central, South-East and South-West, and separate figures were given in published statistics for the Crofting Counties. None of these 'old' regions coincides exactly with any of the 'new' regions, but the core of the new N.W. region is the old Highlands region, that of the new N.E. region is the old N.E. region, and that of the new S.W. region is the old S.W. region, so that, for many purposes, broad trends can be roughly compared.

14. A. M. MacKenzie, *loc. cit.*

15. J. Bryden and G. Houston, *Agrarian Change in the Scottish Highlands*, Glasgow University Social and Economic Research Studies No. 4, p. 6 (1976).

16. D. Turnock, *et al*, *The Lochaber Area — A case study of changing rural land use in the West Highlands of Scotland*, Geographical Field Group Regional Studies, No. 20 (Leicester, 1978). My conclusions are based on an analysis of the farm survey data relating to 1963 and 1974 and recorded in the report of the above study.

17. J. M. Dunn, *loc. cit.* (1976).

18. From the regular series, Scottish Farm Workers' Hours and Earnings, *S.A.E.*, Vol. 14 (1964); *Economic Report on Scottish Agriculture*, Table A 11 (Edinburgh, H.M.S.O., 1982).

19. C. Fraser, *Harry Ferguson, Inventor and Pioneer* (London, 1972).

20. J. Bryden and G. Houston, *op. cit.*, p. 84.

21. Highlands and Islands Development Board (n.d.).

22. *Annual Report*, National Farmers' Union (Scotland) (Edinburgh, 1946).

6
THE SCOTTISH LABOUR MARKET

Laurie Hunter

1. INTRODUCTION

The title of this chapter at once prompts the question: in what sense can we speak of 'the Scottish labour market'? Does such a concept make sense? Some might argue that it does not. Thus the macroeconomist could argue that Scotland is simply an administrative region of the United Kingdom, subject to the influence of national economic policies. In that light, Scotland is just one spatial area which is part of a national labour market system. Arguably, the dominant changes in the Scottish economy over the last thirty years have been those stemming from national political and economic decisions. Divergences between the behaviour of the Scottish and national labour market would therefore be slight and a distinctive analysis of the Scottish labour market dimension unnecessary.

An alternative view might be that the Scottish labour market has no significance in its own right because it is simply an aggregation of local labour markets, each with its own characteristics, such as its industrial and occupational composition, its population density and degree of urbanisation, its particular travel-to-work patterns and other spatial linkages. On this view, differences *between* local labour markets in Scotland would be just as sharp and possibly more important in analytical terms than differences between Scotland and any other part of the United Kingdom. Thus, on the one view, the Scottish labour market is no more than a sector of a U.K. national market, sharing (as it happens) many of the features of that national market and certainly subservient to the same influences from economic policy; and on the other, it is simply a convenient aggregation of a variety of local markets which provide the principal context for decision-taking on both the demand and supply sides of the market place.

To recognise some validity in these arguments, however, does not mean that a study of the Scottish labour market, particularly a historical study, is without interest. Because of the differences among regions in industrial structure, in geographical and geological features, in institutional arrangements, and probably also in social and cultural traits, labour market behaviour and response to general stimuli are likely to show some pattern of systematic variation. In addition, differences in the performance of regional economies, with their associated consequences in economic welfare terms, have often persuaded governments to devise policy measures which are intended to offset the disadvantages or difficulties of certain geographical areas. Thus, over much of the last thirty years, regional economic policies have played a prominent part in the spatial distribution of employment opportunity, and Scotland has been one of the regions which has been the focus of these measures.

In developing this essay, we will have the opportunity to reflect both on the links between the Scottish and the U.K. labour market, and on the differences between local labour markets within Scotland. Over the last thirty years or so, the Scottish economy has experienced major changes, as old-established industries have declined, and as technological change has produced new industries and transformed the production processes and employment structure of others. These changes have been reflected to a large degree in the labour market, and increasing attention has been paid by economists to the way in which economic policies impact on the labour market, with the result that the economic theory of labour markets, and the empirical study of labour market processes have proceeded apace, especially since the mid-1960s. However, although it would be instructive to apply much of this new-found understanding — which is not to say that there are not many problems left! — for the present purpose, this challenge has to be refused. The data which would be required to provide the raw material for such an analysis are quite simply lacking for much of the period under examination, and it is only quite recently that data sets adequate to the demands of the new thinking have begun to become available.

Thus for the most part we will adopt a fairly conservative approach, in which we begin in Section 2 by looking at the growth and development of the labour force. In Section 3 we examine the changing structure of employment, while Section 4 discusses the implications for unemployment and migration. Next, attention is turned in Section 5 to the matter of pay, a context in which collective bargaining plays a significant role. This leads into a discussion of the industrial relations dimensions of the Scottish labour market in Sections 6 and 7. At that point, the main conclusions can be summarised.

Three further points should be made by way of introduction. First, it is not possible in the present compass to provide a detailed treatment of many short-term variations which have occurred over the period. Thus the treatment must at times be in broad-brush style. Second, the problems of achieving a satisfactory level of consistency in statistical series are formidable, and in some cases virtually insuperable. In general, major breaks in statistical series will be pointed out, but minor disruptions will often be ignored, in the spirit of the broad-brush treatment. Third, it may be useful to conceive of the period as a whole as comprising three main phases, broadly corresponding with the separate decades. The 1950s were mainly characterised by post-war recovery gradually merging towards the end of the decade into a period in which living standards were rising and full employment existed. As the 1960s progressed, however, increasing signs of strain on the national economy were to be seen, and with the onset of the 1970s and particularly after the energy crisis of 1973, the strains became increasingly ominous. By the end of the period the real costs of recurrent crises were being displayed, and at appropriate points in the discussion it will be necessary to comment on the continuation of certain trends as they appear in the early 1980s.

2. THE LABOUR FORCE

The primary basis of any country's labour force is the size and structure of its population. The Scottish population has in fact shown remarkable stability since 1950, resulting from a largely offsetting combination of rates of natural increase of population and net emigration, a matter to which we return. Table 1, based on Census of Population data, bears out this stability.

Table 1. *Census Enumerated Population, 1951-81 (Millions)*

	Male	Female	Total
1951	2.43	2.66	5.09
1961	2.48	2.70	5.18
1971	2.52	2.71	5.23
1981	2.47	2.66	5.13

Source: Scottish Abstract of Statistics.

From the standpoint of labour supply, the population of working age is a more precise indicator of the base from which the labour force will be drawn. For the present purpose we focus on the population above minimum school-leaving age (raised from 15 to 16 years in 1973).[1] Table 2 shows that the 15 and over population also exhibited remarkable stability between 1951-71 but rose slowly between 1971-81.

Table 2. *Population aged 15 and over, 1951-81 (Millions)*

	Male	Female	Total
1951	1.795	2.046	3.841
1961	1.797	2.042	3.839
1971	1.796	2.040	3.836
1981[1]	1.874	2.085	3.959

Note: 1. 1981 figures are for those aged 16 and over.

Source: Scottish Abstract of Statistics.

However, there have been some notable variations in the flow of young people entering the working-age bracket, as a result of the post-war 'baby boom' which entered the labour market in the 1960s, and a secondary boom which occurred in the late 1950s and 1960s, the peak effect of which came at the end of the 1970s and which, as it passes, will produce a sharply decreasing inflow of youth labour in the 1980s.

The economically active proportion of the working-age population is subject to influence from demographic, social and economic factors. Thus although the population base has remained fairly constant, we need not expect the same degree of constancy in the active population (defined as those who are

M

employers, self-employed or employed for pay plus those who are actively seeking paid employment). And indeed as Table 3 shows, important changes occurred over the period.

Table 3. *Economic Activity Rates, 1951-81[1] (Percentages)*

	1951	1961	1966	1971	1981
Males					
Economically active as % of population					
15 and over	88.5	87.1	83.7	81.4	—
16 and over	—	86.5	83.9	81.3	76.8
Total economically active (000s)	1,589	1,583	1,503	1,469	1,439
Females					
Economically active as % of population					
15 and over	33.6	35.9	41.2	43.3	—
16 and over	—	35.4	41.2	42.6	45.6
Total economically active (000s)	683	736	840	882	950
Males and females — totally active (000s)	2,272	2,320	2,343	2,352	2,389

Note: 1. Because of the raising of the school leaving age in 1972, activity rates are shown both on the 15 plus and 16 plus age group bases. The 15 plus activity rate follows Census of Population definitions, the 16 plus rate refers to the civilian employment definition, excluding members of the Armed Forces.

Source: Scottish Abstract of Statistics and *E.S.U. Discussion Paper No. 13, 'Labour Supply in Scotland'.*

At the start of the period, the male activity rate (age 15 plus) stood at 88.5 per cent. Since then there has been a marked downward trend, to 81.4 in 1971 and again to 76.8 per cent in 1981 (the latter on a 16 plus age basis to take account of the rise in school leaving age). In contrast, the trend of female activity rates has been upward, starting at 33.6 per cent (age 15 plus) in 1951 and rising to 43.3 in 1971 and again to 45.6 (16 plus) in 1981. In total, then, the active population increased by just under 120,000, but this was compounded by a fall of 150,000 for males and a rise of 270,000 for females, nearly 40 per cent.

These trends are of course a reflection of broader national and international trends, which are dominated by three factors. In the first place, there has been a continuing movement towards earlier retirement among men, resulting in a fall in activity rates at the upper end of the age spectrum, particularly during the 1970s and increasing towards the end of the decade as rising unemployment and redundancy forced many out of the labour market. Secondly, there was a rising activity rate among women, particularly married women who comprised just over 61 per cent of the female active population in 1981. The complex of factors producing this change in the female activity rate is well enough known to require only a summary here. In part, the opportunity for employment during the 1939-45 World War was a launching pad for a change in social attitudes towards women in employment, and improvements in domestic technology made it progressively easier for women, especially married women, to combine domestic responsibilities with full or part-time employment. At the same time, the full employment conditions of the 1950s and 1960s encouraged employers to create work opportunities for women. Further, the changing structure of industry, involving an expansion of light manufacturing and service employment, lent itself to the growth of female employment. The third major factor affecting activity rates was the tendency for young people to remain longer in full-time education. For men this exaggerated the decline in labour force participation; for women it offset the growth we have observed. During the 1960s the number of full-time students more than doubled from 84,000 in 1961 to 171,000 in 1971, which would have reduced activity rates by about 2.0 to 2.5 percentage points. Expansion continued during the 1970s, but at a lower rate, and the main contributory factor in the declining male activity rates was earlier retirement.[2]

It is worth remembering that, as befits the complex factors that determine activity rates, there is considerable regional variation, especially for women. However, the Scottish figures conform quite closely to the national averages. Leser (1954) observed a slightly lower activity rate for both men and women (especially the latter) in 1951, but the rate for males has converged while the female rate, on a recent estimate, now exceeds the British rate by over two percentage points.[3]

An alternative measure of labour supply is the civilian working population, comprising three categories: employers and self-employed, employees in employment and registered unemployed. Table 4 shows a growth pattern broadly correspondent to that for the active population[4] with a reduction in the male labour force of 100,000 between 1951-71, while the female labour force rose by 100,000. During the next decade, the male labour force declined slowly, but the female labour force grew rapidly by 123,000. What these figures for selected years show, however, is that after some slight growth in the male labour force between 1971-79, a fairly sharp fall was registered between 1979 and 1981; while for the first time in many years, the growth of the female labour force was also reversed. This almost certainly reveals the effects of the depression which remained with us in 1983, bringing about a strong 'discouraged worker' effect resulting from lack of job opportunity.

Table 4. *Civilian Labour Force, 1951-81 (000s) (Selected years)*

	Males	*Females*	*Total*
1951[a]	1,509	754	2,263
1961	1,527	805	2,333
1966	1,479	847	2,326
1971	1,409	855	2,264
1971[b]	1,419	831	2,250
1979	1,423	973	2,397
1980	1,420	974	2,393
1981	1,412	954	2,367

[a] Old series
[b] New Series

Source: Scottish Abstract of Statistics.

3. STRUCTURE OF EMPLOYMENT

Over a thirty-year period in which the economy has had to face reconstruction to meet the needs of a changing world and shifts in trading patterns, and to adapt to shocks such as the energy crises of the 1970s, it is to be expected that the structure of the labour force will have shown considerable change. We look first at the industrial structure in broad terms. Because of statistical problems, we begin with a distribution of employment derived from the 1951 Census of Population: the remainder of the figures relate to employees in employment. Despite this difference the data reveal a consistent and clear pattern.

Table 5. *Industrial Structure of Employment, 1951-80 (Percentages)*

Industry Group	1951*	1960	1970	1980
Agriculture, Forestry, Fishing	7.3	4.7	2.8	2.2
Mining and Quarrying	4.4	4.3	1.9	2.1
Manufacturing	35.9	35.0	35.6	26.7
Construction	6.2	7.6	8.3	7.7
Gas, Electricity, Water	1.4	1.4	1.4	1.4
Services	44.7	47.0	49.9	59.9
Total (000s)	2,195	2,096	2,077	2,072

Source: 1951 figures extracted from Leser (1954), p. 67, and relate to working population; other years relate to employees in employment, from *Scottish Abstract of Statistics* and *Scottish Economic Bulletin.*

It was observed in 1951 that 'somewhat over one-tenth of the Scottish working population . . . are engaged in primary production, i.e. in agriculture, forestry, fishing and mining', while just under 36 per cent were engaged in manufacturing.[5] By 1960 the decline in agriculture, forestry and fishing was becoming clear, and this trend continued through to 1980 when just over 2 per cent of employees worked in these industries. The 1960s saw the start of a sharp rundown in mining employment, largely due to rationalisation of coal-mining and the closure not just of many pits but of large parts of the old Scottish coalfields. By 1970 primary employment had fallen to less than 2 per cent of the employee workforce, while the 1970s saw the stabilisation of employment at this level, further falls in coalmining employment being offset by the growth of oil-related employment which partly falls into the extractive industries category. Thus from more than one in ten workers in primary employment in 1951, the situation had changed to one where less than one in twenty were employed in this sector by 1980.

Manufacturing employment, as a share of the total, held up quite firmly down to 1970 at 35-36 per cent, but the 1970s witnessed a sharp fall to just over one quarter of total employment involving a loss of 200,000 jobs. Since these figures relate to employees in employment, and since unemployment has been heavy in manufacturing, they perhaps overstate the change in the industrial structure of the *labour force* but reveal quite accurately the change in *employment* structure.

Construction and utilities have remained stable over the period as a whole, though construction predictably shows considerable cyclical variation. Last but not least, services have steadily increased their share of total employment, rising from under 45 per cent in 1951 to 50 per cent in 1970 and almost 60 per cent by 1980. Within manufacturing and services, which are the main sectors, there have been changes as striking as those in the broad aggregates. Once again, statistical problems bedevil comparisons over time, particularly because of changes in the standard industrial classification of industries. For this reason, we will proceed by discussing two separate sub-periods: 1951-65 and 1966-81.

During the period 1951-65, the economy was generally buoyant and employment was expanding. The engineering, shipbuilding and electrical goods group of industries expanded by over 10 per cent, while lesser gains were made by sectors such as food, drink and tobacco, paper and printing and chemicals. Even at this time, however, industries which were later to suffer major rundowns in employment were beginning to show signs of difficulty. These included metal manufacture, textiles and clothing and footwear. In the service sector the insurance, banking and finance group was growing rapidly, and employment in the distributive trades was also growing in the 1950s.

Between 1966 and 1981, the biggest loss in numerical terms was the metal-producing and using sector which declined by over one-third. Even heavier percentage losses were recorded by the smaller footwear and textiles sector and the bricks, pottery, etc./timber sector, with declines of over 40 per cent, while food, drink and tobacco, and coal and petroleum products and chemicals suffered only moderate employment losses. Within the metal group of industries the heavy losses were in metal manufacture, especially steel, mechanical engineering and shipbuilding. However, instrument and electrical engineering, central to the electronics sector, grew from 54,000 in 1966 to a peak of 78,000 in 1974, slipping back with the recession to 57,000 in 1981.

Another growth sector in manufacturing was the oil-related area, benefiting from the discovery and exploitation of North Sea oil. Employment in companies wholly related to North Sea oil grew from a mere 5,000 in 1973 to 55,000 by the end of 1981, two-thirds of which was located in Grampian Region. In addition it is estimated that at the end of 1979, the total impact of oil-related industry on Scottish employment was in the range 70,000-85,000 jobs.[6]

On the service industries side, transport and communications and the distributive trades experienced modest declines in employment, but these losses were more than made up by expansion in insurance and banking (nearly 80 per cent), professional and scientific services (over 50 per cent), and miscellaneous services (roughly 40 per cent). Public administration and defence (excluding members of the Armed Forces) increased by 30 per cent.

Over the period as a whole, then, the structure of Scottish employment moved from having almost half its labour force in primary and manufacturing industry to a situation where less than one in three was so engaged. Service industry employment, even by 1951 an important source of employment, had further expanded by a third, and six out of every ten Scottish employees now worked in services.

These changes in industrial structure have had their effects also on the geographical distribution of employment and unemployment within Scotland. The West of Scotland, and especially Clydeside with its traditional base of heavy engineering employment in decline, has suffered particularly while the East and North-East have been the main beneficiaries of electronics and oil-related developments. Local government reorganisation makes over-time comparisons of employment and unemployment virtually impossible, but the following figures may serve to illustrate something of the disparities involved.

In 1964, with total unemployment just on the 68,000 mark, the Glasgow Planning Region had a 62 per cent share of Scotland's unemployment while Edinburgh had 16 per cent, compared with employment shares of 51 and 20 per cent respectively. The North-East had 6 per cent of unemployment against a 7½ per cent share of employment. By 1981 when total unemployment exceeded 300,000, Strathclyde Region accounted for 58 per cent of the total compared with an estimated 48 per cent of employment; Lothian's share of unemployment was 12 per cent (15 per cent of employment) and Grampian's was 4½ per cent (9 per cent of employment). These figures suggest the continuing disadvantage of the West of Scotland in terms of unemployment, even while the whole unemployment position has worsened.

4. UNEMPLOYMENT AND MIGRATION

We have now observed that population and the labour force in Scotland have remained fairly stable over the thirty-year period, though the sex structure of employment has changed considerably. These characteristics, together with the changing age structure of employment, consequent on a reduction in activity rates at both ends of the age spectrum, are consistent with national (U.K.) trends. We have also observed significant changes in the industrial distribution of employment which have, however, had a somewhat uneven effect on different sub-regions in Scotland.

In terms of the national economic situation, we know that ongoing structural changes in production and employment have overlapped with irregular cyclical variations in activity, and that this has been reflected at U.K. level in a gradual upward creep in unemployment rates with each successive cycle, which culminated in a sharp rise from the end of the 1970s. Not surprisingly, in view of the importance of macro-economic policy measures in the post-war economy, the Scottish labour market exhibits a very close parallel with the United Kingdom situation.

Figure 1 shows the total numbers of wholly unemployed (excluding school-leavers) for Scotland and Great Britain for 1952-81, together with the male and female components of the Scottish total. The figures for Scotland and

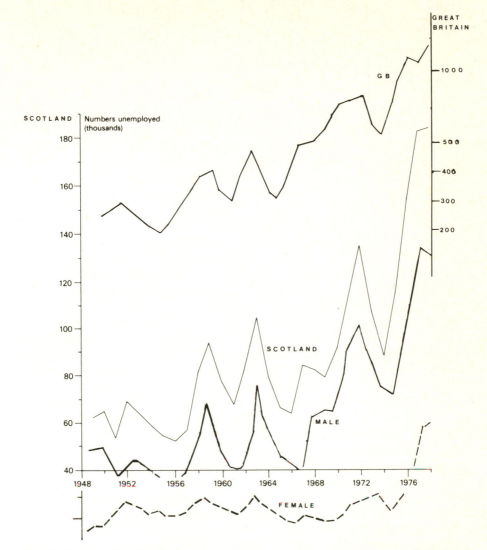

Fig. 1. Number of wholly unemployed, excluding school leavers, Great Britain and Scotland, 1948-1978.

Britain show a striking similarity, and the Scottish male unemployed closely follow the overall trend. Consistent with the growth in female employment, the pattern for female unemployment fluctuates around a stable average of under 20,000 until the mid-1970s, since when the trend has been upward, even during the period 1977-79 when male unemployment stabilised. This no doubt reflects the increased unemployment registration rate for women which followed the removal of the 'opting out' arrangement for National Insurance, available to married women until 1978.[7]

The general similarity of experience might seem to be a convincing

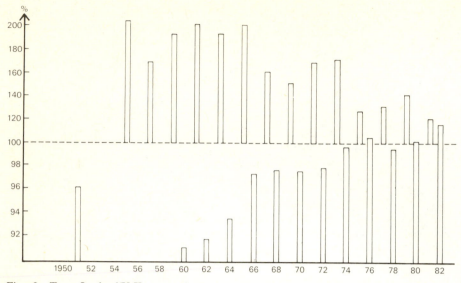

Fig. 2. Top: Scotland/U.K. unemployment relative (annual averages, 1955-1981. Bottom: Scotland/U.K. wage relative (average weekly earnings), male manual workers.

argument in favour of the view, outlined at the start of this chapter, that the Scottish labour market *per se* is not a particularly interesting concept. However, a rather different conclusion emerges from scrutiny of the longer-term historical relativity between British and Scottish unemployment rates. As Figure 2 indicates, in the 1950s and early 1960s the Scottish unemployment rate averaged almost twice the U.K. level. Since then, however, the Scottish rate has converged towards the U.K. rate, especially in the latter 1970s when the differential was reduced to only 20-30 per cent. From one point of view, this suggests a considerable improvement in the Scottish position and might be taken to be one indication of success of sustained regional policies. But against that it has to be remembered that the 'improvement' is only relative, and has to be seen against the background of generally increased unemployment in the U.K. as a whole. In other words, the improved unemployment relative may be more a product of greater deterioration in the rest of the U.K. than a signal of absolute improvement in the health of the Scottish economy.

A rather different aspect of the relation between labour supply and un-employment deserves comment. Given the relatively poor prospects of avoiding or escaping from unemployment in Scotland, as compared with many other parts of the U.K., we cannot be surprised to find that there has been a continual net outmigration of population and labour from Scotland, both to other parts of the U.K. and overseas. This of course is a long-standing trait of the Scottish people. C. E. V. Leser showed that over the period 1861-1951 Scotland lost 43 per cent of its 1.58m. natural increase in population through net migration.[8] Over the period 1951-81, Scottish natural increase in popula-tion was 741,000, while net outmigration was 753,000 (101.6 per cent). In fact,

as Table 6 shows, the natural increase in the 1950s and 1960s was great enough
to outweigh substantial net outmigration, but although emigration fell significantly in the 1970s, the natural increase rate was very small, resulting in a
net population loss of 88,000.

Table 6. *Natural Increase of Population and Net Migration, 1951-81 (Thousands)*

	1951-61	1961-71	1971-81	1951-81
Natural increase	339.3	346.3	55.9	741.5
Net emigration	−282.0	−326.5	−144.2	752.7
Net change	+57.3	+19.8	−88.3	−11.2

Source: Scottish Economic Bulletin.

Over the thirty-year period, almost 45 per cent of the net emigration went to
the rest of the U.K., but in keeping with the relative improvement in
employment opportunity in the 1970s, the rest-of-the-U.K. share fell to 33 per
cent in that decade.[9] The indications are, therefore, that net emigration from
Scotland remains a significant feature, and one which, on the whole, works as
a kind of stabilising mechanism, moderating the natural growth of the
population and labour force to a level more correspondent with the prevailing
availability of jobs. Even so, the migration adjustment has not been quite
enough to redress the longer-term Scottish unemployment differential, nor has
it been anything like high enough to counter the rapid rise in unemployment
in the latter 1970s and early 1980s.

5. PAY

Two aspects of pay are of particular interest. The first is the relationship
between pay levels in Scotland as compared with the U.K. as a whole. The
second is the distribution of pay levels within Scotland itself.

Differences in pay among regions are to some extent a reflection of differences in occupational and industrial structure: thus a region whose
employment is dominated by high-paying industries will have higher average
pay than one with mainly low-paying industries. This point was well recognised by D. J. Robertson when he tried to piece together a picture of the
Scottish pay structure in the early 1950s, in the face of a marked lack of data
— which has since been remedied for later stages of our period.[10]

In the 1950s, Robertson observed, wage rates for manual workers were
fairly well standard throughout the U.K., according to the prevailing industry-
level, multi-employer bargaining. But despite this uniformity of rates, the
evidence suggested that Scottish earnings were below the U.K. level,
especially for men: 'within industries earnings of operatives and of salaried
workers tend to be lower in Scotland, and . . . today the tendency to lower
earnings is spread throughout the Scottish economy'.[11] In part, but only in
small measure, this was attributable to differences in the industrial structure.

Applying Scottish employment weights to 1951 national earnings levels for manufacturing industries yielded lower average weekly earnings for both Scottish men and women: 1.4 per cent for men, and 1.8 per cent for women. But annual wage and salary data, for 1948, suggested an average shortfall in the Scottish case of 5 per cent for wage earners, and 6 per cent for salaried workers, compared with Great Britain as a whole.

How, then, have earnings changed relative to the British average during the last thirty years? The period divides into two contrasting parts. Down to 1960, the adverse differential for Scottish males in manufacturing had increased to 8.9 per cent while the all-industry figure was 8.4 per cent: comparisons here are with the U.K. as a whole. However, as Figure 2 illustrates, the differential then narrowed rapidly down to 1966, stabilised to 1972, then finally caught up and reversed in 1975, both for manufacturing and all industries together. Since then, rough parity has been preserved, taking one year with another.

The reasons for this change are difficult to pin down precisely. The improvement over the 1960s was in some measure due to a closer correspondence between Scottish and U.K. hours of work, including overtime. During the 1950s and early 1960s, the full employment conditions which prevailed for the U.K. as a whole were reflected in an exceptionally high level of labour demand in the Midlands and South of England, which resulted in higher levels of overtime compared with the North and Scotland. Even in the early 1960s, average hours worked by male manual workers in Scotland were up to 2 per cent less than the U.K. average, which with overtime premium payments could account for 2½ to 3 percentage points of the differential.[12] As the 1960s progressed, however, hours of work fell gradually in both Scotland and the U.K., and either because the pressure of labour demand eased more in England or because of real improvements in the activity level of the Scottish economy, a convergence was achieved by 1966 and has been maintained since.

A second factor with some bearing on the improvement of the Scottish relative is regional policy. In the first place, the 1960s witnessed a substantial influx of new industry aided by regional incentives backed up by controls on development in the more prosperous regions. As a result, major new plants were established, some of them in high-pay industries like motor vehicles, and this will have had some effect in improving the structural composition of industry with respect to pay. Again, as part of regional policy, the Regional Employment Premium, which existed between 1967 and 1976, though officially designed to provide a regional subsidy to employment, may in practice have had a leakage effect which increased Scottish wages relative to the average. These factors, arguably, lay behind the pick-up in the Scottish wage relative in the latter 1960s.

The final catch-up, achieved in the mid-1970s, seems more likely to be due to the effects of North Sea oil development and perhaps also the growth of high-paying electronics employment, coupled with the relative decline (and hence a reduced weight in the average) of low-pay industries such as textiles.

For women employees, data for the period as a whole are less readily available. D. J. Robertson noted that 'the average earnings of females in Scotland . . . were higher than those for England if earnings of married women are included and only slightly lower if single women only are considered'.[13] Data for 1949-50 relating to annual earnings showed a 0.7 per cent disadvantage for single women and a 1.4 per cent advantage over all women in the U.K. However, part-time employment was not distinguished separately, and this may have had some distorting effect. Certainly, by the start of the 1970s there was an adverse differential for both manual and non-manual Scottish women, about 2½ and 4½ per cent respectively in 1971. While the women's manual rate followed the male trend in equalling the U.K. figure in 1975 (though tailing off again in 1979-80), the adverse differential for non-manual women remained throughout the decade at around 4½ to 5½ per cent.[14]

Table 7. *Dispersion of Average Weekly Earnings, by Regions of Scotland: Full-Time Manual Workers, 1968 and 1980*

	1968				1980	
	Men	*Women*			*Men*	*Women*
Falkirk/Stirling	106.8	87.7	Central		107.7	93.1
Glasgow	100.5	102.8	Strathclyde		100.0	102.6
Edinburgh	99.1	100.0	Lothian		93.0	91.7
Tayside	94.6	97.2	Tayside		87.5	98.6
North-East	91.4	96.2	Grampian		104.5	98.8
Highlands	89.6	n.a.	Highland		104.9	n.a.
South-West	86.0	n.a.	Dumfries & Galloway		93.8	n.a.
			Fife		101.3	102.0
Borders	83.7	n.a.	Borders		83.7	n.a.
Scotland (av.)	(100)	(100)	Scotland (av.)		(100)	(100)

Source: Scottish Abstract of Statistics.
n.a. = not available.

Within Scotland, much the same factors produce wage and salary differentials as in the comparison between Scotland and the U.K. as a whole. As Table 7 shows, the regional dispersion in 1968 was fairly wide, ranging from 83 to 107 per cent of the average for men, and 88 to 103 for women: by 1980, the dispersion had narrowed somewhat for women, but not for men — though geographical boundary changes make the comparison less than precise.[15]

Because of these boundary changes, too, we must be cautious in interpreting the 1968/1980 comparisons, but for both men and women changes in the ranking order are to be observed. For men, Falkirk/Stirling, roughly equivalent to the Central Region, remained top of the league with a 7 per cent above-average earnings figure, no doubt due to the dominance of petrochemicals, a high-paying industry, in this area. Strathclyde slipped marginally relative to the Scottish average (in which its employment weighting would be substantial). Of major interest was the rise of both Highland (from 6th to 2nd) and Grampian (from 5th to 3rd) in the league — the significance of which is underlined by the fact that their relative earnings position increased from well below the Scottish average to a 5 per cent premium. Tayside and Lothian appear to have slipped in ranking *and* relative to the average, though boundary changes may again provide part of the explanation, especially once account is taken of the new Fife Region in 1973.

Because of limited statistical samples, the evidence for women is less clear-cut. Strathclyde continued to top the league, enjoying a differential of about 2.5 per cent, while the other regions appear to have moved closer to the average.

Overall, it would seem that the oil-related developments, as well as having effects on employment distribution within Scotland, have also had an effect on earnings, particularly for male manual workers.

6. TRADE UNIONS AND INDUSTRIAL RELATIONS

The determination of pay in Britain is heavily influenced by the processes of collective bargaining, which directly or indirectly affects the remuneration and conditions of employment of roughly three-quarters of the labour force. Collective bargaining, in turn, is dependent upon the presence, strength and recognition of the trade union movement — factors which vary considerably across industries, and which may therefore be expected to show some regional variation as a result of differences in industrial structure. In fact, it is far from easy to obtain satisfactory information on many of the industrial relations variables at regional level, especially over a thirty-year span. And in practice, trends in industrial relations over the period have been largely dominated by national forces which have affected regions more or less equally. It is, nevertheless, possible (and of some value) to provide some broad dimensions of the Scottish industrial relations scene, as background to the operation of the labour market.

Fortuitously, an ideal starting point is provided by the results of a survey of trade unionism in Scotland in 1947, and J. D. M. Bell's findings from 1954 provide a reasonably firm base line for the early part of our period. Bell's conclusions can be summarised as follows:

(i) there were roughly 900,000 trade unionists in Scotland in 1947, equivalent to 43 per cent of the insured employee population, compared with 43.9 per cent of the U.K. equivalent. Roughly two-thirds of the male labour force were unionised, against one-third for females;

(ii) union density varied greatly across industries, being close on 100 per cent in coalmining, railways and docks, and high among engineering craftsmen, printers and boot and shoe operatives. In the white collar sectors, teachers and civil servants were highly organised but banking and insurance were low, as was commerce and distribution;

(iii) Bell identified 125 unions operating in Scotland, eight of which had at least 25,000 members in Scotland and together accounted for 53.5 per cent of all Scottish trade union members. The eight large unions were the Transport and General Workers Union (T.G.W.U.), National Union of

General and Municipal Workers (N.U.G.M.W.), Amalgamated Engineering Union (A.E.U.), National Union of Mineworkers (N.U.M.), National Union of Railwaymen (N.U.R.), Union of Shop Distributive and Allied Workers (U.S.D.A.W.), and Amalgamated Society of Woodworkers (A.S.W.) — also at that time the seven largest in the U.K. — and the Educational Institute of Scotland, the largest of the Scottish 'independent' organisations;

(iv) regional distribution of union membership was again variable. Not surprisingly, the highest densities were in the urban, industrialised areas, with about 50 per cent of the total in the cities of Glasgow, Edinburgh, Dundee and Aberdeen. Nevertheless, over the previous quarter of a century there had been a continued and accelerated spread of trade unionism to the previously remote and unorganised areas.[16]

Since 1950, probably the most significant developments in trade union structure and membership at the U.K. level have been an increased rate of union mergers, reducing the number and fragmentation of union organisations and increasing the average size of membership; a growth in total trade union membership, especially rapid during the 1970s but experiencing reversal at the end of that decade as unemployment levels soared; and within that membership expansion, a declining proportion of manual workers and a corresponding increase in white collar employees.

The only reasonably precise data relating to trade unionism in Scotland at the close of the thirty-year period are derived from the Annual Reports of the Scottish Trades Union Congress (S.T.U.C.) which provide information on the number of affiliated unions and Scottish membership. In 1980 there was a total of 73 unions affiliated, with a nominal Scottish membership of 1.07 million, comparing with 1951 figures of 85 unions and 0.73 million members. Thus we observe a process of merger and concentration in the Scottish trade union movement which mirrors the national movement; and a growth in membership of just under 50 per cent. (This, it will be remembered, is against a background of highly stable labour force size.) By 1980, then, roughly 47 per cent of the employee labour force was in membership of S.T.U.C. affiliated unions.[17]

Changes also occurred in the composition of the 'large' Scottish unions. By 1980 there were eleven unions with a membership of over 25,000, accounting for 71 per cent of total Scottish union members. The sharp declines in mining and railway employment removed the N.U.M. and N.U.R. from the list of large unions; the Amalgamated Society of Woodworkers was now a constituent of the new construction union U.C.A.T.T; and the newcomers were the National Association of Local Government Officers (N.A.L.G.O.) (71,000), National Union of Public Employees (N.U.P.E.) (64,000), Electrical, Electronic, Plumbing and Telecommunications Union (E.E.P.T.U.) (40,000), Association of Scientific, Technical and Managerial Staffs (A.S.T.M.S.) (38,000) and the Boilermakers (26,000). The appearance of the white collar and service unions is of course significant in view of the industrial structure

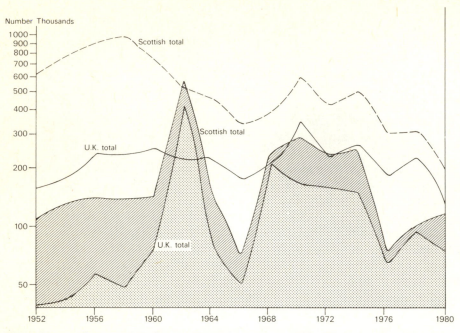

Fig. 3. Top two lines: number of stoppages starting per year, 1952-1980 (even years only). Upper shaded area: workers involved in industrial stoppages, Scotland 1952-1980. Lower shaded area: workers involved in industrial stoppages, U.K. 1952-1980. U.K. figures divided by 11 (even years only).

changes discussed earlier. By and large, however, the observed changes are very much in line with changes at national level, with the union structure being capped with the three large unions, A.U.E.W. (140,000, including T.A.S.S.), T.G.W.U. (134,000) and G.M.W.U. (105,000).

7. STRIKE ACTIVITY

It is perhaps a common view that Scottish workers are among the more militant in the U.K., and that their strike record is worse than average. To some extent this may be a reflection of the 'Red Clydeside' image of earlier this century, and it is perhaps an unfair picture of Scottish industry as a whole. Furthermore, to the extent that the Scottish record is worse, it is necessary to qualify any conclusions by reference to the industrial structure. For there is little doubt that strike behaviour is strongly influenced by industrial organisation, technology, trade union density and other factors which are distinct from any spatial effect. Thus, for example, if industry X tends to have a higher than average strike record, and is heavily concentrated in a particular geographical area, the area will tend to show up as having a poor record for strikes — but that may tell us little about the militancy of the local population *per se*.

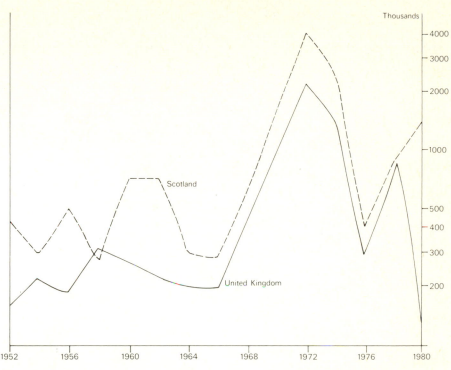

Fig. 4. Working days lost, Scotland and U.K., 1952-1980. U.K. figures divided by 11.

Three measures of industrial stoppages are available: the number of stoppages per period, the number of workers affected, and the total number of working days lost. To facilitate comparison between Scotland and the U.K., we assume Scotland to represent 9.1 per cent of the U.K., and hence dividing the U.K. figures by 11 should give a crude basis of comparison. As we see from Figures 3 and 4, each of the indices shows the Scottish series lying above the U.K. series, almost without exception, indicating that Scotland has a worse record than would be predicted on a purely proportional basis. The number of stoppages averages over twice the U.K. rate, the workers involved average about 40 per cent above the U.K. rate, and working days lost about 55 per cent above. It is noticeable, however, that as the period progresses the series for Scotland and the U.K. move closer — once again suggesting a convergence of Scottish and U.K. patterns.

Further confirmation of the relatively high level of industrial disputes in Scotland emerges from a review of the conciliation work of the Arbitration, Conciliation and Advisory Service (A.C.A.S.) since its establishment in 1974. The number of cases of collective and individual conciliation in Scotland in recent years, expressed as a proportion of all cases in Great Britain, is shown in Table 8. Collective conciliation requests consistently run at over 13 per cent, and individual conciliation cases (primarily unfair dismissal) at over 10 per cent — both significantly over the Scottish employee proportion of 9.3 per cent.

Table 8. *A.C.A.S. Conciliation Cases in Scotland and Great Britain, 1974-81*

	1974-5	1976	1977	1978	1979	1980	1981
Collective conciliation							
Scottish cases as % of British cases	13.0	13.7	12.6	15.1	13.9	13.8	13.6
Individual conciliation							
Scottish cases as % of British cases	n.a.	n.a.	10.8	10.7	10.5	9.2	10.3

Source: A.C.A.S. Annual Reports.
n.a. = not applicable.

Thus the evidence appears to be overwhelmingly in favour of the hypothesis that Scottish labour relations are characterised by a much higher degree of strike proneness. Yet before accepting this conclusion, we have to take into account a number of factors. First, Scotland's traditional industrial base comprises industries — like coal, steel, engineering, shipbuilding and ports and docks — which have a typically high incidence of stoppages. As these have come to occupy a lower proportion of Scottish employment, so have the figures more closely approximated to the U.K. average. Secondly, the very fact that this base has been shrinking rapidly is indicative of a potential conflict situation likely to generate strike action: industrial action is commonly a result of actual or threatened redundancy, especially where the prospects of alternative employment locally are sparse. Thirdly, changed conditions in certain industries will have operated in the direction of reduced strikes: to take just two examples, the level of action over demarcation in shipyards has dropped substantially since the 1960s, with agreements increasing craft flexibility and interchangeability; and in coalmining, the incidence of stoppages, both nationally and regionally, fell dramatically when the piece-rate payment system of the 1950s was replaced in the 1960s by a national day-rate system (which has undergone further changes since).

Thus although the *prima facie* evidence suggests there is an element of truth in the allegations of Scottish labour force militancy and aggression, there is good reason for drawing any such conclusion very cautiously, if at all.

8. CONCLUSIONS

This chapter began with the question whether it was proper to talk in terms of an explicitly Scottish labour market. We have now seen that although the Scottish economy has followed broadly similar paths to that of the national economy in the three decades under review, there are areas in which the relationships between labour market dimensions have changed. In general, it would be fair to conclude that although the major fluctuations in the Scottish labour market have closely reflected the national trends, there has been a gradual convergence of the Scottish and British patterns of behaviour. In particular, this is shown up by the substantial reduction in the adverse unemployment differential, though the Scottish unemployment rate remained significantly above the national average. Likewise, we have seen that earnings levels also gravitated towards the national average. Underlying this convergence there have been perhaps two major forces. One of these is the process of long-term structural change which has affected the U.K. economy at large and within it the Scottish economy, which has simultaneously suffered more than other regions in some respects (such as heavy engineering, shipbuilding and steelmaking) and fared better in others (for example in the oil-related activities). As we have seen, these have had some effect on the internal distribution of employment and earnings within Scotland. The second influence is — perhaps debatably — regional policy, which through a variety of measures, applied with different degrees of intensity, has operated over the whole thirty-year period. It is quite beyond the scope of this chapter to assess the precise extent and incidence of the impact of regional policy measures on the Scottish labour market, but there can be little doubt that the adjustments which the regional economy and labour market have had to make have been helped in some measure by regional aid.

On the industrial relations front, the evidence again points in the same direction of convergence, though there are some indications of a distinctive character to Scottish industrial relations. In much the same way as economic policy at the macro-level has dominated the regional labour market, so it would seem has national industrial relations policy shaped regional response, when allowance is made for the changing industrial structure of Scotland.

What cannot be ignored, however, in the final analysis, is that although convergent trends appear to be prominent, for the most part — North Sea oil aside — Scotland still fell on the 'wrong' side of the balance sheet and still had some leeway to make up. Furthermore, it is necessary to underline the fact that while in some respects the Scottish labour market did show signs of absolute improvement, the convergence was partly to be explained by deterioration in the national economy, particularly in terms of job opportunity and unemployment. It remains to be seen whether a national recovery will be consistent with continued relative improvement or whether signs of divergence will once again emerge.

NOTES

1. A stricter measure of working age population would be 15-64 for men, and 15-59 for women, reflecting normal retirement ages, but a significant number continue beyond these ages. In any event the same overall picture of stability emerges even if the narrower age limits are used.

2. For further discussion, see P. R. Lauener, 'Labour Supply in Scotland', Scottish Economic Planning Department (S.E.P.D.), Economics and Statistics Unit (E.S.U.) Discussion Paper, No. 13 (1982).

3. *Ibid.*, p. 8: subsequent Census of Population results indicate Lauener's estimates may have been somewhat inflated.

4. The differences arise mainly from differences of definition and in the methods by which the data were collected.

5. C. E. V. Leser, 'Manpower', in A. K. Cairncross (ed.), *The Scottish Economy* (Cambridge, 1954).

6. *Scottish Abstract of Statistics* (1981), p. 56, and see Ch. 13 by Stuart McDowall.

7. D. W. Adams, 'The Relationship between Employment and Unemployment in Scotland in the Post War Period', S.E.P.D., E.S.U. Discussion Paper, No. 5 (1980).

8. C. E. V. Leser, *op. cit.*

9. D. W. Adams, 'Migration from Scotland to the Rest of the United Kingdom', S.E.P.D., E.S.U. Discussion Paper, No. 10 (1980).

10. D. J. Robertson, 'Wages', in A. K. Cairncross, *op. cit.*

11. *Ibid.*, p. 168.

12. In 1960, average hours worked in Scotland were 47.1 per week, compared with 48.0 in the U.K. as a whole; *Scottish Economic Bulletin*, No. 8 (1975), p. 11.

13. D. J. Robertson, *op. cit.*, pp. 154-5.

14. Figures from *Scottish Abstract of Statistics*.

15. Considerable caution is required in interpreting these figures, not only due to boundary changes, but also because the data are subject to large standard errors.

16. J. D. M. Bell, 'Trade Unions', in A. K. Cairncross, *op. cit.*, p. 291.

17. Bell's 1947 estimate of 900,000 members comprised 730,000 members affiliated to the S.T.U.C. plus 170,000 'others'. It is difficult to know how far the S.T.U.C. affiliated membership should be augmented to take account of non-affiliated members of *bona fide* trade unions; and we can best proceed by assuming the 1.07 million figure is a minimum estimate.

7

THE HIDDEN LABOUR FORCE: WOMEN IN THE SCOTTISH ECONOMY SINCE 1945

Rosalind Mitchison

Patrick Lindesay wrote in *The Interest of Scotland Consider'd*: 'the Strength, Riches and Reputation, or the Poverty and Weakness of every Country is in proportion to the Industry of the Inhabitants'.[1] I agree with the theme that it ought to pay a country to make full use of its potential labour force. It is, of course, an arbitrary feature of economic calculation that women are considered to be 'working' only when they are doing so for pay, so that, for instance, a woman cooking for a school canteen is 'economically productive' but one working for her own family is not. I do not wish to be held to support this distinction, but I am interested in seeing the changes that have taken place in the size and type of the recognised female labour force since 1945.

There have been, as we all know, demographic and technical developments which have freed many housewives (a census definition which includes some men)[2] from full engagement in household activities. The lowering of the age of marriage which has taken place since 1931, the small family encouraged by the near certainty of rearing, and the trend of relatively healthy adults to have children fairly close together have transformed the family life experience of women. At the same time the increased proportion marrying has made this experience more stereotyped. In the 1981 census 46% of the 20-24 age group were married, which means that few women were still single at 25. At the beginning of this century a woman marrying at 27, a common age for such an event, would in most cases have spent the next fifteen years in producing a family, and would not have been clear of the care of young children until her mid-fifties, at which time she might also be starting to give support to her own daughters as housewives and mothers. The woman of our present period experiences a pattern in which childbearing is usually over by the age of 28, and there is little need of constant personal care of the young by the early forties. So the modern housewife is relatively free from family cares for over half her years in marriage, and even when her daughter marries, the increased mobility of the population may prevent her from being near enough to the new household to give any but occasional support. She herself should expect to live well beyond the arbitrary pension age of 60.

At the same time the burden of housework, particularly of the weekly wash, has become enormously reduced. In the past 'the wash' could easily take a full day's labour and another half-day each week, and it was heavy work. Housework and shopping might take two to three hours daily, though this would be lighter work. Though the direct burden of child care has increased while children are young, for standards have generally risen, all other aspects

183

of domestic work have sharply declined both in the time and the muscle power required. The result of these changes was evident even in the 1951 census, which showed a sharp increase in the proportion of married women in the labour force over 1931: by the 1960s the female labour force was predominantly married.[3]

This development followed similar lines in Scotland and in England, though the pace in Scotland was slightly slower. The collection of studies of the Scottish economy edited by A. K. Cairncross in 1954 showed certain interrelated features:[4] that income in Scotland was markedly lower than for the United Kingdom as a whole, that the birth rate was slightly higher and the proportion of women in employment slightly lower than in England and Wales; and that the emphasis of Scottish industry on heavy industry was still marked. Which of these factors was the cause of others and which derivative is not entirely obvious. Women may have kept out of the labour market either because more of them were tied to small children or because the job opportunities were mainly ones traditionally associated with men.

The heavy industry emphasis of Scottish employment, which had been recognised as responsible for much of the economic discomfort of the interwar period, had received a re-emphasis during the war, for supply needs forced decisions to be made which encouraged the exploitation and development of what was already available. One branch of relatively heavy work, building, which had maintained a low level interwar, expanded in the immediate post-war period when the Labour government put on an extensive housing programme.[5] So the heavy side of industrial work was maintained. But Scotland also shared with the rest of the United Kingdom the twentieth-century trend to more jobs in services and in government, as well as expansion of light industry. This last aspect was particularly exemplified when the post-war plan to deploy the labour force of the largely exhausted Lanarkshire coalfield at Glenrothes in Fife had to be replaced by incentives to light industry once the drainage problems of the area had been shown to be intractable. Much of this light industry was nervous that there would not be labour available, but in fact it found its labour force in women. The labour force expanded as jobs became available. This has also been the experience in the shore-based subsidiaries for the oil fields.

By the end of the 1950s the married woman work force had forced its existence on the notice of even *The Economist*, which could be guaranteed to take an oldfashioned view of society. In 1953 the journal had reported a general shortage of skilled workers in Scotland, and by skilled it meant male. But it also complained of shortage of workers for the jute industry in Dundee, and reported that in the effort to remedy this, one firm had taken to offering to escort small children, presumably to school, and to provide breakfast and tea for them,[6] so here at least the work force wanted was recognised as female and married. It cannot be said that this journal regarded women as having a right to be in the labour force. In a leader in 1956, it made remarks about the tendency of trade unions in Britain to enforce restrictive conditions which kept

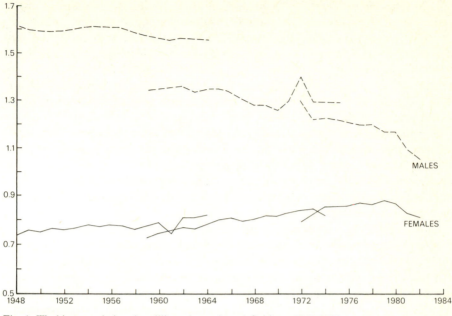

Fig. 1. Working population, in millions, by various definitions, 1949-1982.

out women, which would hardly be received enthusiastically by feminists today. 'Given equal pay, women in employment might serve as a useful buffer; in a slump women, whose rate of absenteeism is usually higher than men's, would often be the first to be laid off.'[7] In 1960 the journal was noticing that in a third of British households there was a working wife, and that there would be more married women working if there were more part-time jobs available. At the same time it still referred to the wages of such women as 'pin money'.[8] This remark shows how deeply entrenched were its writers in middle-class Victorian values, systematically ignoring the contribution made over the centuries by the women of families to the maintenance of a family income. Women's wages in the nineteenth century and since have been of enormous importance in maintaining the standard of living of many families, and also by sustaining purchasing power have had a bearing on the distributive trades. Rarely have pins been more important.

The story of employment to be expected from the general developments since the war is of an expansion of the tertiary sector and of light industry, both to a considerable degree manned by women and continuing through the 1960s and much of the 1970s. This meant a substantial rise in pin-purchasing power. The expansion of employment is shown in Figure 1. (I am ignoring the distinction between full and part-time work because it is arbitrary and also because part-time, except for some people such as academics, is the pattern of the future job.) The confusion of the various lines graphed comes from changing definitions made by the *Scottish Abstract of Statistics*. These do not obscure the general trend. It is impractical to isolate the effects of these changes in family incomes on Scottish industry. The marketing system of Britain was already national in scope before our period. In so far as the United Kingdom becomes part of the E.E.C., this is likely, for geographic reasons, to decrease the impact of enhanced demand from Scotland specifically on Scottish industry. Purchasing power is very largely used for objects produced outwith Scotland. Even food supplies tend to come up the Great North Road in lorries.

The increase in jobs held by women has largely been in part-time ones, and has hardly ever produced an enhanced level of wages earned by overtime. By 1977 in Britain as a whole 57.3% of male workers earned overtime, and only 16.8% of female. Though overtime tends to be concentrated in industries with relatively low pay levels it has, in some of them, been structured in to the regular pattern of work.

The relationship between male and female earnings in full-time work has remained unfavourable to women in Britain as a whole, and has been slightly more so in Scotland. The average of women's incomes in Britain as a whole was 60.5% of men's in 1976, and in Scotland 59.5%. By 1981 the gap between Britain and Scotland had widened, though the percentages had improved. The figures were 65.1% and 62.2%.[9] But an unfavourable trend will set in from the adaptation of employers and trade union officials to the limitations of the Equal Pay legislation of 1975. Ian Watt has asserted that job designation has been used as a means to make clear the segregation of women into a secondary class of employees.[10]

Some idea of the segregation in employment can be gained from looking at the tables of employment in industries given in successive volumes of the *Scottish Abstract of Statistics* and brought almost up to date by figures given to me by the Manpower Services Commission. In 1951 the labour force in the class 'Vehicles' was 8.6% women, in 1983 10.4%. Figures cannot be used over this timespan for the major group of activities covered by the word 'Engineering' because of subsequent change of classification. In another clearly marked group of industry, 'Textiles', the female percentage moved from 62.6 to 56; in 'Distribution' from 47.6 to 58.6; in 'Professional and Scientific', a category which includes both dental workers and teachers, where women have long held a strong position, it moved from 67.3 to 71. What the figures show is that in manufacturing there has been a slight evening out of the sex distribution, though probably not one manifest at the workface, but that the general pattern of where women are employed has stayed much the same.

What this means is that women, particularly part-time working women, have become a group of native *Gastarbeiter*: that is, a labour force tied to particular industries, usually by geographic convenience and by the willingness of particular managements to fix suitable hours for part-timers, and as a result tied also to low pay. The low pay pattern limits mobility, for the workers cannot afford private transport. They tend to be grossly under-represented in or unaided by the established trade unions. Ian Watt has shown that most trade unions in Scotland have made only a token use of women as full-time officials. Since 1897 only two women have served on the General Council of the Scottish Trade Union Congress. The percentage of women officials in trade unions is still low. It need not surprise us, for instance, that there are none in the E.E.T.P.U. (Electrical, Electronic, Telecommunications and Plumbing Union), though women form 13% of the work force in these trades, or only .6% in the Transport and General where they are 16%. These are unions of long-standing, even though the Electricians have changed their initials since the scandal of the 1960s, and long-standing unions tend to be set in their ways. In the relatively new A.S.T.M.S. (the Association of Scientific, Technical and Managerial Staff), women provide 7% of the officials to 18% of the workers. In England an old union with a numerically high proportion of women, the National Union of Teachers, has only 7.7% of the officials female to 75% of the work force.[11] On these figures one would not expect much concern by the unions for the particular needs of women workers. Abandoning statistics for oral history, it is perfectly possible to hear Scottish Trade Union leaders referring to the women whom they are supposed to represent as 'bloody nuisances'. The long-established unions have not much changed their view of society from the days when they killed the Women's Emancipation Bill in 1919 by insisting on the Restoration of Pre-War Practices Act. They still think that the status of labour as a whole is sustained by the protection of the position of male workers, and these male workers are expected to earn enough to support their women folk. But it is in the male-dominated industries — mining, car production, gas and water services, etc. — that the industrial unrest of recent times has occurred. By contrast, things have been tranquil in female-supplied industries. So management has found in married women a flexible and advantageous factor of production. That it has not used any more of it in manufacturing during the 1960s and 1970s is perhaps surprising, but the steady proportion of women in manufacturing masks the collapse of some industries using large women work forces, for instance woollens, and the development of other factories.

So women have gone mainly into service and light industries. It would therefore be expected that women's employment would have been less affected than men's by the enhanced fluctuations of the economy in the 1970s and still less by the depression which set in in 1979. Over a third of male industrial jobs are said to have disappeared since 1979.[12] There has been a major demolition of Scotland's traditional industries, while the areas where women work have been relatively protected: in particular services tend to suffer less unemployment than production in bad times. The official figures of unemployment for the two sexes, available fairly coherently until 1978, before the effect of the various cosmetic reclassifications since, support this view. As can be seen in Figure 1, in Chapter 6, women's unemployment shows no decisive upward gradient until 1976, though it then rose at the same sort of rate as men's. Even so the final recorded level of unemployment for women did not reflect the proportion of women as workers, as can be seen from Figure 1.

This looks a coherent story. But there is no reason to take these unemployment statistics as facts. Here we have to remember the relationship of married women to unemployment benefit. Until 1977 married women had the option between insuring directly only for industrial accident, at a low rate of contribution, and receiving any other benefits nominally as their husband's dependents, or paying full insurance and getting benefits in their own right. It was not even then as simple a choice as that sounds, for a woman making the second choice would not be entitled to her own retirement pension as well as that from her husband's contributions. And in fact the pension as from her husband was not fully based on his contribution. The pension scheme that came in in 1925 relied for solvency on depriving women at marriage of all contributions made on their behalf while single, though in Parliament Neville Chamberlain claimed that the pension of widows was to be paid for by their husbands.[13] The choice was very low contributions and limited rights, or full-scale contributions which did not really produce a pension. In the buoyant economy of the post-war period most married women did not think about unemployment, and took the cheaper option. The only real advantage, apart from unemployment support, that the more expensive choice contained was that they could expect to draw a pension before their husbands retired. In 1977 the cheap option was closed for new entrants to the labour force, but those still in employment for the most part continued to take it, since they were unlikely to have a career long enough to make the other worth while. So most married women even after 1977 have not been eligible for unemployment benefit, and do not figure in the unemployment statistics. They are also unlikely to be eligible for supplementary benefit, unless separated from their husbands, for if their menfolk are at work, receiving unemployment benefit or supplementary benefit, it will be assumed that the male income sustains the wives. Furthermore in 1979 the government knocked all these women who were not insured in their own right off the unemployment books: that is, it deprived them of the information usually sent to those hoping to get jobs. These women could still go and hunt out job notices on their own at Job Centres, but it was being assumed that most married women ceasing work ceased permanently to be part of the work force and were no concern of the Department of Employment. The rough guess made by newspapers is that some 400,000 women in Britain were thus deprived of unemployed status, and, given the disproportion in the total unemployed, the Scottish share of this figure would probably be 50,000. That is one part of the invisible labour force, for these women have disappeared from the statistics.

There are other elements in the system which make the female labour force either invisible, or not strictly comparable with the male. In many matters the statistics for the two sexes are carefully constructed on different bases, so that the male labour force is measured as that between 21 and 65, while the female is that between 18 and 60. I do not understand why a woman as a worker is considered adult three years before a man, unless it is assumed that men are regarded as in training to higher levels of skill, and that this is inappropriate for women. Further invisibility comes from the unwillingness of various people in official positions to recognise that women work. Until very recently normal hospital practice, in gaining information about women patients, was to ask about the husband's employment but not for the employment details of the patient herself: this stemmed from a concern over social class and its different morbidity, a very valuable part of the struggle to improve general health by localising ill-health, but it also reflects a total indifference to the risk of occupational disease for married women. The same indifference is shown in the information collected at registration at death, only in this case it extends to all women. Since an Act of 1953 the occupational information recorded after death for women is, if they are single or divorced, that of their fathers, if married or widowed, that of their husbands. The Registrars General are as unwilling as *The Economist* of 1960 to recognise the reality and scale of women's employment. In the same spirit we have the remark of Sir Geoffrey Howe that there would be no unemployment if married women gave up their jobs, and that of Patrick Jenkin when Minister of Employment in 1979: 'If the Good Lord intended us to have equal rights and to go out to work and to behave equally, He really wouldn't have created man and woman'.[14] In this view, job holding is a secondary sexual characteristic.

Those who hold the view taken by the middle class and the skilled workers in the last century that women should be kept off the labour market except in the category of domestic servant feel very strongly that they should be neither seen nor heard in economic figures. But with home life no longer offering the same scope for activity, and the security of marriage much weakened by divorce, this view is becoming a minority one. The official distaste for recognising that women have a share in the economy has shown itself, rather bizarrely, in the annual *Scottish Abstract of Statistics* in the table of employment for the various groupings of industry. Here the numbers of employees are given under two heads, 'total' and 'males'.[15]

So far I have set out the general picture of what has been happening, with certain warnings that the figures do not represent the truth. The collecting of the information, scanty thought it is, led me to decide that what was best to be done was to try and measure the real potential labour force. By this I mean to try to find out who among women, particularly married women, would probably take a job if it were there. In other words to locate some of the invisibles.

First of all, note must be made of the gap between the figures of employed and unemployed, i.e. the potential work force, as given by the Ministry of Employment, and that set out in the various censuses. In 1961 the census report for Britain as a whole puts this gap at 113,000 men and 576,000 women. If Scotland had its normal share of this, then there were something over 50,000 more women regarding themselves as actively working than were recognised by the Ministry. Perhaps some of these were part of the black economy, doing jobs but paying no tax and making no insurance contributions. In some cases this might be with the active aid of an employer. I can think of various occupations which might produce such a labour force: sweated work at home, part-time typing, child minding, casual domestic work and prostitution; doubtless there are others. And of course some of these workers might work below the level of hours which requires insurance.

For 1981 we can compare the statements of the labour force produced by the Manpower Services Commission with the census figures. The census gives us for April 1981, 286,951 married women working full-time, 260,953 working part-time, and 363,020 single, widowed or divorced women working, a total of 910,924. The Manpower Services Commission has for March 1981 a total of 854,900, a shortfall of 55,924, similar to that estimated for 1961.[16]

But this figure relates only to the most visible of the gaps in information, people actually at work. The next stage is to see how many described themselves as 'economically active' in the census, though not at work. This figure would include those off sick, the disabled or those unable to find suitable work near at hand — many of them being the sort of people knocked off the register of unemployed in 1979. It is true that some of these may have little real capacity for work. Entry into the census is self-originated, though filtered through the person, usually a 'male head of household', who makes up the actual form. Some men may discount the claims of their womenfolk to be economically active. There is a problem here of 'consciousness'; Geoff Payne and Graeme Ford, in a very masculine-orientated paper on unemployment, state: 'a man carries round an occupational identity'.[17] Possibly a woman, at least a married woman, sees her identity first in family terms. Also I do not know if there are women who get themselves labelled economically active but whose normal outside work is in a job for which the retiring age is inescapable, and who are over 60. My own guess is that the additional names of people unrealistically claiming activity are likely to number about the same as those genuinely trying to find work and discounted by their head of household. Still the total claiming economic activity in the census but not in employment is 949,987, a further 39,063 to be recognised as a potential but frustrated labour force.

These figures are all for those who have come to regard themselves as part of the labour force. For the young single woman the definition of potential labour force is those with this opinion. The age-group of the active is smaller at all ages for women than for men, but in the late teens not much smaller. Of those aged 19, the 1981 census has 74.3% of the females and 82.8% of the men as active. By the age-group 30-34 these percentages have changed to 52.9 and 97.5, and it is at this age that the gap is biggest until the different retirement ages for the two sexes produce their own anomaly. But since most women are married before they are 25, and most children are born early in marriage, the women of this age group are probably busy in child rearing. The percentage of economic activity rises for the next age group and for the one after. For ages 40-44 the female figure is 71% of the male figure. Clearly a lot of married women 'return' to work before their children are fully grown up.

What I would like to know is what, given a generous spectrum of job

Table 1. *Scottish Regions*

	% of married women under 60 economically active		% increase	% households with		% population of pension age	% households with	
	1971	1981		children 0 — 4	children under 16		1 car	more
Strathclyde	45.1	56.1	24.4	14.1	36.7	16.1	45.4	9.2
Central	45.7	57.2	25.2	14.0	37.6	15.6	57.2	12.8
Lothians	49.6	62.8	26.6	12.1	32.9	17.2	50.5	10.3
Tayside	53.0	61.5	16.0	12.0	32.7	19.1	52.6	11.4
Fife	46.1	53.0	15.0	13.7	36.2	17.1	55.8	11.0
Dumfries & Galloway	42.3	53.8	27.2	12.4	34.5	20.6	64.1	15.4
Borders	49.3	60.7	23.1	11.1	31.2	21.5	61.6	15.0
Grampians	42.6	54.3	27.5	13.7	35.3	16.9	61.7	15.2
Highlands	37.4	48.1	28.6	15.2	37.5	16.6	64.0	14.0
Islands	29.7	47.5	66.0	15.5	36.6	19.3	63.5	16.0
All Scotland	40.2	48.5	20.6	13.5	35.6	16.8	51.4	11.0

opportunities, would be the percentage of married women choosing to work. From such a figure one could gather the size of the frustrated or as yet 'not activated' female labour force. An estimate of the number of women for whom unemployment is hidden has recently been made by the Henley Centre for Forecasting. They put the level for Britain at 214,000 as the net loss of female labour not acknowledged since 1979. The Scottish proportion of this would probably be somewhat over 10%, perhaps 22,000. But this is a figure simply for those on the books at one time and not now. I want the figure of those who are not on the books, including those who have not yet 'returned' to work, but might be on the books if there were jobs going.

For this I have collected the various regional levels of employment of married women under 60 (itself an arbitrary cut off point) in the two censuses of 1971 and 1981. These are set out as the left-hand columns of Table 1. I have also looked below the regional level to find the districts with the highest percentage of economic activity among women. In 1981 these were, for married women, Dundee at 66.7%, Edinburgh at 64.9% and Roxburghshire at 64.8%. These figures suggest a continued pattern of employment in Dundee and Roxburghshire even after the decline of the traditional textile industries which had made for an unusually large female labour force. For Edinburgh the figure has a different and more interesting base. There is no particular traditional industry accounting for this high level of working. It seems to me to be based on a wide spectrum of jobs and relatively cheap public transport. Edinburgh's economic role has for a long time been as a centre of finance and tourism, with no special tradition of part-time work, and the industries particularly associated with Edinburgh have been printing and brewing, neither conspicuous for female work. The figure of employment is a strong indicator that, irrespective of traditional opportunities, many married women today will choose to work unless prevented by difficulties in finding jobs, or unless there are opposing elements in culture or in family structure.

The rest of Table 1 is an attempt to see if there are such preventive elements in those regions with levels of married women working. Cultural attitudes cannot be assessed numerically. But the percentage increase in these women working between the two censuses in the areas of lowest employment, Highlands and Islands, suggests that women have readily taken to opportunities. In particular the growth rate in the Islands, influenced by the labour shortage consequent on oil development, is striking. In Tayside and Fife, where already in 1971 many women worked, the increase is understandably low. Even the areas with relatively low percentages in 1981 compare favourably with many areas in 1971, and it is difficult not to see this column as showing that many married women everywhere are ready to take jobs, and increasingly so. If the economy were to become buoyant again, the span of the figures of the percentages employed in the regions for 1991 would be slight.

The issue of population structure is more difficult to analyse, largely because the census figures do not differentiate between the older and younger children within the 5-16 age group. It is one thing to expect teenagers to get their own tea, and another for those of primary school age. The areas with low figures in the 1981 column of percentage working are also areas with the highest number of under fives, and also with large numbers of households with older children. We must accept that the Highlands and Islands with a high young child population may also have a higher than average population aged 5-9, an age group which cannot be expected to do without maternal care. This means that up to 15% of women beyond the Scottish norm may not be able to go out to work there. It would be realistic to take the extra percentage not against the whole of Scotland but against those areas of low child population, such as the Lothians, which will bring this up to about 25%. The other population feature, the percentage within the pensionable age, is probably not important, considering that over 46,000 work beyond that age, and also considering the high percentage at work in the Borders, which almost certainly means many over 60.

The final columns of Table 1 attempt to see how far car ownership can be expected to make distant jobs available for women. There is clearly a rational adaptation of car ownership to the various levels of transport problem, with ownership lower in Strathclyde than elsewhere and relatively low in all areas with large urban districts. But even at its greatest level two-car ownership is only at 16%, and everywhere indicates a small minority. In social terms this means that relatively rarely can a woman drive to work unless her husband drives a similar route. Given what we know about the low level of most women's wages and the fact that the largest part of the married woman work force works only part-time, it is not realistic at present to think that most women can equip themselves with a car to make a job available.

One other cultural matter cannot be measured but must be considered. How much are women working at unrecognised aspects of a family economy? It is well known that the wives of ministers are treated by the Kirk as an unpaid labour force, and in rural areas many men working independently may use their wives as unacknowledged telephonists. Since this is not a particularly regional matter, no allowance needs to be made for it. As for the traditional role of crofters' wives as part of the economy of the croft, a matter which is regional, that seems largely to have disappeared with the disappearance of active farming in most crofting communities. Nowadays the crop most likely to be raised on a croft is one of caravans, and these are not labour-intensive.

So we can accept the figures of Table 1 as giving good grounds for assuming that the presence of jobs within reach would bring married women onto the labour market in the proportions they are in the Edinburgh district, except that child care would hold back a proportion in the Highlands and Islands. What figures of unused labour do we then get? The Edinburgh district level of married women working, 64.9%, applied to the figure of Scotland's married women, 1,211,288, would give 786,127. But removing 25% of the extra labour force attributed to the Highlands and Islands would reduce this by 2,153, making 783,974 as the potential work force. Since the number acknowledged as 'economically active' in the 1981 census is 624,321, this new figure would mean that the unused potential is 159,653. This is the real scale of the hidden labour force, to be added to those already acknowledged as frustrated in activity matters: 198,716.

I would stress that most of this labour force is hidden because of lack of opportunity. But some part of that lack of opportunity stems from the prejudiced way in which women workers are treated. If it were normal to pay women the same range of wages as men, more would be at work. It costs to go to work, in terms of transport, of clothing, perhaps of shortcuts in food provision and house care. Some part, perhaps only a small one, of our labour force would not be hidden if there were real equality of opportunity.

NOTES

1. *The Interest of Scotland Consider'd* (Edinburgh, 1733), p. 61.
2. J. B. Cullingworth, *Scottish Housing in 1965* (Office of Population, Censuses and Surveys, 1967), p. 12.
3. See A. H. Halsey, *Trends in British Society since 1900* (London, 1972), p. 116.
4. A. K. Cairncross (ed.), *The Scottish Economy* (Cambridge, 1954), Chapters 3, 4 and 6.
5. The scale of housebuilding in the late 1940s can be seen in G. G. Miller, 'The Scottish Economy under Post-War British Governments', M.Phil.thesis, St Andrews University, 1982; see also Chapter 12 in this volume.
6. *The Economist*, 28 November 1953.
7. *Ibid.*, 21 April 1956.
8. *Ibid.*, 9 January 1960.
9. Scottish Abstract of Statistics (1977) p. 113; and for 1983, p. 133.
10. 'Occupational Stratification and the Sexual Division of Labour: Scotland since 1945', in A. Dickson (ed.), *Capital and Class in Scotland* (Edinburgh, 1982).
11. *Ibid.*, pp. 233-4.
12. Gordon Brown, 'Introduction', in Gordon Brown and Robin Cook (eds.), *Scotland, the Real Divide* (Edinburgh, 1983).
13. *Hansard* 184. 89 (18 May 1925).
14. Quoted in Brown and Cook, *op. cit.*, p. 153.
15. E.g. tables 9.4 and 9.5, 'Employees in Employment . . . by Local Government Regions . . .' and 'Employees in Employment . . . by Industry', in the 1983 volume.
16. Manpower Services Commission, unpublished quarterly statistics.
17. Brown and Cook, *op. cit.*, p. 79.

8

THE ROLE OF GOVERNMENT*

Gavin McCrone

The period chosen for this book has been one of immense change in the Scottish economy. (This chapter and those following illustrate how great has been the transformation not only in structure of economic activity but also in the role of Government and its agencies.) Although Scotland still faces major economic problems, and those problems have a continuity which goes back at least sixty years, the scene described by Sir Alec Cairncross and his colleagues in *The Scottish Economy* was remarkably different from that which faces Scotland now.[1] Scotland's apparently healthy condition then in the midst of a period of fast economic growth and with low unemployment concealed serious structural weaknesses: a continuing heavy dependence on the industries which had brought it past prosperity, an out of date infrastructure and an appalling urban environment giving rise to severe social problems. By contrast Scotland in 1980 was in almost the opposite situation: the worst recession in fifty years causing stagnation of output and intolerable levels of unemployment; but a modernised infrastructure, a much improved environment, and, although some of the problems of the older industries remain, a strong representation of new advanced industry with good prospects of future growth.

The subject of this chapter is the role of Government policy; and it is striking that both the policies and the instruments have changed almost as much as the economy. In 1950 there was no Department within the Scottish Office with responsibility for industry or the economy, no Highlands and Islands Development Board, no Scottish Development Agency, and no Manpower Services Commission. The North of Scotland Hydro-Electric Board had recently been set up, and only two of the five new towns had been established. The Scottish Office officials seconded to the team which prepared the Clyde Valley Plan came from the Department of Health for Scotland, a *provenance* which today seems rather eccentric.[2]

1. THE 1950s: THE LAST FLING OF TRADITIONAL INDUSTRY

Despite the post-war shortages which were still a factor and caused continued rationing, the United Kingdom's rate of economic growth in the period 1945-50 was faster than in any part of the subsequent thirty years: gross domestic product (G.D.P.) showed an average real increase of approximately 4% a year, and industrial production rose by 21% between 1948 and 1951.

---

* The author is Secretary of the Industry Department for Scotland, but the views expressed in this chapter are personal and not necessarily those of the Department.

195

Unemployment in 1950 was only 1.6 per cent of the labour force, or 341,000, and had fallen as low as 75,000 for the whole United Kingdom in 1944.

Scotland benefited considerably from these conditions. A. D. Campbell showed that real income per head of population in Scotland was about 90% of the United Kingdom average in 1948, about the same percentage as it had been in 1924, but higher than it had been in between.[3] Indeed the inter-war period had shown a relative decline in Scotland's economic position, and the 1924 ratio of income per head was only restored as a result of Scotland catching up during the war. Scottish unemployment at 3.1% of the labour force, or 65,000, was very low in historical terms, notably when compared with the 14-18% which was typical of the years immediately pre-war. And of course it was very low by today's standards. But unemployment was nevertheless double the United Kingdom average; and, combined with a substantial rate of net emigration, it showed that the labour market was certainly not as buoyant as in the United Kingdom as a whole.

Despite the obvious contrast with the depressed conditions of pre-war, to more perceptive observers the situation still gave cause for concern because the strength of the economy depended too heavily on the older industries: coal, shipbuilding, steel, textiles, and heavy engineering. Scotland had somehow missed out on the second industrial revolution, the motor car industry and the consumer goods industries of the 1930s, and its prosperity still depended, as both C. E. V. Leser and the authors of the Clyde Valley Regional Plan 1946 pointed out, on the maintenance of demand for the activities with which the process of industrialisation originally began.[4] Indeed as the Clyde Valley Plan puts it:

> The region is dominated by coalmining, metal manufacture, shipbuilding and engineering. These industries in 1939 accounted for 46% of the insured employed population in Lanarkshire, 21% in Glasgow, 58% in Dunbartonshire, 30% in Renfrewshire and 17% in Ayrshire . . . These basic industries are interrelated, the output of one being the raw material of another; as depression in one affects the others, large numbers of men are thus thrown out of work who have no alternative industry to which they can turn for employment.[5]

However, in 1950 these traditional activities were remarkably buoyant. At that time there were few signs that the situation would not last, and so there were many who thought that it was after all the interwar period which was exceptional and that the Government's efforts to diversify the economy no longer need be maintained.[6]

Policies at the U.K. level

The coalition government's White Paper on employment policy in 1944 set the scene for the period immediately after the war.[7] Not only would *'Government accept as one of their primary aims and responsibilities the maintenance of a high and stable level of employment'*, a commitment which became well known, but the White Paper also outlined policies which were to be applied to prevent serious localised unemployment of the kind which had affected Scotland and other depressed areas before the war. These policies stemmed from the report of the Royal Commission on the Distribution of Industrial Population (Barlow Commission) of the 1940s and were set in place by the Distribution of Industry Act of 1945.[8] The principal measures were: provision of Government factories to rent in designated Development Areas; restraining industrial growth in the more prosperous parts of the country, by means first of building licences and later industrial development certificates in order to encourage it to go to Development Areas; the provision of grant and loan finance; and the setting up of Government Training Centres to enable adult workers to acquire new skills.

The amount of grant and loan finance dispensed was relatively insignificant, certainly by later standards, but the provision of factories and the controls were undoubtedly effective, and the policies achieved a substantial impact in the 1940s. Some 46,000 employees were working on Government industrial estates in Scotland by 1954, and some well-known companies whose contribution to Scotland's economic growth in the subsequent thirty years has been substantial took root in Scotland at this time. The most significant examples include I.B.M., Honeywell and Burroughs. Rolls Royce, with its major factory on the Government industrial estate at Hillington, goes back to the years before the war, while Ferranti was set up in Edinburgh during the war. By 1950, however, and more particularly after the change of Government in 1951, the apparent buoyancy of the whole economy, including the former depressed areas, caused this policy to be relaxed. The measures remained in existence, but expenditure on factory building was reduced and industrial development certificates for projects in the prosperous areas became more readily available. No longer could this be described as a priority area of Government policy.

Policy Within Scotland

By any standards the Clyde Valley Regional Plan, which was published in 1949, must be regarded as one of the outstanding regional planning documents to be produced in the United Kingdom after the war. It was concerned not only with physical reconstruction but with strengthening the economy as well; and although its scope was limited to the Clyde Valley, that area was of course then, even more than now, the heartland of the Scottish economy. The plan's high quality undoubtedly stems from the exceptional knowledge and experience the authors had of the area; but to this was added an imagination and perceptiveness which was unfortunately less evident amongst the public authorities and leaders of industry who were in positions of executive authority. As a result some of the problems which the plan addressed have remained throughout the thirty years, only to become the object of more concerted policy effort in the 1980s.

The physical aspects of the Plan were naturally concerned with the problem of overcrowding in Glasgow and other similar parts of the Clydeside conurbation. With densities of 400 persons per acre and up to 700 in places, the city contained some of the worst examples of overcrowding in Europe, resulting in slums, urban squalor and deprivation on a scale which was unsurpassed in any other advanced industrial country. This problem, which was a legacy of the unplanned growth and social inequalities of the nineteenth century, required the city to be drastically replanned and rebuilt if densities were to be reduced. Within the conurbation itself there was to be redevelopment, and there were proposals for recovery of dereliction, the preservation of green space, and facilities for leisure and recreation. Much drastic surgery did indeed take place, sometimes too drastic, and peripheral housing estates grew up lacking social facilities and employment opportunities and with their own brand of intractable problems. Population densities certainly came down but urban deprivation remained, the redevelopment falling short of the standards hoped for in the Plan. Indeed many of these problems remained and became a major activity of the Scottish Development Agency after its creation in the second half of the 1970s. The Plan proposed that this restructuring should be assisted by a policy of building new towns, where overspill population from Glasgow would be housed and new industries attracted to provide employment. Four new towns were proposed at East Kilbride, Cumbernauld, Houston and Bishopton, the first two of which were built, starting in 1947 and 1956 respectively, and they now play a major part in the economy of the West of Scotland.

But it was the Plan's proposals for economic regeneration which are of most interest for this chapter. The need to introduce new industry so as to diversify the economic base of the area was well recognised. Little is said about the type of industry it was hoped to establish, although the underlying assumption is that Scotland needed to make up for its failure to develop the motor and consumer goods industries of the 1930s which had been such a feature of development in the Midlands and South-East of England. But the planning team also addressed themselves to the problems of the older industries. At this time the Scottish coal industry employed approximately 80,000, although its output at 20 to 25m. tons a year was little more than half the peak output achieved in 1910. Until the 1930s labour productivity in the Scottish coalfield had been above the U.K. average, and this was one of the reasons for the success of heavy industry in Scotland. Productivity was now poor by U.K. standards, and the Lanarkshire coalfield was approaching exhaustion. The Plan therefore outlined proposals to base the industry in Fife and the Lothians, anticipating a substantial and sustained reduction in the level of coalmining employment in the Clyde Valley area. Glenrothes new town was started in Fife in 1948 as part of this strategy, originally for the purpose of developing the ill-fated Rothes mine.

The situation in shipbuilding was not dissimilar and is discussed in greater detail in Professor Payne's chapter on the decline of the older industries. At this time there were some 25 separate shipbuilding companies operating on the Clyde, compared with 5 today, and they accounted for a third of United Kingdom output, which in 1950 was as high as 50% of world output. The prolonged boom, stemming from the heavy shipping losses of the war years, was accompanied by a remarkable absence of any foresight on the part of the industry about the problems which lay ahead; it neither seemed to foresee that the situation could change or that when it did it was ill placed to face overseas competition. A remarkable complacency about the industry's effectiveness was shared by management and labour, and not enough was done either to invest in modern facilities or to eliminate restrictive labour practices. Yet the authors of the Plan expressed considerable anxiety about the future of the industry and foresaw the possibility of decline when the post-war backlog was overcome.

Scotland's iron and steel industry had developed in Lanarkshire and at Cambuslang because of the resources of coal and ironstone which were available locally. This had given way to a dependence on imported iron ore for which the location of the industry was, even then, no longer suitable. The Plan therefore proposed the relocation of the industry on a greenfield site on the middle reaches of the Clyde to achieve economies of handling. Its development was to be associated with the new towns of Houston and Bishopton. The choice of site would probably have given rise to serious problems of environmental pollution, and the planners could not be expected to foresee the development of giant ore carriers which would necessitate a terminal even further down the river. But there is little doubt that their instinct to move the industry to a coastal site was the right one. That Colvilles chose, nevertheless, to build their new integrated works at Ravenscraig in Motherwell in the late 1950s instead of on the coast has been one of a number of factors that put the Scottish steel industry at a competitive disadvantage which ultimately came to threaten its existence in the difficult conditions of the 1980s.

Apart from the Clyde Valley, the other area of Scotland which had received particular attention in the post-war period was the Highlands. An area which included Inverness and Dingwall was scheduled as a Development Area from 1948 onwards under the terms of the Distribution of Industry Act of 1945, and this meant that it stood to benefit from the measures which have already been described. But of much greater significance for the Highlands was the development of hydro-electric resources, a programme of investment which was in full swing by 1950. The Cooper Committee of 1942 had concluded that hydro-electricity would be competitive with conventional coal-fired generating plant in post-war conditions and that it had the potential to bring about the economic development of the Highlands.[9] The Committee believed that not only was it desirable for social reasons to improve the living standards of the people of the Highlands but that cheap power offered opportunities for development in the electro-chemical and electro-mechanical industries which could be of great benefit to the United Kingdom as a whole.

The investment in hydro-electricity duly went ahead and, although it proved more expensive than the Cooper Committee anticipated, it was nevertheless developed in very favourable circumstances. As compared with other forms of power generation, hydro-electricity is capital-intensive with a very long life and low running costs. In the post-war years interest rates were extremely low and the capital therefore proved to be very cheap. Thirty years later one can see clearly that this investment gave Scotland its cheapest and most flexible source of electric power. It has therefore proved to be an important asset for the Scottish economy as a whole. The low cost of generation helped to compensate the Hydro Board for high distribution costs in serving an area with such scattered and remote locations.

But ironically the Cooper Committee's industrial hopes were never realised. Principally this was because the Highlands' water resources were limited and the Board felt they should be developed for the area as a whole rather than used to supply power on exceptionally advantageous terms to a small number of power-intensive enterprises whose employment would be relatively modest.[10] But the Board was also prevented by its statute from discriminatory pricing arrangements, and the fact that it was constituted as a monopoly prevented companies from building their own hydro-electric supply. Indeed it is interesting that although the aluminium industry was established in the Highlands, the hydro-electric schemes which serve the Lochaber and Kinlochleven smelters are company-owned and predate the existence of the Hydro Board. The ill-fated Invergordon smelter built in the 1960s was linked with the nuclear station at Hunterston on the Clyde coast since its demand for power greatly exceeded anything which the hydro system could make available to a new customer.

Changing Scene of the 1950s

The first half of the decade saw little change from the conditions which had prevailed in the immediate post-war years. Despite the first post-war recession in 1952-53, demand for the output of the traditional industries was maintained, and unemployment in Scotland had come down to 2.8% or 59,000 by 1954. The Ridley Committee forecast a continuing energy shortage in the United Kingdom and foresaw a need for the United Kingdom coal industry to expand from 220m. tons to an output of 260m. tons a year by 1961 if anticipated requirements were to be met.[11] Steel shortages continued to be a feature of boom years during this period, and the shipyards too continued in a seller's market.

The second half of the 1950s marked a decisive change. Following the post-election credit squeeze in the autumn of 1955, there was a prolonged recession which in Scotland resulted in several years of negligible growth. Oil began to replace coal, causing the latter to reduce output to an extent which was totally unforeseen at the beginning of the decade. Employment in the industry in Scotland had reached its peak in 1952 and thereafter began its long decline. Shipbuilding caught up with the post-war backlog of orders, with the result that there was a substantial slump in the industry and throughout the very wide range of firms in other industries which supplied it. The ending of steam traction brought the demise of the important locomotive industry in Glasgow.

As a result of these changes Scotland's economic performance in the second half of the 1950s was not only weak in absolute terms but poor in relation to the rest of the United Kingdom, as Dr Buxton's chapter clearly shows. Indeed, looking back one can see that, whether measured by employment or income, this was the period during the thirty years when the tendency to fall behind the U.K. economic performance was most apparent. The gap was not enormous: unemployment had only risen to 3.7% by 1960 and G.D.P. per head had come down to 87% of the U.K. average. But the economy was undoubtedly dragged down by the collapse of the traditional industries, and unless there was a major effort to diversify, the situation was bound to get worse.

2. THE 1960s: REGIONAL POLICY AND PLANNING

Already in the closing years of the 1950s there was rising concern at the deteriorating situation in the older industrial areas, in particular Scotland, the North-East of England, Merseyside, and South Wales. The result was to be a decade in which measures to encourage industry to develop in these areas were given a higher priority than ever before. A modest step had already been taken in 1958 when the Distribution of Industry (Industrial Finance) Act was passed and the administration of industrial development certificates was tightened up to favour the Development Areas.

In 1959 a key decision was taken by the Government which was to have far-reaching consequences for the future of the steel industry. The circumstances which led to the building of the strip mill at Ravenscraig in Motherwell and at Llanwern in South Wales are described in Professor Payne's chapter. But in two separate respects this project was expected to be a key decision for the future of the Scottish economy. The first concerned the future of the steel industry itself. Originally the industry had come into being to serve the heavy industries of the West of Scotland, drawing its raw materials from local coal and ironstone. It consisted of a number of small works at Motherwell, Airdrie and Coatbridge, Cambuslang and Glengarnock, each based on the open-hearth steelmaking process and producing a range of products which included plate for ships, rails, sections for the construction industry, various types of forgings and special steels. The industry expanded beyond the needs of the Scottish market, but that market remained its base. The problem was that by the late 1950s it was already becoming clear that the open-hearth method of steel production would be superseded by the basic oxygen process; and that process, while very suitable for bulk steel production, enjoyed economies of scale which required very much larger works. In the long run the small specialist works serving the varied needs of local markets could not survive, since any new works should be designed for a capacity of at least 3 million tons. Given the size of the Scottish market, which never up to this time exceeded about 2m. tons for all steel products together, this meant that it must depend much more heavily on markets outside Scotland.

Strip steel was not a product which had hitherto been produced in Scotland, and at the time of the Ravenscraig decision there was little or no demand for it. No doubt this was the main reason for Colvilles' lack of enthusiasm for the plant. But the view was widely held that if the newer consumer goods industries were to be attracted, notably motor cars, washing machines and household consumer durables, which were the source of economic growth elsewhere, Scotland would remain severely handicapped without a local source of strip steel.

The decisions on the steel industry were followed in the early 1960s by similar decisions on the motor industry. All of the major motor manufacturers were developing plans for expansion in the face of continuing buoyant demand, and the Government intervened by means of the industrial development certificate system to encourage these expansions to take place in Development Areas rather than the existing centres of the motor industry which were the companies' first choice. Substantial financial assistance was made available to make this relocation possible. As a result, Scotland received two major motor industry projects: the Rootes (later Chrysler) factory at Linwood which was to build the new Hillman Imp car, and the British Motor Corporation (B.M.C.) (later part of British Leyland) factory to build trucks and tractors at Bathgate. In the early days of the motor industry Scotland had had at least three companies making motor cars; but apart from the Albion plant at Scotstoun, which had become part of B.M.C. and made components for goods vehicles, these had gone out of production in the 1930s. It was hoped and expected that these new major investments in the motor industry would be the start of further expansion and the source of a growing demand for steel from Ravenscraig, and that they would also result in the gradual development of a motor component industry. Neither hope was to be fulfilled.

Developments in Regional Policy

A series of Acts were passed from 1960 onwards which gave increasing strength to regional policy.[12] The changes in the instruments of regional policy were numerous and complex. But the principal elements were as follows:

(i) after various changes in the early 1960s Development Areas were extended and by the end of the decade covered all of Scotland except the Edinburgh travel to work area.

(ii) grants and differential tax allowances were introduced to encourage new investment by manufacturing industry in both plant and buildings in Development Areas. The Labour Government's Act of 1966 replaced the previous systems with an investment grant at 40% on qualifying investments in plant and machinery — grants of 25-35% were available for buildings.

(iii) a wage subsidy, the regional employment premium, was introduced in 1967 on employment in manufacturing industry. This was partly seen as a substitute for regional devaluation to improve the competitive position of products manufactured in Development Areas and partly to correct the capital bias of the other forms of regional incentive.

Policy Developments Within Scotland

In 1960 a Committee of Inquiry on the Scottish economy (the Toothill Committee) was set up under the auspices of the Scottish Council, but with substantial support from the Scottish Office, and it produced its report in the autumn of 1961.[13] The report came at an opportune time; but it was also a landmark in thinking on regional development and was to set the scene for many of the initiatives which were taken not only in Scotland but in other parts of the United Kingdom as well. The report's principal theme was that policy should have less to do with palliatives for unemployment and give greater emphasis to the promotion of sound economic growth. It was concerned not simply with regional policy, in the sense of incentives to industry, but also laid stress on the linking of infrastructure development to economic needs, something which had been largely ignored since the Clyde Valley Plan in the post-war years.

Within Scotland this meant that economic growth should be encouraged where it had good prospects, rather than concentrating assistance on areas of high unemployment if prospects there were poor. There were obvious difficulties in encouraging new development to go to some of the more isolated mining towns; but the new town programme had already shown itself to be a success and should be expanded. To bring about these changes a re-organisation of the Scottish Office was recommended, and as a result the Scottish Development Department was created with responsibilities for physical and economic planning and the development of infrastructure, including particularly housing, roads and new towns.

The Government's response to the recommendations in the Toothill Report came in the White Papers of 1963 on Central Scotland and 1965 on the Scottish Economy.[14] The 1963 White Paper proposed the establishment of growth points based on the new towns but also on other areas such as the Vale of Leven and North Lanarkshire where economic growth was thought to have good prospects; and an enlarged programme of infrastructure development was proposed with Scotland receiving more than its population share of public expenditure for this purpose. The infrastructure was deliberately intended to enhance the attractiveness of the areas selected as growth points. Growth points of course raise some acute political problems: their selection is bound to be to a high degree subjective, and political pressures are inclined to produce such serious complaints about the areas left out that more are selected than would accord with the original concept. It was perhaps for this reason that the 1965 White Paper, which was produced by the new Labour Government, accorded much less emphasis to growth points and sought instead to cast the development of the Scottish economy in a form which was compatible with the National Plan being produced by Mr George Brown and his Department of

Economic Affairs in London. The White Paper sought to quantify the number of jobs which would have to be created in Scotland to get unemployment and emigration reduced to acceptable levels, and outlined measures — particularly the development of infrastructure related to the economy — which were intended to help realise this goal.

It was in 1962 and 1966 respectively that the new towns of Livingston and Irvine were started in addition to East Kilbride, Cumbernauld and Glenrothes, the existing three. In the mid-1960s also the three major estuarial road bridges were built over the Forth, the Tay, and the Clyde at Erskine, and a start was made on the development of a motorway system in Scotland. A new airport was opened at Glasgow, and the electrification of the Glasgow to London main railway line was started. There can be no doubt that these projects were of the greatest importance to the economic development of Scotland: suffering from an outdated Victorian infrastructure, it acquired a transport system which was better than in many other parts of the United Kingdom and able to meet very adequately the needs of the 1970s and 1980s. Without these developments the economy could never have hoped to benefit from the inflow of overseas investment which has come to play such a major role.

To help tackle the long-standing economic problem of the Highlands, the Highlands and Islands Development Board was set up in 1965.[15] This Board was the United Kingdom's first development agency; its purpose was to promote the economic and social development of the seven crofting counties which comprised 40% of Scotland's total land area but contained only 4% of the population. The area had a very narrow economic base, with little manufacturing industry and a heavy dependence upon poorly endowed hill farming, fishing and tourism. As a result there was a serious problem of depopulation, which throughout much of the area had been continuing for the greater part of a hundred years. The Board was given a restricted budget to start with, but its powers were extensive, enabling it to assist all the main kinds of economic activity in its area. It was able to provide grants on terms which were more flexible and more generous than those available elsewhere, as well as loans and equity investment. The Act establishing the Board provoked a good deal of controversy, which continued throughout its early years of operation. But the powers have come to be seen as justified by the exceptional problems of the area; and the Board has undoubtedly played an important part in the relative improvement of the area's economy in the twenty years since it was founded.

The 1960s in Perspective

The structural change which had started in Scotland in the second half of the 1950s continued unabated in the 1960s. The coal and shipbuilding industries in particular continued their long decline. The difference was that in this decade new growth also came to Scotland: not as much as the authors of the 1963 and 1965 White Papers had hoped for, but on a greater scale than at any other time in the post-war period. But for the fact that serious and recurring balance of payments crises caused measures of restraint to be applied to the United Kingdom as a whole, especially in 1966 and with the further squeeze following devaluation in 1967, the growth would have been even more pronounced. As it was, despite the handicap of its economic structure, the growth of output as measured by Scotland's share of U.K. G.D.P. kept pace with the U.K. from 1963 onwards after some initial loss of ground in the first two years of the decade. G.D.P. per head in Scotland climbed back from 87% of the U.K. average to 91% in 1970. Employment in Scotland grew at a significantly slower rate than in the United Kingdom up to 1966 — 1.8 per cent as compared with 5.7 per cent — but thereafter the decline was slightly less marked, and unemployment, although rising towards the end of the decade, was no longer in the ratio of twice the United Kingdom rate. Emigration, which had touched a post-war peak of over 40,000 a year in the mid-1960s, also began to come down.

Since the declining industries were doing no better than in the 1950s, it can clearly be seen that the improved performance which is illustrated by all these statistical measures was the result of new growth taking place, and this in turn must be ascribed in large measure to greatly strengthened regional policy and the improved infrastructure.

3. THE 1970s: CRISIS, OPPORTUNITY AND INSTITUTIONAL CHANGE

The decade of the 1970s proved to be quite as different from either of its predecessors as they were from each other. Already in 1970 the Bretton Woods international monetary system was breaking down and rates of inflation throughout the world were beginning to climb. This led to quite a sharp recession in the first two years of the decade which was followed by a boom. This in turn was followed by the first energy crisis, when the price of oil quadrupled in 1973/74, leading to a much more severe recession, followed by a second major oil price rise at the end of the decade. For Scotland the adverse effects of the energy crisis were tempered by the discoveries of North Sea oil which led to substantial economic growth. But it was also a period which saw radical change in the institutions of government within Scotland for the promotion of the economy.

North Sea Oil

Although there had been several licensing rounds in the 1960s leading to important gas discoveries in the southern basin of the North Sea, it was not until 1971 that the first oil field, B.P.'s Forties field, was declared suitable for commercial exploitation. The huge fourth round of licences, with 282 blocks taken up, took place in 1971/72, covering a large part of Scottish offshore waters, including much of the most attractive territory in the northern North

Sea and the Shetland basin. As a result, exploration activity was intense from the autumn of 1972 onwards, with something of a goldrush atmosphere: suddenly there were major opportunities both for manufacturing and for services in Scotland. Construction yards for the building of giant production platforms, both steel and concrete, opened in Fife, the Moray and Cromarty Firths, on the Clyde and at Loch Kishorn in Wester Ross. Aberdeen became the forward headquarters and supply centre for the North Sea oil industry, and substantial investment also took place in the development of supply bases at Peterhead and Montrose, and in Shetland. The pressure on the existing infrastructure of the North and North-East of Scotland proved excessive, and crash programmes were drawn up for the building of houses, new roads and the complete rebuilding of the airports at Aberdeen, Inverness and especially Shetland.[16] The development of North Sea oil, despite the exceptionally difficult conditions of the North Sea, proceeded so fast that by the end of the decade production approximately equalled the United Kingdom's annual consumption. Employment in Scotland rose to 38,000 directly employed and 55-65,000 if the indirect effects were included in 1976, with a further increase to 58,000 and 80-90,000 respectively by the end of 1980. Largely because of this activity and the continuing effects of regional policy, the Scottish economy outperformed the United Kingdom's in the first half of the 1970s. Industrial production increased by 4.9% between 1970 and 1975 as compared with 2.4% in the U.K. Thereafter, as a result of the international recession and the second oil shock in 1979, growth was negative, the indices for Scotland and the U.K. showing a decrease of 6% and 3% respectively by 1980. G.D.P. per head rose from 91% of the United Kingdom average in 1970 to 96% by 1980. And although unemployment rose in the second half of the decade to levels which had not been seen since before the war, Scotland's relative position improved so that its unemployment rate was only some 20% above the United Kingdom rate in 1976 and 35% above in 1980.

Institutional Change

After coming to office in 1970, the Conservative Government had abolished the investment grants introduced by its Labour predecessor in 1966 and substituted capital allowances. But these reduced the incentive for investment in assisted areas as compared with the country as a whole; and as the recession deepened, the Government decided that strong incentives both regionally and nationally were required. One hundred per cent first-year allowances on investment in plant and machinery were extended nationwide, and the Industry Act of 1972 established a new system of Regional Development Grants and selective financial assistance which became the basic instruments of regional policy for the next ten years. The Regional Development Grants at rates of 22% in special development areas and 20% in development areas were for investment by manufacturing industry in buildings and fixed plant and machinery; and unlike previous grants they were provided on a tax-exempt basis so that they did not reduce entitlement to depreciation allowances. Previous forms of discretionary financial assistance had been administered from London, and it was a special feature of the new selective system that responsibility for this form of assistance was given to the regional offices of the Department of Trade and Industry supported by local advisory boards. This greatly improved the relationship between those administering the assistance and the companies applying for it, and it ensured that the assessment of cases would be done by people not only knowledgeable about the region but in the best position to judge the prospects for the projects being put forward. In Scotland this financial assistance was administered for the first two years by the Department of Trade and Industry from its office in Glasgow before this function and the office were transferred to the Secretary of State for Scotland.

Increasingly throughout the post-war years successive Secretaries of State for Scotland had become concerned with economic matters, although largely lacking statutory economic functions. During the 1960s, as we have seen, the emphasis was on the provision of infrastructure in support of economic development and on economic planning. The former led to the creation of the Scottish Development Department and the latter to the creation of the Regional Development Division, a small group of officials originally carrying out a role not dissimilar from that of the Department of Economic Affairs in London. But whatever his statutory functions might be, such niceties were not appreciated by people in Scotland who regarded the Secretary of State as having responsibility for Government policy as a whole. The widespread concern with the state of the economy, including such matters as the collapse of Upper Clyde Shipbuilders or the British Steel Corporation's proposals for the modernisation of the steel industry, meant that the Secretary of State had to involve himself, and where appropriate act together with his officials, not only in the decisions but in the work which led up to them.

This role assumed a new importance in 1973 when the Prime Minister announced that the Minister of State at the Scottish Office was to be given special responsibility for co-ordinating North Sea oil development. As a result of this a fifth Scottish Office Department, the Scottish Economic Planning Department, was established which, in addition to the increased work on North Sea oil, took over responsibility for the Secretary of State's interest in regional policy and became the sponsor department for the Highlands and Islands Development Board, the five new towns and the two electricity boards. (*The Scottish Economic Planning Department* was renamed the *Industry Department for Scotland* in November 1983. Throughout this chapter I have used the older name which applied at the time.) In 1975 the Department was further enlarged, and an important addition was made to its functions when the Secretary of State became responsible for the administration of regional selective financial assistance under the 1972 Industry Act and the Department of Industry's Office for Scotland became part of the Department.

There had been pressure from various quarters within Scotland for the establishment of some form of development agency for some time. This was principally because regional policy, as administered from London prior to 1972, had seemed too remote, but also because it was felt that greater emphasis needed to be given to the promotion of indigenous growth within Scotland. It was partly in recognition of this that the administration of selective financial assistance had been transferred to the regions under the Industry Act of 1972. But there were those who felt that a free-standing public agency with its own budget, and less preoccupied with the day-to-day demands of Parliament or serving Ministers, could usefully carry out wider functions, which were important for economic development, than those carried out by the Department. Indeed the authors of the West Central Scotland Plan had argued strongly for the setting up of a development corporation for the West of Scotland in their report of 1974.[17]

These various strands therefore came together in the setting up of the Scottish Development Agency (S.D.A.) in 1975. The Scottish Economic Planning Department (S.E.P.D.) became the sponsor department for the Agency, responsible for setting its operational guidelines and for providing its funds. The Department continued itself to administer grants and low-interest loans to industry, since these had to be compatible with assistance given by Government in other regions of the United Kingdom, if a bidding-up process was to be avoided. But the S.D.A. was given power to provide investment finance either by way of equity or loan on broadly commercial terms and for which financial duties were set; it took over from the former Scottish Industrial Estates Corporation responsibility for the Government's factory estates in Scotland and was expected to formulate its own policy on their development; it was also given power and finance to undertake environmental recovery, the intention being that such recovery should be concentrated in areas where it would improve the prospects of economic regeneration. Unlike the Highlands and Islands Development Board, the S.D.A. therefore did not have wide powers to give grant assistance or soft money on less than commercial terms, although the Act contained a power to grant-aid specific projects with the approval of the Secretary of State. Instead the emphasis was on investment finance, on factory accommodation, and on the environment. To these were later to be added responsibility for the promotion of inward investment from overseas, a function which is now carried out jointly with S.E.P.D. through the Locate in Scotland office.

These various changes greatly increased the Secretary of State's role and that of S.E.P.D. in matters which had previously been the responsibility of the Department of Trade and Industry, but there was one further change which extended it into the realm of the Department of Employment. In the early 1970s the Government had set up the Manpower Services Commission to take over and develop the Department of Employment's functions in relation to training and employment services. Membership of the Commission was drawn from representatives of the Confederation of British Industries, the Trades Union Congress and local authorities with education interests. In due course the Commission established a Scottish committee to advise on its functions in

Scotland, and in 1976 it was decided to transfer responsibility for the Manpower Services Commission in relation to its Scottish activities to the Secretary of State for Scotland with S.E.P.D. as the responsible department.

Thus by the end of the decade the responsibilities of the Secretary of State in economic matters had been immensely increased. S.E.P.D., though still by far the smallest of the five Scottish Office departments with a total staff of just over 200, had a range of functions which corresponded to some of the responsibilities of several different Whitehall departments. These covered regional policy and the provision of financial assistance to industry, and energy policy, including a direct responsibility for electricity and a co-ordinating role in relation to North Sea oil; in addition the Department exercised a sponsoring responsibility for the two development agencies, the Scottish Development Agency (S.D.A.) and the Highlands and Islands Development Board (H.I.D.B.), for the five Scottish new towns, the Scottish Tourist Board, the two Scottish electricity boards, and for the Manpower Services Commission's activities in Scotland. The total funds on S.E.P.D., votes for which the head of the Department as Accounting Officer was responsible to Parliament amounted to some £300 million a year.

4. ASSESSMENT

It is striking that the number in employment in Scotland in 1980, the end of the period with which we are concerned, was not very different from the beginning: 2,072 thousand as compared with 2,024 thousand in 1952, 2,083 thousand in 1961 and 2,003 thousand in 1971. The apparent stability concealed some fluctuation during this period and a peak in the mid-1960s from which there was subsequent decline, but overall the striking feature is stability. Much bigger reductions were to follow in the early 1980s. The numbers unemployed, of course, rose substantially from 65,000 in 1950 to 223,000 in 1980. The working population was therefore nearly 200,000 higher at this end of the period than it was at the start.

But the apparent stability in these figures conceals dramatic change in the industrial composition of employment. Employment in the major declining sectors of coalmining, metal manufacture, shipbuilding, vehicles, textiles and agriculture had fallen by over 300,000, some 15 per cent of total employment in 1980. The expanding sectors were equally striking, electrical engineering (including electronics), North Sea oil related employment, insurance, banking and finance and professional and scientific services showing an increase in jobs of similar magnitude (see the chapters by Professor Payne and J. N. Randall in this volume).

One of the notable features of this transformation is the alteration in the balance of employment towards the services sector, a trend which was evident in the other O.E.C.D. countries as well over this period. In Scotland's case manufacturing employment declined from 36 per cent to 28 per cent of the total, while employment in services rose from 52 per cent to 59 per cent, figures which were close to the proportionate share of these sectors in the United Kingdom.

Scotland's economic structure was widely considered to be a handicap in 1950, and the principal reason for the economy to lag behind the performance of the United Kingdom as a whole in terms of output, employment growth and income level. Various shift share analyses were undertaken during the thirty years, starting with the Toothill Report, and these have generally shown that Scotland's poor growth performance in the 1950s was indeed largely explained by structure rather than by inferior performance sector by sector.[18] Similar studies undertaken in the 1960s showed that Scotland was still handicapped by structure, but that the performance industry by industry was above the United Kingdom average, leading to some reduction in regional disparities.[19] By 1980, however, recent work shows that although the older industries are still somewhat more heavily represented in Scotland than in Great Britain as a whole, the structural effect has become insignificant.[20] There are no doubt a variety of reasons for this, of which the change in structure which had taken place is probably the principal one. But there were also important changes in the relative performance of individual industries themselves. For example, the motor industry which was seen as the best example of a growth sector in 1950 had joined shipbuilding as a problem sector; and it played a much larger part in the economy of some other U.K. regions. This type of analysis has its limitations, of course; a share statistically equivalent to the national average may still conceal a structure handicap if, for example, Scotland has more than its share of unprofitable coalmines, a steelworks which is further than its competitors in England and Wales from its market and a major shipyard making disproportionate losses. But there can be no doubt at all that the structural handicap had been greatly diminished.

Other indicators also demonstrate the changes which had taken place. Scotland's economic growth in the 1960s and 1970s not only kept up with the United Kingdom's, but in the first half of the 1970s exceeded the U.K. rate of growth instead of lagging behind as it had done throughout much of the 1950s. Income, whether measured by gross domestic product per head or by earnings, came closer to the United Kingdom average G.D.P per head by the end of the period, being only some 4% below the U.K. figure. And finally unemployment: although rates of unemployment had moved from being extremely low in 1950 to intolerably high in 1980, there can be no doubt that Scotland's relative position compared with the United Kingdom as a whole had started to improve in the 1960s when unemployment was typically twice the U.K. average, had improved further in the first half of the 1970s and, although it deteriorated slightly in the second half, by 1980 was still only some 35% above the U.K. rate.

By 1980 regional policy measures, in the form of preferential assistance to industry, were costing £198m. a year, of which regional development grants accounted for £113m., selective financial assistance £22m., the loans and grants of H.I.D.B. £11m. and the land and factory building functions of

S.D.A. £47m.[21] Even allowing for the various offsets, whether in the form of interest payments on loans, factory rents or reduced expenditure on unemployment or social security, it is clear that the cost of the policy was substantial. It is therefore important to consider how far the improvements in Scotland's economic performance, as compared with the U.K., were the consequence of Government policy. Obviously the decline in the older industries would have taken place in any event, through the operation of market forces, unless a regime of outright protection had been imposed. It is also striking that so much of the new employment growth was in the services sector when the policies described in this chapter were aimed primarily at manufacturing; and the windfall of North Sea oil, though affected by policy, was certainly not the product of Scottish or regional policies. But of course regional policy and improved infrastructure assisted a whole range of industries, and even if their aggregate employment did not expand, new firms or new investments replaced the old, thereby limiting the reduction of employment which might otherwise have taken place. It would therefore be a grave error to imagine that the only manufacturing sector to show the benefit of regional policy was electronics because its employment increased in aggregate. The effects of regional policy have been subjected to more thorough research than most other aspects of economic or industrial policy. The best-known and most authoritative work is that of Moore, Rhodes and Tyler. This shows that a 330,000 net increase in manufacturing jobs, as compared with the situation which would have obtained otherwise, had taken place in the assisted areas of the United Kingdom between 1960 and 1976 as a direct consequence of regional policy measures and that the total rises to approximately 480,000 if indirect effects are taken into account.[22] Similar studies for Scotland show a corresponding net increase in jobs as a result of regional policy of approximately 90,000. There is no doubt that Scotland gained considerably from the policies adopted.

The movement of employment from one part of the United Kingdom to another has always been, at least in Scotland's case, only one aspect of regional policy and far from the most important. Increasing emphasis has been given to the promotion of growth in companies already within Scotland with the changes made both in the 1972 Industry Act (when responsibility for administering selective assistance to industry was transferred to Scotland), and in 1975 with the creation of the Scottish Development Agency. Furthermore throughout the thirty years Scotland has established a successful record in the attraction of overseas companies, and it is this that has helped to establish Scotland as one of the principal centres of the electronics industry in Europe. By 1980 there were some 270 firms of overseas origin established in Scotland with a total employment of around 80,000, or 17% of the employees in manufacturing industry. Much of this had been achieved as a result of promotional efforts mounted from Scotland itself; but without the incentives available through regional policy, which make it possible to compete with other assisted areas in Europe, notably the Republic of Ireland, the results would have been meagre indeed.

If we accept that in the absence of regional policy the thirty years would have been a period of much more severe contraction in the Scottish economy, with higher unemployment and higher emigration, there can be no doubt that that would have resulted in a substantial waste of national resources. Labour has to be educated and trained, a charge on public expenditure which should be seen as investment. If it is left unused and unemployed skills may be lost, quite apart from lack of output to yield a return. In Scotland's case at least half of the emigration has gone overseas. As it was, some 360,000 left the country out of a total net emigration of 730,000 over the thirty years. Typically, those who emigrate are the more enterprising and the more highly trained. The more that go, the more the countries they go to benefit from the investment in their training which has been financed by the British taxpayer.

Looking back over the thirty years, it is striking not only to see how the policies developed and agencies such as the new towns, the Highlands and Islands Development Board and the Scottish Development Agency came into being, but also to note the extent to which responsibilities were transferred to the Secretary of State for Scotland. In 1950 the Secretary of State's role was extremely modest, the Distribution of Industry Act giving principal responsibility to the President of the Board of Trade. But in successive stages the Secretary of State's role has been increased, first through the Scottish Development Department to co-ordinate infrastructure planning with economic development, and secondly, from 1973 onwards, through the setting up of the Scottish Economic Planning Department and the transfer to it of powers to give assistance to industry. The growth of the various development agencies has also enhanced his role, since all of them are now responsible to him.

Generally this transfer of responsibilities, and the institutional changes which accompanied it, have been widely welcomed as providing a more responsive and understanding system of administration. As a result of entry to the E.E.C., the widespread reduction in trade barriers and currency controls, and of course the economic circumstances of the time, industry faces an extremely difficult and highly competitive international environment. This is in sharp contrast to the situation thirty years ago when the major European powers and Japan were still recovering from the devastation of the war and trade was impeded both by high tariffs and currency restrictions. Scotland's prosperity in the years ahead will depend upon success in exploiting new industrial ideas and an ability to compete in cost, design and quality in those industries that are exposed to international competition. Only those who work in those sectors can take the action that is necessary to meet the challenge. But Government can critically affect the climate in which industry has to operate, and the right forms of support are essential. The policies and structures described in this chapter will no doubt continue to evolve. But the close co-operation which now exists between industry, private sector finance, public agencies and Government departments should be a source of strength for the future.

NOTES

1. A. K. Cairncross (ed.), *The Scottish Economy* (Cambridge, 1954).
2. Sir Patrick Abercrombie & R. H. Matthew, *Clyde Valley Regional Plan 1946*, (H.M.S.O., 1949).
3. A. D. Campbell, in Cairncross, *op. cit.*, pp. 46-65.
4. C. E. V. Leser, in Cairncross, *op. cit.*, pp. 65-84.
5. Abercrombie & Matthew, *op. cit.*, p. 68.
6. *Second Report of the Select Committee on Estimates, The Development Areas*, (H.M.S.O., Session 1955/56), p. viii & p. 264.
7. *Employment Policy*, Cmd. 6527 (H.M.S.O., 1944).
8. *Royal Commission on the Distribution of Industrial Population* (Barlow Commission), Cmd. 6153 (H.M.S.O., 1940), para. 40.
9. *Report of the Committee on Hydro-Electric Development in Scotland*, Cmd. 6406 (H.M.S.O., 1942), pp. 12-18.
10. The Rt. Hon. Thomas Johnston, *Memories* (Edinburgh, 1952), p. 182.
11. *Report of the Committee on National Policy for the Use of Fuel and Power Resources* (Ridley Committee), Cmd. 8647 (H.M.S.O., 1952).
12. Notably the Local Employment Acts of 1960 and 1963 and the Industrial Development Act of 1966.
13. Scottish Council (Development and Industry), *Committee of Inquiry into the Scottish Economy* (Toothill Committee) (1961).
14. *Central Scotland. A Programme for Development & Growth*, Cmd. 2188 (H.M.S.O., 1963); *The Scottish Economy, 1965-70: A Plan for Expansion*, Cmd. 2864 (H.M.S.O., 1966).
15. Highlands & Islands Development (Scotland) Act, 1965.
16. See my paper in A. F. Peters (ed.), *Impact of Offshore Oil Operations*, Applied Science Publishers, on behalf of Institute of Petroleum (1974), pp. 145-161.
17. *West Central Scotland Plan*, Report 1 (1974), pp. 318-9.
18. Toothill Report (*op. cit.*), Appendix 2; A. J. H. Odber, in *Area Redevelopment Policies in Britain & the Countries of the Common Market*, U.S. Department of Commerce, pp. 327-435.
19. See my *Regional Policy in Britain*, (London, 1969), pp. 169-181.
20. See the chapter by J. N. Randall in this volume.
21. *Scottish Economic Bulletin*, No. 28 (H.M.S.O., 1984).
22. B. Moore, J. Rhodes and P. Tyler, 'The Impact of Regional Policy in the 1970s', *Centre for Environmental Studies Review* (July 1977), p. 67f.

9
THE HIGHLANDS AND ISLANDS DEVELOPMENT BOARD

Sir Kenneth Alexander

To review the economic and social changes in the Highlands and Islands of Scotland over thirty years may seem relatively simple. The population is small, the range of economic activities narrow, and the period of time short. This simplicity is deceptive, however. The Highlands and Islands area is large, covering half the land mass of Scotland, is far from being homogeneous in either social or economic terms, and the period between 1950 and 1980 has been one of very considerable change, leaving behind a difficult problem to disentangle: how to allocate the effects to the different causes.

The economic difficulties of the Highlands and Islands are of long-standing. Climate, geology and physical isolation consolidated the conservatism of the people, so that when the efficiency of agriculture increased in the rest of Scotland, the Highlands and Islands lagged behind. The response of many landowners had been to seek rapid change (to increase rents and the return on the land), without consideration for the effects on the lives of the people and on the settlement pattern and level of population. As the rest of Scotland moved towards a structure of employment in which the significance of primary industries contracted substantially, in the Highlands and Islands the very limited size of the local market for goods and services meant that employment opportunities beyond the primary sector expanded very slowly.

The second World War did not change the economic circumstances of the area in a major way, and a 1938 view effectively sets out the background to our period. Although the rate of depopulation was growing, the low proportion of children and persons in the reproductive age groups was alarming. (A survey of five typical crofting parishes showed that males of 55 and over made up 65% of the total male population and females of that age 73% of the female population.) Crofters, smallholders and fishermen made up the bulk of the population, and the main occupations did not provide an adequate income. The conclusion was that 'the establishment of industries of a suitable character becomes a necessity. In addition, transport infrastructure and freight charges must be minimised, modern methods and science must be applied in the primary sector, and the potential of water power must be developed'.[1]

By the late 1940s the slowing down of population decline was continuing, but disaggregated analysis reveals that acute though more localised problems remained, 'For the declining mainland crofting areas of most of Sutherland County, Wester Ross, Wester Inverness (excluding Fort William and environs) and north-west Argyll . . . the decline is so marked, and young able-bodied men so few, more especially in the peninsular areas, that it seems likely that only a small-scale but deliberate re-colonisation will suffice to carry through rehabilitation schemes and radical improvement in employment prospects and living conditions, without which the population of these areas is likely to become almost extinct, and quite unworkable as communities, at the end of the present older generation'.[2]

This was a time when considerable attention was being paid to the possibilities of Highland regeneration, particularly because of the debate which developed around the future of the North of Scotland Hydro-Electric Board (established by Parliament in 1943) in the circumstances of the nationalisation of electricity supply being enacted in 1946 and 1947.

Against this background, the Labour Government of 1950 published a Programme for Highland Development which summarised the then position as follows:

> Fundamentally the Highland problem is to encourage people to live in the Highlands by making it possible to secure there, in return for reasonable efforts, proper standards of life and the means of paying for them . . . Commissions and Committees of Enquiry into the Highland problem or into particular aspects of it have been numerous, but the action taken by successive Governments has been on the whole designed to preserve rather than to construct and has been motivated by social rather than economic considerations. This is true even of the notable Crofters Holdings (Scotland) Act, 1886, which conferred security of tenure and other material benefits on the crofting population in the Highlands following the decline of their customary rights when the clan system was broken down. More positive measures were taken in 1897 when the Congested Districts (Scotland) Board was set up with power to aid agriculture, fishing and rural industries, to acquire land for land settlement purposes, and to assist in the provision of public works such as roads, piers and harbours. But the use made of these powers was related more to the preservation of the existing population in their traditional pursuits than to the building up of a new economy.
>
> For a long time the scope for any more constructive approach was limited. There was little prospect of introducing new economic activity and the agricultural and fishing industries passed through periods of depression which affected their vitality not only in the Highlands but in all parts of the country. In recent years, however, new factors have emerged which provide the basis for a more constructive approach to the Highland problem and for treating it effectively as one of economic development. These new factors are the increased importance of home food production, the necessity for a large scale programme of afforestation, the development of hydro-electric power in the Highlands and the greatly increased importance of the tourist trade. The need now is to re-assess the Highland problem in the light of these new factors and to frame plans for securing the full benefits which they make possible.[3]

The population-holding influence of the security of tenure which the crofting system gave to crofters led to the setting up of a Commission of Enquiry into Crofting Conditions which reported in 1954,[4] and to the establishment of the Crofters' Commission in 1954. The main treatment of land-use in the Highlands is to be found in Chapter 4.

The economic structure of the Highlands and Islands in 1951 is shown in Table 1. The relative weakness of the Highland economy can be judged by comparing the percentage share of the different sectors in the total labour force with the Highlands and Islands share of 5.6% in the population of Scotland.

The years to 1962 did not produce many favourable changes in the economic circumstances of the Highland economy. Table 2 shows how the share of employment in service industries had expanded at a much faster rate than in

Table 1. *Percentage Distribution of insured employees (including unemployed) in broad industrial groups, 1951*

Area	Metal Trades	Textile leather & clothing	Miscell-aneous Manuf.	Total Manuf.	Agric., forestry, fishing	Mining and Quarry-ing	Service Trades	All industries and services
Highlands & Islands as percentage of all Scotland labour force	1.0	1.0	1.8	1.3	12.9	0.7	5.2	3.8

Source: The Scottish Economy, ed. A. K. Cairncross, C.U.P. 1954

Table 2. *Distribution of Employees as Percentage of Total Employees in Scotland and the Highlands, 1950 and 1962*

Category of Employment	1950			1962	
	Scotland	Highlands		Scotland	Highlands
Primary	5.9	22.9		4.3	17.3
Extractive	4.8	0.7		3.8	0.7
Manufacturing	37.0	11.5		34.5	9.9
Construction	7.4	14.6		8.4	15.7
Services	44.9	50.3		49.0	56.4
	100.0	100.0		100.0	100.0

Source: Mackay & Buxton, *Scottish Journal of Political Economy*, Vol. XII

Scotland, and construction had also taken a larger share in the Highlands while falling in Scotland.

The share of primary industry was falling (from a higher base) rather more rapidly than in Scotland, and the share of manufacturing employment in the total Highland labour force had fallen by nearly 15%.

The comparison with Scotland in terms of income from employment in 1959 brings out very clearly the relatively depressed level of the Highland economy. With Scottish income from employment as 100, the crofting counties plus Argyll and Bute index was approximately 63, by far the lowest of all Scottish counties. The gap in total net income per head was not quite so wide, with Scotland at 100 and the Highlands at approximately 77, this narrowing partly explained by the fact that profits and professional earnings per head were actually much higher in the Highlands than the Scottish average, and income from investment much closer to the Scottish average than was income from employment.[5] These monetary differences reflect differences in the social structure of the Highlands, important in a number of ways in considering the developments of the period 1950-1980. Population in the Highlands and Islands in the decade to 1960 had fallen by about 2½% overall, but by approximately 10% in the Islands alone. Just as a Labour government had at the beginning of the decade produced a programme for a period in which it would be out of government, now a Conservative government produced its Review of Highland Policy in 1959.[6]

The most critical review of this period came from academic economists, and is interesting not only for the empirical evidence offered, but also for the policy conclusions drawn. An estimate of £220m. public sector gross fixed capital formation in the Highlands over the period 1951-1960 was contrasted with a population decline of 8.07 thousand for this decade, compared with 3.71 thousand for 1931-1951. Despite substantial government assistance, the number of insured employees in the primary industries fell by approximately 10%. Whereas the rate of unemployment in Scotland rose by 42%, the Highland rate rose by only 14%, but at 6.6% was nearly twice as high as the Scottish average.

It was concluded that '. . . . measured in terms of population, capacity or employment it is clear that the objectives outlined in the 1950 Programme have not been attained. Indeed, it appears as if the general economic situation in the Highlands may have deteriorated from 1951 to 1960.'[7]

This writer and two others[8] had policy proposals to make which coincided in relation to the role of primary industries and appeared to diverge in relation to manufacturing and large-scale developments. Simpson wrote: 'Inefficiency' [in government policy] 'is evidenced in the direction of government expenditures to the declining traditional industries which afford neither profit nor employment in the Highlands, at the expense of industries which provide employment and the prospect of eventual profit . . . it is difficult to find any criteria to justify further investments in agriculture, fisheries and forestry'; and he also expressed concern at the protection of small producers, favouring expenditure to promote industrialisation primarily through foreign private investment.[9] Mackay and Buxton go further: 'what evidence there is available suggests that there is no economic case for the development of the Highland area; . . . the economic solution to the "Highland problem" is to induce the movement of labour out of, and not the movement of capital into, the area',[10] [yet] 'policy remains oriented towards propping up, with increasing Government expenditure, a decaying social and economic order.' Simpson had no difficulty in demonstrating the inadequacy of this approach, but his conclusion that 'discriminatory capital subsidies and current subsidies limited in time' must be offered as an inducement to private industry is arrived at purely by a process of elimination. There is no indication of how many jobs would have to be provided, nor any attempt to indicate what economic costs such a policy would involve.[11] The conclusions reached by these writers on the performance and prospects for each sector of industry within the Highlands were bleak.

Summarised, these were: the probability of the continued decline of crofting; declining opportunities for fishing and ancillary industries; decline of Highland industries even when these were 'growth' industries in U.K. terms; no further growth in public authority employment. Possibilities for expansion of tourism would require a much higher level of capital investment; and its seasonality would make tourism an inadequate basis by which to prevent depopulation. Forestry seemed to be the sole hope for halting population drift. The conclusion was that 'If economic cost is to be counted, the scope for redevelopment is limited in the Highlands and further depopulation is inevitable'.

Politicians were striking a more positive note, but there was pessimism amongst many senior civil servants and politicians about the possibility of reversing these trends and confounding the academics.

Experience in the early years of the sixties was inconclusive. By 1965, population was down 0.7 on the census figures of 1961, the fall being 3.1% for the Islands. Net migration from the Highlands and Islands did not compare unfavourably with that for Scotland as a whole, with a crude loss averaging, over the four years, 1961-64 at 0.45% p.a. compared with a loss of 0.66 for all Scotland. Manpower (employed and unemployed) in the major sectors had changed between 1961 and 1965 as follows: Primary −1,222, Manufacturing +636, Construction −962, Utilities, Distribution and Transport +812, Hotels and Catering +1,284, Miscellaneous Services +805, All Highlands +1,888.[12] Unemployment rates, seasonably adjusted, were unchanged for males and very slightly lower for females,[13] keeping the unemployment relative for the Highlands in relation to all Scotland practically constant.

The Highlands and Islands appeared to be in step with the Scottish economy, which itself was slipping behind, with the ratio of Scottish unemployment to that in Great Britain having reached its highest level in 1960 and returned to that level (a level of more than twice) in 1964. There were also signs that average money income per head was increasing in the Highlands more than in either Scotland or the U.K., the three rates for the period 1960 to 1965 being 43.2%, 37.5% and 35.6%. For the area as a whole, however, a process of agglomeration was at work. Population changes between 1961 and 1965 showed a percentage increase of 4.1% for the burgh of Inverness (1,200 population increase), with an increase also in Caithness (600) within the small overall decline (0.7%), and in contrast to the sharp fall of 3.1% for the Islands.

The area was at the beginning of a new period of substantial change and considerable growth. Several factors brought about these changes, these factors coming together in time but being unrelated themselves in origin and, to a lesser extent, in the nature of the impacts they brought to bear on the economy of the area.

These factors were:

(1) the increase in income and spending power in the U.K. economy over the period 1966 to 1980, and the improved position of Scottish G.D.P. per head as a percentage of the U.K. figure, rising from 89.6% in 1966 to 96.7% in 1975, rising to 98% in 1976, but falling slightly to 96% by 1980. Purchasing power in Scotland is a potent factor encouraging expenditure and growth in parts of the Highlands and Islands, because of close commercial ties, recreational ties and family ties;

(2) the establishment of the Highlands and Islands Development Board (H.I.D.B.) in 1965, bringing not only a marked increase in public expenditure aimed at stimulating economic activity, but also providing leadership and guidance to the development process and giving a substantial boost to morale in the area;[14]

(3) the effect of two major developments on employment and prosperity, the pulp and paper mill at Corpach in Lochaber, creating construction employment from 1963 and going into production in late 1965, and the aluminium smelter at Invergordon, in construction from 1969 and in production in 1972. The building of the experimental breeder-reactor power station at Dounreay between 1955 and 1959 and the build-up of operating staff had already had a major effect on the area around Thurso

(the population of Caithness rising by nearly 200% between 1951 and 1966), and further expansion was to come with the building of a second prototype fuel reactor, announced in 1966:

(4) the onshore impact of oil exploration and exploitation, drilling activity beginning in 1967, the ordering of production platforms beginning in 1972, installations being established in 1974 and production beginning in 1975;

(5) in a minor key, but not without importance, an increasing interest by a limited number of mainly young people in the rural lifestyle and the importance of peace, quiet and beauty as factors determining their decisions as to where to live (a particularly important factor in the growth of the small-scale craft industry).

At the beginning of this period, in January 1966, the Labour Government which had come to office in 1964, produced a five-year *Plan for the Expansion of the Scottish Economy*,[15] including detailed treatment of the Highlands and Islands. The Highland Board, which began work on 1st November 1965, was quoted as joint author of the Highland section of the Plan, published in January 1966. Forestry, tourism and industry requiring water and deepwater facilities were singled out as the most important possibilities for development. Already there were pointers to what was to be the practical experience of the Board: 'Managerial ability . . . is one of the region's weaknesses, and it is significant that although there is a good flow of local applicants interested in starting businesses, many of them fail through sheer lack of training in book-keeping and other aspects of business management'. The Highland section concluded with guidelines:

> First, a policy of concentration on objectives worth investing in, on the points identified as centres of the main labour catchment areas and on those villages and townships in the hinterland which offer the best hope of viability; secondly, the development of forestry and forestry-based industries to give in the long-term the core of employment in much of the region; thirdly, the complementary development of tourism both to assist consolidation in some of the main centres and give a supplementary income to the dispersed population engaged in primary and service industry, large and small and perseverance in attracting outsiders. In the period before a forestry-based industry really becomes established, a modest intermediate expansion of manufacturing employment will also be necessary to ensure that the population structure of the region does not run down to an extent which would jeopardise the ultimate supply of labour on an adequate scale.[16]

The H.I.D.B. in its first Report discussed its preferred range of solutions to Highland problems. In the main, the Board followed the lead of the government Plan, expanding on the forestry, tourism and manufacturing approaches. For manufacturing, the Board elaborated on the growth point approach: 'a methodical programme of building small industrial growth points on a scale with the possibilities of the West and the Islands' coupled with the generation of 'major growth points, involving substantial increases in population wherever the natural advantages of the areas seem to warrant it: the Moray Firth is unquestionably the most important of these areas'.[17]

Reporting on and evaluating the period from the mid-60s to 1980 cannot be

Table 3. *Fisheries, landings by weight, 1966-1980*

	1966	1970	1975	1980
White fish (cwts)	854	984	1710	3115
% of Scotland catch	19%	20%	33%	27.9%
Herring (cwts)	1998	2457	2551	5235
	82%	87%	85%	86.9%
Shellfish (cwts)	83	208	229	790
	38%	47%	54%	57.2%

Source: H.I.D.B. Annual Reports

tackled comprehensively. A few major issues must be covered, and a more general commentary added. Firstly, a sectoral view.

FISHERIES

The number of full-time fishermen increased from 2,513 in 1966 to 2,959 in 1979, against the trend in the rest of Scotland which fell from 5,560 to 4,654 over the same period. There were 533 vessels in the fleet by 1980, about half of which were under 20 tons, and only 26 over 50 tons. In its first five years of operation the Board assisted the purchase of 209 boats, and the volume of white fish landings had risen from 854 cwts. to 984 cwts. in 1970. This growth, from a very weak base, was continued, as the figures for landings in Table 3 show. Despite all the vicissitudes of this industry, of which the rise in fuel costs, the delay in agreeing a Common Fisheries Policy for the E.E.C., and the over-fishing and consequent limits to catching designed to achieve conservation were the most serious, this has been a growth area in the Highlands and Islands, and the clearest case of success achieved as a result of purposeful help from the public sector. The H.I.D.B.'s first major attempt to encourage the opening up of the fishing grounds to the west of the Hebrides to more local fishermen, fishing for blue whiting and ling, failed. It can be argued that it was the conduct of this project (at Breasclete), not the concept, which proved inadequate.[18] The decision in 1984 to develop major facilities at Ardveenish, Barra, for the landing and processing of fish, indicated that the strategy had survived the failure at Breasclete. As an example of an integrated development process, boatbuilding and repairing went ahead in the Highlands and Islands over this period.

MANUFACTURING

The increasing significance of manufacturing is brought out by the growth in employment from approximately 9,600 in 1966 to nearly 17,000 in 1978. However, with an estimated 4,500 of these jobs derived from oil-related manufacturing, the growth is less impressive. In 1978, the share of

Table 4. *Estimates of Manufacturing Employment (000's) Firms employing 11 and over*

	1966	1967	1968	1969	1970	1971	1972	1973	1974	1975	1976	1977	1978	1979	1980
Highlands	5401	5385	5082	5568	5796	6152	7296	8582	9721	11248	11440	11	11.7	11.6	10.6
Units	92	94	90	100	107	103	109	114	114	111	111				
Islands	2031	1855	1942	1943	1986	1982	2067	1946	1981	1967	2017	2.2	2.2	2.4	2.4
Units	52	53	55	55	55	56	64	63	62	59	56				
Scotland	696.6														526.7

Source: Scottish Economic Bulletin No. 21, 1980 & No. 26, 1983

manufacturing in Highland employment was just under half the percentage share for Scotland (14.1% compared with 29.2%), a rise from a third in 1964 (10% compared to 34%). The importance of manufacturing for Highland development has been endorsed in almost every report and study, but the difficulties of achieving a substantial improvement are clearly great. It is in this field of economic activity that the difficulties which arise from the diseconomies of small-scale production (determined both by labour supply related to technology and by market access linked to transport costs) create the greatest barriers to development in the Highlands and Islands. These difficulties can often be compounded by inadequate and inexperienced management, due in part to the early stage of industrial development and the absence of a large pool of experienced managers ready to move over to new and challenging opportunities.

Particularly encouraging are the estimates given in Table 4 of the rise from 1966 to 1980 in employment in manufacturing firms employing 11 and over in the Highlands (+96%) and the Islands (+20%), compared with a decline for all Scotland of 24%. Although these figures are estimated, the differences are wide enough to allow the conclusion to be drawn that, although slowly and unequally, during this period, the Highlands and Islands were overcoming the deficiency in manufacturing industry.

The closure of the pulp mill at Corpach in 1981 cut approximately 400 jobs out of the manufacturing total, and the closure of the smelter at Invergordon took out a further 900. These figures take no account of secondary employment. As far as the pulp mill is concerned, there were early fears that many more jobs in forestry and transport could be lost.[19] In the event the Highland timber was exported to Scandinavia, and the impact of closure was cushioned temporarily at least. The smelter had a much lower multiplier, as a result of there being few local inter-industry linkages; at 1.33 the additional loss of jobs in the area would be estimated at nearly 300.[20] The extent to which this multiplier effect is realised depends in part on the extent to which those made unemployed leave the area. In the smelter case, the movement has not been great.

Different conclusions were drawn from these major economic setbacks, the most fundamental and simplistic being that large-scale industrial development has no place in the Highlands and Islands. An alternative conclusion drawn was that these particular enterprises were never viable from the start, but that other industries could be viable based upon licensing agreements, if necessary publicly owned in part at least, and with government funding the entre-preneurs to run these new plants.[21] A third view was that the failure was due to particular circumstances which might have been avoided. In the case of the pulp mill, for example, it could be argued that the timing of its establishment was wrong. The supply of local timber for pulping was too low to sustain a mill of the optimum size, and the technical process chosen (chemical rather than mechanical) would not have been so rapidly superseded had the establishment been delayed. A later start would also probably have led to a different location, more central, although the increasing availability of timber would have justified two locations rather than one by 1990.[22] In the case of the aluminium smelter, the world price has doubled in less than two years since the closure, despite the continuing world recession. The long history of aluminium smelting in the Highlands at Foyers (1895), Kinlochleven (1909), and Fort William (1929) itself, suggests that it would be mistaken to allow a particular failure to condemn this form of employment for the area under all circumstances.

Whatever policy conclusion is to be drawn on the basis of these major closures in the Highlands, the experience reinforces the importance attached to small and medium-sized manufacturing, capable of location in the small towns in the area, a distribution of industry more likely to hold population throughout the entire area. It is significant that the Board's strategy, published in 1982, recognised this clearly, and at the same time rejected the growth-point strategy which played a central role in the thinking of the mid '60s:

(1) The Board gives special attention and injects a higher level of assistance (per head of population) into the more remote and socially fragile areas in the Islands and the peripheral mainland areas.

(2) The Board rejects the adoption of any rigid strategy based on concentrating investments in growth areas and key settlements.[23]

The evidence that, in the main, (1) above did guide policy is provided in Table 5.

The range of small and medium-sized manufacturing establishments is very wide, from electronics on the technological frontier through food provision, textiles and knitwear to crafts. Within crafts, too, the range is wide, from a substantial company, Caithness Glass, to a large number of very small units, some producing very high quality work and others producing items attractive to tourists as mementos of holidays or as gifts for family and friends. There were over 800 craft-based businesses in the Highlands and Islands in 1980. From 1967 to 1975 (excluding Shetland knitwear and Harris tweed), the total sales in real terms rose from £350,000 to £3.5m. The expansion of this industry benefited from the desire of some to settle and make a modest living in the Highlands. Considerable benefits to peripheral areas came from such settlement, the arrival of young families, some additional employment, a 'demonstration effect' in some cases and a contribution to local leadership in others.

Although a comprehensive treatment of industrial development in the Highlands and Islands is not possible, reference must be made to the Harris tweed industry, an 'appropriate technology' established long before the phrase was applied to third-world problems becoming a major source of secondary employment and income for crofters on Lewis, as well as providing full-time employment for workers in the mills. Securing unique protection with the Orb mark, the industry was nonetheless threatened by competition using more advanced techniques and producing a similar product, and suffered a secular decline in demand over most of the seventies. The turning point came when

Table 5. Board Assistance by statistical area, 1972-81 (at 1981 prices)

STATISTICAL AREAS	No. of cases	Employment created	Employment retained	Population (1974)	Grant equivalence per head of population
Shetland	295	727	432	18,445	198
Orkney	612	779	326	17,462	273
Caithness	465	1,342	406	27,901	192
North-West Sutherland	154	239	57	3,547	451
South-East Sutherland	219	515	202	9,923	192
Wester Ross	250	553	106	4,632	817
Easter Ross	285	1,380	146	33,534	129
Inverness	323	2,180	416	51,897	150
Nairn*	48	117	15	8,906	72
Badenoch	184	625	153	9,043	416
Lochalsh	48	85	32	2,379	191
Skye	284	569	109	7,340	426
Lewis & Harris	353	1,335	730	23,073	235
Uists & Barra	232	578	229	6,987	482
Lochaber	351	1,348	280	19,150	347
Argyll Islands	318	487	206	7,368	494
Oban and Lorn	256	573	262	13,619	258
Mid-Argyll & Kintyre	336	1,512	377	18,612	396
Dunoon & Cowal	166	656	229	17,315	170
Bute*	83	269	41	7,956	129
Arran & Cumbraes	133	171	27	4,787	173
Non-area specific	13	9	0	—	—

Source: H.I.D.B. Annual Reports

Notes: The figures above related to assistance approved by the Board — not payments. Cases withdrawn after approval are thus included. Social development grants are excluded.

Grant equivalence is defined as grant + one-fifth loan.

Part-time or seasonal jobs are valued at half a job, and part-time seasonal jobs at a quarter.

* Nairn, Bute and Arran were not elegible for Board assistance until 1975, and the Cumbraes not until 1980.

in 1975 a large equity investment by the H.I.D.B. in the largest of the then three major companies brought about substantial restructuring of the industry and opened the way to more effective marketing. The influence exercised by the out-working weavers, rooted in their trade association, blocked an attempt in the mid-seventies to change the technology and group the weavers in small factories.[24]

TOURISM

Tourism has shown very rapid growth from 1950 to 1980, reflecting not only the increased investment in tourist facilities in the area but also rising incomes and increased leisure in the U.K., and with a lesser effect, in Europe and North America. Unfortunately, there are no comprehensive statistics, but as an indicator of growth over this period, there were 924,300 visitors in 1955 and 1,664,000 in 1981. Visitors to the Highlands on the average spend longer there than visitors to other parts of Scotland, and with only 5% of the total population of Scotland, the Highlands attract approximately 19% of all tourist expenditure.[25]

A survey for 1982 (the first since 1973) gave the total direct visitor expenditure for that year as £126.2m.[26] Unfortunately quite a high proportion of this expenditure leaks out of the area, but even so the effect on employment and income in the Highland area is considerable. An important influence on the magnitude of the multiplier effect is the category of tourist accommodation used by tourists, and there has been a marked shift away from serviced to self-catering accommodation. A conservative estimate of the employment generated by this £126.2m. expenditure would be that some 70,000 people would be employed, some part-time, many seasonally. The importance of this employment is probably measured more effectively in income terms. Again a conservative estimate would be that the local multiplier effects counteract the leakage effect, leaving the additional gross income enjoyed by Highland residents as a result of tourism approximately the same as the direct expenditure by tourists. This additional gross income falls with any shift from serviced to self-catering accommodation. Table 6 shows how hotel occupancy has been falling in the Highland area, particularly in the tourist season. This reflects both the difficulties faced by Highland tourism generally (higher petrol prices and increased travel costs), but also the increasing attraction of self-catering and other forms of accommodation, a trend which reflects not only taste factors but the more difficult economic circumstances of the latter years. 1981 was a particularly bad year, with the occupancy rate falling as a result both of a reduction in the number of tourists in the hotel sector and the coming on-stream of substantial new hotel accommodation. By 1982 there was a slight increase in the average occupancy rate (from 46 to 52). It will need a continuation of this trend if the view that over-capacity has been increased is to be resisted.

Table 6. *Hotel Occupancy in Highlands and Islands, 1974-1981*

	April	May	June	July	August	September	October	Average
1974	34	47	64	76	76	84	48	61
1975	36	53	67	76	76	80	42	60
1976	33	46	62	74	74	79	38	56
1977	33	46	62	71	74	58	40	55
1978	25	45	59	69	71	57	35	52
1979	33	48	57	65	72	56	39	53
1980	30	41	51	58	64	54	37	48
1981	31	43	46	51	61	53	34	46
1982	N/A	N/A	N/A	N/A	N/A	N/A	N/A	52

Source: Hotel Occupancy Survey, H.I.D.B.

The H.I.D.B. and several commentators were clear by the early 1980s that if the contribution of tourism to Highland development was to be consolidated and extended, it was essential to secure within the area the production of more of the goods and services which the tourist consumed, and to expand tourist expenditures by the provision of more attractive facilities. It was recognised that it might be difficult to achieve this without detriment to some of the characteristics of the area which explain its power to attract visitors.

COMMUNITY CO-OPERATIVES

From 1978, the creation of a new mechanism to encourage development should be noted. Borrowing and adapting from Irish example, the H.I.D.B. made it possible for communities in peripheral locations (beginning in the Western Isles) to establish and run multi-functional community co-operatives. There was an encouraging response, with the great majority of those launched surviving not only the intrinsic difficulties of their location and local economy, but also surviving the additional difficulties resulting from the general depression of the late seventies and early eighties. There were 14 such co-operatives by 1981, plus a number of smaller co-operative ventures. Their contribution to their local communities was fourfold: firstly, the provision of services (shops, plant hire, coal deliveries, minibuses) which otherwise would not have been provided; secondly, the creation of jobs and incomes (full-time, part-time, out-work and seasonal); thirdly, the provision of social activity — building and managing a local hall, organising events; and fourthly, their great importance in providing a boost to morale as a result of successful self-help activities chosen and operated by the community itself. The total economic activity is very small — possibly no greater than 100 job equivalents in communities for which the total population is approximately 9,000 — but the potential is considerable.

TRANSPORT

The importance of transport services and transport costs to the social and economic life of the Highlands and Islands is obvious. For many communities there are considerable distances to be travelled before a town the size of 10,000 is reached, and maybe as much as 200 miles — some over water — before the populated Central Belt of Scotland is reached. That Central Belt is itself regarded by many producers as sub-optimal in terms of the external economies and the markets it can provide. These are formidable obstacles in the way of holding population and sustaining viable businesses. These difficulties were made worse by the substantial series of price rises for petrol and diesel in the seventies. The most acute difficulties are those faced by island communities, and there have been a number of studies and reports suggesting how — in part by subsidy — these difficulties might be minimised.[27] The extent of the subsidy required in some cases was masked by the possibility of a degree of cross-subsidisation, especially during the early years of the Scottish Transport Group which operated both bus and ferry services throughout Scotland. However, national policy moved against cross-subsidisation and towards an insistence that the extent of subsidy required for each service should be known, in part so that the cost could be borne by local (i.e. regional) government rather than national government. Subsidies for ferries have, in the main, remained with national government, but have come increasingly under scrutiny. The policy proposal most favoured for the Islands was 'road-equivalent tariff' (R.E.T.), that is, that passengers and freight should pay what a similar length of journey would have cost on the mainland, with subsidy meeting the rest. This policy had been part of the manifesto of the incoming Conservative government in 1979. Its attraction was that it would provide a clear rationale for subsidy, but it had the serious weakness that it provided no obvious check to the costs, or measure against which these could be assessed. In 1984, Government announced that the earlier intention to adopt R.E.T. had been abandoned.[28]

Despite these difficulties, the period saw a great improvement in ferry services. Changes in some of the main terminals shortened the sea-journeys; extensive capital investment in both terminals and vessels enabled roll-on vehicle ferries to be introduced. Costs, and the consequent impact on prices, remained the problem, however, and although substantial subsidies continued to be provided, a more stable and longer-run solution was widely accepted as desirable.

The growth of air services — passenger and freight — has played a very important role in opening up the Highlands and Islands, both to commerce and to tourism. Here, too, low utilisation of capacity has threatened the continuation of particular services. By the early eighties, the pattern of provision had not settled into a stable, long-term pattern established on a commercially viable basis. Any major curtailment of air services would have very serious effects on some existing businesses and on the prospects for expansion.

CONCLUSION

The period under review has seen a reversal in what had been long-run declining trends in the economy of the Highlands and Islands. The growth in population, employment and incomes in the second half of this period has been particularly marked. One key indicator of regional performance within a national economy is the unemployment relative, which compares movements in the unemployment rate for an area with that for the nation. An independent study, commissioned by the Highlands and Islands Development Board, produced some encouraging information for the period 1954-1980. A summarised version brings out the main trends:

Table 7. *Unemployment Relatives, Seasonally Adjusted June & December*
1954, 1960, 1965, 1970, 1975, 1980

Highland Unemployment % relation to all Scotland

	June	*December*
1954	215	219
1960	189	190
1965	206	219
1970	165	152
1975	111	111
1980	98	92

After three years of deterioration from 1954 to 1957, there was a period of improvement until 1965 (the male relative had been as low as 142 in 1963), but with deterioration setting in again with the male relative higher in 1966 (231) than it had been in 1954. The falling trend continued thereafter, with only minor fluctuations. It has to be remembered that the improvement being measured was in relation to a sharp absolute increase in unemployment in the country as a whole over the later years of the seventies. What these figures do not bring out is the significant reduction in seasonal fluctuations in employment in the Highlands and Islands between 1954 and 1977, an improvement which was held until 1980. Given the more serious problem of seasonal unemployment (about three times the comparable rate for Scotland), this reduction is of great importance. Unfortunately, although female employment grew more rapidly over the period than did male employment, the female to male unemployment relative had worsened from the mid-seventies onwards. Summarising, from 1966 there is a dramatic improvement in the Highland unemployment relative. Some of this is cyclical, the relative falling when unemployment is high in the country as a whole. However, for 1969 there was further improvement which did not appear to be cyclical in character, more evident when the Highlands are compared to Great Britain, but also in relation to Scotland. The improvement in the late sixties and the seventies reflected an improvement in the competitive position of the Highlands and Islands. Additionally, the dispersion of unemployment rates between areas within the Highlands and Islands markedly diminished over this period.

Of particular interest is the extent to which government intervention played a significant part in this reversal of trends. The H.I.D.B. was created midway through the period covered by this review. It is very difficult to estimate the contribution the Board has made to the marked improvement of the area's economy during the period 1966 to 1980. The figures for employment created which have been quoted by the Board in its Annual Reports refer to estimates made at the time when assistance is being sought, and it is made clear that these cannot be relied upon. There are many examples of firms undershooting and overshooting these expectations, and of some failing altogether. The factors which can alter both the absolute and relative prosperity of an area are numerous and complex, and it is virtually impossible to attribute with certainty increases in employment to particular causes. Improvements in transport infrastructure, changes in the capital intensity of production processes and thus in the need for space, new markets arising, for example from membership of the E.E.C., and the uneven regional impact of North Sea oil can all be cited as influences substantially distinct from regional policy. The expansion of employment over the period 1966 to 1978 would be reduced from 33,700 to 15,700 if direct and related employment arising from North Sea oil, plus the additional employment created by the multiplier effect of that part of the earnings from such employment which was spent in the area, were discounted. However, some of this employment had to be attracted to the Highlands or stimulated from within by the efforts of and assistance from the H.I.D.B., so that a reduction by the full 18,000 jobs would be misleading. A comparison on such a basis over a decade or more ignores the job losses which have been replaced. The net gain in employment over a lengthy period in a fragile economy greatly underestimates the job creation process. Additionally, and of particular importance in the Highlands and Islands, these figures do not take account of part-time and seasonal employment, for example in tourism and in agriculture and horticulture.

From 1966 to 1978 the total number in employment in Scotland (itself an assisted area) fell from 2,217,000 to 2,067,000 (−2.25%). Over the same period, employment in the H.I.D.B. area grew from 85,900 to 119,611 (+39.66). That contrast, taken together with the estimates of growth in manufacturing employment for Highland and Island units compared with the decline for Scotland shown in Table 4, and the improvement in the Highland unemployment relative are clear indications of some special factor or factors at work, greatly exceeding the differential impact of oil and oil-related activity on the economic life of the area. That the work of the H.I.D.B. was such a factor would seem to be a reasonable assumption, when the alternatives are considered, although there is no incontrovertible way of demonstrating from published sources that this is or is not the case.

The influence of the Highland Board had a remarkable effect on the growth of private investment in the area. Over the decade 1974 to 1983, the

Table 8. *Structure of Employment, broad sectors, as %age of total employment*
(excluding proprietors & self-employed)

	1961	1966	1971	1978
	%	%	%	%
Agriculture	9.4	7.6	6.7	4.6
Forestry	2.8	2.4	1.9	0.7
Fishing	2.0	1.8	2.2	2.7
Mining & Quarrying	1.0	0.6	0.5	0.4
Total manufacturing	10.2	11.2	12.1	14.1
Total construction	16.6	14.3	11.9	7.7
Total services (excluding utilities)	58.0	61.2	64.7	58.9
Total Employment	100	100	100	100
	(81,700)	(85,900)	(86,400)	(119,611)

Source: H.I.D.B. Annual Reports

proportion of private investment to public grant and loan in Board-assisted developments grew steadily from 54% to 74% (the growth in private investment over the period was 312%, from £15.5m. to £63.9m. measured in 1983 prices).

The statistics which signalled this turn-around in the economic health of the Highlands and Islands have to be qualified with a recognition of the wide divergence of experience in different areas. Despite the efforts of the H.I.D.B. to devote greater attention and higher levels of financial support to the most fragile areas (Table 6), and some signs of convergence within the area (for example in the unemployment relatives), considerable differences in demographic trends remained.

Table 9. *Population present on Census night, % increase or decrease on previous Census*

	1961-1971	1971-1981
Island areas	−7.05	+21.65
Orkney	−8.91	+11.59
Shetland	−2.72	+57.42
Western Isles	−8.34	+6.67
Argyll & Bute	−1.05	+5.82
Highland Region	+7.12	+14.0
All Scotland	+0.96	−1.88

Source: Census of Population, 1981

In its first seventeen years the H.I.D.B. achieved a great deal, but there were acute examples of economic backwardness remaining. The potentialities for development had been demonstrated, but the limits had not yet been determined.

NOTES

1. Scottish Economic Committee, *The Highlands and Islands of Scotland* (1938).

2. A. Geddes and F. D. N. Spaven, *The Highlands and Isles: their regional planning* (Edinburgh, 1949).

3. Scottish Home Department, *A Programme for Highland Development* Cmd. 7976 (1950).

4. Department of Agriculture for Scotland, *A Programme for Highland Development*. Report of the Commission of Enquiry into Crofting Conditions, Cmd. 9091 (1954).

5. For fuller details, see Gavin McCrone, *Scotland's Economic Progress, 1951-1960* (London, 1965).

6. *Review of Highland Policy*, Cmd. 785 (1959).

7. David Simpson, 'Investment, Employment and Government Expenditure in the Highlands, 1951-1960', *Scottish Journal of Political Economy (S.J.P.E.)*, Vol. X, No. 3, (1963), p. 279.

8. D. I. Mackay and N. K. Buxton, 'The North of Scotland Economy — A Case for Redevelopment?', *S.J.P.E.*, Vol. XII, No. 4, (1965).

9. Simpson, *loc. cit.*, pp. 279, 274.

10. Mackay and Buxton, *loc. cit.*, p. 23.

11. *Ibid.*, p. 24, citing Simpson, *loc. cit.*, pp. 277-8.

12. Highlands and Islands Development Board, *Third Report* (1968).

13. P.E.I.D.A., (Planning, Economic, Industrial, Development, Advisors) *Unemployment in the Highlands and Islands* (1978).

14. Writing in 1951, T. A. F. Noble had argued that 'large sums are poured into the Highlands in various forms without any machinery being created to ensure that their expenditure is an efficient investment', 'The Economic Development of the Highlands', Manchester School, Vol. XIX (May, 1951).

15. *The Scottish Economy*, 1965-1970: a Plan for Expansion, Cmd. 2864 (1966).

16. *Ibid.*

17. H.I.D.B., *First Report* (1966).

18. See the *21st Report of the Committee of Public Accounts*, HC. 301, July 1982, for detail on this.

19. One study estimated the regional employment multiplier of the pulp mill as lying between 1.9 and 2.65: M. A. Greig, 'The Regional Income and Employment Multiplier Effects of a Pulp Mill and Paper Mill', *S.J.P.E.*, Vol. XVIII, No. 1 (1971). At the time when the closure was first threatened, the fears expressed were for the much higher secondary employment than this multiplier effect would suggest.

20. G. A. Mackay, 'A Study of the Economic Impact of the Invergordon Aluminium Smelter', H.I.D.B. (n.d.).

21. David Simpson, 'The Lessons of Invergordon', *Quarterly Economic Commentary*, Vol. 7, No. 3 (1982).

22. F. C. Hummel and A. J. Grayson, 'The Future of Wood Supplies in Great Britain', in *Pulpwood Supply and the Paper Industry*, Forestry Commission (1969). The authors demonstrated that by 1990 the additional supply could 'feed a further five pulp mills of the scale of Fort William'.

23. H.I.D.B., *Seventeenth Annual Report* (1982).

24. The earlier history of the Harris tweed industry is covered in Francis Thompson, *Harris Tweed* (Newton Abbot, 1969).

25. R. A. Henderson, 'Recent Trends in Tourism and the Economic Impact of Tourists in Scotland', Scottish Economic Planning Department (S.E.P.D.), Economics and Statistics Unit (E.S.U.) Discussion Paper No. 15 (1982).

26. H.I.D.B., *Seventeenth Annual Report* (1982).

27. *Report of the Highland Panel*, 1961; *Highland Transport Services* (H.M.S.O., 1967); M. Gaskin, *Study of the Effect of Freight Charges on Island Economics*, H.I.D.B. (1971); *Highlands and Islands Transport Review*, H.I.D.B. (1975).

28. See Hansard, House of Commons debate, 21 February 1984, Statement by Secretary of State for Scotland.

10

THE SCOTTISH DEVELOPMENT AGENCY*

Gavin McCrone and J. N. Randall

In the early 1970s opinion in various quarters in Scotland increasingly began to favour the setting up of some kind of public body or agency to promote economic development.[1] There were at least three separate strands of thinking which led to the development of this idea. First, the arrangements then existing for processing loans and grants to industry under the Local Employment Act through an advisory committee in London were too remote and involved too much delay. Although there were Scottish representatives on the advisory committee, this was no substitute for a body which knew the local scene. Secondly, it was assumed that if a Scottish body were set up it would be responsible to the Secretary of State for Scotland, thereby giving him a locus in economic development matters which he previously lacked. And thirdly, the success of such bodies in other countries was beginning to attract attention. In Italy the Casa per il Mezzogiorno with wide-ranging powers and responsibilities for the South of Italy had been in operation for a number of years but — of greater relevance — the Republic of Ireland's Industrial Development Authority (I.D.A.) was making a substantial impact. Starting from a very low base, the pace of Ireland's economic development was attracting considerable attention in the 1960s and early 1970s, and the I.D.A. was able to take a substantial share of the credit for this success. Within Scotland itself the Highlands and Islands Development Board (H.I.D.B.) had by this time been in operation for more than five years, and it was felt that lessons from its operation could be applied elsewhere.

An attempt to meet some of these points was made in the arrangements for administration of selective financial assistance to industry under the Industry Act of 1972. As described in Chapter 8, assistance under Section 7 of that Act replaced the former Local Employment Act loans and grants and was administered within the assisted area regions themselves, including Scotland, from the local offices of the Department of Trade and Industry. These offices were strengthened by the appointment of an Industrial Director, specially recruited for his experience in industry or finance; and advisory boards with membership drawn from the banks, industry and trade unions were established to assist in the processing of cases. As a means of administering selective financial assistance to industry, there is no doubt that these arrangements have proved effective and, apart from the transfer of this office to the Secretary of State for Scotland and its incorporation into the Scottish Economic Planning Department (S.E.P.D.) in 1975, have continued to the

---

* The views expressed in this chapter are not necessarily those of the Industry Department for Scotland.

present time. (Note: In November 1983 the Scottish Economic Planning Department was renamed the Industry Department for Scotland.)

THE SETTING UP OF THE SCOTTISH DEVELOPMENT AGENCY (S.D.A.)

Although the changes introduced by the Industry Act of 1972 were a major step forward in the decentralisation of decision taking in regional policy and in improving its effectiveness, they did not fully meet the arguments of those who were proposing the creation of an agency. Inevitably a Government Department must give priority to the requirements of Ministers and the day-to-day business of Parliament. A public body, while still responsible to Ministers, has its own board specially chosen for their experience and is able to develop its own strategy within the broad objectives set for it. Such an agency would also recruit staff with appropriate qualifications and industrial experience.

In the spring of 1974, the new Labour Administration therefore decided that a Scottish Development Agency should be established. This decision was taken against a background of widespread concern at the industrial situation in Scotland, a dramatic rise in support for the Scottish National Party (S.N.P.), widespread criticism of the handling of North Sea oil policy, and pressure for the revenues from North Sea oil to be used for the regeneration of the Scottish economy. It is perhaps not surprising, therefore, that the Government's announcement of the setting-up of the S.D.A. came first in a White Paper on North Sea oil in July 1974, where the view was taken that it would be neither right nor satisfactory to link the hypothecation of a tax, such as that imposed on North Sea oil, to the funding of economic development in Scotland; and that Scotland's needs would be best served by the immediate establishment of a body charged with that development and with substantial powers and funding.[2]

The Scottish Development Agency Act of 1975 brought the Agency into being in December of that year. As expected, it was to be responsible to the Secretary of State for Scotland, who appointed its Chairman and Board, and it was to work in accordance with guidelines set by him in respect of its principal functions under the Act. It was to be funded primarily by grant-in-aid but also by means of public dividend capital and the National Loan Fund in respect of its investment function, all of these funds being provided through the public expenditure programmes of the Scottish Economic Planning Department (S.E.P.D.).

From the outset the Agency was seen as having two principal functions — furthering the development of Scotland's economy and improving its environment.[3] The emphasis on the environment had not featured significantly in similar bodies elsewhere, but in the circumstances of Scotland the links between economic development and the environment were seen as crucial.

Regional policy over the previous decade and a half had brought about substantial new industrial development in Scotland, and the new towns had been a success story in their own right. It was now time to give emphasis to the older industrial areas which housed a substantial proportion of Scotland's population and whose prospects of new industrial development were blighted by the dereliction of the past. In common with many of the older industrial areas elsewhere in Britain, Scotland had a legacy of spoil and dereliction which, despite the efforts of local authorities and the generous grants available to them, was very far from having been overcome. Accordingly the Agency was given three main areas of activity:

(i)   investment in industry by the provision of equity or loans;
(ii) the provision of publicly owned factories, previously the responsibility of the Scottish Industrial Estates Corporation (S.I.E.C.);
(iii) derelict land clearance and environmental recovery.

This last function was broadened almost immediately to include urban renewal when the Agency was given co-ordinating responsibility for the eastern area renewal project in Glasgow (GEAR). At a later stage the Agency also took responsibility for the promotion of inward investment to Scotland by agreement with the Scottish Council (Development and Industry), which had previously carried out this function.

The S.D.A. was not given responsibility for selective financial assistance to industry under Section 7 of the Industry Act, although such powers were a core function of similar bodies, such as the I.D.A., operating in other countries. The Act did provide for the S.D.A. to exercise Section 7 powers, but only in specific cases and at the express direction of the Secretary of State; this provision was never used and was removed in the amending legislation in 1980. The Act does contain a power to give general grants, but this was intended mainly to assist small enterprises such as craftsmen, and although it has been employed usefully in a number of larger cases, these require the approval of the Secretary of State. Selective financial assistance was retained within Government to ensure that there continued to be broad comparability in its provision between assisted area regions of similar status throughout Great Britain. This is not to say that under existing arrangements identical grants would be offered to a project in, say, the West of Scotland or the North of England, since this would depend on the assessment of the Department's advisory boards. But the rules applied would be the same: bidding-up is avoided, and since the system is directly under the control of Ministers, any interregional difficulties can quickly be resolved. However, the need for a close relationship between the work of the S.D.A. and the provision of selective financial assistance to industry has always been recognised; and it was to provide coherence in the exercise of these functions that, simultaneously with the setting up of the S.D.A., responsibility for Section 7 assistance was transferred to the Secretary of State for Scotland and is administered by S.E.P.D., the S.D.A.'s sponsor department.

On its creation the Agency subsumed three existing bodies: the Scottish Industrial Estates Corporation (S.I.E.C.), the Small Industries Council for Rural Areas in Scotland (S.I.C.R.A.S.) and the Derelict Land Clearance Unit of the Scottish Development Department. These bodies, of which S.I.E.C. was by far the largest, provided the S.D.A. with a core of some 470 existing staff which eased the task of getting the new body underway.[4] S.I.E.C.'s staff had considerable experience of building and estate management which was relevant not only to the continuing function of factory building but to the Agency's land renewal and environmental recovery work. S.I.C.R.A.S., which had been in operation since 1969, was in turn a subsidiary of the Development Commission set up in 1909. Its experience in small business development in rural areas was now extended to Scotland as a whole as it became the Agency's Small Business Division.

THE AGENCY IN OPERATION

The circumstances in which the Agency started its work were far from easy, and this has to be taken into account in assessing its early years of operation. First, the economic climate of the mid-1970s was much more difficult than in previous post-war decades; it was therefore not a time when it was easy to achieve success in any new economic venture. Secondly, the launch of the S.D.A. was attended by much exaggerated expectations. This was partly the result of the S.N.P.'s campaign in relation to North Sea oil and the Government's reliance on the S.D.A. as a counterstroke, but it also stemmed from a very poor understanding on the part of the public as to what could realistically be expected. Thirdly, the launch of the National Enterprise Board (N.E.B.), which had preceded the S.D.A., had been surrounded in controversy. Although the S.D.A. was not given the same objectives, notably buying into the profitable sector of British industry, there was some suspicion of its intended activities in industrial circles. These suspicions were evident in the second reading debate on the Bill, and it was some time before they were allayed.[5]

Industrial Investment

All of the difficulties referred to above focused on the Agency's industrial investment role, its other activities being for the most part uncontroversial and already existing in some previous form. Industrial investment was a new function apart from the loan finance previously provided to small industry by S.I.C.R.A.S. It was therefore an area in which experience had to be gained. In fact, despite the attention focused on it, this function has never absorbed a major share of the Agency's budget, expenditure over the first five years amounting to £25 million against a total Agency budget of £266 million.

The Agency was expected to invest only in viable projects and to earn an 'adequate' rate of return on this expenditure.[6] It was intended that the Agency's funds should be seen broadly as commercial investment rather than financial assistance, which was the province of the Department. The concept of an adequate return was given precision in the financial duty which was set for the Agency by the Secretary of State under the powers of the 1975 Act. This required the Agency to achieve a weighted average rate of return of 15-20% by 1981/82 calculated as the ratio of attributable net income of each company to the Agency's capital employed in the year, for all companies in which it held investments.[7] Steady progress towards that figure in the intervening years was to be aimed at. In practice this was not achieved, the Agency earning a return of 9% in 1977/78 and a negative 14.3% in 1978/79. It became clear that in the difficult circumstances of the late 1970s the target set did not take account of the problems faced. Large parts of the private sector were making losses at this time, and the Agency was not immune; indeed three companies in which it held investments had failed. The financial duty was revised in 1980, and the Agency is now to be guided in investing and in disposing of investments by the aim to achieve, over a rolling five-year period, a cash return at least equal to the cost to the Government of its borrowing over the same period.[8] In addition, a target cash financial return is agreed annually with the Agency for the year ahead and is published after the end of the year in the Agency's accounts. The explicit aim of this revised duty is therefore to ensure that the funds provided by the Agency do not involve a net subsidy.

It may be thought that if the Agency is required to find projects which yield a satisfactory return and yet are not adequately funded by the private sector, the scope for its activity is limited. The role of the Agency's investment finance is fully explored in evidence submitted by the Chief Executive to the Wilson Committee on Financial Institutions, and several points deserve to be emphasised.[9] First, although investment funds are widely available from the private sector, bank finance is predominantly in the form of loans, short-term and against security. Equity finance may be readily available for the larger quoted companies, depending on the state of the market, but it is not nearly so available to small and medium-sized unquoted companies. Despite the welcome part played by the Industrial and Commercial Finance Corporation (I.C.F.C.) and similar bodies, the S.D.A. believed that there was an equity gap for such companies and that this might either put them at risk through becoming overgeared or frustrate expansion altogether. The filling of this equity gap was one of the needs seen by the Agency for its funds and, although it has found scope for loans as well, it pointed to a greater use of equity than loan finance.

Since 1979 the Government has taken a series of important steps to ease the provision of private sector risk capital for small and medium-sized businesses. Notably these include the reduction in rates of personal taxation, the Business Expansion Scheme and the Small Firms Guarantee Scheme. This may have reduced the need for Agency investment funds, and certainly under the revised guidelines of 1980 a somewhat lesser role for Agency investment finance was envisaged.[10] These permit the Agency to invest only if it is satisfied that adequate funds cannot be obtained from the private sector and to seek the Secretary of State's approval for any investment over £1 million as compared with £2 million previously. It is also to seek approval where the acquisition would give the Agency 30% or more of the voting rights, or where the Agency's investment is more than £150,000 and in excess of 50% of the total funding of the company from all sources excluding Industry Act grants.

In step with the change in the guidelines, the Agency's investment philosophy has also evolved. In part this is no doubt the product of experience, in part the consequence of changes in the Agency's top management. Whereas in the early years the Agency made a number of significant investments which put it in a position of overall control in companies, that is now a situation which is as far as possible avoided. Originally the Agency was ready to acquire holdings in ailing companies and to intervene in management in order to effect an improvement in performance; it was also envisaged that it might start up or run businesses on its own account. For a holding company with a range of investments extending across the spectrum of Scottish industry, each requiring specialist knowledge and experience, this is a daunting task, and it is perhaps not surprising that the Agency had some failures. The present philosophy which sees the Agency's role as a catalyst, backing the successful entrepreneur and bridging the gap which makes the commitment of substantial private sector funds possible is undoubtedly more realistic and, on the evidence so far, more successful.

This change in philosophy can be seen from an examination of the Agency's portfolio published in its annual reports. In 1980 it had, apart from the activities of the small business division, investments in 48 companies, some of them picked up on the point of collapse, and in ailing industrial sectors. Since that time the portfolio has expanded to 101, but the new acquisitions are now frequently in high technology companies or in other sectors which the Agency has identified as offering scope for expansion through its various sectoral studies.[11]

Sectoral Initiatives

The Agency has increasingly sought to identify the industrial opportunities which offer the best scope for development in Scotland. This has led it to undertake detailed study of key sectors such as electronics, health care, biotechnology, forest products and oil-related industry. For much of this work consultants with specialist expertise have been employed, and guidance has been sought from the leading companies in the sectors in Scotland. The result has been a series of authoritative reports which set out the best opportunities in these sectors in Scotland, showing how existing strengths can be built on and gaps in industrial structure filled. The aim is to make maximum use of assets such as the strengths of the universities in subjects such as electronics, biotechnology or health care, or the existence of natural resources in the case of forest products or oil-related technology.

There is no doubt that this approach has paid important dividends. Understanding of opportunities has undoubtedly been improved, and this has certainly led to companies exploiting them of their own volition, Highland Forest Products strand board factory at Inverness being a notable example. But it has also enabled the Agency's work to be targeted in a way which increases its effectiveness. Most notably this applies to the investment function, where as explained above Agency funds are increasingly used as a catalyst to encourage private sector investment; but it applies with at least equal force to the work of Locate in Scotland (see p. 242) in inward investment promotion and to a lesser degree to the development of the Agency's industrial property.

Industrial Property

On its formation the Agency inherited a substantial industrial estate from the S.I.E.C. amounting to 2.2 million square metres. But whereas the S.I.E.C. had been an executive agency building and running factories according to a programme decided by the Department of Trade and Industry, the S.D.A. had freedom to evolve its own policy. In the early years there was a significant expansion in the factory programme, but of much greater importance was the change of emphasis. The Agency has increasingly pioneered the development of smaller factories on sites convenient to the centre of urban areas, and when older buildings became available these have frequently been refurbished and subdivided to cater for the needs of new small industry. The effect of this can be seen from the number of factories, which has more than doubled since the Agency was set up while the total floor space has changed very little. In this the Agency has moved closely in step with the needs of the times. In the early decades of regional policy the emphasis was on catering for large plants attracted from other parts of the country and normally accommodated on sites which were peripheral to the main urban areas. By 1980 such moves had become extremely rare, and the need was to provide accommodation for new small business capable of regenerating older areas, or to meet the highly specialised requirements of inward investing companies from overseas. The former can increasingly be seen in such areas as the east end of Glasgow, Leith, Dundee and Clydebank, while the latter cater for the needs of high technology companies, particularly in the electronics industry.

The Agency is required to let its factories in accordance with current market valuations. In a depressed area and particularly where reclamation of derelict land is involved, the market valuation may be below construction costs, in some cases substantially so. Rent-free periods of up to two years may also be given. These arrangements mean that the Agency is unlikely to earn sufficient surplus on its factory-building operation to meet the costs of its investment, and funds are accordingly provided, as they were for S.I.E.C., by grant-in-aid.

In order to regulate the degree of support involved and as a spur to efficiency in construction, the Agency is given a financial duty in respect of its factory operations. In its original form this required it to aim at a return of 4.5% on its factory operations overall, but while this target was generally met, it was recognised to have limitations because of the stock of factories built years previously which had been let on long leases at fixed rents. The duty was accordingly revised in 1982 and in its present form requires the Agency to achieve a rental income from new and modernised premises completed during a rolling three-year period equivalent to an agreed return (initially 7.3%) on the capital investment in such premises; and a financial surplus resulting from the whole operation of its industrial estates and factory provisions at least equal to a target (initially £3.65 per 1,000 square metres of factory space administered) agreed with the Industry Department for Scotland.[12]

Environmental Recovery and Area Projects

Prior to the setting up of the Agency, local authorities had been able to claim grants from central Government for derelict land clearance, the rate of grant at the time being 85 per cent. The central belt of Scotland was of course one of the areas of Britain where the problem of derelict land and urban decay was most severe, a legacy of the area's success in the development of nineteenth-century industry. Although considerable progress had been made in recovery operations, this has been a long way short of adequate; as a result there have been not only adverse consequences for the quality of life in the area, but also for the prospects of attracting industry to sites which might otherwise be suitable.

By funding these operations through the Agency it was possible not only to give a major new impetus to the pace of recovery but also to approach the setting of priorities on a Scotland-wide basis. It was work which the Agency could get under way quickly using the estate management staff it inherited from S.I.E.C., and there are now few parts of industrial Scotland that do not have substantial benefits to show for it. By 1981 some £92 million had been spent on land renewal and environmental schemes.

As the Agency's work developed, however, so did its policy.[13] Soon after it was set up, the Secretary of State asked it to assume the co-ordinating role in the Glasgow Eastern Area Renewal Project (GEAR), an extremely ambitious scheme to mount a recovery operation in one of the most rundown parts of urban Glasgow. The project involved working with the regional and district authorities and with the Scottish Special Housing Association in an operation which went well beyond the S.D.A.'s own powers and resources. Difficulties were inevitably encountered and lessons learned, but the benefits are now coming through and they include not only the substantial refurbishment of a rundown area but also the stimulation and accommodation of new industry. By 1984 some 200 companies had been assisted to locate in the area, providing over 3,200 jobs, the local business community had invested some £50 million in improvements to property and plant and machinery, and private house builders had completed 800 houses.

Other area projects have been on a less ambitious scale, although substantial enough, and following the Agency's experience in GEAR the Agency's role has been more carefully targeted. These include the Glengarnock project set up following the closure of the steelmaking plant, at Clydebank following the closure of Singers, and also at Leith, Dundee, Coatbridge and Motherwell. In each of these a major environmental transformation was a prerequisite for new economic development, and Agency expenditure on this and on factory building was substantial, approximately £70 million by the spring of 1984. But the employment was also impressive, some 7,000 jobs created or provided for and over 500 new companies.

Inward Investment Promotion

The promotion of Scotland as a location for investment from overseas is an important part of economic development which has been undertaken with considerable success since the 1940s. Today there are 270 overseas companies operating in Scotland employing a total labour force of 75,000, equivalent to some 17% of the employees in manufacturing industry. The number of companies is growing all the time, and they are of importance not only for the employment they provide but for the new high technology they bring, many of them being leaders in electronics and oil-related industries.

Originally the promotion of inward investment was undertaken by the Scottish Council (Development and Industry) on a voluntary basis. In the favourable conditions of the 1940s and 1950s its efforts were successful despite very slender resources. The leading U.S. companies which came to Scotland at this time served as an example to the rest and made it easier to build up the impetus of this successful development. By the 1970s, however, other European countries had entered this field, using public bodies for the purpose with much more significant resources than the Scottish Council had at its disposal. The success of the Irish was particularly striking, and their effort is led by the I.D.A. which has several offices and a substantial staff in the United States as well as other countries.

In the early 1970s the Government provided grants for regional promotional bodies in the United Kingdom to undertake this work, the Scottish Council being assisted for this purpose in Scotland. The Council continued its work in the United States and also mounted a campaign in Germany, but the environment had become much more competitive and results correspondingly more difficult to achieve. The creation of the S.D.A. offered an opportunity to strengthen this effort considerably.

The Agency accordingly reached an agreement with the Council to take over this function in 1979 along with several of the Council's key personnel. Two offices were opened in the United States, at New York and San Francisco, together with offices in London and Brussels, and the Agency set about the task of co-ordinating the hitherto independent efforts of local authorities and new towns. Programmes of missions and seminars overseas were organised in which these bodies were invited to take part.

But these arrangements, though stronger than anything which preceded them, still attracted criticism, often exaggerated and unjust, about the number of different bodies involved in this work. In particular it was clearly a serious weakness that the Agency's personnel, having no responsibility for selective financial assistance, were unable to negotiate a financial package with companies and could not therefore see a promotion project through to the point of decision.

The Select Committee on Scottish Affairs examined this subject in detail in 1979/80.[14] Following its Report in which the conclusions of the Committee were divided, the Secretary of State set up Locate in Scotland, an office staffed jointly by personnel working on inward investment drawn both from the S.D.A. and S.E.P.D. but working under a single Director with experience of this work. The first two Directors of Locate in Scotland have been civil servants from S.E.P.D., but the office is housed in the Agency's building. For the work of the office and its expenditure the Director is jointly responsible to the Chief Executive of the Agency in respect of promotion and to the Secretary of the Department as regards the negotiation of financial assistance for companies. For the first time this provides Scotland with an integrated organisation for the attraction of investment and a team both in Scotland and in the offices overseas who can see a project through from the time of first contact with the company to the completion of the negotiations which lead to a successful location decision. The purpose of these arrangements is not to supplant the inward investment work carried out by the Department of Industry and the Consulates abroad on behalf of the United Kingdom as a whole, but to supplement them with the promotion of Scotland which, like Ireland, is marketable in its own right, especially in the United States where there is a large expatriate community. It has taken some time, inevitably, to bring these arrangements to maximum effectiveness, but at the time of writing it had become clear that the impact was beginning to be very substantial. Since Locate in Scotland was established, there has been a 70 per cent increase in the number of overseas companies deciding to set up or expand in Scotland, and this has involved a total investment of £800 million.

CONCLUSION

The Scottish Development Agency was only in existence for the last five years of the period with which this book is concerned. Nevertheless it is clear that its creation was one of the more important landmarks in the development of policy for the Scottish economy. Its significance lies both in the resources it was able to command and in its organisation.

As regards the first, the Agency's gross expenditure in the year ended

March 1977, the first full year of operation, was approximately £19 million, of which £12 was received directly from Government, and by 1980 these figures had risen to £70 million and £65 million respectively. In the early years there can be little doubt that the provision of these funds directly from the Exchequer gave Scotland (and Wales via the W.D.A.) a definite advantage, although in England the grant-aiding of local authorities for derelict land recovery etc. and the operation of the English Industrial Estates Corporation (E.I.E.C.) corresponded with a substantial part of the Agency's activity. More recently the development of inner-city policy in England, particularly the setting up of partnership areas and Urban Development Corporations, has meant that activities equivalent to those undertaken by the S.D.A. in Scotland have increased very considerably. Although there is now no real parallel with the S.D.A.'s investment function, this accounts for only a small part of the total budget, and it is probable that the rest of its activities now have counterparts in England with comparable finance provided.

The organisational importance of the S.D.A. is therefore its key aspect. From the start the bringing together within one body of industrial and environmental functions was a novel aspect, while a close working relationship with Scottish Office Departments, particularly S.E.P.D., has enabled a coherent approach to be developed to many of Scotland's problems in a way which would be much more difficult elsewhere. In particular this structure has permitted an innovative approach within a longer-term perspective which has enabled valuable pioneering work to be undertaken on the opportunities of particular industrial sectors in Scotland and to support these initiatives with investment funds. It has enabled important area projects to be developed where previously there was no instrument capable of circumventing the problems of divided responsibility between different authorities. It is also no accident that it was the S.D.A. rather that its predecessor the S.I.E.C. or equivalent bodies elsewhere which brought about radical changes in factory-building policy. Finally, the arrangements for the promotion of inward investment have also brought a major advance. No doubt the role of the Agency will continue to evolve in the years ahead, depending upon the priorities as seen by its Board and guidelines it has been given by Government. But in a period when the Scottish economy has faced particularly serious difficulties and the world recession has attained depths unequalled since the 1930s, the impetus which the Agency has been able to give to new developments has been one of the brighter spots on the economic landscape.

NOTES

1. Notably the *West Central Scotland Plan* (1974), whose authors proposed the setting up of a Strathclyde Economic Development Corporation. The idea was also advanced by the late Hugh Stenhouse.
2. *United Kingdom Offshore Oil and Gas Policy*, Cmd. 5690, H.M.S.O., para 18.

3. *Scottish Development Agency — Proposals for Discussion*, S.E.P.D. (Jan. 1975). See also Lord Hughes' speech in the Second Reading Debate, House of Lords Official Report Vol. 360, No. 92, 15 May 1975, Col. 845.

4. Scottish Development Agency, First Report (1976).

5. House of Lords Official Report, *op. cit.*, Col. 845ff.

6. *Scottish Development Agency: Industrial Investment Guidelines*, S.E.P.D. 1976. Published also as Annexe F in the Agency's Annual Report, 1977.

7. *Eighteenth Report from the Committee of Public Accounts, Session 1979-80, Scottish Development Agency Accounts*, H.M.S.O., p. vi ff.

8. *Fifteenth Report from the Committee of Public Accounts, Session 1981-82, Scottish Development Agency Accounts*, H.M.S.O., pp. v-ix.

9. Scottish Development Agency, *Evidence to the Committee to Review the Functioning of Financial Institutions* (June 1977).

10. *Scottish Development Agency: Industrial Investment Guidelines*, S.E.P.D. (1980).

11. Scottish Development Agency, *Annual Reports*.

12. *Sixth Report from the Committee of Public Accounts, Session 1983-84*, H.M.S.O. (Nov. 1983).

13. The Agency's work in this area is well described in articles by Stuart Gulliver, 'The Area Projects of the Scottish Development Agency', and Roger Leclerc and Donald Draffan, 'The Glasgow Eastern Area Renewal Project', in *Town Planning Review*, Vol. 55, No. 3 (1984).

14. *Second Report from the Committee on Scottish Affairs Session 1979/80: Inward Investment*, H.M.S.O. (July 1980).

11
NEW TOWNS AND NEW INDUSTRIES*

J. N. Randall

INTRODUCTION

There was a widespread belief in Scotland at the end of the war that industrial diversification was essential if Scotland were to prosper. This view reflected the experience of the 1930s: in a book written at the start of the war James Bowie argued that the boost given to the traditional heavy engineering industries by rearmament and war would exacerbate the long-term problem of over-capacity and eventual rundown of these industries in peacetime.[1] It was reinforced by contemporary assessments of future prospects: for example, Michael Fogarty identified West-Central Scotland as one of the industrial areas of Britain likely to experience long-term unemployment in post-war conditions, partly reflecting industrial structure.[2]

As noted in Chapters 1 and 2, the range of industries represented in Scotland at the end of the war was extremely wide,[3] and at a broad level of industrial grouping Scotland's structure of industry was remarkably similar to that of Great Britain as a whole.[4] But more detailed disaggregation revealed a disproportionate representation of heavy industries such as boilermaking, marine engineering, shipbuilding, locomotive engineering and iron and steel foundries, and an under-representation in the newer light engineering consumer goods industries which had grown most rapidly in the pre-war period.[5] The key feature of the Scottish manufacturing activity identified by A. K. Cairncross, in his introduction to *The Scottish Economy*, was the lack of mass-production methods, a theme which was later developed by the Toothill Committee (1961) in their distinction between small-quantity specialised (often capital) goods — to which the Scottish economy was geared — and large-quantity standardised (often consumer) goods for which location in the south of England seemed to have marketing advantages. Despite this recognition that Scotland's location represents a handicap to the development of some types of industry, the Toothill Report argued that the importance of transport costs was easily exaggerated and that the newer consumer goods industries could and should be attracted to Scotland.[6]

Emphasis on the need to promote new industries in Scotland to offset decline in heavy industry has been a persistent feature both of economic analysis of the problem and of the objectives of regional development policy throughout the post-war period.[7] While the encouragement of indigenous industrial growth has played an increasing part in policy over the period 1950-

---

* The views expressed in this chapter are not necessarily those of the Industry Department for Scotland.

245

80, the main emphasis of policy, particularly in the first half of the period, was on the attraction of mobile industry, whether from the rest of Great Britain or by inward investment from abroad. It was hoped that incoming industry would play a key role in modernising the Scottish economy through the introduction of new technology and management practices, and through the building up of local linkages and the establishment of a complex of industries with output and employment growth potential.

Parallel to this post-war emphasis on industrial diversification there was widespread recognition of the need to modernise and rebuild much of the infrastructure of urban Scotland. The Clyde Valley Regional Plan (1946) highlighted the poor housing conditions and very high residential densities in Glasgow and — in line with contemporary planning philosophy — recommended the creation of four New Towns to help accommodate the overspill of some 250,000-300,000 people who would be displaced from the city on redevelopment.[8] While the specific proposals of the Clyde Valley Plan were implemented only in part, its general approach had a major influence on Government thinking over the next 25 years, and five New Towns were developed — East Kilbride (designated 1947), Glenrothes (1948), Cumbernauld (1956), Livingston (1962), and Irvine (1966). A sixth New Town at Stonehouse was designated in 1973 but abandoned in 1976 before major development got under way.

The New Towns as envisaged by the Clyde Valley Plan were to be self-contained communities in the sense of providing local employment opportunities for the people who moved there. Industry was to come primarily by the steering of some of the incoming industry expected to be attracted to Scotland by Government inducements, and secondly by a limited amount of decentralisation from the congested urban areas. Over time the emphasis on the need to encourage industry in the New Towns as a complement to their primary role in accommodating overspill population gradually shifted to a belief that the New Towns could play a key role in attracting industry to Scotland. The latter role had become dominant by the 1960s, and the New Towns were widely seen as playing a major part in modernising the Scottish economy through industrial diversification.[9]

This chapter describes the pattern of industrial change in Scotland and the New Towns during the post-war period. The two main aims are to consider how far the development of new industries succeeded in overcoming the weaknesses of the Scottish economy foreseen at the end of war; and to evaluate the role which the New Towns played in this process. Reflecting the main emphasis of policy and the availability of data, attention is concentrated on the manufacturing sector. Data availability, particularly in relation to small areas such as the New Towns, also dictates that employment must be used as the main basis for detailed analysis of industrial change. This has obvious disadvantages as an indicator of output performance at a time of relatively rapid growth of labour productivity, although it relates well to a major concern of public policy.

THE COMPOSITION OF MANUFACTURING EMPLOYMENT CHANGE IN SCOTLAND, 1953-78

The major influence on the rate of industrial change in post-war Scotland was the performance of the world and particularly British economies — in 1973 some two-thirds of Scottish manufacturing output went to markets outside Scotland, with over 40% of output going to the rest of the U.K. alone.[10] The two fundamental features of this external environment during the post-war period were: (i) the historically rapid rate of growth of the world economy at least up to 1973; and (ii) the marked and persistent decline of the British economy relative to its main industrial competitors. U.K. Gross Domestic Product (G.D.P.) increased by an average of 2.6% p.a. over the period 1954-78,[11] and Scotland's economic performance has fairly closely paralleled that of the U.K.[12]

Table 1. *Average Annual Growth Rate of Manufacturing Output in Scotland and the U.K., 1954-78*

	1954-58	*1958-63*	*1963-68*	*1968-71*	*1971-78*	*1954-78*
Scotland	1.3	2.6	5.1	3.0	0.6	2.9
U.K.	2.0	3.4	4.4	1.1	0.9	2.9

Source: Lythe and Majmudar (1982)

Over the whole period 1954-78, Scotland's G.D.P. growth rate has been estimated at 2.2% p.a., apparently a little below the U.K. figure, although if the manufacturing sector alone is examined (Table 1), the average rates of output growth in Scotland and the U.K. over this period were identical (2.9% p.a.). Sub-period analysis of manufacturing output trends reveals an unfavourable relative performance for Scotland in the periods 1954-58 and 1958-63, followed by a more favourable relative trend in 1963-68 and 1968-71, and a marginally less favourable trend over the period 1971-78. In both Scotland and the U.K., manufacturing G.D.P. growth was most rapid between 1963 and 1968 and least rapid between 1971 and 1978.

It is helpful to bear in mind this macro-economic background when considering the pattern of manufacturing employment change in Scotland over the period 1953-78. Table 2 sets out estimates of net employment change by industrial Order and by sub-period. Over the period as a whole — during which we can infer from Table 1 manufacturing output is likely to have increased by some three-quarters — employment in the manufacturing sector fell by around 89,000 or 13%, with employment decline particularly rapid since 1968. It is clear even at this relatively broad level of industrial disaggregation that major changes have taken place in Scotland's industrial structure. Employment in Textiles declined by 52,000 or about a half, Shipbuilding by 30,000 or 45%, Metal Manufacture by 23,000 or 40%, and Mechanical Engineering by 17,000 or 17%. These four industries accounted for almost a half of all manufacturing employment in 1953 but only a little

Table 2. Manufacturing Employment Change in Scotland, 1953-78

	1953 Stock		% change in employment					1978 Stock		1953-78 Changes in employment	
	% of all manufacturing employment	Employment numbers	1953-58	1958-63	1963-68	1968-73	1973-78	Employment numbers	% of all manufacturing employment	Nos.	(%)
3. Food, drink, tobacco	12.3	82254	+3	0	+10	+1	-4	89971	15.6	+7717	+9.4
4. Coal and petroleum products	0.7	4448	-6	-29	-12	+7	-3	2716	0.5	-1732	-38.9
5. Chemicals	4.4	29339	-8	-1	-1	-1	+14	29740	5.1	+401	+1.4
6. Metal manufacture	8.7	57678	-4	-18	-10	-3	-11	34771	6.0	-22907	-39.7
7. Mechanical engineering	14.4	96273	+9	-6	-1	-16	-3	79706	13.8	-16567	-17.2
8. Instrument engineering	1.0	6844	+46	+39	+37	-1	-9	17132	3.0	+10288	+150.3
9. Electrical engineering	3.0	19799	+37	+40	+32	+7	-6	50889	8.8	+31090	+157.0
10. Shipbuilding	10.0	66695	0	-32	-5	-6	-10	36501	6.3	-30194	-45.3
11. Vehicles	5.6	37147	-2	+1	+9	-9	-2	33745	5.8	-3402	-9.2
12. Metal Goods	3.6	23714	+2	+1	+6	+3	-6	25101	4.3	+1387	+5.9
13. Textiles	16.0	106407	-11	-3	-8	-16	-24	54071	9.4	-52336	-49.2
14. Leather	0.6	3645	-13	-4	-15	-4	-14	2116	0.4	-1529	-42.0
15. Clothing	4.2	27740	+1	-6	+13	+18	-9	31641	5.5	+3901	+14.1
16. Bricks, pottery etc	2.9	19614	-5	+4	+11	-13	-20	15008	2.6	-4606	-23.5
17. Timber	3.5	23131	-9	-1	+14	-13	-18	16722	2.9	-6409	-27.7
18. Paper, printing, publishing	7.0	46390	+13	+6	-1	-11	-12	42400	7.3	-3990	8.6
19. Other manufacturing	2.4	16049	0	-6	-10	-2	-2	15941	2.8	-108	-0.7
ALL MANUFACTURING	(100)	667167	+1	-4	+4	-6	-8	578171	(100)	-88996	-13.3

Source: Scottish Manufacturing Establishments Record

over a third by 1978. The main job gains occurred in Electrical Engineering (+30,000) and Instrument Engineering (+10,000), both of which more than doubled their employment between 1953 and 1978, and to a lesser extent in Food, Drink and Tobacco which increased by some 8,000 jobs or 9%. The evidence of Table 2 therefore suggests that — in keeping with the objective of diversification — there has been a considerable relative shift away from the traditional heavy industries (together with textiles) towards at least some of the lighter engineering industries. But the rate of job growth in the newer manufacturing industries has been insufficient to offset the job losses in the declining sectors, and the sub-period analysis shows that even in Electrical Engineering and Instrument Engineering the rate of net job growth fell off markedly after 1968, with a net decline occurring between 1973 and 1978.

The scale of the changes which have occurred in the Scottish manufacturing sector is not fully evident from Table 2. A better impression is given by Table 3, which sets out a more detailed analysis of the components of gross job change at the level of individual manufacturing establishments based on the Scottish Manufacturing Establishments Record. It is clear that even in many of the industrial Orders which recorded net employment decline (even in some of those with the largest net declines like Textiles) there was considerable job growth in new openings or expansion of existing units. An extreme example is the Vehicles industry. Between 1958 and 1963 a small net job decline of 4% occurred, but Table 3 shows that this was the balance between massive job losses through closures (equivalent to 31% of employment in the Order in 1958) and contractions (−17%) on the one hand, but also very considerable job gains mainly through new openings which created employment equivalent to 39% of employment in the Order in 1958. This remarkable pattern reflects the decline of the traditional railway locomotive industry (the North British Locomotive Company closed in 1961) and the introduction to Scotland of new motor vehicle plants at Bathgate (1961) and Linwood (1963). Other industries which display particularly high rates of gross job change in relation to net change are Clothing and Timber. The overall pattern is a complex one, and while Electrical Engineering and Instrument Engineering stand out for their relatively high rates of expansion, it is clear that there has been considerable volatility of growth and decline in a much wider range of industries. This would be even more the case at a more detailed level of industrial disaggregation, and the performance of industries such as whisky, food processing and electronics is only hinted at, and of others such as parts of wool textiles concealed, by the level of presentation in Table 3.

Table 3 illustrates the progressive fall-off in the rate of job growth in new openings and (to a lesser extent) expansions since the peak rates achieved between 1963 and 1968 — despite the emergence of new growth sectors related to oil development in the 1970s. This pattern is followed by most of the Orders recording very high rates of gross job increase and which seem to contain the types of activity which can most appropriately be termed 'new industries': in particular, Electrical Engineering, Instrument Engineering and

Table 3. *New Openings, Expansions, Contractions an*

Industry (1968 SIC)	(1) NEW OPENINGS Employment in new openings as percentage of employment in industry at start of period					(2) EXPANSIONS Employment expansions in existing units as percentage of employment in industry at start of period				
	1953-58	1958-63	1963-68	1968-73	1973-78	1953-58	1958-63	1963-68	1968-73	1973-7.
3. Food, drink, tobacco	6	7	11	7	2	16	13	16	16	12
4. Coal and petroleum products	6	2	3	0	0	9	2	14	16	14
5. Chemicals	4	5	7	11	2	7	11	11	13	19
6. Metal manufacture	5	6	3	4	3	6	3	13	7	8
7. Mechanical engineering	4	7	6	6	5	15	7	12	6	13
8. Instrument engineering	3	7	13	11	5	47	36	32	13	7
9. Electrical engineering	11	18	22	12	3	37	32	26	23	16
10. Shipbuilding	1	0	2	5	1	7	1	15	22	6
11. Vehicles	4	39	3	1	1	10	4	18	11	6
12. Metal goods	5	7	12	16	4	12	12	12	9	9
13. Textiles	3	4	6	4	2	7	13	8	7	5
14. Leather	2	18	12	8	3	7	4	7	12	8
15. Clothing	13	8	23	22	8	11	12	14	21	9
16. Bricks, pottery etc.	6	8	18	6	1	9	12	16	9	10
17. Timber	8	10	23	12	3	9	11	15	10	7
18. Paper, printing and publishing	3	2	7	5	1	15	10	8	9	8
19. Other manufacturing	7	6	21	13	4	9	5	12	17	12
ALL MANUFACTURING	5	8	10	8	3	12	10	14	12	10

Source: Scottish Manufacturing Establishments Record (SIC: Standard Industrial Classification)

Vehicles. There is some suggestion of a typical time profile in these industries: the period of most rapid job growth due to new openings is followed by a peak in the rate of expansion, giving way in turn to higher rates of contraction and/ or closure as plants mature. But the predominant impression is one of the complexity of the pattern revealed. Growth has not been confined to one or two 'new' industries or to a few sub-periods, and even industries which have recorded the most rapid net employment decline contain individual units which have opened or expanded in each of the sub-periods.

An alternative perspective on the employment performance of the newer industries is provided by Table 4, which separates out the components of gross job change among incomer units, that is establishments in companies which have moved to Scotland from overseas or the rest of the U.K. since the war. While non-incomer manufacturing establishments declined by 193,000 jobs or 30% over the whole period 1953-78, incomer units recorded a net employment increase of 104,000, divided fairly evenly between units with an origin in the rest of the U.K. (+53,000) and those with an origin abroad (+51,000). Incomer units showed a net increase in employment in each of the sub-periods identified — although only marginally so between 1973 and 1978 — while

Closures of Manufacturing Units in Scotland, 1953-78

| (3) CONTRACTIONS | | | | | (4) CLOSURES | | | | |
| Employment contractions in existing units as percentage of employment in industry at start of period | | | | | Employment in closures as percentage of employment in industry at start of period | | | | |
1953-58	1958-63	1963-68	1968-73	1973-78	1953-58	1958-63	1963-68	1968-73	1973-78
8	8	9	8	10	11	12	7	15	11
7	14	12	6	1	14	19	16	3	16
16	8	10	19	6	4	8.	9	6	2
11	19	13	9	18	3	9	13	5	4
7	14	13	13	12	2	6	7	14	10
2	3	7	16	13	3	1	1	9	9
5	6	8	18	18	6	4	9	9	8
8	30	5	6	11	0	4	17	26	7
8	17	3	12	5	7	31	10	9	4
12	8	7	12	13	2	10	11	10	8
16	10	11	13	16	5	10	11	14	16
14	13	17	6	11	9	13	18	18	19
10	8	11	8	12	13	18	14	17	15
15	10	8	11	16	6	7	14	18	18
13	10	11	12	14	13	12	13	23	18
3	4	6	10	15	1	3	11	14	9
9	13	11	18	12	7	4	12	13	7
10	13	9	12	13	5	9	10	14	10

non-incomers recorded a net decrease in each sub-period, the size of the decline being particularly large after 1968. The relatively more favourable net job performance of incomer units reflects both (a) much higher rates of gross job increase (both new openings and expansions) than in the case of non-incomers (although it should be noted that the absolute scale of gross job increases was larger among non-incomers in all sub-periods); and (b) lower rates of gross job decrease (both contractions and closures). The difference was less marked in the case of gross job decreases, particularly towards the end of the period, but the absolute scale of job losses among non-incomers was massively greater throughout the period.

The pattern of employment change over time in incomer units tends generally to parallel that already decribed in respect of industries with high rates of gross job increase. Job increases in new openings reached a peak in the period 1963-68 (+23,000) and were much lower between 1973 and 1978 (+7,000), while expansions peaked later in 1968-73 (+24,000) and were still running at a high level (+21,000) between 1973 and 1978. In the sub-periods 1958-63 and 1963-68 the great majority of incomer job increases in new openings were in respect of plants with an origin in other parts of the U.K.

Table 4. *New Openings, Expansions, Contractions and Closure*

Type of Unit	(1) NEW OPENINGS Employment in new openings					(2) EXPANSIONS Employment expansions in existing units					(3) CO. Employment co	
	1953-58	1958-63	1963-68	1968-73	1973-78	1953-58	1958-63	1963-68	1968-73	1973-78	1953-58	1958-6
(A) Incomer units[1]												
Nos.	7327	16153	23225	20496	7291	14512	13755	22395	24352	21026	1266	435:
As % employment at start of period	25	34	33	19	6	50	29	32	23	16	4	•
of which:												
Foreign origin												
Nos.	3986	1639	7853	11271	3796	8414	9953	13619	9268	12078	115	127:
As % employment at start of period	35	7	23	22	6	74	43	41	18	20	1	
Rest of U.K. origin												
Nos.	3341	14514	15372	9225	3495	6098	3802	8776	15084	8948	1151	307
As % employment at start of period	19	61	43	17	5	35	16	24	27	13	7	1
(B) Non-incomer units												
Nos.	23045	35318	38355	29923	11281	63823	53184	66620	57538	42079	65566	8047
As % employment at start of period	4	6	7	5	2	10	8	12	10	8	10	1
(C) All units												
Nos.	30372	51471	61580	50419	18572	78335	66939	89015	81890	63105	66832	8482
As % employment at start of period	5	8	10	8	3	12	10	14	12	10	10	1

Source: Scottish Manufacturing Establishments Record

[1] Incomer units are units opening in Scotland since 1st January 1945 with an origin outside Scotland; and units opening

(+30,000) rather than abroad (+9,500); but in 1968-73 and 1973-78 the position was reversed, with incomers from abroad (+15,000) rather than the rest of the U.K. (+12,500) becoming the dominant source of job increases in new openings. Job increases from expansions were greater in incomers with an origin abroad rather than in the rest of the U.K. in all sub-periods except 1968-73 — the latter probably reflecting growth among units which had opened in the previous two sub-periods. Both incomers from the rest of the U.K. and abroad recorded higher gross decreases (both contractions and closures) in the later sub-periods, the trend being particularly marked among incomers with an origin abroad where there was a noticeable increase in job losses over time in proportionate as well as absolute terms. The overall picture revealed is one of gross job increases in incomer units both from the rest of the U.K. and abroad tending to fall off over time, with gross job decreases tending

Incomer and other Manufacturing Units in Scotland, 1953-78

RACTIONS ctions in existing units			(4) CLOSURES Employment in closures					(5) NET EMPLOYMENT CHANGE					
963-68	1968-73	1973-78	1953-58	1958-63	1963-68	1968-73	1973-78	1953-58	1958-63	1963-68	1968-73	1973-78	1953-78
5174	12088	17407	2473	3205	1998	9471	10061	+18100	+22350	+38448	+23289	+2065	+104252
7	11	13	9	7	3	9	8	+63	+48	+55	+22	+2	+361
2960	8674	9256	289	184	11	3278	5119	+11996	+10133	+18501	+8587	+1798	+51015
9	17	15	3	1	0	6	8	+106	+43	+55	+17	+3	+449
2214	3414	8151	2184	3021	1987	6193	4942	+6104	+12217	+19947	+14702	+267	+53237
6	6	12	12	13	6	11	7	+35	+52	+56	+26	0	+303
5876	67195	63655	31803	58725	64531	82471	52852	−10501	−50696	−15432	−62205	−54414	−193248
10	12	13	5	9	11	15	11	−2	−8	−3	−11	−11	−30
1050	79283	81062	34276	61930	66529	91942	62913	+7599	−28346	+23016	−38916	−52349	−88996
9	12	13	5	9	10	14	10	+1	−4	+4	−6	−8	−13

otland with an origin in an incoming unit.

to rise over time as plants opened in earlier periods began to reach maturity and decline.

The broad similarity in the pattern of job change among industries such as Electrical and Instrument Engineering (and to some extent Vehicles) and among incomer units is of course a reflection of the tendency for incoming units to be concentrated in these particular industries. In 1978 incomer units accounted for 133,000 manufacturing jobs in Scotland (23% of the total), the most important sectors being the engineering industries. Of these incoming units, those with an origin abroad accounted for some 62,000 jobs. Employment in all establishments in foreign ownership (a wider grouping including units in foreign-owned companies established in Scotland before 1945) was around 100,000, or about 17% of manufacturing employment by the late 1970s.[13] Overseas-owned establishments form a particularly important and distinctive element in Scotland's post-war economic development. While Scotland did not have the highest share of employment in overseas-owned manufacturing in Britain at this time — this was to be found in South-East England and East Anglia — the Scottish share was above the G.B. average and reflected a very high incidence of openings as distinct from takeovers.

NEW INDUSTRIES IN SCOTLAND — AN ASSESSMENT

Two main conclusions emerge from this description of post-war manufacturing employment trends in Scotland: (i) the very large changes in industrial structure which have taken place, resulting in a considerable diversification of the economy in keeping with the objectives of policy; but (ii) the inadequate scale of new job growth, particularly since 1968, when set against the massive job losses occurring mainly in the older industries but to some extent also among newer industries towards the end of the period.

Structural change has been such that by the 1970s Scotland seems no longer to have been significantly handicapped on this count relative to Great Britain as a whole. This conclusion is supported by analysis both at broad industrial Order level and at the more detailed Minimum List Heading level — and both for all industries and if the manufacturing sector is considered alone.[14] This is not to suggest that structural problems did not remain in relation to particular industries (for example a continuing over-representation of shipbuilding and under-representation in some of the faster growing service industries) or particular parts of Scotland (notably Strathclyde), but the evidence is that Scotland's overall economic performance relative to the rest of Great Britain was no longer dominated by this traditional weakness by the end of the period.

The failure of new job growth to compensate for job losses in the manufacturing sector after 1968 fundamentally reflects slow growth in the British economy, exacerbated by the slowdown in growth in the industrialised world as a whole after 1973. While employment trends in manufacturing must be set in the context of faster growth in services — a marked feature of most developed economies — this does not alter the overall conclusion: total employment in Scotland peaked in the mid-1960s and, apart from a temporary rise in the first half of the 1970s, has been on a long-run declining trend thereafter. Scotland's record of new manufacturing openings in employment terms does not appear inferior to that of other parts of Great Britain,[15] but it seems disappointing that of all manufacturing units employing over 200 in 1974, only around 40 were units which employed under 100 in 1954 or in the second year after opening.[16] Few of the small firms which grew to over 200 during the period appeared to be making products which could be termed technologically advanced, while the majority were taken over by larger companies in the course of their growth. There is also some evidence that new openings in Scotland over the period 1966-75 experienced a higher closure rate than new openings in other parts of the U.K.[17] But in the main inadequate job growth does not seem attributable to less satisfactory performance in Scotland compared with Great Britain, but to economic weaknesses affecting the whole of Britain.

Regional policy has played an important part both in helping to transform the industrial structure of Scotland and in generating additional jobs in Scotland. Estimates based on work by Moore and Rhodes suggest that regional policy may have created some 60-70,000 net additional manufacturing jobs in Scotland (approaching 100,000 jobs in total when multiplier effects on services are included) between 1960 and the mid-1970s.[18] On this basis the effect of regional policy amounted to about 10% of Scottish manufacturing employment in 1975 (compared with around 3% at this date attributable to North Sea oil — although the main impact of oil was on non-manufacturing). Included in the estimate of the impact of regional policy are some of the major initiatives of the 1960s which have attracted widespread publicity, such as the Ravenscraig strip mill, the vehicles plants at Linwood and Bathgate, the Fort William pulp mill, and the Invergordon aluminium smelter; but it should be noted that these plants were together employing around 20,000 in 1975, which (even allowing for multiplier effects on other parts of the manufacturing sector) accounts for well below half of the overall estimated effects of regional policy.[19] Much more important in quantitative terms were the successes of regional policy in smaller projects and in industries such as electrical engineering. The impact of closures in large units tends inevitably to be more severe than that of a number of closures in smaller units because of geographical concentration, particularly in areas such as the Highlands where the large unit dominates local employment. It seems probable that the impact of regional policy has been less since the mid-1970s, reflecting reduced expenditure together with lower economic growth and higher unemployment in the whole of Great Britain and the developed world. But the continuing effect is still positive, and it is clear that without regional policy the ability of the Scottish economy to adapt its industrial structure and generate new jobs would have been significantly less.

The record of post-war industrial development in Scotland also poses a number of more qualitative issues which take on particular importance in a long-run perspective: for example, the type of job opportunities provided in the new industries; the extent to which new industries have led to the growth of linkages with other parts of the economy; and the wider effects of increasing external control of Scottish industry. For example, while many new industries have provided relatively high income employment and diversified the occupational structure considerably, Hood and Young (1976) concluded that the extent of functions such as research and development and marketing exercised in U.S.-owned branch plants in Scotland was limited.[20]

Evidence on industrial linkages in respect of many firms new to Scotland suggests a relatively low degree of integration with other plants in Scotland, despite the efforts which have been made to attract suppliers to the new industries. For example, it has been estimated that U.S.-owned firms in Scotland — which have formed the major part of inward investment since the war — purchased only 25% of their material inputs from plants located in

Scotland in 1969 (compared with an estimate of 45% which can be derived from the Scottish input-output table (1973) for the domestically supplied proportion of all manufacturing intermediate inputs in Scotland); while only 15% of intermediate goods produced by U.S.-owned firms in Scotland were sold to plants located in Scotland.[21] Other commentators have noted the limited extent to which components firms in both the vehicles and electronics industries set up in Scotland to supply the major new plants introduced since the war (for example the Linwood and Bathgate vehicle plants).[22] For electronics, it has been emphasised that local linkage is particularly low in the case of the more sophisticated externally owned plants, although internal company organisation rather than ownership seems a more important determinant of the extent of local linkage.[23] While there is evidence of spin-off effects from oil-related development on local engineering companies in Scotland, it is perhaps disappointing that the very considerable capital investments associated with oil development have not had a greater impact on existing industries.[24] This matter is further considered in the chapter by Stuart McDowall.

The trend towards external ownership of manufacturing industry in Scotland, particularly in the more modern expanding sectors, has been highlighted elsewhere, and the possible adverse effect this could have for the quality of jobs, level of decision-taking and long-run prospects for the Scottish economy has been widely discussed in recent years.[25] We have already seen that the employment performance of incomer units to Scotland (both in new openings and in expansions once established) has been generally much more favourable than that of non-incomers. While takeovers of Scottish companies may lead in some instances to a loss of local decision-taking and a reduction in the range of local job opportunities, it needs to be borne in mind that takeovers may bring financial benefits from membership of a larger grouping — as typified by the experience of many small growing firms subject to financial constraints. Moreover, research published in 1980 on trends in the functions carried out by U.S.-owned manufacturing companies in Scotland concluded that there were some encouraging signs of some research and development functions in Scotland being increased, and that there were no clear signs that Scottish plants inevitably became less important within a wider grouping.[26] That the longer-run consequences of increasing external ownership could be adverse for the Scottish economy remains possible. But the evidence available is by no means conclusive; and in any case, given the strength of the forces making for centralisation and increased economic integration, it seems unrealistic to expect that attempts to counteract the trends by administrative means can do more than have a moderating effect.

This assessment suggests that policy has had considerable success in the number of jobs created and the transformation of Scotland's industrial structure, but that there have also been disappointments. The scale of new job growth has not been sufficient to maintain overall employment levels, and some of the newer industries showed signs of reduced growth or decline by the end of the seventies. The occupational structure has been widened, but the extent of higher-level decision-taking and research and development functions remained limited and subject to forces which may not work in Scotland's favour. Much of the new industrial development has not developed close linkages with other parts of the Scottish economy or reached a stage where it provided a basis for further development or a self-sustaining nature (although there are some hopeful signs that at least in electronics the attraction of plants in earlier periods was leading to spin-offs in the form of new branches in Scotland or the start-up of new companies by entrepreneurs previously employed in the large plants).

Given the slow growth of the British economy and the structural and locational characteristics of the Scottish economy, it is far from clear that a markedly more favourable performance was possible; and the depth and length of the recession in the early 1980s made it inevitable that some major closures would occur, as in other parts of the U.K. But the experience of the post-war period also points to some lessons about the constraints which face policy for industrial development in Scotland. The record of particular industries during these years suggests that Scotland's peripheral location in relation to major markets in the U.K. and Europe remained a general handicap to economic performance — at least relative to other parts of the U.K. — unless it was offset in particular industries by natural resource advantages or special expertise which produced high-quality goods where factors other than price were important marketing characteristics. As already noted, the disadvantage of a Scottish location for industries producing large volumes of standardised items by mass production methods where sales depend critically on small unit cost margins compared with competitors was a feature pointed out by investigations in the 1950s and early 1960s.[27] Even if transport costs form a relatively small proportion of industrial costs and if overall measured transport costs in Scottish manufacturing relative to output and value added are little if at all out of line with the rest of the U.K.,[28] it does not follow that a peripheral location is of no account. For example, the development of industry in Scotland both in terms of the type of new industry attracted and the location of markets served by Scottish industry may adapt to locational circumstances, while there may be other distance costs (apart from those concerning the movement of goods to markets) which operate unfavourably on innovation and revenue growth in a more peripheral area.

Transport costs are clearly more important in industries such as cars and strip steel which have relatively high weight-to-value ratios than in industries such as electronics with a low weight-to-value ratio — although even in the case of standardised electronics components some disadvantage on this count will no doubt arise. At the other end of the spectrum stand industries such as whisky, high-quality wool textiles and certain types of food processing which produce less standardised products for which sales are not dominated by price considerations; these seem good examples of industries for which a Scottish location is not a significant handicap, and indeed a Scottish origin is a powerful marketing advantage. The average size of units in such industries tends to be relatively smaller than in the more standardised volume manufactures where economies of scale are important; and the reduced vulnerability of a whole area to individual closures in these cases seems an additional advantage, particularly in less urbanised areas. To these industries might be added those with a high science and technology content such as health care and biotechnology as well as the more advanced aspects of electronics for which the existence of the Scottish universities and educational background could afford advantages; and service sectors such as insurance and banking which can draw on a strong basis of Scottish expertise. The first decade of oil-related development falls mainly into the category of an industry which has grown because of a resource advantage — the finding of oil close to Scotland — though it remains to be seen whether a level of expertise can be built up in Scotland to provide the basis for further growth (for example in consultancy and specialised technology) when U.K. oil production declines.

Locational factors need to be seen in perspective. Even for those industries where a Scottish location may represent a greater than normal disadvantage, the industry may prosper in circumstances of rapid growth of demand — although in the longer term the weaknesses of its position are likely to be exposed. In the case of the Linwood car plant, factors other than location, including the particular models produced in Scotland, doubtless played a part in the eventual closure. Locational factors do not seem to have been of primary importance in two other major closures of new industries at the end of the period — the Fort William pulp mill in 1980 (which was of course based on the processing of a natural resource) and the Invergordon smelter in 1981. In both cases the predominant factors seem to have been a mixture of unlucky circumstances (for example, the type of processing installed at Fort William and the circumstances of the particular company at Invergordon and the details of the pricing arrangements made for electricity supply) together with developments affecting the U.K. as a whole — for example, the rise in the real exchange rate of sterling at the end of the 1970s and the depth of the recession in 1980-82. Also the large size of these units in relation to their local economies resulted in the impact of closure being exceptionally severe. But for all the qualifications, the pattern of industrial change in the post-war period does suggest that certain types of activity are more likely to succeed than others in the particular locational circumstances of Scotland; and that in the long run policy is likely to be more successful if it gives priority to those developments (whether by adaptation of existing industry or the attraction of incoming firms) which are consistent with the constraints imposed by a Scottish location.

MANUFACTURING EMPLOYMENT CHANGE IN THE SCOTTISH NEW TOWNS, 1953-78

As already described, the role of the Scottish New Towns has shifted over time from one primarily related to the accommodation of overspill population from congested urban areas to one mainly aimed at the attraction of new industry. A comprehensive evaluation of the New Towns would need to take account of their social objectives through the provision of housing and the building up of new communities in an attractive environment, as well as the cost of favouring the New Towns in public expenditure programmes, and is outside the scope of this chapter. The degree of success of industry in the New Towns in generating manufacturing employment is nonetheless an important element in any evaluation, and the aim here is to describe and analyse post-war trends in this particular aspect, using the material already discussed on Scotland as a whole as a context. The main source of data is again the Scottish Manufacturing Establishments Record which allows gross manufacturing job changes to be examined since 1953 for the local employment office areas containing the five New Towns. It should be noted that this procedure will therefore be based on areas slightly larger than the New Town designated areas (except for Irvine) and — more importantly — include trends in these areas prior to the designation of New Towns in the case of Cumbernauld (prior to 1956), Livingston (prior to 1962), and Irvine (prior to 1966). Only in the case of Irvine — which had a substantial pre-designation employment base — is this a significant weakness, and the overall trends for the five New Towns as a group seem unlikely to be seriously distorted.

Table 5 shows the pattern of net manufacturing job change and of the main gross job change components for the Scottish New Towns by sub-period between 1953 and 1978. Over the whole period manufacturing employment increased by some 32,000 (compared with the net decrease of 89,000 in Scotland as a whole already described). The sub-period when the most substantial net growth occurred was 1963-68 (+15,000), but manufacturing employment in the New Towns recorded a net increase in each of the sub-periods, including 1973-78 (+4,000) when Scotland as a whole was experiencing its most rapid net decline. Gross job increases in the New Towns peaked in 1963-68 but continued at a high level after this as a result of increases in the number of jobs created through expansions of existing units (which were greater in 1973-78 than 1963-68) — in contrast with the quite sharp fall off in job increases in new openings after 1963-68. The main reason for the smaller net job gains after 1963-68 seems to be much higher levels of gross job decreases both through contractions and closures recorded after this sub-period.

One method of placing the performance of industry in the New Towns in perspective is to express their components of gross job change as a proportion of the equivalent gross job changes occurring in Scotland as a whole (Table 6), and to compare these New Town shares with their share of Scottish manufacturing employment — which was increasing rapidly from under 2% in 1953 to 6.5% in 1973. It can be seen that the much more favourable net job performance of industry in the New Towns was due mainly to very high shares of gross increases, particularly in new openings but also in expansions (relative

Table 5. *Manufacturing Employment Change in the Scottish New Towns, 1953-78*

Sub-period	Gross job increases			Gross job decreases			Net job change	
	New Openings	Expansions	All gross job increases	Contractions	Closures	All gross job decreases	Nos	(%)
1953-58	1912	2651	4563	1350	512	1862	+2701	+21
1958-63	3235	3705	6940	1414	2123	3537	+3403	+22
1963-68	10734	6607	17341	938	1455	2393	+14948	+79
1968-73	7070	7313	14383	3579	3614	7193	+7190	+21
1973-78	4519	8080	12599	4250	4481	8731	+4119	+10
1953-78 (sum of above)	27470	28356	55826	11531	12185	23716	+32361	+253

Source: Scottish Manufacturing Establishments Record

Table 6. *The Share of the Scottish New Towns of Manufacturing Gross Job Changes 1953-78*

Sub-period	Manufacturing employment in Scottish New Towns as % manufacturing employment in Scotland at start of sub-period	Gross job increases in Scottish New Towns as % in Scotland			Gross job decreases in Scottish New Towns as % in Scotland		
		New Openings	Expansions	All Gross Increases	Contractions	Closures	All Gross Decreases
1953-58	1.9	6	3	4	2	1	2
1958-63	2.3	6	6	6	2	3	2
1963-68	2.9	17	7	12	2	2	2
1968-73	5.1	14	9	11	5	4	4
1973-78	6.5	24	13	15	5	7	6

Source: Scottish Manufacturing Establishments Record

to the benchmark of the New Towns' share of manufacturing employment in Scotland at the start of the sub-period in question). In contrast, the share of gross job decreases was much more closely in line with employment share throughout the period, and it therefore seems that the jump in New Town gross job decreases in 1968-73 and 1973-78 was no greater than would be expected from trends in Scotland as a whole together with the growing size of the stock of employment in the New Towns. Table 6 also shows that even in the period 1973-78 (for which the highest share was recorded) the Scottish New Towns were responsible for only 15% of all gross job increases in Scotland — a very creditable performance given the relatively small stock of employment in the New Towns in 1973, but by no means a dominant element in Scotland's overall growth. In the case of job increases in new openings between 1973 and 1978 the New Towns' share approached a quarter.

Previous studies have concluded that a distinctive feature of the manufacturing employment growth of the Scottish New Towns has been their success in attracting and relative dependence on establishments which are incomers to Scotland, and this is illustrated in Table 7.[29] In contrast to Scotland as a whole, incomers made a larger contribution than non-incomers to New Town gross job increases through new openings in each sub-period, and through expansions in all sub-periods after 1958. Incomers became responsible for more gross job decreases than non-incomers in New Towns after 1968 — and it is noticeable that the rate of job loss in incomers was also rather higher than in the case of non-incomers from this date for both contractions and closures. Table 8 shows the New Towns' share of Scottish manufacturing employment and gross job changes for incomer units. It is clear that the significance of the New Towns in relation to Scotland is much greater for incomer units than for all manufacturing units; in 1973 they accounted for 16.5% of employment in incomers in Scotland compared with 6.5% for all units. The New Towns' share of gross job increases among incomers was much greater still, reaching 26% in 1963-68 and 1973-78, while if analysis is confirmed to gross increases

Table 7. *New Openings, Expansions, Contractions and Closures of Inco*

Type of Unit	(1) NEW OPENINGS Employment in new openings					(2) EXPANSIONS Employment expansions in existing units					(3) C(Employment	
	1953-58	*1958-63*	*1963-68*	*1968-73*	*1973-78*	*1953-58*	*1958-63*	*1963-68*	*1968-73*	*1973-78*	*1953-58*	*1958*
(A) Scottish New Towns												
Nos.	1912	3235	10834	7070	4519	2651	3705	6607	7313	8080	1350	14
As % employment at start of period	15	21	57	21	11	21	24	35	22	20	11	
of which:												
Incomer Units												
Nos.	1269	1733	7965	3644	2503	29	2306	3884	5096	4871	28	
As % employment at start of period	231	95	137	21	12	5	127	67	30	23	5	
Non-incomer units												
Nos.	643	1502	2769	3426	2016	2662	1399	2723	2217	3209	1322	13
As % employment at start of period	5	11	21	20	10	21	10	21	13	17	11	
(B) Scotland												
Nos.	30372	51471	61580	50419	18572	78335	66939	89015	81890	63105	66832	848
As % employment at start of period	5	8	10	8	3	12	10	14	12	10	10	
of which:												
Incomer units												
Nos.	7327	16153	23225	20496	7291	14512	13755	22395	24352	21026	1266	4?
As % employment at start of period	25	34	33	19	6	50	29	32	23	16	4	
Non-incomer units												
Nos.	23045	35318	38355	29923	11281	63823	53184	66620	57538	42079	65566	80?
As % employment at start of period	4	6	7	5	2	10	8	12	10	8	10	

Source: Scottish Manufacturing Establishment Record

Incomer units are units opening in Scotland since 1st January 1945 with an origin outside Scotland; and units openin

in new openings, the share in these sub-periods rises to 34%. In 1963-68 and 1973-78, therefore, the New Towns were attracting over a third of all job increases in incomer units opening in Scotland. But the New Towns' share of gross job decreases in incomer units has also increased rapidly, reaching 20% in 1968-73 and 18% in 1973-78, above their share of employment in these units at the start of the sub-periods. This was due to particularly high rates of job losses in closures of incomer units — some quarter of all such job losses in Scotland occurring in the New Towns.

Non-incomer Units in the New Towns and Scotland, 1953-78

...ACTIONS ...ions in existing units			(4) CLOSURES Employment in closures					(5) NET EMPLOYMENT CHANGE					
3-68	1968-73	1973-78	1953-58	1958-63	1963-68	1968-73	1973-78	1953-58	1958-63	1963-68	1968-73	1973-78	1953-58
)38	3579	4250	512	2123	1455	3614	4481	+2701	+3403	+14948	+7190	+4119	+32361
5	11	10	4	14	8	11	11	+21	+22	+79	+21	+10	+253
363	1958	2335	0	0	187	2268	2490	+1270	+3975	+11299	+4514	+2572	+23630
6	11	11	0	0	3	13	12	+231	+219	+195	+26	+12	+4304
375	1621	1915	512	2123	1268	1346	1991	+1431	−572	+3649	+2676	+1547	+8731
4	10	10	4	16	10	8	10	+12	−4	+28	+16	+8	+71
50	79283	81062	34276	61930	66529	91942	62913	+7599	−28346	+23016	−38916	−52349	−88996
9	12	13	5	9	10	14	10	+1	−4	+4	−6	−8	−13
74	12088	17407	2473	3205	1998	9471	10061	+18100	+22350	+38448	+23289	+2065	+104252
7	11	13	9	7	3	9	8	+63	+48	+55	+22	+2	+361
76	67195	63655	31803	58725	64531	82471	52852	−10501	−50696	−15432	−62205	−54444	−193248
10	12	13	5	9	11	15	11	−2	−8	−3	−11	−11	−30

...land with an origin in an incoming unit.

The relative dependence of the New Towns on incomer units helps to explain other characteristics of their employment structure and performance:[30] the dominance of certain industries well represented among incomers; the tendency for gross job increases to be particularly large (both in absolute terms and relative to the rest of Scotland) near the peak of economic cycles when the level of mobile industry is higher; and the greater degree of volatility in the level of gross job increases from year to year since the number of incomer units fluctuates quite markedly according to economic conditions. By 1978, 39% of

Table 8. *The Share of the Scottish New Towns of Manufacturing Gross Job Changes in Incomer Units, 1953-78*

Sub-period	Manufacturing employment in incomer units in Scottish New Towns as % manufacturing employment in incomer units in Scotland at start of period	Gross job increases in incomer units in Scottish New Towns as % incomer units in Scotland			Gross job decreases in incomer units in Scottish New Towns as % incomer units in Scotland		
		New Openings	Expansions	All Gross Increases	Contractions	Closures	All Gross Decreases
1953-58	1.9	17	0	6	2	0	1
1958-63	3.9	11	17	14	1	0	1
1963-68	8.4	34	17	26	7	9	8
1968-73	15.9	18	21	19	16	24	20
1973-78	16.5	34	23	26	13	25	18

Source: Scottish Manufacturing Establishments Record

manufacturing employment in the Scottish New Towns was in Mechanical, Instrument and Electrical Engineering, compared with 26% in Scotland as a whole at this date (and only 7% in the New Towns in 1953). Research on the period 1950-70 based on annual gross job increase figures found that about 60% of the total gross job increases in the Scottish New Towns was in the Engineering, Vehicles and Metal goods industries.[31] But while it tended to be in these industries that the level of gross job increases in the New Towns was particularly favourable relative to the rest of Scotland, performance in the New Towns (expressed as gross job increases per thousand employees) was also favourable for the majority of industries. The previous research also found that the New Towns' gross job increase performance tended to be more favourable than in the Rest of Scotland for male as well as female employment, for most individual years, and for non-incomer as well as incomer establishments. Within incomer units, the New Towns attracted a disproportionate share of large plants and plants in Electrical Engineering, particularly electronics.[32]

A thorough evaluation of the New Towns' manufacturing employment performance needs to standardise not only for industrial structure (which in the above study was only carried out at the broad Order level) but also for age of plant — since new plants tend to increase employment rapidly in the first few years and the New Towns' high share of new openings would lead one to expect above-average gross increases on this count alone. A rigorous attempt to do this has been made by Robert Henderson, who has examined gross manufacturing job change over the periods 1967-71 and 1971-75 in New Town plants which are at least five years old and compared their performance (after standardising for industrial structure at Minimum List Heading (M.L.H.) level) with similar mature establishments both in the rest of Scotland and in a number of selected control areas in other parts of Scotland which, like the New Towns, have had relatively plentiful supplies of industrial sites and advance factories.[33] The results show that after removing the effect of new openings and their build-up in the first five years, the extent of the favourable gross job performance in the New Towns relative to other areas is much reduced. On balance the record of more mature plants in the New Towns was still rather more favourable in most industries than in either the rest of Scotland or the control areas, but the difference is not statistically significant. Similar results were obtained when the analysis was confined to incomer units.

From these various studies on manufacturing employment change in the Scottish New Towns a number of conclusions emerge. Firstly, it is clear that net job change in the New Towns has been more favourable than in Scotland as a whole throughout the period 1953-1978, but that in view of the absence of a substantial base of existing industry in the New Towns (with the exception of Irvine), which was a handicap to net job performance in other parts of Scotland, an examination of gross job changes provides a fairer comparison. Secondly, gross job change analysis shows that the favourable record of the New Towns is mainly due to very high relative rates of gross job increases, particularly on account of new openings and in respect of incomer units. Gross job decreases were only slightly below the New Towns' share of existing employment, and it is perhaps surprising that the difference was not more marked in view of the New Towns' favourable industrial structure. Thirdly, the record of the more mature manufacturing plants in the New Towns does not seem to have been significantly more favourable than comparable plants elsewhere in Scotland; thus most of the much higher rates of gross job increase in the New Towns seems attributable to the success which the New Towns have had in attracting new openings, particularly incomer units — together with the initial expansion of these plants over the first five years. The importance of relatively young plants in the New Towns may also help to explain why gross job decreases have not been lower, since it is known that young plants are more prone to closure.[34]

Faster than average manufacturing employment growth in the Scottish New Towns may partly reflect non-policy factors. For example, it has been suggested that about half of the more rapid manufacturing growth in the New Towns (throughout Britain) compared with Great Britain over the period 1960-78 can be attributed to the relatively small population size of New Towns, since smaller towns throughout Britain (irrespective of New Town status) have recorded a more favourable employment performance than larger towns and cities.[35] This general shift of manufacturing employment from the conurbations and larger cities to smaller towns and rural areas may reflect factors such as the easier availability of suitable industrial land in small settlements.[36] Caution is indicated in applying these results to the Scottish New Towns, since there have been differences in employment trends between the Scottish and other New Towns in recent years (manufacturing employment continued to increase in the Scottish New Towns over the period 1974-78, whereas it declined in the other New Towns), and a reliable estimate of the population size effect needs to take account of the New Towns' particular industrial structure.

In Scotland the main issue has been the extent to which the success of the New Towns has been at the expense of other parts of Scotland or has resulted in a net addition of employment to Scotland as a whole. Extravagant claims have been made on both sides of the argument. While there is no doubt that the New Towns have been favoured through public expenditure programmes such as advance factory building and Government policy towards the attraction of incoming industry,[37] the decline in manufacturing employment in the older urban areas of Clydeside has been on a far greater scale than the growth in the New Towns; and it has been shown more generally that it is unreasonable to claim that the New Towns have caused the decline of the conurbations.[38] On the other hand it is also misleading to suggest that the New Towns were the only areas of growth in an otherwise declining economy; or that the great proportion of the jobs attracted to the New Towns would otherwise necessarily have been lost to Scotland. It is also clear that the New Towns have not developed as envisaged by some of the early proponents as self-contained centres in relation to either travel to work patterns or growth of a linked industrial complex. In the last resort it is not possible to know how Scotland would have fared without the New Towns policy. While it seems probable that many incoming firms (particularly from abroad) are attracted to the idea of integrated urban development in new settlements co-ordinated by a New Town Corporation, and to the image of success which the New Towns have promoted, we do not know how many of them would have selected alternative locations in Scotland had resources been allocated in a different manner. It seems one of the strengths of New Towns policy in Scotland that a limited number of carefully selected areas have been consistently promoted as centres of industrial growth. The areas chosen for New Towns have the advantage of relatively attractive locations on the fringes of, but accessible to, the major urban areas of central Scotland. Such areas stand to benefit in any case from decentralisation trends as the older urban areas adjust to present economic circumstances. The record of post-war industrial development policy in Scotland suggests that success in providing the basis for long-run growth is difficult to achieve, and much more likely where policy — as in the case of the New Towns — takes account of locational constraints and reinforces existing economic trends.

CONCLUSIONS

Industrial development in Scotland in the post-war period has been faced with a number of severe difficulties: the slow growth of the British economy; an adverse industrial structure for much of the period; and the handicap of a peripheral location both in relation to the U.K. and Western Europe — which has become an increasingly important trading partner for the U.K. over the period. While development in Scotland has been assisted by regional policy and by the discovery of major oil resources in the northern North Sea, the underlying circumstances have not been favourable.

Seen in this light, the record of industrial change over the post-war period is not discreditable. The encouragement of new industries has resulted in the transformation of Scotland's industrial structure. While the scale of job growth has been insufficient to maintain overall employment levels, the extent to which local linkages and higher quality functions have been fostered is disappointing, and it is not clear that it was realistic to expect a much more favourable outcome given the strength of the constraints.

New industries in Scotland appear to have been most successful in the longer run where they have not been significantly handicapped by these constraints, or where they have been based on natural or other local resource advantages. For example, industries or companies supplying worldwide markets have been less affected by slow growth in the British economy. Industries producing specialised goods and services where factors such as design and quality are important seem generally better suited to Scotland's locational circumstances than large volume mass production manufacture where economies of scale and small cost differences compared with more favourably located competitors may be crucial. Among the latter group of large volume manufacture, products with relatively high weight-to-value ratios are at a particular disadvantage, while local economies are more vulnerable when dominated by the large units which are characteristic of such industries.

If we examine the characteristics of industries which have either prospered in the post-war period or seem to have relatively good prospects for the future (for example, whisky, high-quality food processing, some oil-related products, specialised instrument engineering and electronics, high-quality wool textiles, health care and financial services), they seem generally consistent with this analysis. It is clear that many of these industries are not new in the sense of being based on incomer units; and over the period policy gave increasing attention to the opportunities for the development of indigenous industry. But the policy of attracting new industries from outside Scotland also played an important part in strengthening the economy where the fundamental locational and other characteristics of Scotland's circumstances have been recognised.

The record of the New Towns in Scotland's post-war industrial development is also creditable. This is not to say that the New Towns have developed in the way originally envisaged, or that they have achieved all that their proponents have claimed. They have received favourable treatment in the allocation of public investment and have enjoyed additional advantages compared with other areas of Scotland in the attraction of incoming industry. A thorough evaluation of the costs and benefits of New Towns is extremely difficult to make and outside the scope of this chapter. But viewed purely in industrial terms their record of gross manufacturing job increases, particularly through the attraction of incomer units, seems in line with policy objectives. As we have seen, it has not been easy to promote industrial development in the circumstances of post-war Scotland. Against this background the Scottish New Towns, notwithstanding their public expenditure advantages, and their shortcomings and disappointments, can reasonably be counted as one of the success stories. Significantly, the New Towns are an example of a policy which has sought not to override but to operate within the trends of economic geography.

NOTES

1. James Bowie, *The Future of Scotland* (Edinburgh, 1939), and see Ch. 1.

2. Michael Fogarty, *Prospects of the Industrial Areas of Great Britain* (London, 1945).

3. C. Oakley (ed.), *Scottish Industry*, Scottish Council (Development and Industry) (Edinburgh, 1953).

4. C. E. V. Leser, 'Manufacturing Industry', in A. K. Cairncross (ed.), *The Scottish Economy* (Cambridge, 1954).

5. *Ibid.*, and see Table 1, Ch. 1 above.

6. Scottish Council (D. & I.), *Committee of Inquiry into the Scottish Economy (Toothill Committee)* (1961).

7. Ibid; G. McCrone, *Scotland's Future* (Oxford, 1969).

8. P. Abercrombie and R. H. Mathew, *The Clyde Valley Regional Plan 1946*, H.M.S.O. (Edinburgh, 1949).

9. Toothill, *op. cit.*; *Central Scotland. A Programme for Development and Growth*, Cmd. 2188, H.M.S.O. (Edinburgh, 1963).

10. Fraser of Allander Institute, *Input-Output Tables for Scotland, 1973* (Edinburgh, 1978).

11. Central Statistical Office, *National Income and Expenditure*, H.M.S.O. (London, 1980).

12. See Ch. 2 above; and also, C. Lythe and M. Majmudar, *The Renaissance of the Scottish Economy?* (Hemel Hempstead, 1982).

13. *Scottish Economic Bulletin*, No. 24 (1982).

14. 'Employment Trends in Scotland in the 1970s', *Scottish Economic Bulletin*, No. 21 (1980).

15. J. Randall, 'The Comparative Birth Rate of Enterprises New to Manufacturing in Scotland and the U.K.', *Scottish Economic Bulletin*, No. 24 (1982).

16. 'Small Units in Scottish Manufacturing', *Scottish Economic Bulletin*, No. 20 (1980).

17. R. Henderson, 'An Analysis of Closures Amongst Scottish Manufacturing Plants Between 1966 and 1975', *Scottish Journal of Political Economy (S.J.P.E.)*, Vol. 27, No. 2 (1980), pp. 152-174.

18. B. Moore and J. Rhodes, 'Regional Policy and the Scottish Economy', *S.J.P.E.*, Vol. 21, No. 3 (1974), pp. 215-235.

19. W. McNie, 'Industrial Change in the Scottish Economy', unpublished paper, Scottish Economic Society Conference, Stirling (1982).

20. N. Hood and S. Young, 'U.S. Investment in Scotland', *S.J.P.E.*, Vol. 23, No. 3 (1976), pp. 279-294.

21. D. Forsyth, *U.S. Investment in Scotland*, (London, 1972).

22. T. L. Johnston, N. K. Buxton and D. Mair, *Structure and Growth of the Scottish Economy* (London, 1971); David Sims and Michael Wood, *Car-Manufacturing at Linwood: the Regional Policy Issues* (Paisley College of Technology, 1984).

23. P. McDermott, 'Ownership, Organisation and Regional Dependence in the Scottish Electronics Industry', *Regional Studies*, Vol. 10 (1976), pp. 319-335.

24. S. McDowall and H. Begg, *Industrial Performance and Prospects in Areas Affected by Oil Development*, Scottish Economic Planning Department (S.E.P.D.), Economics and Statistics Unit (E.S.U.) Research Paper no. 3.

25. J. Firn, 'External Control and Regional Development: the case of Scotland', *Environment and Planning*, Vol. 7 (1975), pp. 393-444.

26. N. Hood and S. Young, *European Development Strategies of U.S. Owned Manufacturing Companies Located in Scotland*, H.M.S.O. (Edinburgh, 1980).

27. A. K. Cairncross (ed.), *op. cit*; Toothill Committee, *op. cit.*

28. 'Transport Costs in Scottish Manufacturing Industries', *Scottish Economic Bulletin*, No. 22 (1981).

29. 'Annual Gross Change in Manufacturing Employment in the Scottish New Towns and the Rest of Scotland, 1950-70', *Scottish Economic Bulletin*, No. 14 (1978).

30. *Ibid.*

31. *Ibid.*

32. R. Henderson, 'The Location of Immigrant Industry Within a U.K. Assisted Area: The Scottish Experience', *Progress in Planning*, Vol. 14, Part 2 (Oxford, 1980).

33. R. Henderson, 'The Employment Performance of Established Manufacturing Industry in the Scottish New Towns', S.E.P.D., E.S.U. Discussion Paper no. 16 (1982).

34. R. Henderson, 'An Analysis of Closures . . .', *loc. cit.*

35. S. Fothergill, S. Kitson, and S. Monk, *The Impact of the New and Expanded Town Programmes on Industrial Location in Britain, 1960-78*. Industrial Location Research Project Working Paper no. 3, Department of Land Economy, University of Cambridge.

36. S. Fothergill and G. Gudgin, *Unequal Growth: Urban and Regional Employment Change in the U.K.* (London, 1982).

37. R. Henderson, 'The Employment Performance . . .', *loc. cit.*

38. S. Fothergill, S. Kitson, and S. Monk, *op. cit.*

12
POLICY AND PROCESS IN SCOTTISH HOUSING, 1950-1980[1]

Andrew Gibb and Duncan Maclennan

INTRODUCTION

Most cross-sectional or time series reviews of the economic structure of a country include some comment upon the housing sector, for not only are poor housing conditions a cause of major social concern, but the value of the production and consumption of housing are also vast economic magnitudes. In the period which this chapter covers, for instance, housing construction absorbed between 3 and 7 per cent of Gross Domestic Product (G.D.P.), with a tendency for this magnitude to decline over time. In addition, council tenants paid 12 per cent of their gross incomes for housing and new-home buyers 25 per cent. At the same time, spending on housing has comprised up to 12 per cent of total public spending in Scotland (at the end of the 1960s), though it fell by the 1980s to around 5 per cent of public expenditure.

A synopsis of indicators of housing 'need' accompanied with a passing comment on the cyclical role of housing investment and its burden on household incomes singularly fails to catch the breadth of meaning of housing to economies and their development. At the individual scale, housing provides more than shelter. Housing choices and spending also reflect demands for location and access to employment centres, public and private services, demands for neighbourhood quality and the willingness or not to reside with similar social, income, ethnic or religious groupings. In this way individual housing choices may come to reflect or even exacerbate broader social and economic problems, particularly in urban areas. Housing investment and public choices made in relation to it not only reflect the economic wellbeing and tone of society but also shape the structures of the economy, society and polity in which subsequent development occurs.[2]

We do not, in this chapter, seek to provide a detailed synoptic overview of Scottish housing history in the period 1950-80. Rather we are restricted to broad brush impressions organised around the central theme of the evolution of the role of public housing in Scotland. This focus is central to an understanding of the distinctiveness of Scotland within the U.K., and indeed within Western Europe. At the 1981 Census, 54.6% of Scottish households lived in public rental housing compared with 32% in the rest of Britain.[3]

This distinctiveness, although still critical to future policy development, largely emerged in the period 1950-80. The completion of well over one million houses since 1945 has involved the commitment and expenditure of vast financial and human resources. With three-quarters of all Scottish house completions from 1950 to 1980 taking place within the public sector, housing development has involved central and local government agencies and authorities on a massive scale, and in a possibly inextricable commitment. However, by 1980 past patterns of housing investment came to constitute an often problematic structure for the subsequent decade of Scottish housing policy, partly because of its inherent limitations but also because national housing policy had set its face against public sector solutions and averted its eyes from the vast public sectors of Scotland and the North British cities.[4] Thus, examining Scottish public housing not only reveals the nature of housing programmes and conditions and policies but also yields insights regarding the way in which distinctive regional/Scottish programmes evolved within a politically unitary state, the role and perceived limits of the welfare state and the changing pattern of relations between central and local governments. The public sector housing programme in Scotland is an example on the grand scale of the switch from generosity and optimism (perhaps naivety) to meanness and pessimism in public spending coexisting with a sustained willingness to tolerate strategic and operational inefficiency and inequitable policy outcomes. In the 1980s Scottish spending on housing is an example *par excellence* of the tone and spirit of British policy on public spending.

The remainder of this chapter falls into four distinct sections. The next section outlines the context in which housing policy came to operate in the 1950s. Then the period 1950-1969 is examined in detail as it constitutes the main phase of unquestioned commitment to public housing. The decade of the 1970s is then considered in the penultimate section as the period of doubt and uncertainty in housing strategy. The new and anti-public housing certainties of the early 1980s are briefly examined in the concluding section.

PROBLEM ROOTS AND EARLY RESPONSES

The early phasing and rapid pace of industrialisation and urbanisation and their relationship to developing housing conditions in Scotland are already well documented.[5] Although the nature of the economic base promoting expansion varied by area and time period, the century from 1850 to 1950 witnessed concentrated nodes of economic development throughout Scotland. Development of textiles and attractive industries created small and medium-sized towns in Fife, Lothian and Ayrshire. Dundee expanded with the processing of jute and linen, and Aberdeen and Edinburgh developed on a more diverse economic base. Dominating this development, however, was the emergence of the dynamic, dense conurbation stretching from the docks of Greenock through the 'clotted masses' of Glasgow's industries to the coal and steel towns of Lanarkshire.

These developments occurred when levels of personal mobility were low. Economic conditions necessitated a massive development of low-cost, small dwellings for rent (reflecting the income distribution), close to work or, in the later nineteenth century, on public transport routes. Property developments were, therefore, sited in relation to work-centres and also distinctively densely developed. The stone tenement building was the major form of provision, and as a result the Scottish cities developed a dwelling infrastructure distinctive in Britain. Indeed, the built environment of Scottish cities was more akin to major European cities than to English centres. In most urban centres, large or small, the contiguity of housing with poor drainage and sewage, inadequate water supplies, small-scale dairy farming, and numerous industrial 'sweated' workshops, induced major problems of public health. The generally low level of amenities in such areas, other than drinking dens, generated additional environmental difficulties.

Visiting Glasgow in the early eighteenth century, Daniel Defoe had observed that Glasgow was 'the cleanest and healthfullest and best built city in Britain, London excepted'. With the onset of the classical period of industrialisation matters sharply deteriorated. In 1950 Baird noted, 'Scottish housing has long had an unenviable reputation and, rightly or wrongly, the Glasgow slums have widely been regarded as without equal in Western Europe'.[6] This latter comment was made after almost a century of policy intervention to cope with Glasgow's exceptional difficulties, as well as those of the other Scottish urban centres. Local government response at first confined itself to the surgical excision, under City Improvements Acts, of the worst groups of sub-standard dwellings in city cores, with only minor attempts at housing provision.[7] National government intervention first took the form of a Royal Commission on Industrial Housing in Scotland, set up in 1912, and reporting in 1917 to the effect that private enterprise had manifestly failed to meet the housing needs of the working classes, and that only the state, acting through local authorities, could and should take responsibility to meet such requirements.

The Scottish, and particularly Glasgow, manifestation of housing problems had a critical bearing on national U.K. policy in the period 1915-1925. The Glasgow rent strikes were critical in forcing government to introduce the Mortgage and Rent Restrictions Act of 1915, the source of rent control legislation in the U.K. And the Scottish Royal Commission report, as well as the early post-war political climate, were important influences upon the decision to introduce public housing in Britain. Non-market rents and state supply are critical components of the traditions of Scottish socialism, and they have an early manifestation in the Housing Acts of the 1920s.

Public housing provision in Britain has largely been a function of local authorities.[8] Central government, by using standards and financial incentives and controls, has been able to control the scale and mix of council housing output. But local authorities have had, at least historically, an important influence on the cost and scale of public housing. This local discretion, practised under the constant gaze of the Scottish Office which in turn had, and has, some leeway to depart from national policy thrusts, has allowed an important 'Scottish' dimension to emerge in housing policy formulation.

The 'Scottish' dimension had already become apparent in the inter-war period. Between 1919 and 1939, 337,000 houses were built in Scotland, and this total exceeded the quarter million target identified in the 1917 Royal Commission. Notably, two-thirds of the dwellings completed in Scotland were within the local authority sector, in marked contrast to the quarter share of completions of English and Welsh councils in the inter-war years. In this period the role of the state and the owner-occupied sector had already begun to diverge, and this tenure divergence became progressive as political interest and power became consolidated around housing-tenure interests. By 1945, the dependence on state housing and a penchant for low rents (and for smaller dwellings) in Scotland *vis-à-vis* England and Wales were already obvious and important.

1940s Planning and Legislation

While house construction had virtually ceased during the Second World War, it was recognised that advanced planning for post-war needs was necessary. A 1942 survey of housing needs showed a desperate desire among the working population to escape from overcrowded, insanitary tenements after ten or twenty years on the housing list,[9] and a direct response to this need was the 1944 announcement by the Minister of Health that in order to secure the largest possible numbers of dwelling units in the two years after the war, work would proceed simultaneously on the construction of both temporary and permanent houses. At the same time, two reports by the Scottish Housing Advisory Committee introduced a revised scale of overcrowding and proposed the evaluation of housebuilding needs on a national basis, phasing and locating housing development along with industrial development.[10] The two Housing Acts of 1944 at first ignored the latter recommendation, but the 1946 Act included a response to more general housing needs, widening the responsibility and powers of local authorities. As a final crucial step the 1949 Act, by deleting all references to 'working classes', entrusted local authorities with providing for the housing needs of all members of the community, thus firmly elevating the local authority to a position of pre-eminence in the housing field. The total of over one million houses constructed by 1984, over 76% by public sector agencies, provides physical evidence of that pre-eminence

Post-War Housing Needs

The outbreak of war in 1939 brought a halt to the construction of new schemes, and early examination in the post-war period revealed a housing deficit on an enormous scale. In Scotland, over 120,000 unfit houses needed immediate replacement, while a further 200,000 were classified as being overcrowded. War damage and special needs added a further 64,000 to the total, and housing was also required for 134,000 newly formed households. Added to this, houses technically 'fit' but lacking sanitary conveniences or internal water supply provided a further 'need' of c.405,000 houses.[11] A survey of the 'housing needs' of the 17 Economic Council for Europe countries in 1948 indicated that Western Europe's urgent housing need was fourteen million dwellings — clearly Scotland's housing problems were important on a continental rather than merely British scale.

The extent of needs and the difficulties in their solution lay partly in the distinctive character of Scottish housing. The vast proportion of the need lay in urban areas or their satellite zones, and in these areas the bulk of existing housing was tenemental. Problems were generated by structure inflexibility, land-use admixture, and the character of problems generated ranged from overcrowding and sanitation to mixed building ownership, unique to Scotland. There was also the difference in relative degrees of concentration of population (and political power), with the Glasgow conurbation containing 35% of the total population in contrast, to, say, London's 18% of the English population. On a wider scale, 75% of the Scottish people lived in the central Lowlands, and the drift of population to this urbanised core of the nation was still intensifying in the post-war decades. The urban component of the Scottish population amounted to 82.9% in 1951 and had risen to 85.5% by 1961.[12]

This urgent national housing need exhibited an internal pattern which varied greatly from area to area, while the perception of need was rendered more complex by changing standards of evaluation of housing fitness involving the function of rooms within the house and the status of children under 10. The 1951 census was the first occasion when questions were asked on a uniform basis on the availability of conveniences such as piped water, fixed baths and water closets, and together with information on house and household size these provide evidence of a clear hierarchy of need. Table 1 indicates the preponderance of small houses in central Scotland as a whole, but especially in the west-central area, while in contrast the southern and crofting counties were better endowed with larger dwellings. The overwhelming concentration of small houses in urban areas, and especially Glasgow, is indicated in Table 2. Over 78% of Scotland's single-apartment houses and almost 66% of two-apartment houses existed in urban areas, and in the former case Glasgow accounted for almost half of the Scottish population living in single-roomed houses.[13] With over 130,000 houses overcrowded, not to mention thousands of others whose sanitary and other facilities rendered them sub-standard, Glasgow occupied an unenviable position at the top of the hierarchy.[14] Edinburgh, Aberdeen and Dundee came next, where very high proportions of housing stock were classified as unfit. The smallest numbers of houses were required in landward areas of counties, many of which had drawn on inter-war subsidies to greatly reduce their housing needs.

Table 1. *Houses by size and region: Scotland 1951 (% of total)*

No. of rooms*	Scotland	Northern	East-Central	West-Central	Southern	Crofting Counties
1	5.2	2.3	3.5	7.9	1.7	1.4
2	26.3	16.5	26.2	31.3	17.5	12.5
3	31.2	29.7	34.1	30.2	30.3	25.8
4	21.5	25.2	21.8	19.3	24.9	30.6
5	7.7	11.6	6.9	6.2	10.0	13.5
6	3.4	6.2	3.0	2.2	5.8	7.3
7+	4.7	8.5	4.5	2.9	9.8	8.9

* In reckoning the number of rooms in a house, kitchens are counted as rooms, but not kitchenettes, sculleries, closets, bathrooms, landings or rooms occupied as offices, shops, or for other business purposes.

Table 2. *Urban Concentration: % of small houses and population within them: Scotland 1951*

	1 room		2 rooms		3 rooms	
	houses	people	houses	people	houses	people
Glasgow	45.2	49	29.5	32.2	19.3	20
Other 3 cities	16.1	13	18.3	17.3	17.9	17.3
Large burghs	16.9	15.9	18.1	17.8	17	17.4
Counties	21.8	20.7	34.1	32.7	45	45.3

Source: Census of Scotland 1951, Vol. III

Table 3. *Policy and Process in Scottish Housing, 1945-1983*

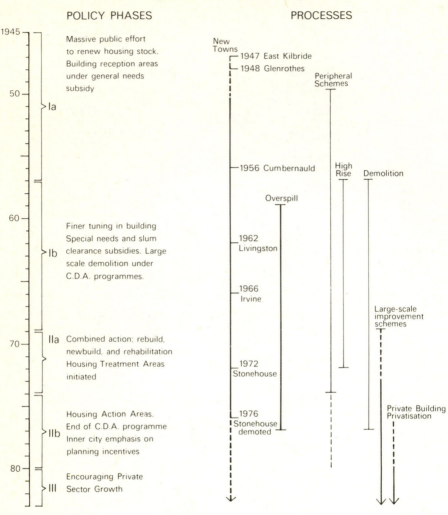

POLICY PHASES — PROCESSES

Phase		
Ia	Massive public effort to renew housing stock. Building reception areas under general needs subsidy	
Ib	Finer tuning in building Special needs and slum clearance subsidies. Large scale demolition under C.D.A. programmes.	
IIa	Combined action; rebuild, newbuild, and rehabilitation Housing Treatment Areas initiated	
IIb	Housing Action Areas. End of C.D.A. programme Inner city emphasis on planning incentives	
III	Encouraging Private Sector Growth	

New Towns: 1947 East Kilbride, 1948 Glenrothes, 1956 Cumbernauld, 1962 Livingston, 1966 Irvine, 1972 Stonehouse, 1976 Stonehouse demoted

Peripheral Schemes

Overspill

High Rise

Demolition

Large-scale improvement schemes

Private Building Privatisation

THE RISE OF PUBLIC HOUSING

The policy response to the inherited housing situation outlined above was urgent and substantial. Conservative and Labour governments alike, nationally and locally, adopted the view that public housing development was essential to ensure an efficient land assembly and construction programme to meet existing needs quickly. Broadly similar responses occurred simultaneously in many European countries, but the subsequent scale of locally provided and bureaucratically managed housing far outreached progress elsewhere. This development dominated Scottish housing policy and provision before 1970. More accurately, this period can be divided into sub-phases 1945-1957 and

1957-69, but it was an era when there was a certainty that public housing investment would end Scotland's housing problems and that sustained economic growth would allow the development to be financed without adverse economic consequences.

In the earlier of these sub-phases a vigorous programme of developments on large-scale suburban greenfield sites was undertaken. Construction then largely consisted of tenemental family houses, built under general needs subsidies to provide necessary reception areas for overcrowded urban slum-dwellers. The second sub-phase, from 1957-1969, was characterised by the introduction of approved houses (Table 3). The high rate of construction continued, but under more specific direction by type, location, function and size of house, including overspill houses or others designed to integrate housing and industrial incentives. Secondly, with peripheral housing schemes, New Towns, and overspill agreements absorbing thousands of families, removal of unfit housing could now begin under comprehensive development area policies.

The effects of the 1957 and 1962 Housing Acts were far-reaching in terms of producing homogeneity and lack of choice within the public sector housing stock. The 1957 Act reduced the basic subsidy to £24, a severe reduction from even the lowest rate of the 1952 Act. At the same time an extra subsidy was made available for houses in blocks of flats of more than six storeys, and with no real possibility of cutting back on their urgent housing programmes, local authorities, especially those of the larger urban areas, committed themselves to the large-scale adoption of high-rise building, a decision reinforced by the provisions of the 1962 Act (Table 4).

Table 4. *Subsidies for Special Needs*

Basic Needs	3 apts.	4 apts.	5 apts.
1938	£10.10/-	£11.15/-	£13 (over 40 yrs)
1946	£21.10/-	£23	£25.10/-(over 60 yrs)
1952	£39.15/-	£42.5/-	£46.15/-(over 60 yrs)

+£12 on each category for houses built for agricultural workers in remote areas.

1957 Basic needs: £24 p.a. regardless of size (approved houses)
      Special needs: £30 — incoming industrial workers
              £36 — agricultural population
              £42 — overspill
              £42 — Development Corporations
Houses in blocks of 6 or more storeys — £24 basic need plus ⅔ of any surplus over average cost of approved houses.

1962 Basic needs subsidies related to financial need of individual authorities; power to reduce existing subsidies.

      Special needs: £32 — incoming industrial workers.

Houses in blocks of 6 or more storeys — basic needs rate increased to £40.

Sources: 9 + 10 Geo. 6 Ch. 54 Housing (Financial Provisions) (Scotland) Act 1946
          15 + 16 Geo. 6 + 1 Eliz. 2 Ch. 63 Housing (Scotland) Act 1952
           5 + 6 Eliz. 2 Ch. 38 Housing & Town Development (Scotland) Act 1957
         10 + 11 Eliz. 2 Ch. 28 Housing (Scotland) Act 1962

U

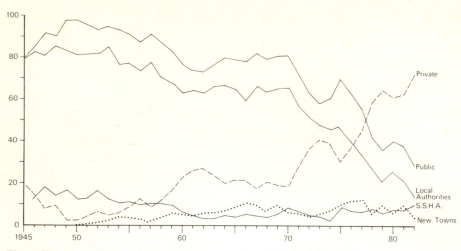

Fig. 1. House completions by agency: percentage of total, Scotland 1945-1982.

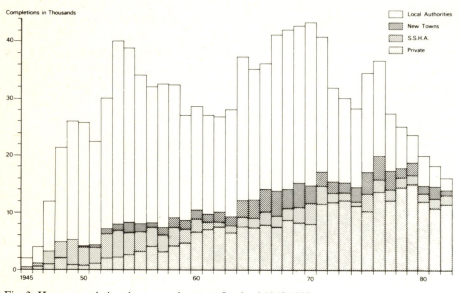

Fig. 2. House completions by year and agency: Scotland 1945-1982.

Housing Supply Response

The subsidy system operated certainly stimulated housing output. Post-war house construction (Fig. 1) shows two major peaks. From 1945 to 1947 completions rose very slowly, reflecting post-war shortages and controls, then surged to over 20,000 per annum until 1952, when a total of 30,000 presaged a decade of building during which totals never fell below 25,000 per annum and sustained levels of over 30,000 for most of the period. The next surge took place between 1964 and 1971, with totals always over 35,000 and for five years over 40,000 per annum. The first major phase produced around half a million new housing units, while the second added a further 400,000. These totals were largely achieved by three sets of agencies, namely Local Authorities, the Scottish Special Housing Association, and the New Town Development Corporations, with the private sector increasing in importance year by year. However, from 1946 until 1970 Local Authorities completed more than half a million dwellings, over 70% of the total (Fig. 2). Thus the immediate post-war Housing Acts in many ways replicated the distinctive inter-war pattern of Scottish housing development. Between 1945 and 1953, the peak year of the first bulge with 40,000 completions, the Local Authority share of building never dropped below 80% and often hovered around 85%. As other agencies, especially the private sector, shouldered an increasing proportion of the burden, this share gradually dropped to below 70% in 1959, and with minor fluctuations stayed in the middle 60s until 1971. While emerging management problems were to call into question the long-term efficiency of massive public housing in a mixed economy, the enormous constructive achievements of thirty-eight years of energetic striving to remove the overall Scottish housing shortage cannot be doubted.

Other public agencies reinforced Scottish reliance upon public housing investment. The Scottish Special Areas Housing Association Limited was established in 1937 to provide homes and employment within the Special Areas designated for economic assistance. It dropped 'Areas' in 1939 and 'Limited' in 1969, to arrive at its present title. Although the 1944 Housing Act allowed the Association to operate throughout Scotland, it concentrated upon areas of greatest need in large cities and in providing overspill housing. From 1946 to 1953 it contributed between 12.5 and 17.5% of annual totals of houses built, dropping to between 9.5-10.5% until 1959 and thereafter contributing a percentage which fluctuated around 6% with peaks of 9% and troughs of 3% (Fig. 1). By 1970 the Scottish Special Housing Association (S.S.H.A.) was the second largest public sector landlord in Scotland, being responsible for around 80,000 units.

The Scottish New Towns, which are discussed in Chapter 11, also constructed 50,000 public sector units to 1970, providing new locations for housing investment and permitting the demolition of older slums, particularly in Glasgow and Edinburgh. The contribution of private sector construction to housing output throughout this period was dwarfed by the public sector but grew steadily in absolute and proportional significance. Home ownership growth throughout this period further relied upon the transfer of rent-controlled dwellings from private renting to owner occupation, thus creating an extremely low-quality and low-value owned sector within the Scottish cities.

In the urban areas, where their greatest potential market lay, the relatively small numbers of builders in the immediate post-war period found their access to prime sites restricted by local authorities, anxious to secure land for their own building programmes. In a number of authorities, most notably Glasgow, there was also a political commitment to preclude private building. At the same time the acute shortage of building materials and labour in the early post-war years found expression in the 1946 Building Materials and Housing Act, which ensured that those in greatest need should have priority and placed the onus for building on local authorities. Among the severe restrictions placed on building for owner-occupiers, private builders had to obtain licences from the local authority, and these were not granted unless exceptional need could be demonstrated. Even when a licence was issued, the size of a house and its selling price were strictly controlled. From 1948 some minor relaxation occurred, but building controls were not abolished until November 1954, and it was only from this time that the private sector began to make an impression on housing development.

Thereafter private completions show a steady climb from the 3-6% of the previous six years to levels of 12-16% between 1956 and 1959, then in the building boom of the 1960s a virtually uninterrupted level of around 20% lasting until 1971 (Fig. 1). During this period the general affluence of a rising middle class was reflected in the proliferation of suburban owner-occupied housing estates. Until this period, the nationally 'underdeveloped' state of the owner-occupied market was reflected in the fact that building societies were substantial net exporters of funds from Scotland to the U.K. as a whole.

Growing Reservations

The strong and consistent thrust towards public housing development was not without its critics, from both pragmatic and ideological perspectives. In the formulation of the Clyde Valley Plan, between 1944 and 1947, a number of the critical planning officers involved were dissuaded from advocating rehabilitation strategies by the political representatives involved. Clearly politicians, at that time, did not believe that revitalisation of older neighbourhoods was the desired approach because residents would remain at the mercy of private landlords or because of poor local environments. Also, at that time, the already developed areas of public housing had not manifested the environmental and social problems which subsequently developed. The grass was still greener on the peripheral estates.

By the early 1950s a number of academic commentators were already drawing attention to the negative impacts of urban renewal in central Glasgow. For instance, in 1957, Brennan argued:

> One may therefore ask whether adaptations could not be made to improve conditions sufficiently in the present area at something less than the cost of tearing the whole place down.
>
> All kinds of changes have taken place in Gorbals and places like it since the time when 'No Mean City' presented a fair picture of life there. These changes are still continuing and others could be encouraged. Many of the unpleasant features of life in the Gorbals were the result,

not of bad housing, but of poverty and lack of education. Life in one or two rooms is likely to be squalid for a family with young children who are inadequately clothed and fed, badly trained and often ill, and where the mother is trying to make a meal out of bacon bones and potatoes over an open fire in a badly ventilated room hung with damp washing. It is a different matter for two or three adults who have more efficient equipment in the home and sufficient income to buy in prepared food: who also have their clothes washed at the laundry or launderette and are able to spend their recreational time in cinemas and clubs.[15]

However, such dissent did not influence policy until the 1970s, and Conservative as well as Labour local authorities promoted public housing schemes, although, especially in Glasgow and Edinburgh, occasionally with less enthusiasm. The national level attempt to restrict public development and revitalise private renting, in the period 1957-1960, had markedly lesser impact in Scotland than in the rest of the U.K. By then public housing had come to form a critical affiliation with Labour Party policy, and past housing developments had created political constituencies clearly identified, indeed polarised, by housing tenure. The association of a single or dominant housing tenure with a particular political party is heavily pronounced in Scotland in comparison with other areas of Britain, even in depressed regions such as South Wales or Northern England. Scottish MPs, to a much greater extent than their southern counterparts, have been able to identify single-tenure dominance and policies within their areas. Housing issues have always figured critically within Scottish politics, and Scottish central and local politics have been and are Labour-dominated. Until the late 1970s this political perspective, combined with the growing power of the Scottish Office and the expanding role of local government, allowed public housing development to override, or at least frustrate, Westminster opposition to the programme (and indeed it still does in most Scottish authorities!).

By the end of the 1960s, however, the euphoria of the new development phase evaporated sharply, and growing doubts about the impact of the programme began to be widely expressed. The pressures for a more considered approach to housing provision arose from a number of factors. Concern came to be expressed about the nature of the dwelling structures and neighbourhoods created and their evolution over time, and by the 1970s dwellings less than two decades old were already unlettable. Technical problems were, in many areas, reinforced by the style of management and the inadequacies of management systems. The external policy environment was also changing, and the case for rehabilitation and inner city investment gained credibility and political support. Such new ideas for housing provision and the increasingly ailing public sector have had to compete for shrinking public investment resources as housing programmes, after 1975, became the leading sector in the attempt to reduce public spending.[16] These changes are worth considering in more detail, and it is also noteworthy that such issues are not restricted to Scotland or indeed the U.K. The problems associated with the financing and management of public or social rented housing in Europe, developed in parallel to Scottish policies but on a smaller scale, have recently been concisely reviewed by Harloe.[17]

The Structures Created

In the introductory paragraphs of this chapter we mentioned the complexity of housing and the range of household activities with which it is critically linked. This broad view of housing attributes was not adopted in the development of public housing, indeed it is only now gaining credence. Political activists were concerned with raising resources for new housing, and design decisions were largely left to technocrats. The professions involved, especially the architects,[18] had scant regard for the way in which new housing developments created new spatial, social and economic structures and problems. Commenting on the development of social housing in Hungary after 1950, Szelenyi suggests that in socialist housing systems aiming for large and rapid housing output targets, the technical staff involved are inevitably alienated from the final consumers and that repetition of insensitive design mistakes and lack of variety of output are characteristic.[19] Post-war public housing development in Scotland was on a proportional scale similar to that prevailing in Hungary, and many of the processes and outcomes have a similarity.

The majority of inter-war council houses were in relatively high-quality structures with moderately low density layout. However, between about 1965 and 1972, the adoption of system building techniques introduced into Scottish housebuilding the potential for a whole crop of problems. A Scottish Office circular of 1965 described nine different designs of system-built dwellings with factory-made components, and encouraged groups of housing authorities to get together to choose one and cut costs by mass purchase.

Building designs originating in Scandinavia and Western Europe and embodying features totally unsuited to the Scottish climate (let alone temperament) were symptomatic of the lack of architectural conception and commitment. Flat roofs failed to shed heavy rainfall and acted as reservoirs for rainwater which inevitably percolated to the houses below. Cladding slabs were secured by ferrous pins which rusted rapidly in the moist climate. Steel-framed windows which no amount of painting could protect from corrosion, and which acted as magnets for condensation, thin interior divisions which provided no insulation against noise, and insubstantial exterior walls which permitted heat to drain away were but a few of the basic structural drawbacks. In addition to these, underfloor electric heating which produced differential expansion cracks (in the cases where householders could afford to use it), uninsulated water tanks and pipes which were liable to burst in frost, and ineffective ventilation systems which encouraged severe levels of condensation were among the catalogue of architectural absurdities which perhaps reached their nadir in systems provision for high-rise buildings. Windows lacking safety catches, common landings with no access to fire-doors save through houses, steel fire doors on the main walls of bedrooms, elevators never designed to cope with twenty-four hour usage, metal rubbish chutes and doors seemingly designed to provide the maximum noise above ground level and a noisome eyesore on the ground, ludicrously inadequate drying and storage facilities and noisy plumbing systems which provided perfect fire transmission ducts, were built in as additional features of frustration.

The initial conception of design may have been shallow enough, but these inadequacies were compounded by lack of quality control at the component fabrication and assembly stages. Mass production of components, often by a range of manufacturers, shoddy workmanship and inadequate quality control ensured sufficient sub-standard items to provide a scattering of malfunctioning systems and crumbling, cracking or corroding structural members throughout a diversity of housing types. Pressure to meet contractual deadlines, careless and slipshod assembly of prefabricated components, and poor standards of finishing combined to ensure a further group of future problems. At all stages, from design through production and construction to mute consumer acceptance, quality was sacrificed for false economy, engendering an unwelcome legacy of uninhabitable dwellings, many of them destined for demolition before the interest on their construction loan was paid, and the remainder constituting an architectural timebomb, ticking towards an estimated cost (in 1983) of £3,000 million nationally for rehabilitation to a habitable standard.

In spite of the limitations of dwelling structures, it was solely concern about dwelling size and sanitary standard which shaped investment decisions. A narrow and misleading conception of housing and housing needs had shaped the programme. The provision of visual amenity and neighbourhood amenities, both public and private, was sadly neglected, and inadequate transport systems exacerbated the problems of peripheral estate living.[20] Further, relocated households had their social and labour market ties disrupted, and for many households the net benefits of the rehousing programme were markedly reduced by the failure to see public housing investment in its broader context.

Over time social and economic changes have exacerbated these initial difficulties. Changing demographic structures have called into question the size structure of dwellings developed, growing real incomes have altered the demand for housing attributes, and expanded activity patterns and changing energy costs have reduced the liveability of many of these dwellings. Of course not all such developments were foreseeable but, in effect, badly planned structures have become even less appropriate over time. Tenants may like the concept of subsidised council housing, many do not like their council houses, and the estates they live in.

By the early 1970s maturation of the council housing stock had produced sharp variations in housing quality and socio-economic structure across Scottish public sectors. Areas of high-quality council housing, often inhabited by higher-income tenants paying modest dwelling rents, contrasted markedly with rundown neighbourhoods often on the outer edge of the city which contained low-income, large families in modern dwellings. In many areas the 'solution' rapidly became the 'problem', although a strategy for 'outer city' problems was still only in its infancy in Scotland in 1980. Such estates developed in large and small housing authorities in Scotland, but they became particularly obvious in Glasgow and Edinburgh. In the mid-1970s more than half of Glasgow's tenants were on the transfer list, and analysis of the spatial structure of requests to leave and requests for entry revealed massive variations in estate popularity. Public sector vacancy rates also rose alarmingly, and public sector abandonment became a major issue in the 1970s.

Management Styles and Feasibility

The centralised bureaucratic structure of Scottish housing management, as in other parts of the U.K., reinforced the problems of stock structure. The simple conception of needs generated simple rules for eligibility of access to public housing and allocation within it. Sensitivity to the selection and placement of tenants was absent, and there were no direct feedback mechanisms for the housing service to record and assess tenant dissatisfaction (to our knowledge no Scottish local authority has ever asked its tenants how they feel about their housing and housing service). Societal commitment to develop public housing was not matched by a similar attitude to managing the dwellings provided. As noted above, lack of detailed planning, an absence of concern over the process of service delivery and no attention to efficiency are hallmarks of British public provision which are at their most apparent in Scottish public housing.

Bureaucratic centralism and a narrow focus upon houseletting and rent collection were the characteristics of most Scottish housing departments in the 1970s. Aside from general style and structure, the detailed procedures of management were also open to criticism. Allocation procedures, apart from excluding important 'needy' groups from the public sector (the young, the mobile, the unmarried), are also reputed to have contributed to social differentiation within the sector. Rent fixing policies, which have only ever been systematically addressed by the 1972 Act, have produced outcomes where the relationships between dwelling quality (as viewed by tenants) and rent levels may be perverse and where higher-income tenants enjoy higher levels of subsidy and housing quality. The public housing effort has not always produced decent housing (broadly defined) which is equitably distributed.

The Rise of Inner City Policy

By the 1970s the academic warnings of twenty years previously regarding the impact of demolition on inner areas had been widely justified. In the three main cities, but most obviously Glasgow, the clearance-demolition process had a number of observable and negative effects. Clearance and overspill had disrupted existing communities and contributed to social, spatial segregation. Within cities, public rehousing had removed younger households (of a conventional format) with families and left behind small elderly families and a growing number of students and young professionals. Overspill and New Town selection schemes catered systematically for higher-skilled and qualified labour market groups.[21] At the same time, blighted stock awaiting demolition, gapsites and derelict land all amounted to discouraging eyesores for remaining residents.[22]

The systematic analysis of small-area data from the 1971 census confirmed the then widespread local view that inner city areas, or more correctly older residential neighbourhoods, in Scottish cities still constituted nationally (U.K.) significant foci of urban deprivation.

However, this view, which was later to be usefully contrasted with the new abundance of North Sea oil resources, by Scottish politicians seeking Westminster revenues, did not lead to an unqualified call for re-expansion of the clearance and demolition process. Rather, rehabilitation of existing dwelling units became a growing and important concern. This switch of emphasis in housing investment priorities reflected considerations other than the problems of inner cities and public housing provision noted above. At a national scale, it was increasingly recognised that there could be a strong case for housing rehabilitation. Locally it was recognised that many of the very worst, smallest houses had been removed and that a significant proportion of remaining dwelling units could be rehabilitated. This new approach to housing improvement was first recognised in the 1969 Housing (Scotland) Act.

Thus, at the beginning of the 1970s growing problems within public housing, sustained interest in and growth of the owner-occupied sector, and the recognition that new approaches to meeting housing needs, particularly via rehabilitation, were desirable, all set the tone for a reappraisal of Scottish housing policy.

PLURALISM IN POLICY, 1970-1980

The Changing Public Sector

The 1970s witnessed a sustained retreat from a simplistic approach to Scottish housing policy. Within the public sector new approaches to management were slowly introduced which stressed the importance of service decentralisation and the importance of tenant participation, and there was a new emphasis on the training of housing staff. Changing circumstances, most notably the passing of crudely measured 'housing shortage' (indeed the occasional manifestation of surplus appeared), saw housing authorities extending housing offers to previously excluded social groups. Central government, in conjunction with local authorities, gave a new thrust to housing the most unfortunate of all groups, 'The Homeless' — by 1980, 8,000 households were being permanently rehoused annually under the 1978 Homeless Persons Act. Most housing authorities recognised that, with past completion records, their development programmes would contract, and forward attention focused upon the renovation of existing stock and provision for 'special needs' groups. A temporary, but important, exception to this diminishing role was the timely public provision of dwelling units in the oil development areas of Scotland, where between 1970 and 1977 almost half of housing completions were in the public sector.[23]

Whilst letting conditions and government circulars encouraged housing authorities to adopt a 'comprehensive lettings' policy, central government also encouraged a new approach to housing planning. In most areas, as will be indicated below, housing authorities were having to increasingly compete or cooperate with housing associations and the private sector. The Scottish Office promoted a series of studies and circulars to encourage local authorities to make comprehensive needs assessments and plans for their areas. This novel, rational and pluralistic approach to local housing policy was formalised in the Scottish Housing Plan system, first introduced in 1978-79. This plan provision and submission system, which was to underpin the allocation of capital for housing policy purposes in Scotland, marked two important changes in housing policy. First, central government was effectively recognising that local authorities, and not the Scottish Office, were the most efficient identifiers of housing problems and strategies to deal with them after the removal of crude shortages. Second, it reflected a major shift in the way in which central government was to control spending on council housing.

The funding of council housing in Scotland, as in the rest of Britain, was, prior to 1974-75, notoriously complex. The overall amount of subsidy flowing from the Scottish Office to a local authority was determined by the range, age, type and relevant Acts for its dwelling stock. These dwelling subsidies, of which there were a considerable number in 1970, were fixed in money terms and received annually for a period of, often, sixty years. It had long been recognised that this system subsidised neither the neediest authorities (in terms of income per capita) nor authorities with building requirements. However, it was not these concerns but the inflationary environment of the mid-1970s which destroyed the old subsidy system.

From 1974 to 1976 central government was concerned, particularly in Scotland, that rises in council rents would fuel wage demands and undermine incomes policies. Thus rent rises were severely limited from 1974-76 but, at the same time, costs of management and maintenance rose ahead of the general price level. In order to avoid growing rate contributions to council housing, central government directly financed an increasing proportion of a growing bill for operating the council sector.

The post-1976 attempts to reduce public spending in Scotland had an immediate impact upon capital spending,[24] but also generated significant rent increases and a new subsidy system. The Housing Support Grant System was introduced in Scotland in 1978 and was a deficit subsidy reflecting, in effect, the difference between an authority's reckonable income and eligible expenditure. 'Reckonable' and 'eligible' were to be assessed by the Secretary of State, and the system was promoted on inter-authority equity grounds rather than as an instrument of macro-economic control. Since 1980, of course, the Housing Plan and Housing Support Grant Systems, particularly the latter, have been the major devices by which central government has made housing spending the lead sector of public sector contraction.

The Scottish Green Paper on Housing Policy, introduced in 1977, reflects the high point of explicit central government discussion of a housing policy for Scotland. Its publication, separate from the Green Paper for the rest of Great Britain, reflected not only the distinctive nature of Scottish housing but the then strong pressures for Scottish devolution. The Green Paper was also important in that it marked a broader-balanced approach to housing policy for the Labour government. Selective sales of council housing were countenanced, a passing reference was made to the possibility of reviving private rental housing with institutional finance, an increased role for housing associations was proposed and, for the first time in Scotland, it was argued that the promotion of owner-occupation should be considered, particularly in the larger cities. The latter two concerns are important and deserve further consideration.

The Scottish Rehabilitation Movement

In the previous section we considered the broad factors which promoted a shift from demolition-renewal to *in situ* rehabilitation. The 1969 Housing (Scotland) Act first encouraged local authorities to indentify unfit tenements and undertake grant-aided work within Housing Treatment Areas. By the early 1970s many local authorities had not used the legislation or, as in the case of Glasgow, recognised that their operational procedures were not sufficiently flexible to promote rapid progress. The 1974 Housing (Scotland) Act was promoted in order to remove a number of difficulties in the rehabilitation process. Local authorities were allowed to declare Housing Action Areas (HAAs) based on the sub-tolerability of tenemental dwellings. Preferential grant aid for improvement within HAAs was made available to private owners, local authorities or housing associations. The distinctively Scottish response, at least in the three largest cities, has been to build HAAs into territories of between 1,000 and 2,000 tenemental dwellings which are then progressively rehabilitated by locally based, resident-managed housing associations. In 1970 there were fewer than six such associations involved in rehabilitation in Scotland, by 1980 there were more than 50 (28 in Glasgow). Using the provisions of the 1974 Housing Act, registered Housing Associations receive funding, and scrutiny, from the Housing Corporation. Scotland has certainly received generous funding from this national quango, and undoubtedly the inflow of additional capital funds to tackle acute housing problems has been welcomed — equally the major role of housing associations reflects a mature willingness of local councillors to cede some sovereignty over housing issues in order to secure progress. This was in marked contrast to the 'centralist-socialist' ideology of the period 1950-1970.

The detailed activities and effectiveness of housing associations in Scotland are assessed elsewhere.[25] Here only the broad patterns of progress are noted. Between 1974 and 1982 almost 20,000 tenemental housing units were rehabilitated, and another 10,000 properties were in the planning phase by 1984. Programme funding grew from £5m. to £90m. by 1983, and housing associations by this date were undertaking more than a third of 'public' investment in housing in Scotland. The Housing Corporation's programme in Scotland was 'bent' towards rehabilitation and towards Strathclyde region. As a result it became the major dimension of urban revitalisation policy in Glasgow. Aside from improvements in dwelling quality and the retention of original residents, the concentrated pattern of improvement encouraged wider neighbourhood revitalisation and acted as a 'growth pole' for private residential investment in previously rundown areas. A movement which was young and hasty in the 1970s had acquired a mature significance by the 1980s, although an initial preoccupation with residential unit improvement resulted in some difficulties for comprehensive neighbourhood improvement.

The Growth of the Owner-Occupied Sector

The emphasis in this Chapter, so far, on council housing reflects the distinctive Scottish dimension in housing provision. However, by the end of the 1960s the margin of change in tenure shares in Scotland began to approximate to national developments. From 1970 the owner-occupied sector, though accounting for a small share of housing in Scotland (at around 30 per cent of households), grew at approximately the national rate. Sector growth in Scotland was, however, much less dependent upon council sector sales, and cycles of output and price inflation rates were less severe than in England and Wales. That is, there were local as well as national and secular as well as cyclical influences promoting ownership growth.

The 1977 Green Paper recognised the apparent desire of many Scottish households to own their own dwellings. However, government then only seemed to recognise a single major cause of this growing demand — sustained income growth was allowing the fulfulment of tenure preferences. Undoubtedly this view had some validity, as there had been sustained real income growth in Scotland between 1950 and 1975. But there were other disequilibrium features of the national economy and the local housing sector which also promoted tenure change. During the 1970s the building societies progressively increased their share of personal sector liquid assets but, with few exceptional quarters, were pressed to meet the demand for mortgages. General price inflation was not fully reflected in interest rates, and hence the mortgage rate — indeed the real mortgage rate was negative throughout most of the 1970s. At the same time rising nominal incomes, marginal tax rates and house prices increased the real value of mortgage interest reliefs in Scotland and the rest of the U.K. Thus the macroeconomic environment, even with rising real house prices, in Scotland acted to encourage households with borrowing capacity to switch from rented to owner housing — an international phenomenon in the 1970s.

Research on tenure change in Scotland[26] indicates that there were few moves from council to owned housing by middle-age, middle-income families with children. Scottish council tenants received relatively deep subsidies and, via transfer and allocation processes, established households received relatively better council housing. As a result tenure change in Scotland was particularly associated with new household formation, and the Scottish house price inflation rate was, in comparison with other regions, acutely sensitive to the marriage rate.[27] Demographic trends in Scotland, from 1970-1985, clearly facilitated intergenerational tenure switches, and changes in the proportion of single-person households sustained a similar shift.

Examination of census data on the socio-economic profile of residents by tenure in Scotland confirms that, by national standards, council housing contains a relatively large proportion of 'higher' socio-economic groups. The Scottish council sector is far from being 'residualised', and since the inflationary environment of the 1970s did little to promote tenure switch by mature households, it is highly unlikely that rapid decline in council sector scale will occur in the 1980s.

The distinctive tone of development of owner-occupation in Scotland has had pronounced housing market effects. Detailed research in Glasgow and Aberdeen indicates that the growth in first-time purchaser/new households had a particularly strong impact in the bottom half of the house price distribution. At first the surge in housing demand in lower-value tenements was sustained by local authority lending, but by the late 1970s building society activity, and then bank lending, in downmarket areas increased, especially as grant aid for home improvement and repair expanded rapidly.[28] Housing prices in such areas increased more rapidly than for the Scottish cities as a whole and Scotland became, by the end of the 1970s, the most expensive housing price region outside the South-East of England.

Taking the decade of the 1970s as a whole, a number of trends are apparent. A more planned and considered approach to housing policy developed, both in the Scottish Office and in many local authorities. There was a genuine attempt to devolve housing strategy formulation to local authorities, and housing 'management' broadened its scope and improved in quality. In broad outline, and with local variations such as the rehabilitation programme, Scottish housing policy became more similar to (indeed often served as a testing place for) national policy developments. However, since 1980 the inherited structure of housing policies and local politics in Scotland has created new divergences between Scottish and English policy developments.

New Certainties?

The planned, pluralistic approach to Scottish housing policies has now been swept aside. With the return of a national Conservative government committed to privatisation and growing home-ownership, in conjunction with increased Labour support within Scotland, consensus on housing policy development has, in many areas, disappeared.

It would not be unfair to suggest that the Scottish Office, following Treasury restrictions, now has to establish the housing spending implications of government cuts rather than develop a purposive housing policy *per se*.

Council house rents have doubled since 1980, though the effects of this change have been greatly ameliorated by the introduction of the Housing Benefit System. Capital cuts have been even more pronounced, with spending on housing now running at a quarter of 1976 levels. The early phases of adjustment to a monetarist strategy also reduced the rate of growth of home-ownership, by creating positive real interest rates and greatly reducing house price inflation.[29] Council house sales in Scotland have proceeded slowly by English standards. Housing policy may now be producing divergent effects in Scotland and England.

The lack of public resources for the revitalisation of council dwellings is of particular concern in Scotland, and the generosity of the 1950s may have inadvertently created the squalor of the 1990s. Central government cannot continue to ignore for much longer the Scottish inheritance of vast public sectors. But there have also been positive aspects of policy since 1980. Local authorities have been required to work with the private sector, and new routes for joint/public private actions are constantly being developed. New private housing investment has generated benefits in previously rundown inner city neighbourhoods.[30] Indeed, through housing association investment, home improvement grant policy and private sector initiatives the inner area of Glasgow in particular is being transformed. This inner-city, private sector bias in policy contrasts markedly with policy of the period 1950-75. However, the critical policy concern for the next decade will be the outer, public city. A planned and purposive policy for public housing which learns from as well as deals with the failings of the past must be a paramount concern for Scotland in the 1990s.

NOTES

1. We are grateful to a seminar audience at the University of St Andrews and to a number of colleagues at Glagow University for helpful comments.

2. There is a marked tendency amongst housing analysts to focus upon the last decade of events and to discuss the British housing system as if it were a single entity. However, there are important and longstanding differences in housing policy in Scotland, Northern Ireland, and England and Wales. It is particularly regrettable that we lack a detailed economic history of housing and housing policy in Scotland.

3. The proportion of households living within the public sector in Scottish District Councils ranges from around 20 per cent in a number of smaller rural authorities, to almost 90 per cent in smaller authorities on the edge of conurbation areas.

4. The apparent disregard for large public housing sectors should not be a source of Scottish paranoia. Rather, since housing policy is often more rooted in ideology than the consideration of circumstances, and since the Department of the Environment have largely foregone housing research since 1979, it is hardly surprising that central government policy is dominated by southern-British vignettes. Such ignorance is not the preserve of central government, however. In establishing its review of British housing, chaired by the Duke of Edinburgh (the only Scottish connection!), the National Federation of Housing Associations included no members currently working outside the South or Midlands. Indeed, their publicity notes refer to Birmingham as the largest public housing authority in Britain. This is an accolade of some dubiety, but there is no doubt that the honour rests with Glasgow District Council and the Northern Ireland Housing Executive.

5. For example, in A. Gibb, *Glasgow; the Making of a City* (London, 1983), Chs. 5-7.

6. W. Baird, 'Housing', in A. Cairncross (ed.), *The Scottish Economy* (Cambridge, 1954).

7. For an early discussion of the possible roles for local authorities in housing provision, see W. A. Smart, *Housing and the Municipality* (Glasgow, 1902).

8. For a brief discussion of the evolution of this role, see D. Maclennan, *Housing Economics: An Applied Approach* (Harlow, 1982).

9. D. Chapman, *Wartime Social Survey; the location of dwellings in Scottish towns* (Edinburgh, 1943).

10. Scottish Housing Advisory Committee 1944.
    (a) 'The Design, Planning and Furnishing of New Houses in Scotland'.
    (b) 'Distribution of New Houses in Scotland'.

11. Scottish Housing Advisory Committee 1944(a), *op. cit.*, pp. 10, 11.

12. Census of Scotland, *Enumeration Abstracts*, 1951, 1961.

13. A. Gibb, *The Development of Public Sector Housing in Glasgow*, University of Glasgow, Centre for Urban and Regional Research, Discussion Paper No. 6 (1982).

14. J. Cunnison and J. Gilfillan (eds.), *The Third Statistical Account of Scotland: Glasgow* (Glasgow and London, 1958), Table LXXIV, p. 469.

15. T. Brennan, 'Gorbals; a study in redevelopment', *Scottish Journal of Political Economy*, Vol. 4, No. 2 (1957), p. 122.

16. D. Maclennan, 'Public Cuts and Private Slump', in M. Cuthbert (ed.), *Public Spending in Scotland* (Edinburgh, 1982). D. Maclennan and A. J. O'Sullivan, 'Housing Policy in Britain since 1979: an overview' (University of Glasgow, mimeo, *n.d.*).

17. M. Harloe, 'Trends in Social Rented Housing in O.E.C.D. countries', Paper presented at O.E.C.D. Experts Meeting (March, 1984).

18. P. Dunleavy, *The Politics of Mass Housing in Britain, 1945-1975* (Oxford, 1981).

19. I. Szelenyi, *Urban inequalities under State Socialism* (Oxford, 1983).

20. I. M. L. Robertson, *Accessibility to Social Facilities in a Peripheral Housing Estate; Drumchapel, Glasgow*. University of Glasgow, Centre for Urban and Regional Research, Discussion Paper No. 3 (1982).

21. E. Farmer and R. Smith, 'Overspill Theory: a metropolitan case study', *Urban Studies*, Vol. 12 (1975).

22. D. Maclennan, M. Brailey and D. Lawrie, *The Activities and Effectiveness of Housing Associations in Scotland*. The Scottish Office (Edinburgh, 1982).

23. C. Jones and D. Maclennan, *North Sea Oil and the Aberdeen Housing Market*. Final Report to Social Science Research Council North Sea Oil Panel (1983).

24. D. Maclennan, in M. Cuthbert, *op. cit.*

25. D. Maclennan, M. Brailey and D. Lawrie, *op. cit.*

26. D. Dawson, C. Jones, D. Maclennan and G. Wood, *The cheaper end of the owner-occupied housing market: an analysis for the city of Glasgow, 1971-1977*. Scottish Economic Planning Department (Edinburgh, 1982).

27. I. D. MacAvinchey and D. Maclennan, 'A Model of Regional House Price Inflation in Britain', *Urban Studies*, Vol. 19, No. 3 (1982).

28. D. Maclennan, in M. Cuthbert, *op. cit.*

29. I. D. MacAvinchey and D. Maclennan, 'Regional House Price Inflation: a response', *Urban Studies*, Vol. 21 (1984).

30. D. Maclennan, D. Lamont and M. Munro, *New Private Housing in the GEAR area. The GEAR Report*. Scottish Development Agency (Edinburgh, 1982).

13

COAL, GAS AND OIL: THE CHANGING ENERGY SCENE IN SCOTLAND, 1950-1980

Stuart McDowall

There were major changes in the patterns of both production and consumption of primary energy in Scotland during the period 1950-1980. These changes had profound consequences in the employment provided by the primary energy industries. In Chapter 3 the decline of the Scottish coal industry was analysed within the general context of the failing heavy industries of the country. Within the context of the changing production and consumption of primary energy, however, the decline of coal is only one of a number of significant events. The most important of these were: (a) the steady decline throughout the period in consumption of solid fuel by all categories of consumers; (b) the replacement of town gas by natural gas in the 1970s; (c) the increase in . consumption of liquid fuels by all categories of consumers, especially transport and industrial consumers; and (d) the discovery and subsequent exploitation of oil and associated gas in the northern North Sea. These trends in energy consumption in Scotland are illustrated in Table 1. It is our purpose in this chapter to describe and to trace the consequences for the Scottish economy of these important events in the field of energy production and consumption.

Table 1. *Heat supplied to Scotland: million therms. Industrial, Domestic, Transport and Miscellaneous Consumers Selected Years, 1952-1976*

	Solid	Gas	Electricity	Liquid	TOTAL
1952	4,037	232	173	103	4,545
1958	3,407	208	245	878	4,738
1962	2,771	195	389	1,400	4,755
1968	1,740	325	602	2,448	5,115
1972	1,102	469	733	2,841	5,145
1976	945	655	843	2,888	5,331
1978	812	833	875	2,882	5,402
1980	709	963	875	2,627	5,175

Source: S. F. Hampson and L. H. Thomson, *Recent Trends in the Scottish Energy Market*, Economics and Statistics Unit (E.S.U.) Discussion Paper No. 1, Scottish Economic Planning Department (S.E.P.D.), 1978, and *Scottish Economic Bulletin* No. 28, December 1983

COAL

The decline in the output of coal in Scotland was the result of a combination of factors operating on both the supply and the demand sides of the market. On the supply side, Scottish-mined coal is and has been for decades high-cost coal because the Scottish pits are smaller than the U.K. average, which has imposed a cost penalty on their operations, and they have suffered from geological problems to a greater than average extent. Moreover, in Scottish pits, larger-than-average numbers of non-face workers have been required to support the coal-winning workforce. This is, to some extent, a consequence of their size and geology.

Since the Second World War, a number of trends may be discerned on the demand side: railways and gas manufacture, both traditional markets, ceased to demand coal; domestic consumers, for a variety of reasons, including the clean air legislation and the increasing demand for automatic central heating systems, switched from solid fuel to electricity, gas and oil; furthermore, industrial consumers, partly because of relative costs, switched from solid fuel, especially to natural gas, when this became available. Natural gas was relatively cheap until the late 1970s. In the 1950s and 1960s, because of relative costs, there was a marked trend for electricity boards to install oil-burning generating sets. In 1973/74, there was a dramatic change in relative costs in favour of coal which, by 1980, had become much cheaper than oil as a primary fuel for power stations (see Table 2). Over a twenty-year period, the Scottish coal industry increased its sales to electricity boards from around 2½ million tons (15% of total coal output) in 1955 to 8 million tons (over 70% of total coal output) in 1981. Oil-burning in Scottish power stations is probably at an irreducible minimum level today. The major outcome of these trends was that, by 1980, increased sales to power stations had been greatly outweighed by reduced sales to industrial, transport and domestic consumers. The Scottish coal industry, moreover, had become extremely dependent on sales to electricity boards. Its chief rival in the medium to long term must be nuclear power generation, especially in view of the increasing concern in North-Western Europe about the effects on the natural environment of acid rain which can be attributed in large measure to the emissions of coal-burning power stations.[1]

Table 2. *Costs of Fuel to S.S.E.B: pence per G.J., 1964-1977*

	Coal	*Oil*	*Coal : Oil (%)*
1964-65	20.6	22.1	93
1967-68	24.1	21.5	112
1970-71	25.9	21.7	119
1973-74	29.7	34.9	85
1976-77	76.9	110.7	69

Source: Annual Reports of South of Scotland Electricity Board

Scottish coal output fell from 23.5 million tons in 1951 to 7 million tons in 1981, a decline of over two-thirds, with an accompanying drop in employment from 82,000 to 18,000. The fall in employment of almost four-fifths exceeded the fall in output which indicates an increase in output per employee over the

Table 3. *Average Number of Unemployed Scottish Colliery Workers: 1955-1970*

Year	Number
1955	115
1956	100
1957	146
1958	280
1959	497
1960	384
1961	175
1962	730
1963	1,443
1964	631
1965	260
1966	132
1967	125
1968	262
1969	276
1970	195

Source: Manpower Services Commission

period. In fact, this was quite modest, the average increase being only three tons per employee per annum.

The total loss of jobs in the industry of about 65,000 between 1955 and 1981 represented an annual rate of loss of 2,500 jobs, but the annual rate of job loss was much higher, about 3,500, during the early part of the period from 1955 to 1970. Two points are worth making here. The first is that this fairly rapid fall in employment was achieved very smoothly for the most part, causing little hardship in the form of unemployment to coalminers and, until the close of the period under review here, little overt industrial conflict. Throughout the period of heaviest job loss, from 1955 to 1970, there were typically no more than a few hundred coalminers registered as unemployed in Scotland (See Table 3). It has to be remembered, of course, that this rundown was taking place in a relatively buoyant labour market in Scotland, with new jobs being created at a historically high rate, especially in those areas where mines were being closed. This was a special feature of regional policy at the time. Much credit must go, however, to the National Coal Board for its policy of securing as many transfers as possible and for making early retirement a genuinely attractive option for older miners, of which the industry had (and still has) a disproportionately large share. From 1950 to 1970, the average age of employed coalminers in Britain increased from 40.3 to 43.9 years. In the latter year, 38 per cent of coalminers were aged 50 or over.

The second point to be made about the decline of coalmining employment is that there were significant differences in the regional impact of the decline ranging from 83 per cent in Lanark to 52 per cent in Midlothian between 1951 and 1971 (see Table 4).

It is important to see the loss of jobs in coalmining in perspective. Where a

Table 4. *Fall in number of coal miners by area of Scotland: 1951-1971*

Area	Percentage fall
Lanark	83
Stirling	73
West Lothian	72
Fife	67
Midlothian	52

Source: Census of Population 1951, 1961, 1971

strong trade union exists, there tends to be a good deal of publicity surrounding decline. Other sectors of the Scottish economy have suffered job losses at least as severe as those in coalmining (as other heavy industries) with much less publicity and with the redundant employees receiving much less generous treatment in terms of severance allowances. The Dundee jute industry lost 85 per cent of its jobs between 1970 and 1981. Between 1971 and 1980, the Scottish hosiery and knitwear industry lost 20,000 jobs, which represented a rate of job loss twice as great as that in the coal industry over the period.

When an industry such as coalmining sheds employment there are, of course, both direct and indirect effects which are felt throughout the regional economy. The coal industry was firmly embedded in the Scottish economy and had many long-established backward and forward linkages with other industries and activities. The coal industry has a higher than average regional employment multiplier, perhaps around 1.7. To the 65,000 jobs lost in the coal industry over our period must, therefore, be added a further 45,500 elsewhere in the Scottish economy, giving a total job loss of over 105,000.

GAS

At the beginning of our period, gas was produced largely from coal. Indeed, it represented a very important market (about 11 per cent of total demand) for the coal industry. A small amount of gas was produced from oil, and many gas boards also bought gas (more cheaply than they could themselves manufacture it) from coke ovens and from refineries. In Britain, gas was produced for local consumption in over 1,000 local gas works, the majority of which had a capacity of less than 500,000 therms a year. There was nothing resembling a national gas grid. Nationalisation of the industry created a number of separate regional gas boards of which the Scottish Gas Board was one. In 1950, the gas industry in Scotland employed some 10,500 people and its output was valued at £6m. The total market for gas was virtually static during the 1950s, and there was little technical change in the industry except for the introduction of the Lurgi gasification technique, designed to be used at opencast coal sites, and the development of oil-based gasification.

The industry was transformed by the discovery of large deposits of natural gas in the North Sea, with the result that, today, the gas industry has ceased to be a secondary source of manufactured energy and is a distribution channel for a source of primary energy. Scottish Gas is merely a part of this national distribution system. The Scottish Gas Board lost its autonomy in 1973 when it was merged, along with the other twelve gas boards, into the British Gas Corporation. Local production of gas is now quite unimportant. The first supplies of natural gas came to Scotland from the southern North Sea but (as will be explained later in this chapter) Scotland, along with the rest of the United Kingdom, is also being supplied with natural gas from the large Frigg gas field and with gas found in association with oil in many fields in the northern North Sea.

Conversion to natural gas, which began in England in 1967, started in Scotland in 1970. The first to be converted included a number of major industrial users, some of whom took the opportunity to switch from solid fuel. By the end of 1977, the conversion programme was complete. Taking Britain as a whole, over 13 million customers had been converted from town gas to natural gas in a decade, which was a major technical and organisational achievement although it was not accomplished without hitches or incidents. The speed of conversion in Scotland may be illustrated by the figures for gas sent out to consumers. In 1970, natural gas represented only 1 per cent of all gas sent out. By 1976, it accounted for 83.5 per cent. As early as 1972, 26 per cent of domestic consumers had been converted.[2]

Natural gas, as a primary energy source for industrial use, however, is less important in Scotland than it is in England. In 1975, for example, gas provided 12.7 per cent of the total heat supplied to industrial users in Scotland; the corresponding figure for the United Kingdom was 25.0 per cent. There is a very significant non-energy use for gas in England, one particularly important use being the manufacture of fertilisers.[3]

By 1980, natural gas had completely taken over the market once occupied by town gas, and it had made heavy inroads into the traditional industrial and domestic markets of the coal industry. The coal industry had also, of course, lost its gasification market. The gas industry, however, has never been and and is not now an important Scottish industry in terms of employment. The number of jobs provided has been fairly steady at between 7,000 and 8,000 in the 1970s. This represents about half the jobs provided by the electricity industry.

Gas from the North Sea is, in terms of cost of production, a very inexpensive energy source, being roughly comparable, per therm delivered to the United Kingdom, with onshore Middle East oil. It is much cheaper than coal, either British or European. Its present relatively high price to consumers is due entirely to Government policy which, effectively, places a tax on North Sea gas to bring its price into line with that of oil. The medium-term outlook for supplies of natural gas is good and estimated reserves are promising.

OIL

The discovery of oil in Scottish waters was undoubtedly one of the most significant economic events for the United Kingdom and for Scotland in the second half of the twentieth century. The most important consequences for Britain have been and will continue to be the macro-economic effects on the balance of payments and on the flow of tax revenue to the Government. North Sea oil has not been a major generator of new jobs, although it would be wrong to suppose that the numbers generated are insignificant. Seen against the massive loss of jobs in manufacturing industry which took place in the late 1970s, however, oil-related jobs, in total, could not be said to have turned the tide of mounting unemployment in Scotland. The most noteworthy aspect of the employment created by oil developments is its geographical concentration in the North and North-East of Scotland, where the impact has been sharp and far-reaching.[4]

It is necessary to point out that the oil and gas which comes ashore in Scotland is not counted, for the purposes of national income accounting, as part of Scotland's regional product. The Government has invented a new region of the United Kingdom, the United Kingdom Continental Shelf (U.K.C.S.) to which is allocated the entire output of oil and gas from the U.K. sector of the North Sea. This does not, however, apply to employment. All jobs are allocated to the place where the appropriate wages and salaries are paid.

In this section we shall be concentrating on the aspects of North Sea oil developments which have been most important in Scotland, and these will concern mainly changes in employment and their effects on local economics. Scotland is, however, completely integrated into the United Kingdom economy and is consequently not insulated from the macro-economic effects of oil. We have already identified these as being balance of payments effects and government revenue effects. The balance of payments benefit to the British economy amounted to about £7,000 million in 1980 (estimated to rise to £10,000 million in 1984). This benefit will, naturally, fluctuate with the world price of oil, to which North Sea oil is closely tied, and with the sterling/U.S. dollar exchange rate, since North Sea oil is valued in U.S. dollars.

The flow of taxation from the companies operating in the North Sea yielded nearly £8,000 million in 1982-83. It results from a complicated set of arrangements which include royalty payments, Petroleum Revenue Tax (with Advance P.R.T. from January 1983) and Corporation Tax. If all these are levied at their full rate, the marginal rate of taxation is about 88 per cent. The average rate is much lower, however, since there are special allowances and deductions which vary from field to field. The total amount of revenue, which in 1982/83 represented more than half of the entire national defence budget, is highly significant, taking pressure off the Public Sector Borrowing Requirement and easing the Chancellor of the Exchequer's problems with taxation from other sources.

Table 5. *North Sea Oil*

Oil fields in production and under development in the U.K. sector of the northern North Sea[1]

a. Oil fields in production

million tonnes

Field	Operator	Discovery date	Reserve estimate[2]	1975/1976	1977	1978	Oil Production 1979	1980	1981	1982	Total[3]
Argyll	Hamilton Bros.	1971	7.3	1.6	0.8	0.7	0.8	0.8	0.5	1.0	6.2
Auk	Shell	1971	8.8	1.2	2.3	1.3	0.8	0.6	0.6	0.6	7.4
Beatrice	BNOC	1976	17.0	—	—	—	—	—	0.2	1.6	1.8
Beryl 'A'	Mobil	1972	66.0	0.4	3.0	2.6	4.7	5.4	4.7	4.4	25.2
Brae South	Marathon	1975	40.0	—	—	—	—	—	—	—	—[6]
Brent	Shell	1971	230.4[4]	0.1	1.3	3.8	8.8	6.8	11.1	15.4	47.3
Buchan	BP	1974	7.7	—	—	—	—	—	0.9	1.4	2.3
Claymore	Occidental	1974	54.0	—	0.3	3.0	4.0	4.4	4.5	4.8	21.0
Dunlin	Shell	1973	41.5	—	—	0.7	5.7	5.2	4.7	3.9	20.2
Forties	BP	1970	261.0	9.2	20.1	24.5	24.5	24.6	22.8	22.1	147.8
Fulmar	Shell	1975	56.0	—	—	—	—	—	—	2.6	2.6
Heather	Unical	1973	8-12	—	—	0.1	0.8	0.7	1.2	1.7	4.5
Magnus	BP	1974	75.0	—	—	—	—	—	—	—	—[6]
Maureen	Phillips	1973	21.0	—	—	—	—	—	—	—	
Montrose	Amoco	1969	12.1	0.1	0.8	1.2	1.3	1.2	1.1	0.9	6.6
Murchison	Conoco	1975	42.7	—	—	—	—	0.4	3.1	4.4	7.9
Ninian	Chevron	1974	143.0	—	—	—	7.7	11.4	14.3	15.0	48.4
North Cormorant	Shell	1974	53.5	—	—	—	—	—	—	1.4	1.4
N W Hutton	Amoco	1975	37.5	—	—	—	—	—	—	—	—[6]
Piper	Occidental	1973	94.0	0.1	8.6	12.2	13.2	10.4	9.8	9.8	64.1
South Cormorant	Shell	1972	26.8	—	—	—	—	1.1	0.7	0.9	2.7
Statfjord	Mobil	1974	384.0[5]	—	—	—	—	0.5	1.2	1.8	3.5
Tartan	Texaco	1974	8.2	—	—	—	—	—	0.7	0.6	1.3
Thistle	BNOC	1973	60.0	—	—	2.6	3.9	5.3	5.5	6.0	23.3
Total				12.7	37.2	52.7	76.2	78.8	87.6	100.3	445.5

b. Fields under development

million tonnes

Field	Operator	Discovery Date	Reserve estimate[2]	Planned production start date
Alwyn North	Total	1975	26.2	1987
Beryl 'B'	Mobil	1975	39.9	1984
Brae North	Marathon	1975	23.97	1988
Clyde	Britoil	1978	20.5	1987
Duncan	Hamilton Bros.	1981	2.9	1983
Hutton	Conoco	1973	31.8	1984

1. Including natural gas liquids (condensates).
2. Operator's estimate of proven recoverable reserves.
3. Cumulative total to end of 1982.

4. Stabilised crude, excluding natural gas liquid.
5. Total production and reserves of field including Norwegian sector.
6. Field started production during 1983.
7. Condensate.

Source: Department of Energy

There is considerable debate about a third macro-economic effect of North Sea oil which originated with the work of P. J. Forsyth and J. A. Kay.[5] Their principal argument was that the impact of North Sea oil was and would continue to be felt on the sterling exchange rate, causing an upward movement equivalent to a 22.5 per cent revaluation. This would lead to a fall in the competitiveness of British manufactured exports and to an acceleration of the de-industrialisation process which was already under way in the country. Obviously, Scotland would not escape the effects. There was, in fact, a strengthening of sterling against most other currencies from 1977 to 1980, but it is possible to attribute this to high U.K. interest rates and the Government's deflationary policies. Certainly the decline in competitiveness which accompanied the rise in the value of sterling was much more the result of the very rapid increase in labour cost per unit of output in Britain accompanied by a very sluggish increase in productivity. It is far from clear that the decline in employment in manufacturing industry in Scotland can be attributed to the exchange rate effects of North Sea oil on competitiveness.

Before we deal specifically with the particular industrial impact of North Sea oil in Scotland it would probably be instructive briefly to trace the development of the industry during the 1960s and 1970s. It was an extremely rapid development.

The event which triggered the major exploration effort was the onshore discovery by Shell/Esso, in a joint venture, of the giant Groningen gas field in the northern Netherlands in 1959. This encouraged oil companies to believe that gas might well be found in the southern North Sea in similar geological structures. The first concessions to explore were granted in 1964. Gas was the objective; it was thought much less likely that oil would be found. The first gas, in the West Sole field, was found by BP in 1965 followed by further significant finds in 1966, including the Leman field which is today the world's largest-producing offshore gas field. As we explained earlier in this chapter, the conversion of the British gas industry to natural gas began with the arrival ashore of the first North Sea gas in 1967 and was virtually complete in 1977, whereupon natural gas output from the North Sea flattened out and remains at about 3,500 million cubic feet a day.

The move northwards into deeper and stormier waters in the search for oil was encouraged, first, by the discovery of the Ekofisk oil field in the Norwegian sector of the North Sea in 1969 and, secondly, by the fact that oil companies were highly dissatisfied with the price which the British Gas Council, which had been granted monopoly buying rights by the Government in 1964, was paying for natural gas. The move soon bore fruit. The first oil field found in British waters was Amoco's Montrose field in 1969. 1970 and 1971 saw the discovery of the two largest fields so far found in British waters, BP's Forties and Shell/Esso's Brent, which were significant finds on a world scale. All the indications were that the northern North Sea was a prolific oil-bearing province and, by 1973, a further five fields, all with estimated reserves of over 40 million tonnes, had been discovered.

The first oil, from the small Argyll field, came ashore early in 1975, followed later in the same year by oil from the giant Forties field reaching the pipeline terminal at Cruden Bay. By the end of 1982, the number of offshore wells drilled had passed the 2,000 mark, 20 British oil fields were in production and a further 6 were being developed. By 1980, North Sea oil output represented 4.0 per cent of British G.D.P. Table 5 illustrates, in detail, the build-up of output from 1975 to 1982. The northernmost field, Magnus, which lies well to the north of 61°, was producing by 1983. Its single steel production platform stands in 612 feet of water and the reservoir depth is 9,500 feet. Its oil goes 56 miles by 24″ diameter pipeline to join the Ninian system before travelling the final 100 miles by 36″ diameter pipeline to Sullom Voe.

Apart from the Frigg pure gas field which lies mostly in the Norwegian sector, many North Sea oil fields have associated gas. In the early days, most of this was flared. Even in 1980, around 12.5 million cubic metres of gas, worth over £1 million, was being flared every day. Increasingly, however, the associated gas is being piped ashore or re-injected into the structures for later recovery. In 1982, the first gas from Shell/Esso's Brent field came ashore at St Fergus, which also takes gas from the Frigg field. At least seven other fields, including Magnus, are being linked into a pipeline system known as FLAGS, Far North Liquids and Associated Gas System.

The short timescale of all these events is worth emphasising. The first oil discovery in the North Sea occurred in 1969. In 1974, Britain was still importing all its oil requirements. The first oil came ashore in 1975. By 1980, Britain was self-sufficient in oil, by 1981 a net exporter and by 1983 producing a surplus of over 50 per cent. Apart from its general economic consequences, this represents a technological achievement of enormous proportions.

It seems pretty clear that the pace of development of the North Sea oil province was accelerated by the OPEC price increases of 1973-74. In early 1973, the international price of crude oil was about $2.50 a barrel, at which level many of the North Sea oil discoveries were uneconomic to develop. By late 1974 the price was over $11 a barrel. These OPEC price increases had two effects: first, about 50 per cent of the discovered oil reserves became commercially viable and secondly, the U.K. Government, concerned with the acute balance of payments consequences of the price increases, was strongly motivated to press ahead as fast as possible with exploiting the North Sea reserves.

Let us turn now to a consideration of the effects of this unparalleled sequence of events on the economy of Scotland. The first point to make is that, given the location of the oil fields and the technology of offshore oil operations, there was bound to be geographical concentration of the impact. The industry requires highly specialised equipment. For some of this equipment, such as mobile (semi-submersible) drilling rigs, there is considerable choice in the location of manufacture. Proximity to the oil fields is not a vital consideration. Many of the mobile drilling rigs deployed in the North Sea are not of British, let alone Scottish, manufacture. By contrast, the very large structures of steel or concrete used as fixed production platforms have to be towed from the place of construction to their final location. The shorter the towing distance the better, other things being equal. Steel platforms require about 30 feet of water to permit towing out, and the steel platform yards are on the east coast of Scotland to permit easy access to the oil fields. They are at Nigg Bay, at Ardersier and at Methil, in Fife. Concrete platforms on the other hand require deeper water than is present on the east coast. They were, therefore, located on the west coast at Kishorn and Hunterston. Concrete platform building yards were also constructed at Portavadie and at Ardyne Point. The former never received an order and the latter is now closed. There was considerable over-estimation by the Government of the demand for production platforms in the mid-1970s. Yards for the construction of smaller steel structures or modules are located in Dundee, Stornoway and Burntisland.

A brief examination of Map 1 will persuade the reader that support and supply functions to North Sea offshore operations would ideally be located in the North-East of Scotland and the Northern Isles. For these functions, distance can be a critical factor, especially for helicopter flights. An exploration rig or a production platform, when drilling, requires 2,000 to 3,000 tonnes of pipe, drilling mud, food, water and other materials every month as well as maintenance and other services. Storage space being extremely restricted on these offshore structures, rapid, reliable, land-based support facilities are essential. It is not surprising to find, therefore, that of the 19 supply bases in operation in 1980, 8 were in Aberdeen, 2 in Peterhead and 5 in Shetland.

Study of Map 1 will also make it obvious that given the very high cost of laying undersea pipelines and given that oil and gas found on the U.K.C.S. had to come ashore in the United Kingdom (Petroleum and Pipelines Act, 1975), landfalls for pipelines and the terminal facilities associated with them would also be located in the North-East of Scotland or in the Northern Isles. Pipeline landfalls, terminal and storage facilities with, in the case of oil terminals, tanker loading facilities for export are located at Sullom Voe in Shetland with a capacity of 1.41 million barrels of oil and natural gas liquids a day, Flotta in Orkney with a capacity of 310,000 barrels a day, Nigg on the Cromarty Firth (100,000 barrels a day from the Beatrice field), Cruden Bay which takes 24 million tonnes a year of oil from the Forties and Brae fields for onward transmission by pipeline to the BP refinery at Grangemouth or for export by tanker from Hound Point in the Forth and St Fergus, in Buchan, which takes almost 100 million cubic metres of gas each day from the Frigg, Piper, Tartan, Brent, Cormorant and other fields.

Given the North-East Scotland orientation of land-based activities required to support offshore operations, it is not surprising to find that Aberdeen emerged as a focus of these activities. Aberdeen was reasonably well served by rail and road links in the mid-1970s and, most importantly, it had an airport which could accommodate medium-haul jet

Scottish oil fields and North Sea gas (1983).

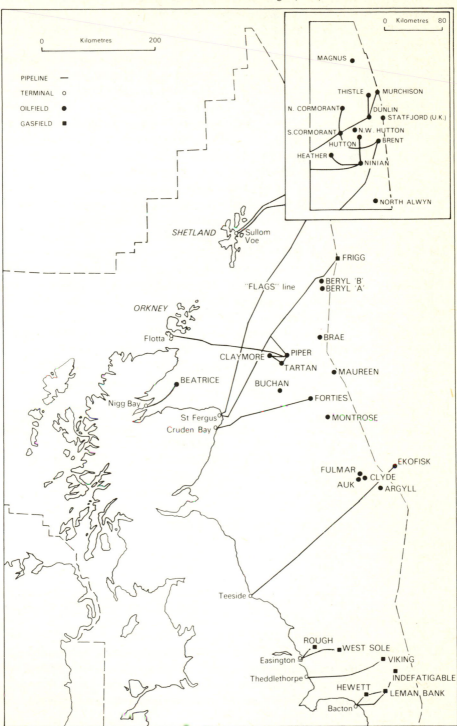

aircraft. The local authorities in Grampian Region were also enthusiastic and cooperative. By 1980, a very high proportion of the Scottish jobs involved in the service, supply and service functions for the North Sea oil province were located in and around the town.[6]

It will be clear from the foregoing discussion that the immediate economic impact of the discovery and exploitation of oil in Scottish waters was highly concentrated geographically. The logistical reasons are obvious.

The offshore location of the oil fields also meant, of course, that a considerable number of offshore jobs would be generated. In the event, the largest single category of employment associated with North Sea oil is offshore employment. It is worth pointing out, however, that the extraction of oil is an activity of strikingly low labour intensity. Wages and salaries account for roughly 3 per cent of value added in the oil and gas sector, compared with 60 per cent in mining and 70 per cent in manufacturing. Employment is always allocated for official purposes to the place where the appropriate salaries or wages are paid. Thus, since most of the offshore workers in Scotland, wherever they may live, are paid in Aberdeen, that city is credited with the employment. Since only one quarter of the offshore workers resided in Aberdeen or the Grampian Region in the early 1980s, this exaggerated the number of oil jobs concentrated in the area. Even taking this fully into account, however, there is no doubt that the employment effects of oil developments have been concentrated in the Grampian Region and, especially, in the city of Aberdeen.

Table 6. *Estimates of Wholly Oil-related Employment in Scotland: end-1980*

Region	Oil-related employment (Nos.)	Percentage of Total oil-related employment	Percentage of Total Scottish employment
Grampian	39,200	57.6	8.5
Shetland	7,800	11.5	0.5
Strathclyde	6,800	10.0	49.5
Highlands	5,300	7.8	3.3
Tayside	2,800	4.1	7.4
Fife	2,300	3.4	6.2
Lothians	1,800	2.6	16.3
Western Isles	1,300	1.9	0.2
Orkney	500	0.7	0.3
Others	300	0.4	7.8
	68,100	(100)	(100)

Source: Various Scottish Economic Bulletins, Scottish Economic Planning Department, 1981 and 1982

It might have been expected that the traditional centres of engineering, metal working and manufacturing in Scotland would have quickly felt some beneficial impact from the arrival of this new industry. In fact, only a relatively small number of jobs were generated outside those areas in which the employment clustered as a result of logistical and technological factors. Tables 6 and 7 illustrate this. A high proportion of the jobs are to be found in the service and construction sectors. In the manufacturing sector, most of the jobs are in platform and rig building yards which have their locations determined by geography. Apart from its demands on the engineering industry for rigs and platforms, the North Sea oil industry has made relatively few demands on the traditional, indigenous manufacturing industries of Scotland.

Table 7. *Wholly Oil-related Jobs: Scotland, 1979*

	Thousands
1. Offshore	12.1
2. Onshore	
Engineering and Metal Manufacture	
(mainly rig and platform construction)	20.0
Other manufacturing	4.4
Construction	5.5
Services	17.2
3. Total	59.3

Applying a conservative employment multiplier of 1.3 to the above total, we arrive at a figure for direct, indirect and induced employment arising from wholly oil-related jobs of about 77,000. Perhaps a further 12,000 jobs were partly related to oil.

Source: *Scottish Economic Bulletin* No. 21, Summer 1980, Scottish Economic Planning Department

From the early days of oil development in the North Sea, the Government was concerned to maximise the benefit to British industry. The Offshore Supplies Office was established in Glasgow in 1973. It was charged with the responsibility of attempting to ensure that as many orders as possible for the requirements of companies operating in the North Sea were placed with U.K. companies. In the early days, not unexpectedly, the Americans, with 25 years of offshore experience, albeit in relatively shallow and sheltered water, had a great advantage, and British firms, given their almost total lack of relevant experience, faced a considerable entry barrier. It was clear, moreover, that there had to be a substantial and rapid advance in technology to cope with the deep and stormy waters and the high winds encountered in the northern North Sea. The Americans, at least, had a technological base on which to build. An agreement was reached with the United Kingdom Offshore Operators' Association (U.K.O.O.A.) in 1975, under which British industry was to be given the opportunity to compete with overseas companies for orders on the U.K.C.S. This is known as the 'Full and Fair Opportunity' (F.F.O.) policy.

Many American companies set up manufacturing subsidiaries in Scotland; others formed consortia with U.K. companies. Most of these were highly successful, a good example being Brown and Root of Houston who, with George Wimpey, set up Highlands Fabricators at Nigg Bay whose major achievement to date has been the huge steel platform for the Magnus field.

Despite encouragement from the Offshore Supplies Office, both the British Steel Corporation and British Shipbuilders were very slow to grasp the opportunities presented by the offshore market. British-based industry, nevertheless, has gradually increased its share of the offshore market from 35 per cent in 1973 to over 70 per cent in 1980, in which year the total market was worth around £2,500 million. It is estimated that Scottish companies had about 15-20 per cent of this total.

One consequence of the influx of U.S. oil industry companies, such as Brown and Root, Baker Oil Tools and McDermotts, into Scotland has been a considerable increase in the already significant penetration of Scottish industry by U.S. companies. After 1975 there was a noticeable increase in the share of Scottish manufacturing industry which was controlled from the United States. Of all the regions in Britain, Scotland had by far the largest proportion of U.S.-owned subsidiary companies, with almost one-half of the electrical engineering and one-third of the mechanical engineering industries foreign-owned by the early 1980s.

The general impact of North Sea oil developments, therefore, was not widely diffused through the Scottish economy either industrially or geographically. In total, by 1980, about 68,000 directly related jobs of all kinds, including construction of terminals, pipelines, etc. had been generated. 68,000 jobs, while being considerably fewer than half the jobs lost in Scottish manufacturing over the same period, represented, nevertheless, about 3 per cent of total Scottish employment. Most of the jobs could be accounted for in three ways: offshore operations, onshore service and supply activity directly linked to North Sea offshore operations and, thirdly, rig and platform construction yards. Long-term oil-related employment which could survive the exhaustion of the North Sea province because it is involved in supplying an international market for oil goods or services has, so far, been very slow to develop. It seems unlikely that it exceeded 5,000 jobs by 1984.

The geographical impact, as we have explained, was highly concentrated, and this concentration was the cause of major transformations of the local economies in which it occurred. Parts of Highland Region, notably at Nigg, Ardersier and Kishorn, where large platform building yards are sited, were affected, as was the economy of the Orkney Islands by the construction of the terminal at Flotta which takes oil from the Claymore, Piper and Tartan group of fields. The two local economies which best exemplified the impact of oil developments were those of Aberdeen and the Shetland Islands, and we consider these in turn.

ABERDEEN

Until the 1970s Aberdeen was the centre of a relatively sparsely populated, rural region whose industrial structure was very largely resource-based. The city provided central facilities in administration, education, professional services, retail distribution and entertainment. Apart from these central-place, service activities, its manufacturing base was in fish- and food-processing, paper-making, textiles and shipbuilding. There was, of course, a sizeable fishing fleet operating from the port. Over the years, the Grampian Region had experienced high levels of population emigration, and Aberdeen itself had scarcely maintained its population over the post-war years.

All this was to change with the advent of the oil industry. As we have seen, in 1980 Grampian Region had 57.6 per cent of all Scotland's oil jobs. No less than 90 per cent of these were to be found in Aberdeen where, by the end of 1980, there were 31,500 jobs in companies wholly related to the oil industry. Of these, 11,500 were offshore, 5,000 were in manufacturing, and 15,000 in services. The service employment covered a range of activities, some of them traditional, such as marine transport, catering services and warehousing services. Others, however, were quite novel, even exotic in an Aberdeen context, such as diving services, mud logging and well-testing, barytes and mud chemical supply, and oil-tool equipment supply. Around 10,000 jobs were to be found in this new category. It should be noted that the rapid build-up of oil activity and employment in Aberdeen did not begin until the mid-1970s.

Table 8. *Aberdeen: Some Indicators of the Effects of North Sea Oil*

	1971	*1981*
Population of Aberdeen (S.P.A.)[1]	254,866	284,028
Employees in Employment (S.P.A.)	108,800	132,212
Oil-related employment (S.P.A.)	1,000	44,000
Earnings relative to G.B. average (%)	89	108
Unemployment relative to G.B. average (%) Aberdeen T.T.W.A.[2]	93	58
Passengers through Dyce Airport	119,500	1,448,000
Housing Stock	90,000	112,500

[1]Structure Plan Area
[2]Travel to Work Area

Source: Grampian Regional Council, Aberdeen City District Council, Manpower Services Commission, British Airports Authority

The wholly related jobs, however, do not exhaust the employment impact of oil. G. A. MacKay estimated that a further 9,000 jobs in Aberdeen were provided by companies which were partly related to oil (N.E.S.D.A. (North East Scotland Development Agency) lists 700 such companies in the Grampian Region).[7] In addition we must include all the employment generated indirectly in non-oil activities as a result of the additional population and expenditure in such sectors as retail distribution, professional services, hotels and catering, etc. These were estimated by Grampian Regional Council (G.R.C.) in 1980 to amount to about 3,500. In total, it appears that by the end of 1980, oil developments had brought to Aberdeen about 44,000 additional jobs, divided as follows:

Offshore, registered to Aberdeen	11,500
Onshore wholly oil-related	20,000
Onshore partly oil-related	9,000
Onshore indirect employment	3,500
	44,000

Grampian Regional Council estimated in 1980 that of the 20,000 wholly oil-related jobs, 7,750 were in the 14 major oil companies present in Aberdeen, 3,500 in drilling companies, 1,300 in helicopter support and 2,500 in catering for offshore workers. This increase in employment should be seen against a total of 108,000 jobs in the Aberdeen Structure Plan Area (S.P.A.) in 1971. Oil-related jobs represented, in 1980, 40 per cent of total employment in 1971. If we exclude three-quarters of the offshore jobs, there was still a 32 per cent increase.

Such a large increase in employment cannot be accommodated in a relatively small economy without major disruption of labour and housing markets or without imposing considerable strains on the existing social and economic infrastructure. The people of Aberdeen experienced those problems which might be seen as the price to be paid for rapid growth in average earnings.

The population of the Aberdeen S.P.A. increased by around 30,000 from 1971 to 1981, and average earnings in the Grampian Region rose from being 89 per cent of the British average in 1971 to 108 per cent in 1980. This had severe effects on the competitiveness of Aberdeen's traditional non-oil manufacturing industries. Research has revealed the considerable disruption of labour markets which adversely affected indigenous manufacturing industries.[8] Skilled labour of all kinds was attracted into the oil sector, and a dual labour market emerged in which the oil industry captured the high-quality labour and the established indigenous industries were left to fight for the remainder. Traditionally Aberdeen manufacturers had been able to compensate for the disadvantages of their peripheral location by paying lower wages than the national average. This advantage was extinguished by the impact of incoming oil-related employers on the local labour market. Despite the oil boom, Aberdeen lost manufacturing jobs towards the end of the 1980s at a rate higher than any other of the Scottish City Districts. This does not bode well for the long-term future of Aberdeen's economy.

22,500 new houses were completed between 1971 and 1980, increasing the City's housing stock by 25 per cent. Even so, there were shortages in some sectors of the housing market, especially the private rented sector. House prices in Aberdeen rose by 5½ times over the decade of the 1970s, roughly 40 per cent more than the British average. In the later seventies, as the oil fields came into production, the major oil companies, following the clustering principle, settled more firmly and in larger numbers in Aberdeen, building their own office accommodation. They raised the new office space occupied from 4,300 sq. metres in 1974 to 85,000 sq. metres in 1980. The number of hotel beds increased from 1,100 in 1973 to 2,400 in 1980, with six large new hotels built. One of the most telling indicators of oil's impact on Aberdeen was the transformation of Dyce Airport. The total number of passengers handled in 1970 was 119,500. By 1980, this had increased to 1,448,000, a twelvefold increase. The number of air transport movements increased from 4,000 to 74,000, and in 1980 there were 28,500 helicopter flights into and out of Aberdeen — roughly 80 a day.

There is no doubt that Aberdeen became the oil capital of Western Europe, but its prosperity rested rather precariously on the supply of services directly and exclusively to the North Sea oil province. The oil industry had yet to put down real roots in the Aberdeen economy to create significant and permanent backward linkages. There remained the possibility, probability even, that when the oil ran out in the North Sea, the industry would fade quickly away, leaving almost no trace, except empty offices and warehouses.

SHETLAND

In the remote, scattered and climatically hostile Shetland Islands in 1971 there lived 17,300 people. The working population of 6,400 were employed mainly in fishing and fish-processing (1,800), knitwear (350 plus 2,300 home knitters) and in the basic services essential to survival in a peripheral community. Hundreds were part-time crofters. Broadly speaking, average earnings were about 70 per cent, and unemployment about 123 per cent, of the U.K. average. By 1980, the resident population of Shetland had grown from 17,300

Table 9. *Shetland Islands: Some Indicators of the Effects of North Sea Oil*

	1971	1975	1980
Population	17,300	19,000	22,300
Employees in employment	5,000	—	14,000
Oil-related employment	0	935	8,590
Non-oil earnings relative to G.B. average (%)	70	—	100
Unemployment relative to G.B. average (%)	123	—	45
Housing Stock	5,787	—	8,182
Passengers through Sumburgh Airport	70,000	—	623,000
Local Government income from rates	—	£433,000	£23,000,000
Local Government expenditure	—	£6,200,000	£34,300,000

Includes about 6,000 temporary construction jobs at Sullom Voe held by non-Shetlanders.

Source: Registrar General, Scottish Economic Planning Department, Manpower Services Commission, Civil Aviation Authority, Shetland Islands Council

to 22,300, an increase of 5,000 in a decade, and the total workforce on the Islands had increased to 14,000. It should be noted, however, that about 6,100 of these jobs were temporary and taken by *immigrant labour* on the construction of Sullom Voe Terminal. The vast majority of these men lived in the two work camps near Sullom Voe which had been specially built to house them and to provide a high standard of accommodation, entertainment and cuisine.[9]

By 1980, unemployment had fallen to 45 per cent of the British average and average earnings in the non-oil sector had caught up with the British level. Significantly, employment in non-oil manufacturing had *fallen* by 28 per cent from 1,300 to 940. By 1980, the housing stock had increased from 5,787 to 8,181 (41 per cent), passengers through Sumburgh Airport had increased from 70,000 to 623,000, private vehicle ownership had doubled, and primary school rolls had increased by 36 per cent. How did this apparent transformation take place?

It was in 1971 that exploration activity in the East Shetland Basin began in earnest. Shetland had obvious logistical advantages for companies operating above latitude 59°N, and forward supply and helicopter bases were established. These might well have been only temporary, but it quickly turned out that the East Shetland Basin was a major oil province. Shell/Esso's huge Brent field was discovered in 1971, followed by five further large fields within two years. Quite clearly, Shetland was the only serious contender for a pipeline terminal if oil was to be got ashore that way.

The Zetland County Council as it was then (now the Shetland Islands Council) was determined to seize and to retain control of all oil developments in the Islands, to minimise the disturbance to the community and the economy and to maximise the financial benefits which it could extract for the community from the oil industry. To a very great extent, to a remarkable extent indeed for such a small authority, it succeeded. It secured the passage in 1974 of the Zetland County Council Act which gave it powers of compulsory purchase of land likely to be needed for oil developments, and it acquired rights as the harbour authority for such developments. The major Shetland development, the £1,200 million Sullom Voe Terminal, is sited some 28 miles north of Lerwick. In Lerwick itself there are five service and supply bases, employing about 300 people in 1980, and there is a small base at Sandwick. The main airport development was at Sumburgh, where over 700 people were employed in 1980. There were significant new developments at Lerwick Harbour. The total number of wholly oil-related jobs in Shetland, excluding the temporary jobs at Sullom Voe, was of the order of around 2,500. Most of these were in various kinds of service activity or in construction. Very few were in manufacturing where there had been, as we have already noted, a net fall in employment of about 400 jobs.

It would be idle to suppose that this transformation could have been achieved without some upheaval and disturbance. On the whole, however, the disturbance was minimised, especially the kind of social disturbance which could have arisen as a consequence of the employment of thousands of migrant workers at Sullom Voe. An old wartime fighter airstrip near Sullom Voe, at Scatsta, was reconstructed around the requirements of the HS748 aircraft. Dan Air was given the contract, and all the men were flown in and out directly to and from Glasgow without ever going near Lerwick. In 1980, around 2,600 passengers a week were handled at this airstrip. Furthermore, Shetland Islands Council took large shares in companies set up to perform some of the key operations, such as towage and pilotage, at Sullom Voe. The Islands Council has been subject to serious criticism about some of its handling of the oil industry; for example, there was considerable delay in reaching agreement with the operators about the terms of the lease. Many of its critics think it has been too greedy, but in the matter of minimising disturbances it has performed remarkably well. Of course, geography has protected many parts of Shetland from disturbance. Unst, Yell, Fetlar, Whalsay, Out Skerries — these islands have seen very little change except for rather more income being available as a result of men moving over to the mainland for spells 'at the oil'.

In 1983 ninety per cent of Shetland's rate income came from oil activities, no less than eighty-five per cent from Sullom Voe itself, and domestic ratepayers in Shetland paid by far the lowest rates in Scotland. Earnings by 1980 had reached average British levels and unemployment was well below the U.K. average. No disinterested observer could conclude that the impact of oil on the Shetland economy had been anything but beneficial. Although employment in the Islands' traditional manufacturing activity had fallen by 1980, the sensible use of the monies steadily accruing to the community as a result of the agreements reached between the Islands Council and the oil companies (amounting to several million pounds each year) ought to make it possible fully to restore the fortunes of these industries and to attract to the Islands other suitable sources of employment for the increased working population.

NOTES

1. Emissions from nuclear power stations do not cause acid rain.
2. British Gas Council, *Annual Reports*.
3. S. F. Hampson and L. H. Thomson, *Recent Trends in the Scottish Energy Market*, Scottish Economic Planning Department (S.E.P.D.) (Edinburgh, 1978).
4. M. Gaskin and D. MacKay, *The Economic Impact of North Sea Oil on Scotland* (Edinburgh, H.M.S.O., 1978); C. A. Walker, *The Impact of Offshore Oil on the Scottish Economy*, S.E.P.D. (Edinburgh, 1979).
5. P. J. Forsyth and J. A. Kay, *Fiscal Studies* (June, 1980).
6. H. M. Begg and S. McDowall, *Aberdeen Manufacturing Industry. A Study conducted for the City of Aberdeen District Council* (1983); S. McDowall and H. M. Begg, *Industrial Performance and Prospects in Areas Affected by Oil Developments*, S.E.P.D. (Edinburgh, 1981); G. A. MacKay and A. C. Moir, *North Sea Oil and the Aberdeen Economy* (Institute for the Study of Sparsely Populated Areas (I.S.S.P.A.) Research Paper, 1980); John Whiteman, *North Sea Oil and the UK Economy* (National Economic Development Office, 1981).
7. G. A. MacKay and A. C. Moir, *op. cit.*
8. S. McDowall and H. M. Begg, *op. cit.*
9. Elizabeth Marshall, *Shetland's Oil Era* (Shetlands Islands Council, 1981); T. Strachan and M. Bruce (eds.), *Scottish Petroleum Annual* (Aberdeen, 1982).

INDEX

Abercrombie, Patrick, Sir, 21, 22, 23, 30, 32
Aberdeen, 304-309
Acts of Parliament
    Crofters Holdings (Scotland) Act (1886),
        215
    Distribution of Industry Act (1945), 29,
        69, 199
    Distribution of Industry (Industrial
        Finance) Act (1958), 69, 201
    Finance Act (1972), 70
    Hill Farming Act (1946), 153
    Homeless Persons Act (1978), 285
    Housing Acts (various), 273, 277, 280,
        285-288
    Hydro-Electric (Scotland) Act (1943), 27
    Industrial Development Act (1966), 69
    Industrial Act (1972), 70, 72, 206-208, 211,
        232
    Local Employment Act (1980), 69
    Mortgage & Rent Restrictions Act (1915),
        272
    Scottish Development Agency Act (1975),
        234
    Special Areas (Development & Improve-
        ment) Act (1934), 17-18
    Special Areas (Amendment) Act (1937), 17
    Special Areas Reconstruction (Agreement)
        Act (1936), 17
    Town & Country Planning Act (1932), 20
    Town & Country Planning Act (1947), 22
    Women's Emancipation Bill (1919), 187
    Advisory Council of Ex-Secretaries of State
        on Post-War Problems, 22-3, 27-8
Agriculture
    (general), 22, 24, 60-1, 141-162
    Multiplier effects of, 67
    Antibiotics & hormone promoters for
        animals, 143
    Area of land, 147-149
    Arable & crops, 141-2, 144-5, 147-9, 150,
        155
    Beef, 142, 144-5, 152
    Breeds: use of continental cattle, 151-2
    Dairy, 144-5, 150
    Effects of changes in, additive, 142, 159
        161
    Environmental damage by, 142-144
    Farmers, social differentiation, 143, 148,
        154-157
    Fertilisers, 142, 150
    Incomes, 144-147
    Interest payments, 146
    Machinery, 142, 150, 158-9
    Milk, 143-145, 150
    Outputs: concentration on large farms,
        44-5, 148, 158-161
    Pigs and hens, 154-5

Potatoes, 144-5, 148
Potato Marketing Board, 148
Prices, 142
Regional Aspects, 141-158
Rent, 146
Research spending: bias in, 158
Sheep, 142, 148, 153
State support system, 141-3
British Sugar Corporation, 149
Sugar beet, 149
Wool, 153-4
Aircraft & aerospace, 2, 4, 10, 33, 35, 64
Aluminium, 34, 49
Arbritration, Conciliation & Advisory Ser-
    vice, 179-180
Armaments & defence, 1, 4, 18, 35, 49
Association for the Preservation of Rural
    Scotland, 27

Babcock & Wilcox, 14, 34
Balance of payments, 204-5, 297, 301
Banking & finance, 35, 63, 114-140
    Adam & Company, 125-6
    Assets & reserves, 120-121
    Clearing banks, 115-6
    Clydesdale Bank, 116, 123, 125
    Competition & credit control, 118, 119-20,
        126
    Deposits & note issues, 116-119
    Bank of England, 17, 119, 122
    Innovations in lending, 122-4, 127
    Lending to manufacturing, 124, 127
    Money markets, 118
    National Girobank, 124
    Retail banks, 114-5
    Royal Bank of Scotland, 116, 131, 138
    Secondary banking crisis, 140
    Bank of Scotland, 116, 127
    Supplementary special deposits, 118-9
    Trustee Savings Bank, 114-5, 124
    Wholesale and merchant banks, 115, 125-
        128
Barber boom (1971), 121
Bathgate, 49, 95, 202, 249, 255-6
Beardmores, 9
Bellahouston Park Empire Exhibition (1938),
    14
Bilsland, Sir Steven, 15
Board of Trade, 1932 report on SW Scotland,
    5
Board of Trade control of factory & storage
    premises, 10, 28
Brassert, H. A. & Co. (1929), 94, 98, 109
Brennan, Thomas, 280-1
British Motor Corporation, 95, 202
British Iron & Steel Federation, 94, 98
British Shipbuilders Ltd., 106, 108

British Steel Corporation, 80-1, 95-7, 99
Building societies, 114-5, 118, 125, 129-30, 136, 288
Building Societies Association, 130
Building trades, 28, 30, 36, 62, 67, 71, 169, 184, 219, 282-3

Cairncross, Alexander, 195, 245
Canada, 3, 34
Carron Company, 49
Casa per il Mezzogiorno, 233
Census of Production, 1924, 1930, 1935, 1948, 1-4, 6-9, 11, 24, 30, 36-7, 38-42, 43(n), 51
Chamberlain, Neville, 19
Chemicals, 9-10, 64
Clydesdale & North of Scotland Bank Index, 4
Coal
    Coalfields & reserves, 84-5, 88
    Coalmining, 24-5, 28, 42, 60, 74, 83-93, 292
    Machinery, 84-5
    Markets for, consumption by sector, 85-6, 292-294
    Outputs, 79-80, 198, 293-4
Collective bargaining, 164
Colvilles Ltd., 93-5, 98, 103, 199
Conservative Party & Government, 13, 70, 99, 206, 217
Conservative views on women, 189
Cooper, Lord (hydroelectricity), 27, 199-200
Council for the Preservation of Rural England, 20
County Councils Association, 18-19, 23

De-industrialisation, 49, 56-7, 60
Derelict Land Clearance Unit, 236
Development Areas, 28, 31-2, 69-70, 77, 202-3
Dollar shortages, 34
Dounray reactor, 219-220
Dundee investment trusts, 133

Earl of Elgin, 3, 15
Economic growth & performance, 4, 11, 36-42, 47-8, 50, 54-5, 200-1, 267 (see specific sectors)
    Comparisons with other countries, 47, 54-5
    Indicators of, 50-56
    Regional comparisons, 11-12
Economist, The, 184-5, 189
Electrical engineering, 2, 10, 34, 56, 65, 169, 209, 248-9, 253, 265
Electricity, 36, 83, 88, 108, 292
Electronic data processing in banks, 117, 137
Electronics, 34, 56-7, 64, 66, 170, 174, 224, 238-9, 257, 265, 268
Employment (general), 49, 53, 55-6, 58-9, 64, 163-194

Agriculture, 141, 146-7, 158-160, 168, 214
Banking, 115, 136-7, 169
Branch factories (see Multinationals)
Coalmining, 79, 80, 84, 168, 198, 293-295
Economic activity rates, 166, 174
By industry and sectors, 31, 33, 35-6, 61-2, 65, 167-8, 209, 217, 221-4, 247-268, 294-5, 308-9
Highlands industries, 217-9, 231-2
Manufacturing, decline in, 61-3, 209, 310
Public sector, 49, 169
Scottish oil, 59, 168-9, 206, 221, 297, 304-7, 308-11
Services, 35, 65, 169-70, 186
Shift to foreign firms, 56
Women, 56, 165-6, 171-6, 183, 229
English Industrial Estate Corporation, 243
Engineering (general), 24-5, 29, 35, 42, 55, 60, 83, 109, 306
Entrepreneurship & business psychology, 10, 14, 26, 47-8, 55, 64, 66, 83, 103-4, 109-10, 220, 284-5
European Economic Community (general), 4, 64, 74-6, 186, 212, 221, 230
    Agricultural Policy, 74-5, 142-144, 148-9, 153-4, 158, 160-162
    Coal & Steel Community, 74-5
    Regional Fund, 74-5
    Social Fund, 74-5
    Scotland transfers, 74-6
    Sheepmeat subsidies, 153
European Currency Units & Eurocurrency, 74, 118, 126, 128
European Investment Bank, 74
Exports, 28, 36, 63 (and see specific sectors)

Factory completions & licences, 29-32, 239-40
Federation of British Industries, 16, 20-21
Finance (see Banking)
Fishing, 60-1, 221
Foreign capital, 47, 60, 122, 204, 211, 252-258
Forestry, 61, 67, 238 (Highlands & Islands)
Fort William, 27, 49, 56, 224, 255, 258
Fraser of Allander Institute, 63-64, 66-67
Fuel (see sector)

Gas:
    North Sea, 60, 292, 295-6, 297-300, 302
    Town, 88, 292, 295
General Strike, 84
Glasgow East End Area Renewal, 235, 240-1, 290
Glen Affric, 27
Gollan, John, 30
Government (see Scottish, State)
Gross Domestic Product, Scottish, 49, 51-4, 60, 63, 64-5, 71, 201, 205, 219, 270

Heavy (staple) metal industries, 11, 47, 51-54, 57, 60, 79, 83, 184, 195-6, 201, 245 (see sectors)
Henderson, Robert, 265
Highlands & Islands (general), 18, 157, 160, 192-3, 214-232, 301-311
　Agriculture, 160, 214, 219
　Community Co-operatives, 227
　Crofting, 193, 214, 217-8, 309
　Employment structure, 214-216, 217, 221-226, 229-232
　Physical, 214-5, 220
　Tourism, 218, 226-227
　Transport, 228
Highlands & Islands Development Board, 69, 72, 195, 204, 207-9, 210-212, 219, 220, 221, 225, 230, 233-244
Hirshman, A. J., 67
Housing, 278-290, 308, 310
　Demolition, excessive, 198, 280-1
　Investment, 270-290
　Overcrowding, 197-8, 271-2, 273, 280
　Owner-occupied, 288-9
　Policy & process, 276, 280-290
　Public-owned & sector, 270-288
　Quality, lack of, 282-3
　Subsidies, 277-8
Howard, Ebenezer, 20
Hunterston ore terminal, 96-7, 99
Hydro-electricity, 22, 26-28, 199-200, 195, 215

Imports, 36, 64 (and see sectors)
Inchinan aerodrome, 14
Incomes, per capita, 48, 52, 63, 71, 196, 219
Incoming firms, 64, 249-264 (see Multi-nationals)
India Tyre & Rubber Co., 14
Industrial & Commercial Finance Corporation, 237
Industrial Development Boards, 70
Industrial Development Certificates, 69
Industry
　Closures, rate of, 71, 249-263, 294-5
　Diversification, 14, 26, 35-6, 47, 51, 54, 236-8, 248-269
　In Highlands, 217-9, 231-2
　Index of, 54-5, 59
　Linkage, 9, 63, 67-8, 255-6, 294-5, 297, 302
　Location, 24
　New, 2, 4, 10-11, 13, 33-35, 61, 209, 233-242, 245-269
　Production, 50-1, 56, 61-2, 65, 167-8, 209, 217, 221-4, 247, 250-268
　Structure, 47, 60, 61, 65, 69, 247
Input-output analysis, 61-68
Insurance, 63, 115, 131-2, 136-7, 169
Invergordon, 49, 200, 219, 223-4, 255, 258
Investment trusts, 115, 132-3, 137

Ireland: Industrial Development Authority, 233, 235, 241

Keynes, J. M., 13, 26
Korean War, 56

Labour Government & Party, 3, 26, 105, 142, 220, 234, 278-79, 281
Labour Transference Scheme, 17
Leser, C. E. V., 85, 172, 196
Linwood, 95, 202, 249, 255-6, 258
Llanwern, 95, 99, 201
Lloyds Insurance, 103
Locate in Scotland, 208, 239, 242
Location quotients, 65-66
Lurgi gasification technique, 295

McCance, Sir Andrew, 95, 98, 109-110
McCrone, Gavin, 51
Manpower Services Commission, 186, 190, 195, 208-9
Marine engineering (see shipbuilding)
Marine underwriting, 132
Mears, Sir Frank, 23
Migration, 4, 49, 73, 163, 170-173, 212
Millan, Bruce, 48
Ministry of Health, 15, 28
Ministry of Labour, 2, 15
Ministry of Supply, 10, 28
Ministry of Town and Country Planning, 22, 29, 33
Moore & Rhodes, 70, 73, 211, 255
Motorway system, 204
Multinationals and branch factories, 14, 28, 29, 33-34, 47-48, 56, 59, 64, 122, 249-269, 305-306
Multiplier effects, 63, 66-68, 226, 295

National Coal Board, 85, 88, 90-1, 108, 294
　Accounting procedures, 92(note)
National Enterprise Board, 236
National Government, 12
National Shipbuilders Security Ltd., 101
Nationalisation, 12, 88, 97-8, 64, 74
Nationalism, Scottish National Party, 15, 132, 234, 236
New Towns, 1, 2, 198, 235, 246-268, 278-290
Non-ferrous metals, 10
North America, 2, 14, 47 (see USA, Canada)
North British Locomotive Company, 249
North British Rubber Co., 14, 34
North East Scotland Development Agency, 307
North Hillingdon Trading Estate, 17, 25, 33, 197
Northern Ireland, 70-1
Nuffield, Lord, 17

Oakley C. A., 3
Oil (see Scottish oil)

Political factors and economic growth, 79, 95, 99, 105, 109-10, 218, 233, 234-5, 236, 276-7, 281, 296
Population & Census, 165, 173, 189-90, 192, 216-220, 270, 274, 309
  Highlands & Islands, 214, 231
  New Towns, 265-266
Post-war conversion policy, 28
Protectionist tariffs, 16-17
Public Works Loans Board, 126

Railways & locomotives, 5, 10, 35, 88, 245, 292-3
Ravenscraig, 56, 95, 97-99, 199, 201-2, 255
Recession, post-1974, 47, 49, 55, 59, 167, 195
Regional policy, 48-51, 54-6, 65-6, 70-74, 163, 174, 181, 202-205, 210-212, 235-269
Regional Planning Committees, 23, 27
Regional Policy, special assistance, 32, 71-2, 174
Registrar-General, 3
Rolls-Royce, 33
Royal Commissions & Government Reports:
  Royal Commission on the Distribution of the Industrial Population (Barlow) (1940), 3, 11, 15-22, 44(n), 197
  British Shipbuilding 1972: A Report to the Department of Trade & Industry by Booz, Allen & Hamilton International B.V. (1973), 109
  Commission of Inquiry into Crofting Conditions (1954), 215
  Committee to Review the Functioning of Financial Institutions (Wilson) (1977), 237
  Report of the Committee on National Policy for the Use of Fuel & Power Resources (Ridley) (1952), 200
  Plan for Coal (1950), 85
  Report of the Scottish Coalfields Committee (1944), 85
  Central Scotland: A Programme for Development & Growth (1963), 203-4
  Clyde Valley Regional Plan (Abercrombie) (1946), 3, 23-26, 29, 43(n), 195, 196-9, 203, 246, 280
  Geddes Report on Shipbuilding, 105, 109
  A Programme for Highland Development (1950), 215
  Review of Highland Policy (1959), 217
  Housing Policy: Green Paper (1977), 286
  Royal Commission on Industrial Housing (1912), 272
  New Towns (Reith Committee) (1945), 22
  Report of the Committee on Land Utilisation in Rural Areas (Scott), 22, 24
  Plan for the Expansion of the Scottish Economy (1966), 220

Radcliffe Committee (1959), 135, 137
  Committee of Inquiry into the Scottish Economy (Toothill) (1961), 203, 210, 245
  Report of the Committee on Compensation and Betterment (Uthwatt), 22, 24
  West Central Scotland Plan (1974), 208
  White Paper on Employment Policy (1944), 25, 29, 196
  White Paper on Industry and Employment in Scotland (1946), 29, 42(n)
  White Paper on the Scottish Economy (1965), 203-4

Scottish Building Committee, 22
Scottish Co-Operative Wholesale Society, 10
Scottish Council (Development & Industry), 32-33, 42, 241
Scottish Council on Industry, 22
Scottish Development Agency, 64, 70-2, 128, 195, 208-9, 211-2, 233-244
Scottish Development Council, 12-17
Scottish Development Department, 207, 236
Scottish Development Financial Trust, 15
Scottish Distribution of Industry Panel, 22
Scottish Economic Committee, 12-19
Scottish Economic Planning Department (now Industry Department for Scotland), 51, 207-8, 233-5, 240
Scottish Housing Advisory Committee: reports of, 273
Scottish Industrial Council, 22
Scottish Industrial Estates Corporation (Ltd), 14, 17, 30-1, 235-6
Scottish Manufacturing Establishments Record, 259
Scottish Office, offshoots and influences, 12, 18, 26-7, 32, 34, 42, 195-212, 214-231, 233-290
Scottish Office, Index of Gross Domestic Product, 51
Scottish oil (general), 50, 52-3, 59, 60, 127, 174, 205-6, 209, 211, 230, 234, 236, 292-311
  Banking and, 127-9
  Exploration, 64, 220, 298-303
  Linkage to local industry, 59-60, 205-6, 221, 238-9
  New name for: U.K. Continental Shelf, 297, 302
  Prices, 93
  Reserves, 63, 297-299, 303
  Revenues, 63, 297
  Switch to oil in late 1950s, 88
Scottish Physical Planning Committee, 22
Scottish Special Housing Association, 240, 279
Scottish Tourist Board, 209
Scottish Trades Union Congress, 176, 187

Service sector, 35, 49, 54, 57, 61-62, 65, 69, 211
Shetland Isles, 309-311
Shift share analysis, 68-9, 73
Shipbuilders Conference, 1928, 101
Shipbuilding, 1, 4, 10, 24, 28-9, 35, 42, 56, 60, 80-2, 101-110, 198-9, 207, 245
  Advantages of foreign yards, 103-5
  Employment, 81-2, 169, 247
  Fairfields, 105
  Industry Board, 106
  Output, 80-2, 102-3, 107
  Scott-Lithgow, 106, 108
  Shipowners, 105
  Shortages of skilled labour, 103
  World production, 102-3, 107
Singers, 14, 34, 241
Small Industries Council for Rural Areas in Scotland, 236
Social Deprivation, 3, 49
Socialist movements, 12
Special Areas Acts & Commissions, 12, 15-17, 19
State planning, 12, 16, 18-19, 23-25, 42, 48, 195-212, 233
  in housing, 272-290

Steel & iron trades (general), 5, 10, 25, 28, 34, 79-81, 93-101, 108-110, 199, 201-2
  Employment, 80-2
  Output, 80-81, 96, 100
Stock Exchange, 115, 134-5, 137
Strike activity, 178-180

Technology, 60, 64, 66, 84
Textiles & machinery, 5, 9, 14, 56, 60, 247, 257, 268
Town & Country Planning, 2, 12, 16, 18-22
Trade Unions, 12, 98-9, 176-79 (named), 187

Vale of Leven, 3
Vehicles, 2, 4, 34-5, 55-7, 66, 193, 209, 249, 265

Wage relative, 172
Wages & earnings, 58, 60, 71, 84, 158, 172-6, 184-5, 192-3, 304
Wages, women, 174-5, 184
Wales, 12, 70, 95
Welsh Development Agency, 243
Women & the economy, 165-176, 183-194
  (see Employment, sectors)